THE RISE OF DAVID DUKE

THE

RISE

OF

DAVID

DUKE

TYLER BRIDGES

UNIVERSITY PRESS OF MISSISSIPPI
JACKSON

9 2
D8773 b (handwritten)

Library of Congress Cataloging-in-Publication Data

Bridges, Tyler.
    The rise of David Duke / Tyler Bridges.
        p.   cm.
    Includes bibliographical references and index.
    ISBN 0-87805-678-5 (alk. paper). —ISBN 0-87805-684-X (pbk. : alk. paper)
    1. Duke, David Ernest.   2. Politicians—Louisiana—Biography.   3. Ku Klux
Klan (1915–   )—Biography.   4. White supremacy movements—Louisiana—
History—20th century.   5. Louisiana—Politics and government—1951–
6. Louisiana—Race relations.   I. Title.
F376.3.D84B75   1994
976.3'063'092—dc20   93-43873
[B]   CIP

British Library Cataloging-in-Publication data available

I hope that if somebody writes my epitaph some day, that it will be that David Duke was a person who stood up honestly for what he believed, he spoke honestly and courageously for the values he believed in.

—DAVID DUKE, 1988

To my

M O T H E R

and

F A T H E R

Who taught me the love of reading and writing

CONTENTS

PREFACE

Whacked-out supporters of David Duke would insist later that I had been brought to New Orleans as part of a Jewish conspiracy to bring him down. But when New Orleans' daily newspaper, the *Times-Picayune*, hired me in October 1988, I was a free-lance reporter covering the presidential election in Venezuela and had never heard of Duke, who was running a little-noticed presidential campaign of his own on the independent Populist party ticket.

I cannot remember exactly when I first heard of Duke. It was undoubtedly soon after I arrived in New Orleans in mid-January 1989. With his past as a grand wizard of a Ku Klux Klan faction, Duke was making news as a state legislative candidate from the New Orleans suburb of Metairie. My first distinct memory of him is from a couple of days after he ran first in the January 21 primary. I had lunch that day with Ed Renwick, Louisiana's top pollster, to get a briefing on the state's politics, and I remember someone telling Renwick that the way to beat Duke was by emphasizing his Klan past.

The four-week runoff campaign drew considerable interest not only in New Orleans but throughout the state and country. I paid little attention to it. I was too busy getting settled in a new job in a new city. My only brush with the race came on a Sunday six days before the election when I covered a speech by Mordechai Levy, the head of the radical Jewish Defense Organization. Levy had come to New Orleans several days before to attack Duke, much to the consternation of Duke's opponents, who feared—correctly, it turned out—that he would create a backlash. I got the assignment only because, as the new kid on the block, I had to work on Sundays.

I don't remember my response, if any, to the news on February 18 that Duke had won the election to the Louisiana state House of Representatives by 227 votes. The news, however, shocked the political establishment, and Duke's opponents began to ask themselves how he had pulled off the upset victory. They blamed many people and institutions, including the *Times-Picayune*. Critics said the newspaper had not fully exposed Duke's notorious past. In fact, the paper had treated the special election pretty much like any other, assigning it to the suburban East Jefferson bureau because it fell within East Jeff's geographical boundary. East Jeff's reporters were not as experienced in covering politics as reporters in the paper's main newsroom.

The criticism of the *Times-Picayune*'s election coverage stung the paper's editors, as I soon learned. One morning in early April, six weeks after Duke's victory, Metro Editor Jim Amoss and Editor Charlie Ferguson called me into Ferguson's office. As soon as I sat down, Ferguson got to the point. "We didn't take Duke seriously enough during the election," he told me. "We think there's more to David Duke than we currently know. As the local paper, it's our job to know who he is. Find out everything you can about Duke that the public should be aware of. He's never had a regular job. Where does he get his money? Is he living off donations from his supporters? Is he part of an international conspiracy of racists? Was Duke's race planned by some outside group or person? Is he expanding his network of support?" As I left the meeting, I was a bit worried that I wouldn't be able to answer all of Ferguson's questions. I knew little about Duke.

When I began my research, I had never seen Duke in person. But a few days later, I learned that he had scheduled a rally at an elementary school in his Metairie legislative district as part of his campaign to defeat a tax measure up for a statewide vote in a few weeks. The measure had been sponsored by Governor Buddy Roemer and approved by the Louisiana legislature earlier in the year. Duke, seizing on an issue of intense public interest, was traveling the state, denouncing the measure, not entirely accurately, as a tax increase foisted on the middle class. When I took my seat in the elementary school auditorium and saw Duke standing a few feet away, waiting to speak, I was surprised at his clean-cut appearance. I had expected him to look rough and tough, like the cartoon image I had of Klansmen. But wearing a white jacket, dark pants, and a red handkerchief in his breast pocket, he looked quite dapper and seemed unthreatening.

Still, that evening I also witnessed the darker emotions that Duke could unleash. As he denounced Governor Roemer and the tax measure, I felt a raw anger fill the packed school assembly. It made me uneasy. Duke then turned his fire on my employer, calling it "The Times-Pick-Your-Nose." As the crowd howled in delight, one man shouted, "The *Times-Picayune* lies!" I slumped in my chair, fearful that someone would expose me as a *T-P* reporter and I would face the wrath of the crowd. No one recognized me.

Shortly afterward, Louisiana voters defeated the tax measure 55 percent to 45 percent.

Duke had proven the experts wrong in his 1989 legislative race, and voters had defeated the tax measure he campaigned against. But when he announced for the United States Senate in December, elected officials, political consultants, and pollsters dismissed his candidacy. They derided him as an amateur, a political freak, a man who couldn't stand the rigors of a Senate campaign, especially when the truth about his past became public. When I pointed out that he had been underestimated in the Louisiana house election, they waved me off.

As Duke campaigned around the state, holding old-style political rallies, I began to realize that the political experts were wrong, that he was not just another candidate. This point was driven home for me on a warm April night in 1990 when 600 people packed the Rice Festival Building in the southwestern Louisiana town of Crowley to hear Duke speak. A few years before, the hall would have filled for Edwin Edwards, a Crowley native son who would become the only man elected governor of Louisiana four times. But on this evening, Crowley belonged to the former Klan grand wizard. Chants of "Duke! Duke! Duke!" rocked the Rice Festival Building. As I drove home that night, I began to realize that Duke was tapping into a rich vein of frustration among whites. I realized he was becoming the most effective spokesman for disaffected whites since Alabama governor George Wallace nearly a generation before.

As the Senate campaign wore on, more and more information about Duke's past racist and anti-Semitic statements and activities became public, fueling attacks not only from his opponent, incumbent senator J. Bennett Johnston, but also from a group formed by local academicians and ministers to oppose him— the Louisiana Coalition Against Racism and Nazism. And yet Duke's support grew. Indeed, Duke repeatedly used developments that were expected to hurt his campaign as ways to reinforce his claim that he spoke for frustrated white people. When other elected officials refused to endorse his candidacy, Duke used this as a weapon, asserting that this showed he was a foe of entrenched interests, an outsider—just like them. "The special interests attack me because I threaten them," Duke said time after time.

On election day, he showed again that he had been underestimated. He nearly defeated Johnston and, in the process, captured a stunning 59 percent of the white vote. In defeat, he had won big, establishing himself at age forty as a potent force in Louisiana politics. He followed up the Senate race with a bid for governor in 1991. Duke succeeded in knocking Governor Roemer,

President Bush's candidate, out of the race by finishing second to former governor Edwards in the October 1991 primary. But he lost to Edwards in the runoff a month later, 61 percent to 39 percent, in an election followed closely by the entire country.

Duke had lost, but he had again won a majority of the white vote and had received so much media coverage that he was now better known than all the Democratic presidential candidates. Shortly afterward, he announced his candidacy for president at the National Press Club in Washington, D.C. Interest in him was high. More than 100 reporters—representing all the major newspapers and television stations—covered the press conference. It seemed for a time that Duke might present a credible challenge to President George Bush from the Right. But conservative commentator Pat Buchanan also entered the race, and Buchanan advocated many of the same positions as Duke—with none of the baggage. Duke's presidential campaign fizzled. Shortly after his dismal showing in the southern primaries held on Super Tuesday, he dropped out of the race. He said he planned to take a sabbatical from politics but promised to return one day.

A striking truth about Duke is that, despite the thousands of articles written about him, he has been misunderstood repeatedly. Reporters always note his past racist and anti-Semitic activities, but few of them have gone beyond the caricature of the Klan or neo-Nazism to understand the man or explain what drives him. And reporters have focused so much on the notoriety of the Klan and its racist legacy that they have too often missed Duke's darker and deeper fears about Jews.

This book is based on interviews with his sister, his father, and hundreds of people who have known Duke since he was a skinny youngster in New Orleans: schoolmates, teachers, one-time members of the American Nazi party, policemen who tracked him in the Klan, former Klan members, ex-girlfriends, campaign aides, his political opponents. Many of my best sources were reluctant to be interviewed at first, fearful that if their names appeared in print, Duke or his supporters would retaliate. But most spoke openly, once assured that I would protect their anonymity. I came to be struck by the similarity of their accounts as they discussed Duke: they had originally seen him as a knight in shining armor but in time had become disillusioned by his arrogance, self-centeredness, and lack of integrity.

This pattern of disillusionment has been particularly true among men who still openly proclaim their allegiance to white supremacy and National Socialism. I have gotten to know nearly all the leaders of the neo-Nazi movement, most of whom have been friends with Duke at one time or another. Even though they knew I did not share their racist or anti-Semitic views, they were almost always helpful—once they overcame their initial suspicions. For example, it took more than a year of correspondence before Karl Hand, Duke's right-hand man in the Klan in the late 1970s, who was serving time in a Louisiana prison for attempted second-degree murder, agreed to be interviewed. And once Hand had agreed, it wasn't easy to talk to him. Prison officials did not allow me to interview him in person and did not permit me to call him. Hand would call me collect from the prison, but we could never talk long—either because other inmates wanted to use the phone or because he had to line up for a head count.

But some of Duke's more fervent supporters refused to help or were openly hostile. James K. Warner, a former lieutenant in the American Nazi party whom Duke recruited into his Klan in 1975, told me in early 1990, "You're working for the Newhouse people [the owners of the *Times-Picayune*]. They're agents of Israel and avowed enemies of the white race. Don't you feel like a collaborator, writing articles against your own race? You're no different than the journalists in Romania who were writing articles for the state paper against the people. Some day the white race will again take control."

In another phone conversation, after telling me that Jews should be prohibited from owning property in the United States, Warner said, "You've sold out your race and you've sold out your culture. You know, they rounded up the collaborators in France after World War II. They took them out and shot them. Aren't you afraid somebody will exact retribution against you?" At Duke's 1990 Senate election-night rally, Bernie Davids, another Duke supporter and one-time American Nazi party member, shouted at me, calling me "scum" and "slime." He also accused me of being an agent for the Mossad, Israel's intelligence agency. But neither Davids nor any of the other Duke supporters who screamed insults ever tried to strike me, for which I was thankful.

Along with the hundreds of interviews I conducted, this book is based on my coverage of Duke in the Louisiana legislature in 1990 and my coverage of the 1990 Senate election, the 1991 gubernatorial election, and his aborted 1992 presidential campaign. I have interviewed him dozens of times in person and on the telephone and have attended many of his campaign rallies. During the three years I covered him, he frequently lashed out at me. The first time was on August 8, 1989, when I revealed in a front-page article that Duke had secretly funneled money from his political campaigns and his political organization, the National Association for the Advancement of White People, to a company I linked to Duke. The article indicated that he made a living off his supporters' contributions.

Duke called a press conference that day to blast me and the paper—and to admit that he owned the company. "There's a vendetta by the *Times-Picayune* against myself, and it's a way to attack the issues I'm trying to stand up for," he said. "The *Times-Picayune* is a New York-owned newspaper, and they have a reporter [he pointed at me] doing nothing but trying to dig up things with which to twist and hurt me. . . . I say that the *Times-Picayune* is more beholden to the morals and values of New York City." In the following weeks, he denounced me as a "liar" and "dishonest" and hung up on me in phone conversations or simply refused to speak to me. "You're just trying to hurt me," he told me one time before slamming down the phone.

While he often lashed out at me in public or simply refused to talk to me during 1989 and 1990, he promptly returned my phone calls during the 1991 gubernatorial campaign. Perhaps this was because he had no choice, since I was writing for Louisiana's biggest newspaper, or perhaps it was because he was trying to win me over. After one long interview six weeks before the 1991 primary election, he turned on the charm and spent several minutes drawing diagrams on his living room table as he described how to win at craps, a favorite pursuit. After the gubernatorial campaign ended and he was running for president, he said he no longer had to talk to me and called me "hatchet man."

Other major sources of information for this book are: thousands of newspaper articles describing Duke's activities since he was a sophomore at Louisiana State University in 1969; dozens of videotapes and cassettes of Duke rallies and interviews dating as far back as his Klan days; copies of his Klan newspaper, the *Crusader*; and copies of the newspaper of the National Association for the Advancement of White People, the *NAAWP News*.

Duke has been profiled in one biography, published in 1990 by Michael Zatarain, and in one long chapter of a 1978 book on the Klan by Patsy Sims. I found neither very helpful in understanding Duke. Zatarain, while proclaiming his book an "unauthorized" biography, relied almost exclusively on newspaper clippings and on Duke himself, who gave Zatarain access to his files. In sum, Zatarain's *David Duke: Evolution of a Klansman* is essentially Duke's story as told by Duke. Sims's profile, meanwhile, while filled with good details, made no attempt to analyze Duke. It merely summarized his views and described him in action.

Capturing the real David Duke is not easy. He is a complex man. On the surface, he is charming, friendly, boyishly handsome. But beneath the mask lurks a twisted fanatic. With views like Duke's, virtually anyone less captivating or cunning would have been laughed off the political stage. That he has won massive support among whites, despite attacks and defeats that would destroy almost any other politician, attests to his political skills. It also shows an enduring faith in himself and his belief that history is destined to turn his way. In the end, he fervently believes, he will be elected president, and he and the white race will prevail. David Duke's success is also a chilling illustration of how messages of hate can be packaged to appeal to many white voters, people who would never don a Klan robe but are nonetheless receptive to thinly veiled racist cant that is offensive to virtually all blacks.

The banner of right-wing hatred in the United States will not be borne in the future by the Ku Klux Klan or the American Nazi party, with their crude rhetoric and violent tactics. They have too negative an image and too few members today to warrant much concern. The future of such hatred lies in David Duke, who is espousing many of the same beliefs today that he held when he was a neo-Nazi and grand wizard of the Knights of the Ku Klux Klan in the 1970s. These views have made him a hero to many whites, not only in Louisiana, but also throughout the United States.

ACKNOWLEDGMENTS

I owe a large debt of gratitude to the many people who helped me over the four years it took to report and write this book. At the top of the list are *Times-Picayune* editors Jim Amoss, Charlie Ferguson, Peter Kovacs, Jed Horne, and Greg Roberts, who oversaw my coverage of David Duke. They allowed me time not only to report the daily stories but also to dig into Duke's past.

I'd also like to thank the many people who generously gave their time to help me better understand Duke. Lance Hill, executive director of the Louisiana Coalition Against Racism and Nazism, provided badly needed insight into the far Right. Beth Rickey, who courageously stood up to Duke when other Republicans cowered, kept me abreast of developments within the GOP. Irwin Suall of the Anti-Defamation League and his assistants, Tom Halpern and David Lowe, provided me information time and time again from the group's voluminous files on Duke. Evelyn Rich, who combined a scholar's curiosity and personal charm to get Duke in 1985 to lay out his deepest beliefs in National Socialism, was always willing to answer another of my questions. Gwen Udell, who shared with me her extensive knowledge of Duke when others who knew far less remained fearful and silent, provided a unique vantage point on him.

Jim McPherson always treated me decently and sat for three long interviews even while other Duke aides refused to talk to me. Van Loman was candid in his knowledge of Duke, despite knowing that he and I share few political views. Duke's sister, Dotti Wilkerson, and his father, David Hedger Duke, each gave me several long interviews that helped me understand young David Duke. Mike Wells, Wayne Arnold, and Dorothy Singelmann dug into their memories to describe Duke during his teenage years. Others who helped me include: Joe Roy and Danny Welch of the Southern Poverty Law Center, Lenny Zeskind of the Center for Democratic Renewal, the Reverend James Stovall of the Louisiana Coalition Against Racism and Nazism, Ralph Forbes, Karl Hand, Jerry Dutton, Richard Barrett, Tom Metzger, Mick Mixon, Spencer Robbins and Pete Cicero.

Many other people—both Duke supporters and Duke opponents—gave hours of their time to discuss Duke's later political elections and their role in them. For the section on the District 81 race, I'd like to thank: Neil Curran, Sandy Emerson, John Treen, Jim Donelon, Ed Renwick, Donna Randall, Debbie Thomas, Roger Villere, Bobby Savoie, and Delton Charles.

For the chapter on the Senate race: Bob Mann, Hal Kilshaw, Jim Oakes, Billy Hankins, Thomas Cochran, Rusty Cantelli, Geoff Garin, Billy Nungesser, and J. Bennett Johnston, Jr.

For the chapter on the governor's race: Al Donovan, Billy Broadhurst, Bob d'Hemecourt, Billy Rimes, P. J. Mills, Sam Dawson, Gordon Hensley, Raymond Strother, Steve Lombardo, Buddy Roemer, Edwin Edwards, David Treen, Caroline Roemer, Harry Lee, Pres Kabacoff, Darryl Berger, Moise Steeg, Jr., David Dixon, Henry Dillon III, Deno Seder, David Touchstone, Mark Heller, Jim Nickel, Donald Spector, and Norman Robinson.

For the chapter on Duke's presidential campaign: Jewel Tardiff, Marc Ellis, Frank Luntz, Charles Black, Carole DiFalco, Colette Rhoney, Mary Matalin, and James Carville. Peter Brown, chief political reporter for Scripps Howard, and Robert Shogan, a correspondent with the *Los Angeles Times*, helped me understand Duke in a national political context.

Many others provided immeasurable assistance but on condition of anonymity, so I thank them while continuing to respect their wishes.

I'd also like to thank the many librarians who helped out: Nancy Burris, Danny Gamble, Karen Cooksey and Amy Wahl at the *Times-Picayune*; Bill Menary, archivist at the Political Ephemera Collection at Tulane University's Howard-Tilton Memorial Library; Andy Simons, archivist at Tulane's Amistad Research Center; and Ken Owen, archivist at the University of New Orleans Earl K. Long Library Louisiana Collection. I'd also like to thank those who read drafts of my manuscript and improved it immensely: Jed Horne, Rick Meyer, Tina Rosenberg, C.B. Forgotston, Lanny Keller, Betsy Mullener and Adam Nossiter. Thanks to John Donahue for proofing the manuscript and to Kurt Mutchler and Doug Parker with photographs.

This book was supported by a grant from the Louisiana Endowment for the Humanities. Thanks to Michael Sartisky, the endowment's executive director, for his help in securing the grant.

Thanks to Richard Abel and Seetha Srinivasan of the University Press of Mississippi for making this project see the light of day. Shelly Bell provided needed understanding and humor that sustained me.

THE RISE OF DAVID DUKE

CHAPTER ONE

THE MAKING OF A FANATIC

By late 1971, the Vietnam War was winding down and with it the protests that had rocked college campuses. But opposition to the war still burned strong enough even at conservative institutions like Louisiana State University for antiwar radical Jerry Rubin to pack the ballroom at LSU's student union when he appeared there on November 14 of that year.

Six students stood out from the motley throng of hippies, peace activists, and hangers-on who had come to cheer on Rubin. The six were neatly dressed and wore armbands with a cross inside a circle. It denoted their membership in an anti-Jewish, white supremacist group named the National party recently formed in New Orleans. Earlier in the day, the National party members had picketed the governor's mansion, protesting Rubin's visit to LSU. They had also picketed the student union before Rubin's speech. The six people were led by a pale, thin twenty-one-year-old named David Duke. This would have been Duke's senior year at LSU, but he was taking the year off from school to organize the National party.

Even though Duke had been away from LSU since May, many students in the crowd recognized him and eyed him warily. During the previous school year, he had become the most controversial person on campus by giving impassioned speeches every Wednesday at Free Speech Alley—LSU's version of the Speakers' Corner in Hyde Park—to denounce Jews and blacks for what he believed was the rapid decline of the white race and the United States. And now as Duke sat in the student union, waiting to hear Jerry Rubin, he eagerly anticipated the chance to confront Rubin during the question-and-answer period—as he had two other recent antiwar speakers he also considered Communists, Dr. Benjamin Spock and black activist Dick Gregory. But when Rubin finished his speech, he refused to take questions and walked off the stage. Duke was furious. He rushed after Rubin, catching up with him in the student union foyer. Fourteen years later, Duke recalled the incident with glee.

"I walked right up to the little bastard. I said, 'Jerry Rubin! Aren't you that big, tough Jew Revolutionary? Jerry, you've got a fascist right in front of you! Why don't you show your followers how tough you are? You talked a pretty good fight up there on the podium. You got a fascist right here. I tell you I'm a fascist and you're a Jew pig! You're a Jew pig! You want to debate, I'll debate you. You want to come on physically. . . . we'll go outside right now. Right here! I don't give a shit. We'll see how tough you are. Jew bastard!' That's what I told him! Right to his face! He turned white as a sheet and turned around and made a beeline for the door. And all his little Commie followers were there, and they couldn't believe it. It was the most hilarious thing you ever saw."

With a large crowd gathered around, Duke decided to press his advantage and make a speech outside the student union. Duke gave himself a glowing review when he wrote about the incident several months later. "Standing on a bench, surrounded by NP members, Duke exposed Rubin's lies to an audience of nearly 500 students," he wrote. "Except for a few loud-mouthed Jews and Gentile dupes, the audience was quite attentive. The hecklers, I might add, were unable to refute any of the points made by Duke."

Twenty years later, on November 16, 1991, David Duke received 680,000 votes in losing the Louisiana gubernatorial runoff to former governor Edwin Edwards. This included a stunning 55 percent of the white vote. Duke's support was remarkable for a candidate who had been openly racist and anti-Semitic for twenty years and who had faced a barrage of attacks during the campaign because of his past as a grand wizard of the Ku Klux Klan and his Nazi activities. It was also remarkable because only five years before, after having become a nationally known Klan leader in the late 1970s, he had drifted into such political obscurity that he had nothing better to do than play golf every day on the public links at New Orleans' City Park. Moreover, his showing came only two years after an abysmal campaign as the 1988 Populist party's presidential candidate—a candidacy that Duke hoped would mark his political comeback. He got a scant 48,000 votes out of the 91 million cast.

How had he traveled so far in three years? Had he changed? Or had America changed? That a former grand wizard of the Ku Klux Klan could win a majority of the white vote—what did that say about relations between blacks and whites in the United States? That he found a way to make his message appeal to so many voters—what does that tell us about political discourse? Or about American voters? Or did it simply reflect the genius of David Duke?

Who is he, anyway? Why had he become a Nazi as a young man? Why had he joined the Klan and left it several years later? What drove him to seek political office? Was he still a Nazi and Klansman who simply had gotten a haircut and dressed up his old views in new clothing, as his opponents maintained? Or had he matured to become the spokesman for the conservative white majority, as he claimed? And a more basic question: what had led this handsome, articulate man—who was intelligent enough to have been successful in any field he chose—to decide that the most noble thing he could do with his life was engage in political warfare against blacks and Jews?

As Duke told the story many years later, the seminal event in his youth came in 1964 when he was a fourteen-year-old ninth grader at Clifton L. Ganus School, a small, all-white Christian academy in New Orleans. His civics teacher assigned him to write a term paper opposing integration, a major issue at the time. According to Duke, he had been given the assignment because he supported the civil rights movement so outspokenly. "In those days," he said, "I held liberal views because that's the pablum that's fed to you." Duke said he went to Ganus's library but found little prosegregation material. By chance, he read an article in the *Times-Picayune* reporting that a white-rights group called the Citizens Council had held a meeting to oppose forced integration of public education. The next day, he said, he took a bus to the Citizens Council's downtown New Orleans office.

The first book Duke read was a 118-page volume called *Race and Reason*, by Carlton Putnam. Popular among the white supremacy movement in the 1960s, *Race and Reason* would become one of his favorite books—"the first eloquent challenge to forced race-mixing," he said in offering it as part of his bookselling operation in the 1970s and 1980s. "Must reading for racial understanding." Putnam provided a theoretical defense of segregation by arguing that whites and blacks were biologically different and that blacks were inherently less intelligent than whites. As a result, Putnam argued, integrating schools would worsen education for whites, because teachers would have to lower standards so that black students could cope. Society overall would lose. "I read the book carefully," Duke said later. "I thought that I would find nonsense, but the book was extremely well written. I couldn't put it down. The author was sensitive and intelligent, and there wasn't a shred of the hatred that I expected to find in it. It didn't convert me, but it began an intellectual odyssey into the other side of the race issue."

Like many of Duke's accounts of his life, this story has some truth but also some rewriting of the facts to suit his political needs. Duke did apparently first begin to develop his race theories by reading *Race and Reason*. But there is no evidence that Duke was liberal on racial issues before reading the book. Neither his sister, nor any of his ninth grade classmates, nor his ninth grade civics teacher, who supposedly gave him the book assignment, remember him as being liberal on race. Instead, they say, he was steeped in a society in which southern whites openly used the word "nigger" and fought to block integration of their schools and public facilities. Duke had no black friends. He lived in all-white neighborhoods until he left for college and attended all-white schools until twelfth grade.

Duke also worshiped his father, David Hedger Duke, a highly conservative man who favored segregation, and tried to imitate him whenever possible. For example, in 1964, David Hedger Duke favored the archconservative Republican presidential candidate Senator Barry Goldwater, and so did his fourteen-year-old son. And years later, as Duke's father described his views of blacks, one could hear the echoes of his son's beliefs. "I'd like to preserve our race," David Duke's father said, "I've always felt that way."

Duke's father said he opposed interracial marriages and preferred to have white neighbors, although he did not mind living next to Hispanics and Asians. "[They] fit in," he said. "Blacks don't." He also said he favored segregated public schools. "Whenever there's a school with 40 percent blacks, the value of education goes down," he said. "The good teachers choose schools that aren't mixed. They feel like they can accomplish more" at white schools. He said there were fundamental differences between blacks and whites. "Blacks in general are not as adept as whites in computers and mathematics," he said. "Most blacks don't fit into supervisor jobs."

Beyond the influence of his father's beliefs, additional clues help explain why Duke developed such a hatred of blacks and Jews. He grew up in a dysfunctional family that provided little love or nurturing at home. School gave him no respite. Classmates shunned him as a pushy know-it-all. At the same time, Duke's personality—he was hyperactive, compulsive and obsessive in his thirst for knowledge and his desire to impress his views on others—seemed likely to inspire fanaticism. It almost seems inevitable, in retrospect, that Duke should end up at one extreme or another. Perhaps his father's strong conservatism ensured that he would head to the Right rather than to the Left. "My brother had no guidance," says his sister, Dotti. "There was no one there to teach him to be a balanced human being, no one there to slow him down and channel his energy into something positive. He's a natural leader. Had he had someone to direct his energy into becoming more of a well-rounded person, he could have moved mountains, done wonderful things. He could have been president."

David Duke's father was born in 1912 in Blue Rapids, Kansas, the great-grandson of Scottish immigrants. He grew up in Kansas. In 1937, while at the University of Kansas, he married a fellow student, Maxine Crick, who was a year younger and had grown up as a neighbor of Harry and Bess Truman in Independence, Missouri. The Dukes were to have two children, Dorothy, born in 1945 in Seattle, and David Ernest, born on July 1, 1950, in Tulsa. Shortly after graduation from college, the elder Duke began working as an engineer for Shell Oil. He was a member of the ROTC at Kansas and was called up for active duty by the army in December 1940. An antiaircraft officer, he spent most of the war in the United States but was promoted to major and was reassigned to the Philippines in anticipation of the planned invasion of Japan. The atomic bombing of Hiroshima and Nagasaki ended the war before he could engage in actual combat. In 1946, he returned to Shell and was transferred from city to city in the oil boom states. Tulsa was one of his stops.

In 1954, David Hedger Duke accepted a position at Royal Dutch Shell's headquarters. The family moved to The Hague in the Netherlands, where young David went to kindergarten. But in 1955 the family moved to New Orleans. The Dukes purchased a tidy, two-story house at 4768 St. Ferdinand Street, in an all-white, middle-class neighborhood known as Gentilly Woods. David spent his grade school years at William C. C. Claiborne Elementary School, which was several blocks away. In 1963, the family moved to suburban Metairie, where David attended seventh grade at Metairie Junior High School. A year later, the Dukes moved back to New Orleans, this time to a larger, one-story brick house at 235 Jewel Street near the huge lake on the city's northern border, Lake Pontchartrain. Their new neighborhood was also all white but more upscale.

A thin man who stood a couple of inches above six feet, Duke's father was a strict disciplinarian with an aloof manner and a hardheaded belief that he was always right. Unemotional and tight with his money, the elder Duke barked commands at his children. Over and over, he lectured them on the need to be self-disciplined and self-reliant. "My father was conservative to the max," Dotti recalled years later, "much, much more conservative than what you would now call a Reagan Republican." She attributes her brother's studiousness to her father, who was an education taskmaster. "If we had no homework, he'd give us three hours' worth of reading to do," Dotti said. "We had to read summers and before we could watch TV on Saturdays. Even one time when we went to the beach. My brother David was very intense, very studious, a bookworm. He never played."

Dotti, who shares few of her brother's traits, rebelled when her father gave her homework. But her brother did not. "He loved it," she recalled. "It was a way to please my father. Even when he was 12, it was read, read, read. Most kids would want to look at kids' things. He wanted to go to a museum, ask about the exhibits, try to absorb everything. It was boring to me." On a trip to the Grand Canyon, "We'd look at the scenery and enjoy it. He'd look down at the rocks under his feet and say he wanted to dissect them to learn more about them. David was on the track of, 'How much information can I put in my brain?'"

Duke would later describe his youth as "a Beaver Cleaver childhood. We rode bicycles, and we played baseball on the front grounds of the Baptist Seminary near my house. I even chipped my front tooth playing football in the street." He remembered having a number of pets, including 100 white rats he kept in the garage. He recalled swimming in Lake Pontchartrain while his dog, Frisky, ran along the shore. But Duke's boyhood was clearly less idyllic than he recounts. He had few friends and spent much of his time alone. His father was often gone, either traveling for Shell or fulfilling his commitment to the army reserves. Duke's sister left home when he was twelve. Afterward he was alone with his mother.

A tall, thin woman with a patrician air, Maxine Crick Duke came from a well-to-do family and inherited a good sum of money. But her husband lost it through bad investments. "She never had a single piece of new furniture after marrying my father," Dotti said. Duke's mother had once been vivacious, active, and an excellent golfer. But during the 1950s, she began to drink heavily, Dotti says, partly to cope with her husband's long absences, partly to cope with losing her sister in a plane crash, and partly because she had trouble adjusting to motherhood. "My father used to buy her books on parenting, and she'd never read them," Dotti says. "When she wanted to tell me about sex, she bought me a book." By the early 1960s, Duke's mother was alcoholic and was taking dozens of pills a day. Frequently bedridden and unable to care for her children, she rarely left home except to play golf on Wednesdays, when it was ladies day at New Orleans's City Park. But her game suffered from the drinking.

Dotti was badly scarred by her mother's alcoholism. "I remember being very alone," she said of her childhood years. "I never had a mother to nurture me. You didn't want to invite anyone home. Everyone in the neighborhood knew that she drank. I had a girlfriend whose mother wouldn't let her play with me—'like mother like daughter,' she said. It was devastating to me." Dotti fled home at the first opportunity, eloping at age seventeen. The marriage ended in divorce a few years later. With Dotti gone, her twelve-year-old brother felt the full force of the family's problems. When she saw her brother in California several months after her elopement, he leaned over the back seat of the family car and confided in her. "You know, Dotti," he said. "I never realized what hell you went through until you left home and it all fell on me."

The following year, after the family had moved to near Lake Pontchartrain, young David was enrolled in Clifton Ganus School for eighth grade. There were only sixteen students in his class. The yearbook photo shows that his ears stuck out and that he wore his hair like the other boys—close-cropped and slicked back. He was a reserve on the basketball team and threw the discus on the track team. But he was scrawny and uncoordinated, not a good athlete. During ninth grade, he again played for the basketball team—the Eagles—and was a member of the school's drama and bowling clubs. The future politician was not a member of the student council during either of his two years at Ganus.

Perhaps the reason was that he could not be elected—for he was estranged and spurned by his peers. Duke had but one friend at Ganus, a tall classmate with wire-rim glasses named Mike Wells. "Nobody liked him," Wells recalled. "No one would talk to him. He was a reject and an outcast. The other kids called him 'Puke Duke,' or 'Duke Puke.' They'd say it to his face. He didn't mind. He probably preferred the abuse to total rejection." Duke's classmates liked to tease each other, play games in the schoolyard, and daydream. But Duke was quiet and serious—unless the subject was politics or history. Already reading the newspaper and closely following political affairs, he'd leap at the chance to forcefully express his views.

His ninth grade civics teacher, Mary Elizabeth Gill, at first encouraged his interest in politics. But she soon found that Duke insisted on interrupting other students to make his views known. If anyone disagreed with him, he insisted on arguing with them until they backed down. "It was, 'It's my way or none at all,'" a classmate remembers. And when Gill wanted the class to move off politics and onto another subject, Duke would resist. "It was the same thing every day—wanting to discuss politics," she remembers. "He'd have an opinion on every subject. The other kids weren't interested. They were talking about sports, making friends, a date—things other teenagers were interested in. I wanted to see him fit in, but he was very preoccupied with what he was trying to figure out. He was looking for direction."

Mike Wells felt sorry for Duke. Wells, who was deeply involved in the Church of Christ, decided it was his Christian duty to befriend his outcast classmate. In the summer of 1966, he sponsored Duke's baptism in the Carrollton Avenue Church of Christ in New Orleans. It was a fleeting commitment, however, for Duke quickly drifted away from the church. Shy and sensitive, Wells was shocked when he visited Duke's home. "Everyone in his household hollered," Wells says. "His mom had a high-pitched voice and was always yelling at him for something. She'd yell, 'David, I told you to get your shoes out of the living room.' She'd yell it again. And again. He would ignore her. He'd turn to me and say, 'Let's get out of here.'"

At tightly knit Ganus, Duke's classmates rarely saw his parents, and he almost never mentioned them. Wells met his mother several times at Duke's house. She always seemed to have a cigarette in one hand and a glass of bourbon in the other. "David didn't want to go home unless he had to," Wells says. "He was embarrassed about her." Nearly thirty years later, Wells, the father of a seventeen-year-old son, shook his head at the memory. "I never saw any love in that home of any kind," he said. "I've always thought his family turned him into who he is."

In the fall of 1964 Duke walked into the Citizens Council's New Orleans office for the first time. He had somehow obtained the council's newsletter, which mentioned *Race and Reason*. Duke asked the Citizens Council's secretary, Dorothy Singelmann, if he could see the book. She got it from a bookshelf. After he read it for a few minutes, he looked up and said, "Mrs. Singelmann, this book is wonderful, I'd like to buy it." Duke returned several days later and asked if he could read other Citizens Council books. Soon he was coming to the office every day after school. Sometimes he just did his homework or chatted with Singelmann and her husband, George, the group's executive director. Reciting what he had learned in *Race and Reason*, Duke began telling them that blacks had smaller brains than whites and that integration of schools would lead to race mixing.

"David, the day is coming when all schools will be integrated," Dorothy Singelmann told him one day.

"I don't think I can stand that," he replied.

Duke was always clean-cut and polite, but he annoyed Singelmann by constantly pestering her. When he began telling her about his problems at home, however, she softened. One time he told her that his mother had been too drunk the night before to eat dinner and had locked herself in her room, where she kept her whiskey. He knocked on the door, but she didn't answer. Afraid that she was seriously ill, he pulled the hinges off the door only to find her in a drunken stupor. "He was a very sad boy," Singelmann said. "I thought he should be around young people. He was never one, like other kids, to talk about a football game or the parties he'd been to."

The Citizens Council had been formed after the Supreme Court's 1954 decision in *Brown v. Board of Education*, which outlawed segregation in public schools. The council was a more reputable opponent of segregation than the Ku Klux Klan, and many of its members were respected citizens. Prominent segregationists spoke at their meetings. Speakers at 1964 Citizens Council meetings in New Orleans included: former Mississippi governor Ross Barnett, who had challenged the integration of Ole Miss in 1963; Lester Maddox, who had recently closed his Atlanta restaurant rather than serve blacks and who would soon be elected governor of Georgia; and John Rarick, a Louisiana state judge who would serve in the United States House of Representatives from 1967 to 1975 and would be active in Duke's political campaigns in the early 1990s. While the Citizens Council's mission was to fight integration, Duke broadened his concern to Jews. Exactly why is not clear. Singelmann said Duke told her that his paternal grandfather had instilled in him a belief that Jews were evil. Dotti, however, says their grandfather was not anti-Semitic.

David Hedger Duke, unlike his son, was not concerned about Jews. His father's sister was, in fact, married to a Jewish man. "He's a fine man," David Hedger Duke disclosed privately. "I'm glad to have him in the family." When he said in 1991 that his son had a Jewish relative, he asked that it not be mentioned to his son. "It'll just embarrass him," Duke's father said. David Hedger Duke rebuked his son the one time he began spewing anti-Jewish views. "He didn't bring it up again," Duke's father said, "because I thought it was nonsense."

Why Jews? Deeply angry and full of rage at his mother's alcoholism, and disappointed with his father's frequent absences, Duke was probably looking for a scapegoat for his unhappiness and for someone—or something—to provide order in his life. The search may have led him to Nazism, which offered a rigid orthodoxy and a clear-cut analysis of the world's problems and clearly defined solutions to those problems. A scrawny kid with no friends, he was ready to fantasize a heroic life for himself, and comments of his in later years show that he pictured himself as an Aryan warrior: brave, handsome, blond, tall, ready to do battle with enemies. Duke's unhappiness at home may also have caused him to idealize a previous, happier era—in this case the era of Nazi Germany. Just as his sister had eloped at age seventeen because of her desperate desire to leave home, Duke may have found his own kind of elopement when he took refuge in Nazism.

Children of alcoholic parents frequently become overachievers and seek attention to overcompensate for what they don't receive at home. Neither a great student nor a great athlete, Duke might have become a Nazi in order to stand out.

Duke began bringing a tattered copy of *Mein Kampf*, Hitler's bible, to the Citizens Council office and praising the Nazi leader. Singelmann was horrified and often ordered him out of the office. But he kept coming back. "He never gave up trying to convince my husband that the American Nazi party was the grandest thing in the world," Singelmann said, "that Nazis were the only pure white people left in the world and should be preserved. My husband told him, 'David, you may not realize it, but you're making a terrible reputation for yourself.'"

George Singelmann was not alone in trying to warn Duke away from Nazism. His mother came to the Citizens Council office once and pleaded with the Singelmanns to persuade her son to end his fascination with Nazism.

"I've told David many many times that he was ruining his life," George Singelmann told her.

"Yes, I know he is," Duke's mother replied. "That's why I'm here."

Ganus School ended after the ninth grade, so David Duke for his sophomore year enrolled at Warren Easton High School, a hulking red brick building near downtown New Orleans. It had the dubious distinction of having had President Kennedy's assassin, Lee Harvey Oswald, as one of its students fifteen years before. For Duke, it was nothing more than a place to attend school. He was a quiet student and participated in no after-school activities; he wasn't even pictured in the yearbook. He continued to spend most of his afternoons at the Citizens Council office, where he delved more deeply into Nazi theories.

After Ganus, Mike Wells went to a school other than Warren Easton, and he and Duke didn't see each other much. Still, Duke used to call him often. They usually talked about girls, but Duke was so enthused about *Mein Kampf* that he would frequently read excerpts of it to his friend. Wells, who abhorred Duke's views, dreaded the calls. He routinely walked away from the phone for minutes at a time while Duke droned on. Occasionally, before Wells returned to the phone, Duke realized that he had walked away. "I'd hear him yelling over the phone," Wells said. "I'd rush back to the phone and say, "Sorry, David, I had to go get a drink of water.' And he'd say, 'Well, I'm going to back up because you missed a good part.'"

With his wife incapacitated by alcohol and drugs, David Duke's father was not happy at home either. He would try to sober her up by putting her in a New Orleans sanitarium. "But they can only hold you three days against your will," Dotti said, "so after three days, she'd check herself out and march to an attorney and file for divorce. My dad would talk her out of it. 'I don't want a divorce, I want you sober,' he'd say. 'The attorney would take all the money.' I can't tell you how many times that happened. He'd have to wait on her hand and foot. I remember him telling me, 'I'm not cut out to be a nursemaid. I just can't keep watching her go down the tubes.'"

At the same time, David Hedger Duke's career at Shell had stagnated. He blamed this on his wife's being drunk at company functions. In 1966, he took early retirement and accepted an offer from the United States Agency for International Development to work as an civil engineer in Vietnam. Many AID employees in Southeast Asia during the Vietnam War were CIA agents, and David Hedger Duke's long experience in the military would have made him a likely candidate, especially since he went into AID in a top-ranking position. He has denied, however, that he was a CIA operative.

It must have been difficult to leave his son behind, but his marriage had disintegrated, and he wanted to join the war against Communism. He would remain in Southeast Asia for nine years, visiting New Orleans on leave every six months or so. His son, meanwhile, ventured deeper and deeper into a world that lurked on the fringe of society.

David Duke's father knew that his departure had left a huge void in his son's life. To try to make up for his absence, and aware that his son had visions of becoming a career officer, he sent him to Riverside Military Academy in Gainesville, Georgia, for eleventh grade. Located in the foothills of the Blue Ridge Mountains, Riverside is a strict school, where student cadets wear uniforms, live in barracks, and follow a set regimen every day. The cadets are divided into companies. Duke was in Company D.

School records show that Duke went AWOL shortly after school began in early September but that he returned within ten days. Duke told one interviewer years later that he had trouble adapting to the regimented life initially and was hazed by older, bigger cadets from the Northeast because of his racist and Confederate sympathies. But, Duke added, by the middle of the year he had won over the other cadets and orchestrated a huge barracks party to celebrate Robert E. Lee's birthday.

Several of Duke's fellow cadets at Riverside tell a different story. They say he did not have many friends and did not stand out. Spencer Robbins, who was a year ahead of Duke, remembers him because of a specific incident. One Sunday, during the regular room inspection, school authorities found a flag with a swastika on Duke's dorm room wall. They gave him so many demerits, Robbins says, that Company D lost several school privileges to other companies. Not surprisingly, this episode did not make Duke popular with the other seventy-five cadets in Company D. The company's cadet officers met, Robbins says, and decided to give Duke what was known as "a blanket party." This was a ploy by which officer cadets at Riverside traditionally brought wayward cadets into line. At 1:00 A.M. several nights later, a group of cadets burst into Duke's room, smothered him with a blanket and pounded him with their fists. "The goal of a blanket party wasn't to hurt anyone but just send him a message," says Robbins. "I bet Duke stayed awake during the next few nights in fear that he would be visited again." (There was no second visit.)

Duke did not hang the swastika on his wall simply because he admired its design. Glenn de Gruy, who lived on Duke's hall, remembers that Duke had a stack of Nazi pamphlets in his room. Duke, says de Gruy, also tried to convince him that whites are the master race. De Gruy, more interested in sports and girls than Nazi theories, waved him off. "I don't know who had gotten ahold of his mind," de Gruy recalls, "but they had made a real imprint."

The 1966–1967 Riverside yearbook contains two photographs of Duke. One is his class portrait. In it, he is wearing his cadet uniform and looks younger than his sixteen years. In the other, he is standing with the other members of the scuba diving team. Duke, like the others, is bare-chested. But, unlike the others, he is wearing a Nazi Iron Cross around his neck. Duke said in an interview that he was promoted to corporal before the end of the school year. But school records show that he finished the year as a private first class. (He would have been promoted had he not gone AWOL, a school official said.) Duke was an above-average student and was invited back to Riverside, but he returned to New Orleans.

Duke has said he spent only a year at the military school because he disliked the regimented life and wanted to go to school with girls again. For twelfth grade, he was enrolled in John F. Kennedy High, the public school closest to his home. While Duke was glad to be back in New Orleans, relations with his mother, which had been tense, worsened with his father thousands of miles away. He hated his mother's drinking and yelled at her that she was a drunk and had to stop. Once he threatened to set her on fire if she did not quit drinking, according to the family's black maid, Florence Parker. David Duke's mother was so afraid of her son that she often accompanied Parker for the weekend to her home in a New Orleans housing project. "She couldn't stand David," Parker said. "She once said she must have gotten ahold of the wrong child."

One day while no one was at home, Parker beckoned to Phyllis Wilenzick, the mother of a family next door on Jewel Street and asked her to come over. Parker led Wilenzick to Duke's room. It was decorated with a Nazi helmet and a Nazi flag. Wilenzick, who was Jewish, was shaken. Wilenzick instructed her children to stay away from Duke. "If he was in the front, I was in the back," she said. "If he was in the back, I was in the front. If he was outside, I wanted to be inside."

Just before he began his senior year, a news report from Arlington, Virginia, carried tragic news for Duke: George Lincoln Rockwell, commander of the American Nazi party, had been shot and killed by a disgruntled follower. Duke called Dorothy Singelmann. "The greatest American who ever lived has been shot down and killed," he said, sobbing.

Duke did not fit in at JFK High during his senior year any better than he had at Riverside. His interests were not the same as those of the other students. He wore a ring with the swastika insignia and carried around *Mein Kampf* as if he would be lost without it. One of his teachers at JFK High was still shaken more than twenty years later by having had Duke as one of her students. "He was the most memorable student I ever had," she said. "What a cross to bear."

Other kids would seek her out after class to talk about homework. Something else weighed on Duke's mind. "It was always the same thing: that the problems in the world were the result of Jews, blacks, and Communism," she said, still incredulous at the memory. "He'd tell me that if the Nazis had won World War II, Hitler would have taken care of the Communists and Jews in Europe and the blacks afterward in the United States. He'd say it was too bad that Hitler had lost." The woman's husband and brother had fought the Nazis in World War II, and her brother had been badly wounded. "It was very unsettling talking to [David]," she said. "The frightening part was that he wasn't a redneck, didn't use four-letter words, was clean-cut. He was so logical and calm—like a simmering kettle waiting to explode. He has the most evil nature of anybody I've ever known."

Duke on prom night hosted an open house. One of his classmates who visited, Chris Champagne, was also disturbed to see the Nazi flag in his room. Champagne remembers: "I thought it was kind of strange." Duke during his senior year was a member of JFK's first integrated class. It was the first time he had gone to school with blacks. Because Duke mainly kept to himself, he was involved in only one racial conflict that black students can remember. When the Reverend Martin Luther King was assassinated in April 1968, Duke was one of the white students who argued against lowering the school's flag. This dispute divided the school's whites and blacks for several days.

Duke's black guidance counselor, Vidal Easton, had no problems with Duke. But Easton remembers him for an unusual comment he made. "You'd ask kids what they planned to do," Easton said, "and they'd say, 'I want to go into the family's business or go into medicine or be a businessman.' But David said he wanted to go into right-wing politics."

Duke's high school grades were good but not exceptional. His grade point average, combined with his family's modest means, led him to enroll at

Louisiana State University in Baton Rouge, a sprawling campus shaded by oak and magnolia trees with an enrollment of about 25,000 students. After spending the summer selling vacuum cleaners door to door and then painting houses, Duke entered LSU in September 1968. Protests against the Vietnam War were inflaming campuses across the country. At LSU, many students passionately opposed the war, but perhaps even more favored it. Duke sat out the debate during his freshman year. He preferred to stay in his cramped, single-person dorm room in LSU's football stadium, where he read books that fed his growing conviction that Jews and blacks presented a mortal threat to the white race. When other students visited him, he pressed his Nazi views on them.

When a sophomore named Jim Beckham accompanied his roommate once to Duke's dorm room, Duke played a record featuring a speech by George Lincoln Rockwell, the slain commander of the American Nazi party. With a laugh, Duke showed photographs of Jewish corpses from Nazi concentration camps.

"Why did you laugh?" asked a perplexed Beckham.

"They'd laugh at you," Duke replied.

Beckham had grown up in New Orleans and was used to racist whites. "But I had never run into hatred of Jews like that," he recalled. "I thought it was bizarre."

Beckham ran into Duke a few times on campus after that, and Duke always tried to convert him. "He would pull out a book and point to a passage where it said Jews had been responsible for Communism," Beckham said. "I told him it was foolish, and after a while he wouldn't talk to me anymore."

Duke was required to take ROTC and a standard curriculum, which included a course in European history. He got a D— in the course. "As a freshman, he was unable to avoid mixing real strange neo-Nazi opinions with standard historical data," said his professor, James Hardy, Jr. "He was obviously a kid with a quirk. When everyone else looked like a shepherd, he wore a coat and tie. The majority of the kids were going one way and he was going the other way." But while Duke may have been a strange kid with a quirk to the students and professors he met during his freshman year, by the time the school year ended, he had done little to distinguish himself on campus and had given few signs that he was to become one of LSU's most famous alumni.

In his sophomore year, Duke, however, set out to lose his anonymity, and he succeeded with a vengeance. The vehicle would be a public forum called Free Speech Alley. For years, anyone wanting to voice his views on any subject could stand on the soapbox at Free Speech Alley in front of the LSU

Student Union. Held every Wednesday afternoon for two hours, the sessions were generally low key, attracting at most fifty spectators. Duke had gone to Free Speech Alley as a freshman but had never gotten up on the soapbox to speak. But one Wednesday afternoon in the fall of 1969, his sophomore year, he mounted the soapbox and delivered the first of the thousands of speeches he would give in his life. As he recalled in 1985: "One day I said, 'To hell with this. I've got to do something sometime with my life.' And I got up and said, 'I'm just going to say everything I know and just spout it all.'"

Free Speech Alley speakers typically complained about student matters or debated the preeminent political issue of the time, the Vietnam War. Duke, too, wanted to talk about a war, although not the one in Southeast Asia. His war was the one that he thought needed to be waged against Jewish influence. When he spoke at Free Speech Alley on November 12, Duke charged that Jews had founded the Communist party and still ran it. He contended that the Soviet Union was aiding Israel against its Arab neighbors because "Brezhnev is married to a Jew and his children are Jewish." When the crowd, which now numbered hundreds of people, expressed astonishment at these statements, Duke explained that "in this country your press is controlled by Jews. You are victims of suppressed news." Asked what he would do to thwart the Jewish Communist conspiracy, Duke said he would prohibit Jews from holding high appointive positions in government and would eliminate the "negative" influence of Jewish culture.

When he was asked by members of the crowd whether he was a Nazi, Duke replied, "I am a National Socialist. You can call me a Nazi if you want to."

The largest outcry from the crowd came when Duke said that whites are "the master race. We should have the right to keep the race white."

Carl Tickles, a black student, challenged Duke's statement. "Look at my hands," Tickles told Duke. "What's the difference?"

"They're black," Duke replied.

Tickles took a knife from a spectator and offered to compare the color of his blood with Duke's.

Duke refused.

A white student joined Tickles. They cut their fingers to show that both bled red.

Duke wasn't impressed. "I could go across the street to the scientific laboratory and get the biggest, hairiest, dirty rat that you could find and slit that and it's going to bleed," he shouted. "It's a rat! What the hell does that prove?"

Most of the crowd jeered him. But their scorn only seemed to spur him on, as did the large numbers of people turning out each week to hear him.

He spoke again at Free Speech Alley the next Wednesday and repeated his claim that Jews were behind world Communism. Three weeks later, when he was asked for proof of this claim, he said that page 29 of *Who's Who in Jewry* listed Herbert Apthecker, a prominent Jew, as a theoretician of the American Communist party. That day, December 10, Duke also called Nazi Germany "the ideal country."

Tempers flared the following week at Free Speech Alley when Duke handed out copies of the *Liberator*, a newsletter of the National Socialist White People's party, the successor to the American Nazi party. A black student named Zebedee Dilworth took issue with the publication, which featured an advertisement for tear gas that read: "Negro control equipment, guaranteed to drop the most vicious buck in his tracks." Dilworth lit a copy of the *Liberator* on fire and approached Duke and the speaker's stand.

"I'm sick of all this," Dilworth cried—and grabbed a stack of the newsletters. He set them on fire. Shouting broke out in the crowd. Dilworth told Duke that he had once kept a pair of blacks from killing him. But he predicted that Duke would be murdered one day.

Duke responded coolly. "The way to show me that I'm wrong is not to beat on me or burn papers," he said, "but to persuade me in a debate."

While a star, albeit an infamous one, at Free Speech Alley, Duke was a loner who had few friends at LSU. He was so filled with anti-Semitic fervor and love for Nazi Germany that other students always rebuffed his overtures. One student who lived two doors down from Duke in West Graham dorm in the summer of 1970 gave Duke a wide berth after seeing a photograph of Hitler on his desk, a poster of a Nazi soldier on his wall, and a swastika draped over his windows. "We were all interested in girls and had *Playboy* centerfolds on our walls," the student said. "The consensus was that he was strange."

When Duke returned to LSU for his junior year in the fall of 1970 and began speaking again at Free Speech Alley, spectators began complaining that it had degenerated into a one-man show. They also complained that the student newspaper, the *Daily Reveille*, gave Duke too much publicity. Duke was no longer a funny novelty. On one Wednesday in October, he was booed off the soapbox under new rules that allowed the crowd to determine whether a speaker could proceed. Duke complained that the crowd had lost what he called the "real meaning of free speech." But one student told the *Daily Reveille*: "We wanted David off the box because we were tired of listening to his tirade against Jews."

Duke would not be deterred. On December 9, 1970, he gave an impromptu speech after the regular Free Speech Alley. He got into a heated discussion with a Jewish woman. She jumped on a bench and began hitting him on the head and chest, the *Daily Reveille* reported. Duke doubled over and called for aid. Campus security officers finally pulled the woman away. When Duke later wrote about the incident in the *Racialist*, the newsletter of the White Youth Alliance, a group he had founded in January 1971, he told a different story. "She jumped on the bench and tried to kick Duke between the legs," Duke wrote, referring to himself in the third person. "He just held her back with one arm and turned sideways. Police . . . quickly moved in and removed the Jewess from the bench."

"Jewesses" were not alone in countering Duke at LSU in 1970. He also faced opposition from an unlikely source: the commanders of the ROTC program. ROTC was mandatory both freshman and sophomore years at LSU. Although he hated the regimen at military school when he was sixteen, Duke still dreamed of becoming a career officer. He loved ROTC. And he was good at it. In fact, he was so good that when his commanders during his sophomore year reviewed his academic grades, his military grades and his leadership ability, they ranked him highest in a class of about 2,000 cadets. His commanders gave him the Outstanding Basic Cadet award and promoted him to sergeant major. He was the only sophomore to reach that rank.

Normally, Duke's lofty standing would have automatically advanced him to the upper division ROTC program for his junior year. But in a highly unusual move, his commander, Colonel Joseph W. Dale, refused to promote him. Dale knew of Duke's Nazi pronouncements from the *Daily Reveille* coverage at Free Speech Alley. Dale also discovered that Duke had a Nazi flag, a Nazi uniform, and other Nazi paraphernalia at his Baton Rouge residence.

Duke appealed the decision of a review board not to advance him, but Dale upheld its ruling. Duke then sought assistance from the American Civil Liberties Union—a group he would later assail publicly—but it told him it could not help. His military career was over. "Duke had outstanding leadership potential," Dale remembered. "But his activities did not lend themselves to the United States Army."

Duke's Nazi pronouncements in college came to haunt him later in life despite his efforts to dismiss them. During his 1990 United States Senate campaign, Duke readily discussed his Klan activities but glossed over his Nazi activities. When questioned, he denied having been a Nazi party member and deflected further probing by saying he had been too "strident" and "intolerant" as a youth. In a laughable understatement, he also said he had been "a bit of a rascal" as a young man. Asked in a 1989 interview about having passed out Nazi literature at LSU, the most Duke would concede was: "I had all kinds of right wing materials. I had stuff from Klan groups and all kinds of different organizations, Posse Comitatus, so many different groups. There might have been some of that in there."

On a 1990 radio talk show, when asked about his Nazi activities at LSU, Duke replied: "There's no question about the fact that I had a controversial youth. When I was a youngster, I explored lots of different political opinions and values and organizations." What Duke did not say is that from 1969 to 1971 he headed a succession of groups at LSU that had close ties to the National Socialist White People's party, the successor to the American Nazi party.

Because of the Ku Klux Klan's notoriety, Duke's views toward blacks have received the most attention. But he has always viewed Jews as a far greater threat to the white race than blacks. As an LSU sophomore, he founded the National Socialist Liberation Front, a student chapter of the NSWPP. In a signed column that appeared in the *Daily Reveille* on November 19, 1969, Duke said that the NSLF would work to prevent Jews from destroying the white race.

He had yet to hone his message into simple language. National Social-ism "stands for cultural, spiritual and racial values to become the primary emphasis of a system," he wrote. "It stands for instilling into our people the self-discipline, self-respect and personal toughness which we need to build a society which gives the individual a positive relationship between himself, his community, his race and Nature." But his message came through: "The Jewish people as a whole control both systems [Marxism and capitalism] and have been a driving force for the disintegration and degradation of Western Civilization and the white race."

The January-February 1970 issue of *White Power*, a publication of the National Socialist White People's party, applauded Duke's activities. "By seizing every available opportunity to present National Socialist ideas to his fellow students, Duke, a pre-law sophomore, has made the Party a real issue on his campus." The August 1, 1970, issue of the NSWPP's internal news-letter wrote approvingly of Duke's most infamous act, the picketing of leftist lawyer William Kunstler on July 23 at Tulane University in New Orleans. Sporting a swastika armband, a brown shirt, and black storm-trooper boots, Duke carried a placard reading, "Kunstler is a Communist Jew" on one side and "Gas the Chicago 7" on the other. The latter reference was to the group of demonstrators—Jerry Rubin and Abbie Hoffman among them—who had been arrested at the 1968 Democratic Convention in Chicago. Kunstler was their attorney.

The Kunstler protest would bedevil Duke for years. His opponents regularly brandished photographs of him wearing the Nazi regalia and holding the placard aloft. Reporters, meanwhile, invariably questioned him about the incident. For years, Duke passed it off as "guerrilla theater . . . a stunt . . . it was neat," as he told one 1980 interviewer.

A decade later, as he sought mainstream acceptance, he changed his tune and called it a mistake. But even then he said he regretted dressing in the Nazi garb only because the questions it provoked deflected attention from issues he preferred to discuss. He never apologized for the hatemongering itself.

Certainly, to his NSWPP comrades in 1970 he was a godsend—a young, energetic activist organizing college students. NSWPP Commander Matt Koehl was so pleased with Duke's activities that he invited him to the second annual North American Congress of the World Union of National Socialists on Labor Day weekend in Arlington, Virginia, where the NSWPP was based. Koehl also had Duke speak at a public rally in Washington's L'Enfant Plaza on September 6, 1970.

The speaker's platform at the rally was flanked by a security force of nearly fifty stormtroopers and decorated with a huge swastika and a banner proclaiming "National Socialism Is for the White Man." The September 1 party bulletin reported: "In his remarks, Dave Duke appealed to the anti-establishment sentiments of young people present by emphasizing that National Socialists also want to smash the System. He pointed out that unlike our Bolshevik opponents, we recognized the true nature—the Jewish nature—of the System and that therefore only we could be considered true revolutionaries capable of destroying that System. Duke was really making points with a large number of the young persons when a fresh rain of bottles from Jewish agitators in the crowd caused a police lieutenant to halt the rally."

As he began his junior year at LSU in September 1970, Duke changed the name of the National Socialist Liberation Front to the White Student Alliance and formally linked it up with the NSWPP. Students wanting to join were invited to send five dollars to the NSWPP's Arlington headquarters. By January, Duke had changed the name of his group again, this time to the White Youth Alliance. People wanting to join were now directed to write Duke directly at LSU. The NSWPP's newsletter *White Power* hailed the formation of the new group as a counterweight to the leftist Students for a Democratic Society and the Black Student Union. Copies of the newsletter turned up in the files of the FBI, which had been keeping close tabs on Duke.

David Duke would soon formally cut his ties to the NSWPP, but he would maintain private contacts with neo-Nazi leaders for years. When asked publicly, however, he would downplay his Nazi past, quickly changing the subject to a topic that put him on firmer ground. More ambitious than the white supremacy movement's other leaders, Duke was willing to go to almost any lengths to avoid being labeled a Nazi.

"I hate to be Machiavellian, but I would suggest you don't really talk much about National Socialism . . . publicly too much," he said in 1986, interrupting an interview being conducted with Joe Fields, a member of the National Socialist party. "You need to leave your options open. . . . If they can call you a Nazi and make it stick . . . , it's going to hurt. It's going to hurt the ability of people to open their minds to what you're saying. It's going to hurt your ability to communicate with them. It's unfortunate it's like that."

Duke headed the White Youth Alliance at LSU until his junior year ended in May 1971. In the final copy of the group's newsletter, the *Racialist*, Duke told his readers that he was about to travel overseas for four months. And when he returned, he added, he would not enroll for his senior year at LSU but would move the WYA to New Orleans.

CHAPTER TWO

THE RACIALIST IDEAL

As a youngster, David Duke liked to work on science projects at a home laboratory. He read *National Geographic, Science Digest,* and *Popular Science.* So it was not surprising when he was drawn to racist theoreticians who dressed up their bigotry in the trappings of scientific fact. White supremacy was a biological fact, *Race and Reason* argued, in updating the racial theories that had impressed Hitler.

Duke's belief that he had developed his views through scientific study rather than gut-level emotion made him all the more unshakable in his racism. It also made him feel that no one could rightly call him bigoted. After all, he thought, hadn't he developed his views through logic and reason? By the time he was twenty, Duke was using an impressive-sounding phrase to describe his views on race: "racial idealism." He called himself a "racial idealist," a term that he borrowed from the National Socialist White People's party. For years, he would deny that he was a racist and instead call himself a "racialist."

In the September 1970 issue of the *Racialist*, he gave the first full definition of his views. He relied on obtuse, academic phrasing, but his statements formed the core of a philosophy that he would espouse for years. "Racial idealism, or racialism, is the idea that a nation's greatest resource is the quality of its people," he wrote. "It means examining all questions of government on the basis of whether the proposed measure is good or bad for our race. It means that racial interests should never be subordinated for momentary materialistic advantage. And it means that although economics must play a vital role in our system, the primary emphasis of our system must be the physical, mental and spiritual health of our people. . . . Neither Communism, Capitalism, nor any other materialistic doctrine can save our race; our only racial salvation lies in a White racial alliance uniting our people with the common cause of racial idealism."

Duke held that the primary goal of government should be furthering the interests of the white majority. Whites, he reasoned, had founded the United States and were responsible for the laws that had made it the greatest country in the world. But now antiwhite elements had taken control. "Through courage, strength and idealism, our White race fought disease, famine and a savage non-white population to build this nation out of the wilderness," Duke wrote in the *Racialist*. "Unfortunately, political power in America today is held by the ANTIWHITE minority, which not only controls the government, but also the powerful media of publications, radio and television. The plain truth is that our race is losing. We're losing our schools to Black savagery, losing our hard-earned pay to Black welfare, losing our lives to NO-WIN Red treason and Black crime, losing our culture to Jewish and Black degeneracy, and we are losing our most precious possession, our White racial heritage, to race-mixing."

Duke was in the forefront of an anti-Jewish/white supremacist pseudointellectual movement. The movement's ideas were expressed most thoroughly in a 584-page book published in 1972 called *The Dispossessed Majority*. It was written by a mysterious man who used the pseudonym Wilmot Robertson and who published an anti-Semitic newsletter called *Instauration*. "I think this is the most important book since the Second World War," Duke said of *The Dispossessed Majority* in a 1985 interview. "It's a brilliant book. The scholarship in it is intense."

Robertson argued that it was no accident the white race was losing ground. He thought it resulted from a deliberate strategy by Jews to make themselves the dominant race. Worst of all, he said, the conspiracy was working. A key part of the strategy, Robertson wrote, was to control the media. By owning the nation's newspapers, television networks, motion picture companies, publishing houses, and magazines, he said, Jews acted as a kind of thought police to brainwash whites into accepting what he called nonwhite values.

"The Jews control what we read, what we see, what we know," Duke explained in a 1980 interview. "The top man at ABC is a Jew, Goldenson. The top man at CBS is a Jew, William S. Paley. Eight men all together—Goldenson, Rubenstein, Westin, Paley, Salant, Sarnoff, Silverman and Crystal—all of them are Jews, and they determine what over two hundred million Americans know about what happened in the world each day. Who owns *The New York Times*? A Jewish family. Who owns *The Washington Post* and *Newsweek*? A Jewish family."

Although he did not make the distinction publicly because it was clumsy to identify whites as Caucasians or Aryans, to David Duke Jews were a separate race—and a money-grubbing race at that. He said Jews would do practically anything to make a dollar. The July 1976 issue of the *Crusader*, his Klan newspaper, even accused them of introducing the slave trade to the United States. The newspaper said five Marano Jews on Columbus's initial voyage had captured 500 Indians and sold them in Spain. "Columbus did not receive any of the money resulting from the sale of the slaves but became a victim of a conspiracy of the Marano Jews and was imprisoned," the *Crusader* said. "This episode was the beginning of the slave trade in America." (Maranos were Jews who, faced with death by the Spanish Inquisition if they did not renounce Judaism, converted to Catholicism but secretly continued to practice their faith.)

Duke believed Jews were engaged in a conspiracy to weaken the white race by using the media to promote integration and race mixing. Through integration, whites were forced to accept blacks at their public schools. As *Race and Reason* had taught, blacks were less intelligent than whites and inevitably attacked teachers and white students—so integration produced a lesser education for whites. Race mixing, Duke believed, was inevitable when whites and blacks lived in close proximity because lust and rapes could not be suppressed even between the races. Race mixing, according to Duke, meant white genocide. "The blood that flows in our veins, our genetic makeup, is the product of thousands if not millions of years," he said in a 1974 interview. "And we feel like that to cast this out, to race-mix, is to destroy something that is very sacred."

Race mixing inevitably caused the decline of white nations, Duke believed, because the children of interracial couples, by definition, were lesser beings. "There have been studies confirming, for instance, the much higher frequency of mental illness and retardation among the offspring of interracial couples," he wrote in 1986. While promoting race mixing between blacks and whites, Duke argued, Jews assiduously kept themselves pure. "The Jews are constantly talking about preserving their 3,000- or 4,000-year-old culture and values," Duke noted in a 1982 interview. "In Jewish publications, you always see reiteration of the dangers of intermarriage—how this will hurt the Jewish people in the long run. . . . But meanwhile, they tell us Gentiles that we don't have the right to preserve our culture as European people."

In the early 1970s, Duke suggested several ways to curb the power of Jews and reverse integration. To force Jews like Secretary of State Henry Kissinger out of government, Duke favored prohibiting Jews from holding high government positions. He was not sure exactly how to end Jewish economic control, but he anticipated that the United States economy was about to plunge into such a deep depression that whites would be called upon to replace Jews in positions of financial influence. If whites were superior, how did they come to be controlled by Jews? Duke had an answer for this vexing question. "It's an affirmation of the goodness of our own people," Duke told an interviewer in 1985. "The whole chivalric medieval type of morality, for instance, is a good example of white morality compared to a Jewish type of morality—an openness, an honesty. You're not necessarily nice. But if a white guy stole something, he'd steal it. He wouldn't sneak up behind you . . . and steal [somebody's] wallet while he's not looking."

Duke said that Jews were sneaky and did not play by the rules as whites did. "So we're not psychologically equipped to deal with the entry of the Jews," he said. Once whites had broken the hold of Jews, they could reverse the integration forced on them by Jews. Duke favored partitioning the United States by race and eventually shipping blacks back to Africa. Blacks in New Orleans, for example, would be relegated to the central city, he said in a 1975 interview.

As a short-term solution, he favored a voluntary separation of the races. This, of course, meant repealing civil rights laws that prohibited segregation. Duke thought integration was a Jewish plot to force black crime and sloth upon whites as a means of weakening the white race. He believed that whites and blacks preferred to live apart. "I am certain that the masses of Whites would prefer for their children to go to White schools, and blacks would prefer for their children to attend black schools," Duke said in 1977. "Both races would prefer to live in neighborhoods that reflect their own culture and values. I think that people should be given a choice.

"If a few people want integration in the major cities, put a couple of schools aside for them and let them have all the integration they can stand. Those blacks who want to have their own schools, which reflect their own particular needs, let them have them. Whites who want schools that reflect our culture, our heritage, our values and our needs, can have them also." He added in a 1984 interview: "The federal government and local government today is coming in and forcing the races together, and this is causing more problems than it's solving."

Duke blamed Jews for pollution, saying it reflected their greedy, capitalistic ways, and from his LSU days on called for a clean environment. "I want to see a clean society—clean up the pollution, and in concert with the environment, not trying to get out as much bucks as you can to pursue some Jewish dream," Duke said in a 1985 interview. Duke thought that pollution interfered with what he called Nature—his mystical belief that if it weren't for the interference of Jews and minorities, whites would live in a clean, pure society, like the Nazis under Hitler. The Nazis, he said in the 1985 interview, had "a real sense of unity with nature and believing in non-pollution and relocating factories to the countryside and creating a whole community around nature walks and that outlook on life."

Duke expressed admiration for such black nationalist leaders as Malcolm X in the 1970s and Louis Farrakhan in the 1980s because they supported racial separation. Duke thought blacks and whites preferred separation because there were inherent cultural differences. Blacks were good at music, sports like track and basketball and heavy labor work, he said. Whites, he said, were better suited to employment as professionals.

Throughout the 1970s and 1980s, Duke's newsletters published articles complete with diagrams from scholars of dubious distinction showing that the skulls of blacks and whites were different—with the skulls of blacks appearing to be apelike. Other diagrams showed teeth of blacks resembling those of apes. Duke didn't just cite discredited theories to prove that the races should be apart. "Separation or segregation is also promoted vigorously in the Bible," he wrote in 1986. "There's nothing in the Bible which sanctifies integration," he said in an interview the year before.

Duke said government policy should reflect the differences between the races. Not only should whites not be forced to go to school with blacks, he argued, but they also should not be required to hire them. In what would become one of his main political issues, Duke argued passionately against affirmative action and minority set-aside programs, which were designed to offset past discrimination by giving blacks preference in hiring and the awarding of government contracts.

Duke believed that an employer should hire the best qualified person, regardless of color. While Duke may have seemed to be inviting businesses to employ blacks, he was not: because he believed whites were inherently more intelligent than blacks, whites would naturally get the jobs. Only when the government forced companies to follow affirmative action and minority set-aside programs, which he thought were a form of reverse discrimination against whites, did blacks get the jobs. Duke acknowledged that blacks had faced discrimination—but only when they were slaves. He was blind to the injustice and oppression that blacks have suffered since, and he saw no reason why whites today should be punished for their forefathers' sins.

Duke's dread of racial mixing was not confined to Jews and blacks. Latin American immigrants appalled him because he thought they brought disease, crime, and laziness—all of which were spreading throughout healthy white communities. He rejected the view that the Latin Americans would invigorate the United States much as the Irish and Slavs had before them. The government was accepting so many undesirable, nonwhite immigrants, he said, that the inscription at the base of the Statue of Liberty should be rewritten to say: "Give me the wretched refuse of your teeming shores, the bones, the scabs, the whores; anything that can walk, crawl or make it by U.N. flight; anything, that is, but a healthy intelligent man who is white."

Duke was a true believer. As he explained in a 1985 interview: "Once I learned about the race issue, I felt any other pursuit in my life would almost be meaningless if the white race didn't win the . . . struggle to see the continuation of our culture and heritage and the enrichment of those values."

When David Duke told members of the White Youth Alliance in May 1971 that he was going overseas, he did not disclose his destination. In fact, he was headed for Vientiane, the capital of Laos. He was joining his father, who was working in Vientiane as an engineer for the State Department's Agency for International Development. David Hedger Duke, after four years in Saigon, had transferred in October 1970 to Laos, where he oversaw the building of bridges and roads. By now a colonel, David Duke's father had grown increasingly worried as he heard more and more reports about his son's open identification with Nazism. While he was home at Christmas in 1970, Duke's father asked him to spend the summer with him in Laos. He could easily find David a job, he said. After demurring initially, David in March agreed to go when the semester ended.

Duke in later years would use his visit to Laos as a weapon to ward off his political foes. He would tell audiences and reporters that he had served his country during the Vietnam War by teaching anti-Communist Laotian military officers. He would also say he had risked his life to push sacks of rice out of planes flown by Air America, a Central Intelligence Agency subsidiary, as they supplied anti-Communist rebels in the countryside below. He may not have called himself a war hero, but he certainly left the impression that he was one—and that he had served in uniform. Laos provided the perfect foil against suggestions that his Nazi activities—especially his protest against William Kunstler in 1970—made him unpatriotic. "I did my part for this country (in Laos)," he said at one point in 1989. "What the opposition doesn't say is that I stood up for America," Duke said in 1989. "I went behind enemy lines and brought rice to anti-Communist insurgents in that country." He said he spent nine months in Laos—"a normal tour of duty."

The truth is rather different. Laos had been part of French Indochina until France granted it independence in 1949. While first the French and then the United States tried to prevent Ho Chi Minh's North Vietnamese Communists from taking over neighboring South Vietnam, the Laotian government tried to remain neutral. But this neutrality became increasingly difficult to maintain in the late 1960s as the United States poured more troops and weapons into Vietnam. By the time Duke and his father were in Laos in 1971, Communist guerrillas controlled most of the countryside, and the United States was secretly financing the Laotian government and a band of anti-Communist rebels fighting to reclaim the countryside. Vientiane remained safely in the government's hands.

When David Duke arrived there at the beginning of June 1971, his father secured him a job teaching English at the Defense Department's American Language Institute. It was a job many parents found for visiting sons and daughters, because the language school was always looking for instructors. The job required little more of teachers than giving rote lessons in military English to about ten Laotian officers. The pay was $2.20 an hour for six hours a day.

In Vientiane's tightly knit American community, David Hedger Duke was well respected. But his son did not fit in. David Duke's fellow teachers quickly decided that their new colleague was strange and avoided him whenever possible. "David always pushed things too far," said a fellow teacher, who, like Duke, was a college student visiting his parents. "We all thought, 'This guy is some kind of heavy duty radical.'" Charles Green, the head of the language school, oversaw hundreds of teachers during the five years he held that position, but twenty years later David Duke still stood out in his mind.

One day Green was making his rounds at the school when he passed Duke's classroom. He glanced in and stopped in horror. Duke had drawn a Molotov cocktail on the blackboard. Green walked into the classroom, asked Duke to erase the drawing and said he wanted to see him after class. Green, who had participated in three wars, knew that such a drawing could encourage an impressionable soldier to make Molotov cocktails—and Molotov cocktails could be very dangerous in a strife-torn country. After class, Green fired Duke—who became the only American instructor he ever axed. Duke had been on the job only six weeks.

Duke's claim that he delivered rice to hungry anti-Communist Laotian guerrillas seems fanciful. In 1990, he told an interviewer that he had gone on about twenty flights. They were at night, he added, and after spotting its target, each plane would fly only ten feet off the ground to deliver its cargo. On one such flight, Duke said, mortar fire hit his plane, and he narrowly escaped serious injury when a piece of shrapnel lodged in his belt.

Two Air America pilots in Laos at the time, however—Leon LaShomb and Gene Landry—say there were no unauthorized passengers on Air America flights and that, because of the mountainous terrain, the rice drops were made in the daytime from at least 500 feet. LaShomb said Duke might have gotten a friendly pilot to let him ride along once or twice—but no more—and then only on "milk run" flights over safe areas. No pilot, LaShomb added, would have allowed Duke to push the rice off the plane.

When these doubts were raised during Duke's United States Senate campaign in 1990, he showed aerial photographs of rugged terrain and claimed that he had taken the pictures during rice runs. But he had no proof that he was the photographer—or that the photos had been taken in Laos from planes delivering rice. In addition, Duke's normally extraordinary memory failed him when he was asked the name of the airfield from which he had taken his twenty flights. (The Air America planes delivering rice flew from Watty Airfield.)

Duke's later attempts to portray himself as a war hero in Laos—and his calls at the time for an all-out effort to defeat the Communists in Vietnam—were particularly ironic, considering that he had been drafted and could have been fighting had he wanted to. Duke was classified 1A—ready for induction—on August 21, 1968, seven weeks after he turned eighteen and was required to register for the draft. But he wasn't inducted because he was attending LSU. He received two student deferments in 1969.

When Duke left school after his junior year in May 1971, he lost the student exemption. As a result he was called up for active duty. But Duke requested another student deferment, and the induction order was canceled on March 4, 1971. Two weeks later he received the student deferment, draft records show. He didn't lose his student exemption until February 4, 1972, when he was reclassified as 1A. By then, the draft was winding down, and he was not called again. When it was revealed during the 1990 Senate campaign that Duke had dodged the draft, he said he had wanted to serve but had been prevented from doing so by the military because of his "racist activities." This statement was untrue.

Duke's racist activities got him kicked out of the ROTC but not out of the army. In 1971, the final classification he received to avoid the draft—a 1S(C) classification—was granted only at a student's request. Students rejected by the army were given a 4F or a 1Y classification. Duke's Selective Service record showed that he had been deemed fit for induction—"physically," "morally," and "mentally"—in the three categories in which would-be inductees were tested. (He took his induction physical on December 17, 1970.) The record showed he received the passing "X" mark in each category, not the "Y" or "Z" mark that would have disqualified him. It was Duke's decision not to serve.

Not only did Duke lie twenty years later about why he opted out, but he also apparently failed to notify the draft board that he had left school in May 1971—a violation of the draft law. Duke was required to notify his draft board within ten days of leaving school, which would have caused the draft board to reinstate the 1A classification almost immediately, said Eileen Wagenhauser, secretary of his draft board. Paper notification would have meant almost certain induction. Twenty years later, Duke would portray himself as a great friend of the military and of veterans. But in 1971 when he had a chance to go to Vietnam as a soldier to do his part to defeat the Communists whom he regularly denounced while at LSU, he chose not to do so. In sum, David Duke was one of the many Americans who evaded the draft.

Duke left Laos soon after he was fired from his teaching job in July 1971, and he spent the next three months traveling throughout Europe and India. He claimed that throughout the trip he met with right-wing politicians and professors to discuss race issues, although he never provided any evidence that he had done so. He wrote later that his visit to India played an important role in what he called his "racial odyssey." In a 1982 article, he wrote that he came to realize that the poverty and filth in India resulted from the inexorable decline in the racial purity of the white-skinned Aryans who had ruled India centuries before. "Only a tiny percentage of any generation had sexual liaisons with the lower castes, but over hundreds of generations a gradual change in the racial makeup occurred, imperceptible in a generation, but dramatic after a millennium," he wrote. His visit to the Taj Mahal left him depressed, believing that the Aryan culture that could build such a magnificent structure had given way to the rot of a mixed society. "I saw it as a funerary monument to the memory of a people who gave the earth great beauty," he wrote.

A couple of days later, Duke visited another ancient temple and had an encounter "that will forever remain etched in my memory." Duke said he saw "a dark brown, poor little half-caste Indian girl." She was emaciated, riddled with sores, covered with flies, and begging for rupees. Duke wrote that he gave her all his Indian coins and "stumbled into the hot Indian sun with my eyes full of tears." The brief encounter, Duke wrote, steeled his resolve to devote himself to the cause he had already been pursuing since age fourteen. "I wondered if, a few hundred years from now, some half-black ancestor of mine would be sitting in the ruins of our civilization brushing away the flies," he wrote. "Every day our nation grows a little darker from massive non-white immigration, high non-white birthrates and increasing racial miscegenation, and with each passing day we see the quality of our lives decline a little bit more. . . . The Brahmins of America are becoming replaced by the Pariahs, the Untouchables, and seeing that child in that setting was my passage into a future time that can happen to America unless everyone who has racial understanding acts to shape, with the power of his will, a future not of racial decadence, but of racial excellence and achievement. . . . I had already committed myself to the struggle for our racial survival long before I saw that child in the ruins, but that experience changed an intellectual commitment into a holy obligation. I realized in the hot Indian sun that I would never abandon this cause. The flame that burned in me that hot August day in 1971 is white hot and unquenchable."

Duke had returned to New Orleans from his overseas sojourn by November 1971. He was now twenty-one years old, sporting a small blond mustache and combing his hair Hitler-style straight across his head. He wasted no time in reviving his work to save the white race. Duke had promised members of his White Youth Alliance that he would continue the group, but once again he changed its name, this time to the National party. In a letter to WYA members that included a National party membership form, he explained that the name change would broaden the group's appeal beyond just students. "The WYA served like a lighthouse in the foggy murk of modern day democratic-liberalism . . . ," he wrote. "But, my friends, the great political victory that we long for won't generate from just a student organization. We must be youth oriented, but all our people are needed in the struggle."

The National party was similar to the White Youth Alliance. Its goals were the same—curbing the power of Jews—and it had a publication that Duke edited, the *Nationalist*. The newsletter used a format that Duke would use over the next twenty years in tabloid-sized newspapers he would publish for the Ku Klux Klan and the National Association for the Advancement of White People. The *Nationalist* attacked Jews and blacks, blaming them for every problem faced by the United States, while it hailed whites as responsible for all of the country's accomplishments.

Like other anti-Semites at the time, Duke paid homage to aviator Charles Lindbergh, whose praise of Nazi Germany and efforts to keep the United States out of World War II had greatly diminished the hero worship that had greeted him after he became in 1927 the first person to fly across the Atlantic Ocean. In March 1972, the *Nationalist* featured a story headlined, "Lindbergh: Man of Wisdom." Lindbergh's diaries, the story said, "on several occasions point out that Jewish propaganda was behind Roosevelt's foreign policy and was designed solely to save Russia and the Jews. As years pass, it becomes more and more clear that Lindbergh was right [in opposing United States entry into World War II]."

The *Nationalist* also advertised videotapes of speeches by George Lincoln Rockwell, an early hero of Duke's who had been commander of the American Nazi party until his 1967 assassination. "Rockwell at Brown University, Rockwell vs. Carmichael, Rockwell vs. NAACP, Rockwell Lynchburg

Speech. Order one today: $4," the advertisement read. Duke continued selling these tapes well into the 1980s. Like his later newspapers, the *Nationalist* also carried many photographs of Duke and heaped adoring praise on his every public appearance. "David Duke, 21, has made each meeting come alive with a speaking talent unequaled," one issue gushed. "Certainly he will probably be one of the greatest public speakers of our time. At each meeting in which Duke speaks, about 90 to 100 percent of the new people present become members."

But the *Nationalist* also showed Duke at his crudest, a far cry from the sophisticated pamphleteer he would become. The March 1972 issue offered several jokes:

"Q. What do you get when you cross a nigger with a gorilla?

"A. A retarded ape."

"Q. Why are synagogues round?

"A. So the Jews can't hide in corners when they pass the collection plate."

The April 1972 issue featured cartoons depicting blacks as thick-lipped savages and Jews as big-nosed swindlers.

Because Duke was no longer in school, he was able to work full time for the National party. As a result, the group was more activist-oriented than the White Youth Alliance. One of the group's first activities was the November 14, 1971, picketing of Yippie leader Jerry Rubin at LSU, where Duke called him a "Jew pig!"

On January 21, 1972, Duke organized a torch-lit parade in New Orleans from City Hall to historic Jackson Square in the French Quarter. Ostensibly, the march was organized to protest the killing three weeks earlier of a seventeen-year-old white high school student. Duke blamed an unspecified black person for the slaying, although no suspect had been named. With a light rain falling, about eighty-five people marched in the parade. They chanted, "Two, four, six, eight, we don't want to integrate!" and screamed, "What do we want? White Power!" They carried National party flags, which featured the cross-wheel insignia that Duke had unveiled at the Rubin protest and banners saying, "America for Whites, Africa for Blacks."

At Jackson Square, Duke gave a speech attacking his familiar targets. "This is the beginning of the end of nigger rule," he cried. He blasted New Orleans mayor Moon Landrieu, a white, calling him "Moon the Coon" for trying to block the march. "They didn't want to see us out here," Duke said, "but rain isn't going to stop us. Words won't stop us. Fights won't stop us. And bullets won't stop us. We're gonna keep on going 'till we win political power in this country. You can boil down the problems (of the country) into two words:

Jews and niggers. Every great institution and American tradition is being attacked and is being befouled by these people who are determined to destroy this country."

Few people paid attention. But Duke portrayed the march as a great victory. "The parade seemed almost like a huge living thing," he wrote in the *Nationalist*. "It was alive with chanting and singing. 'White Power! Glory, glory, separation, we don't want a nigger nation! White Victory!' filled the whole downtown area of New Orleans. At the end of the march, a great rally was held and we hit point after point. Finally at the close we let out the loudest chants of 'White Victory' this country has ever heard."

Preparations for the march were marked by Duke's first arrest. He and three other National party members were taken into custody three days before at party headquarters, 3210 Dumaine St. in New Orleans—a small, wooden structure that doubled as Duke's home. The charge: violating a city ordinance that prohibited filling glass containers with flammable liquids because they could be used as Molotov cocktails in a riot. Duke was jailed briefly until James A. Lindsay, a man who had come to play a key role in his life, posted bail. The charges were dropped after Duke convinced authorities that he and his friends were making Mardi-Gras-style flambeau torches.

Duke has said he met Lindsay during his senior year at JFK High School. While most people thought that Lindsay was simply a real estate developer, he in fact led a double life as a racist and anti-Semite under the pseudonyms Ed White and Jack Lawrence. To try to keep his identity hidden at one Klan rally, Lindsay ducked his head under his coat when authorities tried to photograph him. Until Lindsay was shot dead with three bullet wounds at his Metairie real estate office in 1975, he was Duke's political mentor and surrogate father, providing him with advice and money. (Lindsay's estranged wife was acquitted of the murder, which remained unsolved. There is no evidence that Duke was involved.)

Duke was arrested again four months after the National party march. He and three others were charged with soliciting money for the presidential campaign of Alabama governor George Wallace while pocketing the money. Police said the Wallace campaign reported that none of the $500 collected by Duke and the others had been forwarded. Again, Lindsay bailed Duke out of jail. Lindsay also persuaded Wallace campaign officials to tell authorities that the National party members had been collecting money for them. The charges were then dropped. But the arrests had taken their toll on Duke, and he soon disbanded the National party.

One of those arrested in June was an LSU graduate named Chloe Hardin. The daughter of a used car dealer in West Palm Beach, Florida, she had been active with Young Americans for Freedom and the Young Republicans at LSU. Opposed to integration and mistrustful of blacks, the petite student with straight blonde hair had been intrigued by David Duke at Free Speech Alley. One day in early 1970, one of Duke's friends loaned her a copy of *White Primer*, an imitation of George Lincoln Rockwell's *White Power* that Duke had written under the pseudonym C. W. Bristol. Several days later she telephoned Duke to pay for the book. He asked her out to dinner, and they began dating.

Hardin's roommate at the time, Marilyn Memory, was stunned. Memory's boyfriend was Mike Connelly, the head of the conservative Young Americans for Freedom at LSU, who frequently clashed with Duke over political issues. Duke's influence on Hardin was immediate. Soon after they began going out, Marilyn Memory returned to their dorm room and found a huge picture of Hitler covering Hardin's bulletin board. She immediately took it down. The two never discussed the incident and indeed stopped talking to each other.

Chloe Hardin graduated from LSU in December 1971 with a degree in home economics. She and Duke decided to marry. They exchanged vows in a West Palm Beach church on September 9, 1972. Duke's best man was an older friend named Ray Leahart, who worked as a foreman at a trucking company. Leahart, who was convinced that the white race was heading toward extinction, was friends with Matt Koehl, the commander of the National Socialist White People's party. Leahart had met Duke while Duke was at LSU. Leahart would become a den leader in Duke's Klan and would remain faithful in succeeding years while others turned against him.

For their honeymoon, the young couple traveled across the United States, camping in Yellowstone and Glacier national parks. They ended up in Seattle, where Duke's sister, Dotti, was living. By now, the newlyweds had run out of money. They both got jobs, Chloe working as a waitress and her husband as a bellhop. Dotti at first was glad to see her brother and his bride. She had had little contact with him since eloping a decade earlier, having lived in Japan and California. But when he began expounding his antiblack and anti-Jewish views, she was horrified. "We'd get in the same room together and argue," she says. "We didn't really have a whole lot in common. I could never understand how he was so one-subject-oriented. He was like a stranger to me. I believe that putting anybody down about race, creed or color is wrong."

They rarely talked to each other in succeeding years. During that time, Dotti brought her mother to live with her in Oregon and weaned her from alcohol and drugs. Deeply spiritual and active in adult children of alcoholics programs, Dotti raised a family of four and became the director of an institute that strengthened ties between Japan and the United States. She and her brother reconciled in 1987, but the gulf between them remained too great. Dotti often suggested that Duke would benefit from attending adult children of alcoholics meetings, as she did. But he always resisted. Love and frustration were mixed in her voice when she described a disagreement over this in 1992. "I told him it's impossible to live in a dysfunctional family and not have scars," she said. "I told him he should deal with it. But he won't. He does not accept that my mom's drinking has had any effect on him. He's wiped that out as an adult. My brother is very surface with his feelings. He's too much into having to be in control, not showing weakness and faults. We had an argument about that."

Three months after Duke and Chloe came to Seattle in 1972, they had saved enough to return to Baton Rouge. In January 1973, Duke enrolled at LSU for his senior year. He was ready again to undertake his life's mission: winning "victory" for the white race.

CHAPTER THREE

KNIGHTS OF THE KU KLUX KLAN

In time, David Duke would claim that the White Youth Alliance and the National party had simply been fronts for the Ku Klux Klan and that by 1973 he had decided that the best course of action was to openly proclaim his allegiance to the Klan. He would say that he had actually joined the Knights of the Ku Klux Klan when he was seventeen while a senior at JFK High School but that at his father's insistence he had agreed not to identify himself as a Klansman for several years.

When he joined the Knights of the Ku Klux Klan, Duke would say later, he was simply rejoining the group. Duke would claim that the Knights of the Ku Klux Klan had existed for years—that its headquarters were moved from Nashville, Tennessee, to Baton Rouge in 1973 by Imperial Wizard Ed White, who was actually Jim Lindsay disguising himself to hide his activities. Duke would contend that Lindsay was so busy with his real estate business that he had let the Knights grow moribund and that Duke in late 1973 offered to revitalize it by reviving its newspaper.

Duke's assertion that the Knights of the Ku Klux Klan had existed for years may have seemed unimportant to outsiders. But it was a crucial claim for a twenty-three-year-old Klan leader competing for legitimacy and attention against more established Klan groups. In fact, it was a false claim, according to three men who served as officers in Duke's Klan. James K. Warner, whom Duke recruited into his Klan in 1975, said in a 1987 interview that Lindsay did not head the Knights of the Ku Klux Klan, that Ed White was a fictitious name invented by Duke, and that it was Duke who formed the group. "He made up the story," Warner said, "to get rid of criticism by other Klan leaders that he had an upstart Klan."

Jerry Dutton, who was grand wizard of the Knights of the Ku Klux Klan for about six months in 1976, said that the National party's collapse in 1972 led Duke to join a New Orleans Klan group headed by a man named Roswell

Thompson. Dutton said Grand Dragon Frank Widenbacker kicked Duke out a few months later for trying to upstage him. "Duke stormed out of the headquarters vowing that he would start his own Klan," Dutton said. "Jim Lindsay was never a member of the Klan. Instead, he was a member of several other right-wing organizations and was a personal friend of Duke's."

A third former Klan member, Gregory Durel, contradicted Duke's story that the Knights of the Ku Klux Klan had existed in Tennessee before being moved to Louisiana in 1973 by Ed White. Durel said Lindsay indicated to him that Ed White was a nonexistent person. "Ed White was a straw man," said Durel. "Lindsay told me that people wouldn't understand if we told them the truth." Duke's stories that he joined the Klan at age seventeen and that the Knights of the Ku Klux Klan moved from Nashville served two purposes. Not only did it make his Klan seem more legitimate, but it also served to deflect attention from his open embrace of Nazism from 1969 to 1971 at LSU. More so than the Klan, his Nazi activities would later become a political embarrassment, requiring that he do everything he could to hide them.

The Ku Klux Klan had been founded on Christmas Eve, 1865, by six former Confederate military officers in a law office in Pulaski, Tennessee. The Civil War had been over for eight months, and the young men were looking for a way to relieve their postwar boredom. Someone suggested that they form a club. One man suggested they call themselves "The Merry Six," but that stirred no enthusiasm. Another of the six, who had studied Greek and Latin, suggested the Greek word "kuklos," meaning "band" or "circle." That caught their fancy, and they soon settled on the alliterative—and mysterious sounding—Ku Klux Klan.

The six then designed a suitable outfit: a white robe, a mask with holes cut out for the eyes, and a tall headdress, built up with cardboard to make the Klansman look taller than he actually was. They next produced a list of nonsensical titles—grand cyclops, grand turk, grand scribe—that deepened the mystery. Members, called ghouls, were bound together by an oath of secrecy. The group started off as pranksters, terrifying freed slaves during evening rides by pretending to be ghosts of the Confederate dead. A favorite trick was to ask a black person for a drink of water and then drink a bucketful—by pouring the water into a secret receptacle hidden into the robe. The Klansman would then say: "First drink I've had since I was killed at Shiloh." If the white robes could scare blacks so easily, why not use the Klan to maintain white supremacy—especially since the Reconstruction government, at the insistence of the northern states, was giving political power to blacks? Many whites felt this political power belonged to them.

As the Klan spread, its members began attacking blacks. Lynchings became common. Violence became so synonymous with the Klan that in 1869, Klan Grand Wizard Nathan Bedford Forrest, the Confederacy's greatest cavalry commander, officially ordered the Klan's dissolution. The violence ebbed gradually as white southerners regained control over their land from the hated northern carpetbaggers and blacks. The Klan lost its reason for being and died out. It was dormant for fifty years. Its revival began in 1915. A southerner named William Joseph Simmons fulfilled a boyhood dream by recruiting fifteen friends to climb to the top of Stone Mountain, Georgia, on the outskirts of Atlanta. By the light of a burning cross, they launched a new Klan.

Simmons's action coincided with the release of an epic motion picture, *Birth of a Nation*, which was the brainchild of a talented young director named D. W. Griffith. Based on a historical novel, *The Klansman*, written by Thomas Dixon in 1906, *Birth of a Nation* captured Griffith's vision of southern history on camera.

Griffith blended the romantic appeal of the prewar South, the heroics of the Confederate Army, and a vision of the South rising again by throwing off the northern carpetbag government during Reconstruction thanks to the exploits of the Ku Klux Klan. The movie was a hit. Using innovative filmmaking techniques, Griffith, the son of a Confederate officer, told how the South was being trampled by power-mad black Reconstruction legislators and soldiers. The greatest indignity came when the demure sister of the hero leaped to her death to avoid being raped by a hulking black man. When the Klan rode to the rescue, audiences were so stirred that spectators often grabbed their guns and fired shots into the motion picture screen.

With favorable publicity from *Birth of a Nation*, the Klan caught the public's fancy after World War I. As part of the country's "return to normalcy," the Klan rode the wave of a xenophobic movement spurred by a backlash against European immigrants. An estimated 5 million people joined the Klan's ranks, including senators and congressmen. Vigilante-style beatings, lynchings, and floggings returned—and by the Great Depression, the group had again gone out of favor.

In the 1950s, the Klan once again enjoyed a comeback as racist southerners latched onto a vehicle to oppose the federal government and the Supreme Court, which were upholding efforts to integrate public schools, lunch counters, buses, and other public facilities. But when the Klan was unable to stem the tide of integration through legal methods, Klansmen again resorted to bombing and murdering blacks. By 1965, the FBI had infiltrated many Klan groups and was arresting members who resorted to violence. By the time Duke identified himself as a Klansman in 1973, the group had been discredited and membership had shrunk to about 3,000 from roughly 50,000 in 1965.

Perhaps because his unhappiness at home made him yearn for a golden time of the past, Duke bought completely into D. W. Griffith's celluloid image of the Klan—the dashing young men saving the South from the dastardly Reconstruction government and its carpetbag leaders who let the freed blacks rape and murder white Southerners. In line with this view, Duke idolized Nathan Bedford Forrest, not William Joseph Simmons. Duke described the original Klansmen as cultured and intelligent, much as he liked to think of himself. For years, Duke sold portraits and busts of General Forrest, and as late as 1989 he displayed a bust of the original Klan grand wizard in his home.

His romanticized view of the Klan—"a fantastic heritage," he called it—attracted Duke to the Klan in 1973. Having disbanded the National party in late 1972, he was looking for another vehicle to promote his racial politics. He was attracted to the Klan also because he thought that it could generate the media coverage needed to spread his views. Initially, his title was grand dragon. Jim Lindsay, who was operating under his pseudonyms as grand wizard, asked Duke to produce a newspaper for the Knights of the Ku Klux Klan. He published the first edition in the fall of 1973. The newspaper was called the *Crusader*.

The front page of the first issue was headlined "Who Shot Wallace? Was the White House Behind It?" Duke had no doubt. He wrote, "As time goes on, it becomes obvious who would have gained from the assassination of George Wallace—the Committee to Re-elect the President and the entire Jewish Power Structure." Duke believed that Communists—i.e., Jews—had co-opted President Nixon. Jews were behind Nixon's decision to establish ties with China, Duke believed. Another article in the first issue of the *Crusader* called the NAACP "[a] Jew front." The article said two Jewish brothers had founded the group and had run it until 1966, when a rich Jewish shoe manufacturer, Kivie Kaplan, became president. The article also said that the head of the NAACP's Legal and Defense Fund was another Jew, "Jake [*sic*] Greenberg."

Duke was clearly awed by the overwhelming power he attributed to a worldwide Jewish conspiracy. But he was not without hope. The present power structure was so rotten that it would collapse under its own weight, he believed, paving the way for whites to reclaim their rightful position on top. In the meantime, he advised, whites must build a political machine. "It must be recognized, that at this time, any violent White Revolution against the MINORITY MACHINE that rules America is doomed to fail. . . . We must

(1) work to gain as much power as possible in every legal way, and (2) prepare for the coming economic collapse and the total breakdown in Law and Order that will result," he wrote in the *Crusader*.

"How can we obtain power legally? The Jewish superstructure of power can never be brought down from the inside. They have not and would not permit one of our people to become more powerful than themselves at their own game. Witness the shooting of George Wallace. . . . Because of the Jews' basic alien nature, the weakest link in his power structure is between himself and the masses of [white] Americans. Beginning at the lowest levels, we must get between the Jews and our people. Jewish power comes from a national level downward with only its weakest tentacles reaching down to the local community. Local politics, working upward, is the soft underbelly of their empire, one that can be pierced."

It was fitting that the first issue of the *Crusader* carried an ad for the NSWPP's *White Power* newsletter. After all, it was George Lincoln Rockwell, the slain American Nazi party leader, who had urged fielding white candidates in local elections. In *White Power*, Rockwell advocated winning a series of local elections as the first step to regaining control of the government from Jews. Duke had left the American Nazi party behind because he thought the stigma associated with Nazis was too great to overcome. But in joining the Klan, he hoped to steadily build a white political movement with himself at its head that would become so powerful that Klansmen would win elective office.

Duke's appeal for a political—and legal—approach to taking power marked a sharp departure for a Klan group. Leaders of other Klans seemed to be doing little more than holding cross burnings and ranting against "niggers" and "integrationists." There were at least a dozen Klans in 1973, but only two had more than a handful of members. These Klans were led by long-standing grand wizards Robert Shelton and James Venable.

Shelton, forty-four years old in 1973, was imperial wizard of the United Klans of America. A tough, taciturn, good ole boy from Alabama, Shelton had been the best-known Klan leader for years—and by 1973, he had the largest Klan. He had founded his Klan in 1961 and had been jailed for contempt of Congress for nine months after refusing in 1966 to turn over records of United Klans to a congressional committee. Shelton's jailing—and his harassment by the FBI— seemed to sap his energies, and by 1973 his Klan was in decline. Shelton had taken an instant dislike to Duke, whom he called a Nazi. Shelton also dismissed Duke as a mail order Klansman because Duke accepted applications to join the Klan through the mail without inducting everyone through the traditional secret ritual.

James Venable, the granddaddy of Klan leaders, had joined the National Knights of the Ku Klux Klan in 1924, and his family owned property at Stone Mountain, where he hosted annual Klan cross-burning ceremonies. His Klan had once been considered dangerous by the Anti-Defamation League. But by 1973, he was seventy years old and was slowing down. Venable also detested Duke, complaining that he did not defer enough to Klan tradition and ritual.

Duke initially proclaimed allegiance with members of the other Klans, calling them "Klan brothers, for we are all fighting for the same cause." He wrote that he would not tolerate criticism of the other Klans because "the enemy would like nothing more than for Klan groups to slander, redicule [sic] or smear other Klan groups." But he soon abandoned this stance and began sniping at the other Klan leaders. The animosity developed from differences not only in style but also in ideology. Shelton and Venable were generally red, white, and blue segregationists, focusing their energies on damning integration in the United States. Only occasionally did they mention Jews, and calling them Nazis would have been an insult. Duke, in contrast, was to change the Klan's ideological focus and to usher in a new era—a Nazification of the Klan—based on his conviction that Jews posed the greatest threat to the white race. Many of his early Klan speeches were practically word-for-word recitals of speeches made by George Lincoln Rockwell.

His mentor, Jim Lindsay, donated money to the National Socialist White People's party, the successor to the American Nazi party, and was a secret admirer of Adolf Hitler. At a 1974 Ku Klux Klan meeting, where *Birth of a Nation* was supposed to have been screened, Lindsay instead showed newsreel footage of the Nazi leader. A Klansman who attended recalls that "Lindsay was sitting in the front row saying what a great leader Hitler had been, what a great orator he'd been."

Most of the key members that Duke recruited into the Knights of the Ku Klux Klan were from the NSWPP or other neo-Nazi groups. One key recruit was Don Black, a veteran anti-Semite. Black, the son of a conservative construction contractor, had become active in racist activities while still a teenager in Huntsville, Alabama. He had been a member of the NSWPP's National Socialist youth wing when he met Duke in 1970. Black nearly died that year when he was shot by Jerry Ray, the brother of the Reverend Martin Luther King's assassin, James Earl Ray, while Black was trying to steal the membership list of a rival neo-Nazi group, the National States Rights party. Like Duke, Black had been denied advancement in ROTC while a student—at the University of Alabama—because of his neo-Nazi activities. He joined the Knights of the Ku Klux Klan on July 27, 1975, the day before his twenty-second birthday, and became Duke's Alabama grand dragon. Black was noted for his tall, erect bearing and piercing eyes. When he wasn't wearing his white robe, he worked as a medical technician for a Klan sympathizer.

Duke also recruited William Grimstad, another NSWPP veteran, to write a column for the *Crusader*. A former reporter for the *San Diego Union* and the *Minneapolis Tribune*, Grimstad was one of the hate movement's most prominent propagandists. He had been editor of the NSWPP newsletter, *White Power*, and had been the author of several anti-Semitic books published by Noontide Press, the publishing house of longtime anti-Semitic propagandist Willis Carto, the leader of the Liberty Lobby. Grimstad's most noted book was *The Six Million Reconsidered*, which was published anonymously in 1977. The book, which became a classic in anti-Semitic circles, argued that the Holocaust was a Jewish myth. After registering for a short time as a foreign agent for Saudi Arabia, Grimstad in 1979 became editor of the *Crusader*.

Another Duke recruit was Tom Metzger, a stocky television repairman. Metzger, who had grown up in Indiana and had moved to Fallbrook, California, in 1968, had been a member of the far-right John Birch Society. Metzger had refused to pay federal income taxes for several years in protest of continued American involvement in the Vietnam War. Metzger thought the war was a conspiracy to bankrupt the United States. To collect the back taxes, the federal government briefly seized his home.

In 1974, Metzger met Duke at James K. Warner's North Hollywood home. Like Warner, Metzger was a minister in the Klan's newly developing religion, the Identity church movement. Soon afterward, Metzger, who wore a pistol at home, joined the Knights of the Ku Klux Klan, and became Duke's California grand dragon.

In the early 1960s, Warner had been an officer in the American Nazi party under George Lincoln Rockwell. He had been arrested numerous times for his extremist activities, including a 1963 conviction for conspiracy to interfere with the integration of Birmingham's schools.In 1961, Warner had been ordained as a minister in the Church of God, and in 1970 he was ordained in his own Identity church, the New Christian Crusade church. He met Duke in 1974 when Duke spoke at Identity meetings in the Los Angeles area. Warner was impressed with Duke's appeal to young people, since Klansmen tended to be older men who had joined in the 1960s. In 1975, Warner accepted Duke's invitation to move to New Orleans and become the Louisiana grand dragon of the Knights of the Ku Klux Klan.

With the Nazification of the Klan, the Identity movement became its unofficial religion. Identity was based on an obscure nineteenth-century theory called "British Israelism" holding that the people of Britain or northern Europe were the true descendants of the Ten Lost Tribes of Israel. Identity had been brought to the United States by Gerald L. K. Smith in the 1930s and popularized by a notorious anti-Semite, the Reverend Wesley Swift, during the 1940s and 1950s. Using selected biblical passages, Identity taught that whites descended from northern Europeans, not Jews, are the "chosen people" and that Jesus was an Aryan, not a Jew. Identity preached that nonblack people of color—like Latin Americans, American Indians, and Asians—are "mud people" and exist on the same spiritual level as animals. As a result, race mixing for whites is a sin.

Identity further held that Adam was not the first man but the first white man. It taught that Eve was physically seduced by Satan, to whom she bore Cain, the forebear of a hybrid race, the Jews. Thus Jews were literally the children of Satan. Identity newspapers, like Warner's *Christian Vanguard*, were filled with articles alleging that Jews tortured and mutilated children. Identity taught that one day not only Jews but also all minorities would be destroyed in a worldwide race war that would leave only the "true Israelites," white Anglo-Saxons. Identity preachers urged their disciples to arm themselves and stockpile food in preparation for the coming race war.

The Identity movement coined a phrase to capture its belief that the federal government was effectively under the control of Israel. They called the federal government the "Zionist Occupational Government," or ZOG. In October 1974, Duke incorporated an Identity church, the Christian Crusader church, with the Louisiana Secretary of State's office, and he spoke at Identity meetings that year and the next. Also in 1975, he claimed, he had received an honorary doctorate from Los Angeles Christian University, an Identity church. In the 1970s, Duke was a minister in a mail order religious group based in Goodlettesville, Tennessee. He never publicly discussed this activity, which was apparently a way to make a little extra money. He claimed privately to have presided at ceremonies at which Klan couples reaffirmed their vows.

Despite his flirtation with Identity, he never adopted its beliefs. He was trying to tap into a new audience that would be receptive to his views. Duke, in fact, was suspicious of Identity and contemptuous of organized religion in general. He had his own form of religion: trying to preserve the white race. Duke had been baptized in the Church of Christ as a sixteen-year-old in 1966, but sometime afterward he switched his faith, because during the 1970s and 1980s he told interviewers that he was a Methodist. He rarely went to church during those years, however, and expressed nothing but contempt for Christianity.

In fact, Duke told many people over the years that he was an atheist and believed that Christianity was created by Jews to control white people. He was particularly scornful of the Old Testament because it called the Israelites a "chosen people." In a 1986 letter to his followers, Duke said "the major organized Christian churches have been converted into a deadly enemy against the White race. The National Council of Churches, for example, has funded black, communist, athiest terrorists in Africa who have murdered White Christian missionaries!" But if Duke was an atheist, he was an atheist with a twist. He had a mystical belief in what he called Nature—the white race was the product of Nature, and if Nature's laws were followed, whites and blacks would follow their true instinct and choose to live apart, leaving whites free of the pernicious influences of blacks.

When Duke was starting out with the Klan, it served his purposes to be friendly with the Identity movement, so the first issue of Duke's newspaper, the *Crusader*, in the fall of 1973, carried an advertisement for James K. Warner's New Christian Crusade church. The ad offered such books as *Reopening the Trial of Jesus Christ*, by Dr. Wesley Swift. It was described as "a gripping review of the viciousness and illegality of the most famous trial in history, with devastating proof that the Jews were totally and solely responsible for the murder of Christ!" The first *Crusader* also carried an ad for *Attack!*, the newspaper of the National Youth Alliance, as well as several articles from *Attack!* One reprinted article detailed how Jews dominated the business of pornographic books and films.

The National Youth Alliance, later to be shortened to the National Alliance, was headed by William Pierce, a former physics professor at Oregon State University who had turned into an anti-Semitic propagandist. Duke first made contact with Pierce at age sixteen when he wrote him a letter. "He was an intelligent, interested teenager who wanted my views on some things," recalled Pierce, who was ideological director of the George Lincoln Rockwell's National Socialist White People's party at the time.

The *Crusader* reprinted more than a dozen of Pierce's articles. But Pierce's major contribution to the hate movement was writing a novel called *The Turner Diaries*, under the pseudonym Andrew Macdonald. *The Turner Diaries* "fantasizes about the overthrow of the American government by superpatriots who kill Jews and non-whites, destroy Israel and establish an Aryan nation and world," the Anti-Defamation League reported. "*The Turner Diaries* served as a blueprint for The Order, an underground terrorist group founded by members and former members of the National Alliance and the anti-Semitic and racist Aryan Nations. The Order was responsible for a string of criminal and terrorist activities in 1983–84," including the 1985 murder of Alan Berg, the acerbic host of a Denver talk show. After Robert Mathews, the leader of The Order, was burned to death in a fire during a shootout with the FBI in December 1984, most of the other members were captured and sentenced to lengthy prison terms.

The *Crusader* printed a glowing review of *The Turner Diaries* by Nick Camerota, one of Pierce's associates, who wrote that he especially liked the book's drawings. "The one of the *Washington Post* blowing up was delightful," Camerota wrote. "Come to think of it, the drawing depicting the charred ruins of the FBI building was pretty good too." In a note at the end of the review, Duke offered copies of the book for $4.95. Pierce also wrote another influential pamphlet, *Who Runs the Media?*, which argued that the country's major media outlets—the *Washington Post*, the *New York Times*, the Newhouse newspaper chain, the major networks and others—were owned and controlled by Jews. Duke began selling the pamphlet, but he put his own name on it as the author. "I chastised him a few times for not giving me credit," said Pierce. Nonetheless, they remained close allies throughout the 1970s and 1980s.

Another Duke ally was Willis Carto, described by the Anti-Defamation League as "probably the most influential professional anti-Semite in the United States." Carto in 1961 had founded the Liberty Lobby, which sought to neutralize Jewish power. In 1979, he would establish the Institute for Historical Review, which promoted the view that the Holocaust was a myth propagated by Israel.

Giving the Klan a distinct Nazi flavor was not the only way Duke revamped the invisible empire in the 1970s. In an effort to modernize the Klan and broaden its appeal, he also opened his membership to women, Catholics, and teenagers. Before Duke, women could be only auxiliary members of most Klans. But Duke gave them full membership and claimed in the mid-1970s that 40 percent of his members were female. Duke not only invited women into the Klan but also gave them leadership roles. He named Sandra Bergeron, a housewife, as area coordinator for New Orleans, and he bestowed the title of "grand geni" on his wife, Chloe. Duke's views regarding women, however, were hardly progressive. More than anything else, he wanted them to be Klan mothers of large broods. "We need women to breed Klan babies," he said in a 1976 interview, "raise their children to become Klan members and exert their great moral force to make the rest of the nation see our purpose."

While the Klan had been virulently anti-Catholic in the past, Duke realized that the ranks of his Klan could not grow without Catholics. Southern Louisiana, where Duke was based, is heavily Catholic. It was also necessary to dampen anti-Catholicism when he began looking to the northeastern United States to recruit blue-collar workers angry with court-ordered busing and crime.

Duke instituted a Klan Youth Corps for white students between twelve and seventeen years old. The youth corps was a continuation of Duke's effort to exploit racial tensions in New Orleans by recruiting at high schools in 1972 while he headed the National party. In the late 1970s, Duke had youth corps chapters scattered throughout the country, and occasionally they would make news by handing out Klan leaflets. Another major innovation Duke brought to the Klan was artful manipulation of the media. While Robert Shelton avoided reporters whenever possible, preferring to hold secret meetings and cross burnings in cow pastures, Duke sought media exposure—and exulted when he received it.

Duke believed that because Jews controlled the media, he would never get fair treatment. But he knew he needed media attention to promote his Klan. And as time went on, Duke realized how easily he could manipulate the media. The Klan was a compelling story. Morever, many reporters did not do their homework—and were thrown off track when he effortlessly parried their hostile questions and articulately outlined his views. Reporters invariably focused on Duke's appearance. "He is an earnestly handsome young man, handsome enough to turn women's heads," wrote one reporter in 1979. "He has long, dirty-blond hair that he keeps pushing out of his face and a very becoming blond-reddish mustache. At 28, he is disarming and eloquent and looks like your ordinary Middle-American Jaycee out pushing the latest raffle or perhaps making his first stab at politics."

Duke came to realize that he could especially beguile an audience on television. He quickly mastered the quotable sound bite—the brief, concise comment that plays well on the 6:00 P.M. news. He learned that by looking good and sounding reasonable, he could win half the battle, since reporters and television viewers expected him to fit the Klan stereotype of looking and sounding like an overweight redneck. Duke was always neatly groomed in a coat and tie and spoke earnestly without raising his voice. "The media can't resist me," he boasted in a 1978 interview. "You see, I don't fit the stereotype of a Klansman. I don't have hair cropped so close to my head my ears stick out two or three inches. I'm not chewing tobacco, and I don't have manure on the bottom of my shoes."

Duke got his first chance to publicize himself and the Klan on "Tomorrow," NBC's late-night talk show hosted by Tom Snyder. It was a popular show in its time. After seeing a segment on devil worshipers, Duke wrote Snyder daring him to interview a Klansman. Snyder accepted the challenge, and the show was broadcast on January 7, 1974. Duke, then twenty-three, had done only one television interview before, with a Baton Rouge station, so he was "scared shitless," as he said later, before the hour-long show began.

But he gave an extraordinary performance. Snyder was expecting someone he could dominate. But instead it was Duke who easily handled the talk-show host. In fact, Duke grew so confident as the show progressed that at one point he admonished Snyder for talking too much. Surprised by Duke's performance, Snyder late in the show told him, "I'd always thought of the Klan as being a bunch of old fogies who were concerned with yesterday. But you're intelligent, articulate, charming."

Duke had prepared for the show with a question-and-answer session at a friend's house in Baton Rouge. He also drew upon his debating experience at Free Speech Alley. Snyder was expecting to discuss the Klan's hatred of blacks, but Duke shifted the debate to whites' becoming second class citizens in the United States—the dispossessed majority—because of integration and Jewish control of the media.

"We have a situation in this country where the white people, the majority that built this nation, has been continually downgraded by the media," Duke said. "Our heritage, our racial and cultural heritage, is misrepresented in many cases, distorted. White people are told that they are exploiters, that they should be ashamed of the fact that they're white. One of the leading authors in this country, Susan Sontag, writes that the white race is the cancer of history. It's the kind of a minority racism that dominates a great deal of our country today."

Duke said FBI statistics showed that blacks commit more serious crimes on a per capita basis than whites. He would continue to make this argument for years. "Now you can say, 'Well, it's because they've been oppressed or because they've been discriminated against, that they're committing this crime.' But the actual fact of the matter is that places where the Negro has been given the most freedom, where they've been initiated or gathered into society the most is where you have the biggest problems." He cited a recent attack by blacks against a white fisherman in Boston. A flustered Snyder responded, "When you talk about crime, it's difficult to argue your points."

Duke picked up steam as he switched to his preferred theme, the excessive influence of Jews. He called Secretary of State Henry Kissinger "a Zionist Jew" and said Kissinger had a conflict of interest. "When he goes and does the State Department work, he's also doing the bidding of Israel." The Jewish-controlled media also did Israel's bidding, Duke said. "I believe that the media in this country . . . do not really reflect the ideals of our Western, Christian civilization and culture. I believe they're very anti-white in many ways." He said Hollywood was part of the conspiracy and called it "the most kosher thing that I've ever seen."

These were standard arguments he would repeat for years. But on "Tomorrow," he also condoned violence against blacks, a position he soon dropped when he realized that it undercut his image of a "new" Klan. When Snyder asked whether he would participate in a lynching, Duke said he would not because it would hurt his Klan if he went to jail for forty years. But he said he favored lynching a black man who he said had recently raped and murdered two women in Baton Rouge but had gotten off on a legal technicality. When Snyder asked how he was preparing for the revolution he expected, Duke said he and his followers were stockpiling weapons and food in rural areas. "Two hundred years ago, our forefathers fought a revolution to become masters of their own destiny," he said. "And the white people in this country [are] going to have to realize that we're going to have to fight if we want to maintain our society."

Duke's appearance—he was seen by millions of people—was an overwhelming success for the young Klan grand dragon. Calls and letters poured into the Knights of the Ku Klux Klan office asking Duke to appear on radio and television talk shows and to give speeches at universities across the country. (For years he sold an audio cassette of the show for five dollars.) The Anti-Defamation League was furious with the show. Shortly before signing off for the night, Snyder had invited Duke to return. But the ADL pressured NBC to retract the invitation.

Duke had launched his career as a media star. First, though, he had to finish his studies at LSU. Having begun his senior year in January 1973—which he financed with a $1,400 student loan from the state of Louisiana—he graduated with a degree in history in May 1974. Neither of his parents attended the graduation ceremony. Colonel Duke was in Laos, and Maxine was bedridden at home. Nevertheless, it was a triumphal day for Duke. His degree gave him added respectability, and now he could devote all of his time to the Klan.

He didn't have long to wait for an opportunity that would bring him the wide exposure he had been seeking. The city of Boston was tense in September 1974. United States District Judge Arthur Garrity's order requiring the busing of nearly 20,000 of Boston's 94,000 schoolchildren to achieve racial balance had left the city in turmoil. Whites were particularly angry, wondering why a federal judge was telling them where their kids had to attend school. Didn't he realize, they asked, that busing their kids to black schools meant they'd get a lousy education and might even face physical harm?

Two thousand miles away in Baton Rouge, David Duke followed the events in Boston and decided to try to exploit the white rage. He had already spoken forcefully against busing, believing it to be yet another way that the Jews who controlled the United States were weakening the white race. On

September 17, he announced that 300 Klansmen were heading to Boston to help organize white resistance against the forced busing. He said the Klansmen were undertaking "Freedom Rides North," a wordplay on the trips made by blacks and whites who traveled to the South in the early 1960s to try to force integration. "We feel like Boston is a signal," Duke said, "a turning point in this fight against forced race-mixing."

Duke's announcement showed his ability to push hot-button issues. It also revealed a shrewd effort to move the Klan beyond attempting to halt desegregation—he knew that battle was lost—to exploiting contemporary issues that inflamed whites. Finally, the Boston announcement showed that at age twenty-four Duke had already learned how easily he could manipulate the media.

There were no 300 Klansmen heading to Boston. There weren't even 30. There were but 2—Ken Perry and Gregory Durel, the Baton Rouge and New Orleans organizers, respectively, for the Knights of the Ku Klux Klan. There were no buses, either. When Duke spoke, Durel and Perry were on their way to Boston in Perry's battered Ford Maverick. The Maverick didn't even make it. It broke down in Pennsylvania, forcing Perry and Durel to rent a Monte Carlo. They finally checked in at their Boston motel only to discover that police intelligence officers were staking them out. Boston police had taken Duke at his word and thought that Perry and Durel were only the first of a horde of Klansmen descending on the racially troubled city.

The two Klansmen did everything they could to encourage this deception. As Durel and Perry drove around Boston, they honked and waved at every passing car with an out-of-state license plate. For a while, the policemen busily jotted down the license plate numbers, thinking these, too, were Klansmen. Duke arrived in Boston on September 19. A crowd of reporters, television cameras, and FBI agents met him at the aiport.

That night, Duke held an antibusing rally at a park in south Boston, a Catholic working class neighborhood that was the stronghold of the white opposition. More than 2,000 people turned out. "Two hundred years ago our ancestors stood up and fought against the tyranny of the British bayonets," Duke told the cheering crowd. "Our struggle is much harder. The federal government is taking money out of your pockets to finance the production of thousands of little black bastards. The real issue isn't education. The real issue is niggers!"

Duke whipped the crowd into such excitement that afterward a throng of people besieged him, wanting to sign up in his Klan. He led them down a hill from the park to his car to get sign-up sheets. But the car was locked—and Durel, who was still at the park up the hill, had the keys. Duke could not get in. When he met up with Durel an hour later, he was furious. Without the sign-up sheets, Duke had written names on scraps of paper, his coat sleeve, anywhere possible—but had not been able to collect the initiation fee of ten dollars per person. "Do you know much money you cost us?" he shouted at Durel.

The next day, Duke planned to lead a motorcade through the city to protest busing. Mounted police came up to the Klansmen and their supporters in a park and began trampling on the signs they were making. The police had seen enough and told Duke, Durel, and Perry that they had better leave Boston immediately. Duke caught a plane to Louisiana. Durel and Perry climbed into their rented car for the long ride home, stopping in Pennsylvania to pick up the Maverick. Duke was elated by the trip. With only two Klansmen, he had held a large rally in Boston and had fooled the media into giving him nationwide coverage.

With the Boston trip, Duke discovered a formula for winning attention that he followed throughout the remainder of the 1970s: tap into white fears and frustrations by seizing hot issues and relying on the media to publicize his views and activities. Over the next six years—before quitting the Knights of the Ku Klux Klan amid an embarrassing scandal—he would make headlines and TV and radio appearances across the nation. In the process, he would win credit for revitalizing the Klan. During this time, he would publicly decry Jewish influence—but he would never identify himself as a Nazi sympathizer or willingly discuss his Nazi activities at LSU.

After graduating from LSU in May 1974, Duke began to put into practice his strategy of building a white political machine. He and Jim Lindsay began holding meetings at metropolitan New Orleans motels to attract recruits. Because the motels would not rent meeting rooms to the Klan, they advertised themselves as the Louisiana Taxpayers Association. At one meeting, on August 23, 1974, at Metairie's Ramada Inn, Lindsay greeted people at the door, calling himself Jack Lawrence. About 150 people paid $1.50 each to enter the meeting room, which was decorated with Klan flags featuring the cross-wheel insignia. There were middle-aged, plain-faced couples and young people, many with beards and long hair. Many of them said they came out of curiosity, that they were worried about the country's direction.

At one point, a local black television reporter tried to enter the meeting but was barred. Soon after, Duke bounded onto the stage, a bundle of nervous energy wearing a blood red sportcoat. "The time for decision, the time for action is now," he shouted. "We must get together as white people and take back our country. You'll soon find that the white man is a minority in his own country." Duke spoke of the era of Reconstruction—an unfortunate period, he said, when the white man was disenfranchised and the black man controlled the government. "But then," he said, picking up the pace, "a secret weapon was sent to the white people of the South, a miracle from God. The Klan swept across the South like wildfire." Return to those days, Duke urged. "When in the hell are we going to fight? When are we going to do something?"

People leaped to their feet. "Now, now, now!" they chanted. Duke plunged into the crowd, shaking outstretched hands. "I hope I've convinced you to join us," he told person after person. "Have you filled out the application? I hope you'll stay with us."

In October, after returning from Boston, Duke seized on an incident in Destrehan, a town thirty miles up the Mississippi River from New Orleans, to bluff the media again. A thirteen-year-old white boy named Timothy Weber was shot at Destrehan High School as his parents were taking him and his sister away from the school, where hundreds of white and black students had scuffled throughout the day. The shot came from a bus filled with black students that whites were pelting with stones. (Gary Tyler, a sixteen-year-old black student, was arrested and was later convicted of the murder, although many people in Louisiana rallied to his defense and said someone else had shot Weber.)

With whites outraged by the murder, Duke announced he would send armed Klan "security teams" to patrol the area. "We're not down there for violence," Duke told reporters. "We're down there to protect white people from black savages and murderers." The police, fearing that the Klan's presence could cause tension to explode into violence, mobilized their forces in response. Dozens of officers cruised throughout Destrehan and set up checkpoints at eight areas in anticipation of the arrival of Duke and the Klan security teams. Throughout the day, estimates of how many Klansmen Duke would bring ranged from a dozen to forty-eight. Rumors flew around the command post and up and down the main thoroughfare, called the River Road. Every few minutes, it seemed, there was a report about a Klan sighting, and the police would brace themselves.

But the reports were always false. As in Boston, there were no Klan security teams. Duke brought only three Klansmen. When they finally arrived in Destrehan, reporters and television cameras swarmed around Duke. "Our presence here should have an inhibitive effect on the blacks," he told them.

Police officers were disgusted. "It's nonsense," one said. "He was supposed to bring an army, and he couldn't, so he's making one up." But it did not matter. Duke had won the publicity he wanted.

Slowly, however, the police were learning not to be fooled. Because of the

Klan's reputation for violence, they kept Duke under close surveillance almost twenty-four hours a day, and undercover agents from both the Jefferson Parish Sheriff's Office and the New Orleans Police Department infiltrated the Knights of the Ku Klux Klan. For a while, an undercover agent even lived with one of the high-ranking women in Duke's Klan.

Not only did the police try to keep constant tabs on Duke but they also tried to disrupt his activities. At public demonstrations Duke sponsored, uniformed policemen, angered that they had to be there in case of violence, frequently whispered to undercover agents in the Klan that they should have kept Duke from holding the event. The undercover agents were under orders to try to undermine Duke's credibility by responding that Duke was actually a police informer. "We'd say, 'Hey, he's with us.' It wasn't true, but we hoped word would get out so he'd have less credibility [among his own supporters]," said Fred O'Sullivan, who headed the New Orleans police intelligence unit when Duke got his start in the Klan.

O'Sullivan and Jefferson Parish deputies suspected that Duke was providing information to the FBI for money, but they never had any specific proof. "The Klan didn't seem like a well-heeled organization," said another former New Orleans policeman who kept close tabs on Duke. "But he lived a middle-class lifestyle and traveled a lot. I just kind of figured he was providing information to [the FBI] for money." FBI officials in New Orleans denied that Duke was an informant for them.

During the six months after the Destrehan incident, Duke spoke on at least six college campuses across the country, appeared on radio and television talk shows whenever possible, and held occasional Klan rallies. He was particularly hopeful about attracting college students to the Klan. He would speak at any university that would pay his expenses, although he also asked for a fee of $800—and he often received it. His college appearances frequently drew at least 1,000 students, but hecklers usually proved too disruptive for Duke to finish.

When Duke spoke at the University of North Carolina on January 18, 1975, for instance, about 2,000 students packed an auditorium. But they did not get to hear him because a group of 200 blacks shouted him down. The incident became a major topic of debate at UNC, with many students and professors condemning the hecklers for trampling on Duke's First Amendment right to speak. Duke, of course, agreed with this view. But he carried their argument one step further and said the incident provided further proof that blacks were inferior to whites. "Finally, it came time for me to speak and unfortunately, the blacks acted in accordance with their primitive nature," he wrote in an "ACTION" bulletin distributed to his Klan members.

"They yelled obsenities [sic], shouted, blew whistles and generally acted like apes. The PA system was simply not powerful enough for the audience to hear even one single word.

"As the blacks chanted, jived and danced, I tried to reach the crowd by a gesture. I acted niggerish and mimicked the ape-like actions of the blacks— inverting my lips and sticking out my chin with their chants. The white audience loved it—rose to their feet, cheered and clapped with their hands over their heads. The audience began to yell at the niggers—telling them to shut up. But all this was to no avail, and although it was obvious to all intelligent people that the blacks would come out of this worse if they persisted—their thick primitive skulls just couldn't understand that."

Duke expressed other crude views of blacks. The *Crusader* ran blatantly racist jokes under the label "Good Old Fashioned Humor." "A man was walking his alligator on a chain," one joke went. "He became thirsty and pulled into a local tavern. Approaching the barkeeper, he asked, 'Do you serve Negroes here?' The barkeeper answered, 'Why Sir, of course we serve Negroes.' The gentleman with the alligator then replied, 'Give me a scotch and give my alligator a Negro!'"

Another joke went, "Klansman: 'How do you save a Negro from drowning?'

"Liberal knee-jerk race-mixing pinko: 'I don't know.'

"Klansman: 'GOOD.'"

Following Duke's aborted appearance at the University of North Carolina, his next big splash came on April 4, 1975, in the rural Louisiana community of Walker, forty-five miles east of Baton Rouge. There he hosted perhaps the biggest Klan rally since the 1920s.

The organizer for the event was Bill Wilkinson, who had joined the Knights of the Ku Klux Klan the previous December as its "giant," or organizer, in Livingston Parish. While in the navy, Wilkinson said later, he had become "nauseated" at the sight of "coloreds and whites dating. It stunned me. I was a plain old country boy, and I asked myself, 'What's going on here?' It repulsed me and made me sick to my stomach. I drew my own conclusions about integration. I knew it was wrong." By the time Wilkinson joined Duke's Klan and organized the Walker rally, he was an electrical contractor in Denham Springs, a suburb of Baton Rouge.

The Walker rally filled all 800 chairs in the Old South Jamboree hall, and another 1,900 people filled two sets of bleachers. Klan banners, Confederate and American flags, and White Revolution posters were displayed throughout the hall. The 2,700 people in attendance heard a prayer from a Baptist minister—"God save us all from the Mongrelization of the white race"—and heard Wilkinson's vision of a white Christian America, freed from the "tyranny of niggers, Jews" and the "Jew-socialist" federal government.

The crowd also heard a brief speech from a surprise speaker: Mary Bacon, then one of the country's leading female jockeys. Duke, whom Jefferson Parish deputies had observed spending the night at Bacon's apartment, had persuaded her to endorse the Klan publicly. "Maybe when your wife or daughter or neighbor gets raped by a Negro, you'll get smart and join the Klan," was all Bacon said. But it was enough to cost her mounts as a jockey and several commercial endorsements.

All evening, as part of Duke's effort to refurbish the Klan, speakers had struggled to use the words "black" or "Negro" rather than "nigger"—but the crowd was not satisfied. "Use the right word," one man screamed repeatedly. "Use our word." When Duke spoke, he asked the crowd for its solution to racial problems.

"Kill the niggers," the crowd cried.

"Get your guns!" Duke yelled. "No, no, wait, I'm not saying it's time for killing yet. We can't say that. But get your guns ready!" It was one of the few times Duke spoke publicly in favor of violence. As part of his effort to give the Klan a facelift, he sought to erase its violent image. He portrayed himself as a new breed of white-rights advocate who sought to win supporters with reason, not guns. In interviews, he would emphasize that he opposed violent acts.

But Duke, in fact, seemed ambivalent about violence. He was not known to have engaged in any typical Klan acts, like beating or shooting blacks. But two of his Klansmen were arrested during the October 1974 flare-up in Destrehan for carrying an illegal gun. And Duke and the *Crusader* were highly sympathetic to former and current Klansmen who were accused, tried, or convicted of violence.

In 1974, Duke asked *Crusader* readers to mail contributions to Robert Miles, a longtime Klansman who had been indicted for bombing school buses in Michigan in opposition to school integration. Duke called Miles a "Christian Patriot." The *Crusader* blamed his arrest on an FBI frame-up and lambasted the "biased Jew Judge Gubow," who presided over the trial. Miles was convicted and spent six years in jail. Duke also accused the FBI of framing Byron de la Beckwith, who had been tried twice for the 1963 murder of Mississippi NAACP leader Medgar Evers. Both trials ended in mistrials when the all-white juries could not reach verdicts.

De la Beckwith found himself in trouble again when he was arrested on his way to bomb the home of I. A. Botnik, the regional director of the Anti-Defamation League in New Orleans. Calling de la Beckwith "one of the most vocal defenders of the White race and our Christian civilization," the *Crusader* reported that Duke said he had protested "the excessive bail and the obvious frame-up of Mr. de la Beckwith. As a result of the uproar Mr. Duke stirred up, the judge had no choice but to lower the bond to $25,000 and drop all charges except 'possession of a bomb.'" Duke asked for contributions to be sent to de la Beckwith in Mississippi.

The same winter 1974 issue of the *Crusader* included a glowing tribute to Kathy Ainsworth, who had been killed by the FBI while trying to blow up the home of a Jewish resident of Meridian, Mississippi. Ainsworth, the *Crusader* eulogized, was "an innocent, pregnant Christian girl" and "a patriot." Over the next several years, the *Crusader* regularly reprinted its tribute to Ainsworth.

When J. B. Stoner, chairman of the National States Rights party, was tried and convicted in 1977 for the 1958 bombing of the Bethel Baptist Church in Birmingham, Alabama, Duke's Klan proclaimed his innocence. Duke and Don Black, his Alabama grand dragon, also sponsored marches for Robert Chambliss after he was charged with a Birmingham church bombing in 1963 that killed four young black girls.

Duke also leaped to the defense of Klansmen arrested following a shootout in Greensboro, North Carolina, in 1979 that left five members of the Communist Workers party dead. "Free the Greensboro 14!" read a banner headline on page one of the *Crusader*. Duke said the Klansmen had killed the CWP members in self-defense.

In addition, two of Duke's Klansmen were arrested at a cross-burning rally in New Orleans in 1978 for shooting at police officers as they approached the site. With the police beating a hasty retreat—but not before they sent a code red signal (all units needed immediately, officers are in trouble)—Klansmen began panicking. Prominent citizens who did not want it known that they were Klan members began throwing their white robes and membership cards into the fire. Dozens of police units descended on the open field. Duke ended the tense standoff by handing over the two men who had fired the shots. Charges against them were later dropped.

In 1982, after Duke had left the Klan to form the National Association for the Advancement of White People, he campaigned for the release of two brothers convicted of conspiring to use explosives. An article referred to the two men, John and Ed Gerhardt, as "white political prisoners" and identified them as founders of the American White Nationalist party. The Anti-Defamation League identified them as neo-Nazis. In Texas in the late 1970s, Duke's grand dragon, Louis Beam, ran a paramilitary camp. Klansmen participated in army-style maneuvers and practiced with assault rifles fitted with a special grenade launch attachment. "I don't know what half our people are doing," Duke said when asked about it.

During the last half of 1975, David Duke suffered several setbacks. On June 12, a month after the Walker rally, Duke's mentor, Jim Lindsay, was murdered. Lindsay, forty-nine years old, was shot three times at his small real estate office in Metairie. His estranged wife, Peggy, was arrested and charged with second-degree murder. The police believed she shot him in a fit of anger when he demanded a divorce. Because he was extremely conscious about his safety and always had a gun nearby, police thought that he would let his guard down only with someone he trusted. During the trial, Peggy Lindsay testified that she had been with her husband for two hours before his death. They had talked about a reconciliation, she said, and then had sex on a couch.

Minutes later, as she was getting in her car to go home, she said, she heard gunshots and a male voice saying, "Give me your money." Mrs. Lindsay was acquitted, and the murder remained unsolved. Duke's name never came up in the trial and he was not linked to the murder.

Duke made no public comments at the time about Lindsay's death. The *Crusader* did not mention the killing—or even whom he was replacing—when it announced that Duke had been elevated to grand wizard, the top position in the Knights of the Ku Klux Klan. But Duke was still mourning Lindsay's death in interviews years later. "He was almost like a dad to me," he said in 1985, "a real fine gentleman."

In August, two months after Lindsay's murder, Duke legally incorporated the Knights of the Ku Klux Klan at the Louisiana secretary of state's office in Baton Rouge—further evidence that the group's genesis dates to the mid-1970s and not earlier. Duke would later claim that his Klan had been incorporated in 1956 when he tried to show that his Klan group was the most legitimate because it had existed longer than his rivals'. But secretary of state records show that a different Knights of the Ku Klux Klan was incorporated then and that this group was no longer active in 1975.

In his 1975 incorporation, Duke listed himself as the founder and national director and his wife, Chloe, as the secretary. He declared that "this corporation is organized to bring peace, harmony and prosperity to these United States of America and her people, and to advance the cause of Fraternity, education and charity of all Americans."

Duke next turned his sights on electoral politics. In the fall of 1975, he declared his candidacy for a state senate seat from Baton Rouge. His opponent was the conservative incumbent, Kenneth Osterberger. Duke threw himself into the fray. He brought Tom Metzger from California to manage his campaign and quickly built up a loyal cadre of supporters that consisted mainly of Klansmen. Years later, Metzger, by then a Duke critic, still marveled: "There were a tremendous amount of people in the streets for David. I've never seen such a committed group of people, they worked night and day."

Running as a Democrat, Duke gave a preview of the campaigns he would run more than a decade later that would make him a household word. Against Osterberger, he campaigned on a platform that combined traditional conservative positions and a strong dose of white rights. He opposed new taxes—so that the Jewish-controlled government would have less money to promote integration and to hand out to blacks—called for halting the growth of the state welfare program, endorsed harsher punishment for perpertrators of brutal crimes, and demanded less government interference and bureaucracy, positions he would take in his 1989 Metairie state house election, his 1990 United States Senate race, and his 1991 Louisiana gubernatorial campaign.

In the 1975 race, Duke opposed reverse discrimination against whites in employment, promotions, and scholarships, also a favorite issue in his later races. In 1975, Duke also opposed forced busing of schoolchildren and said public schools should "reflect the heritage, traditions and ideals of our nation"—by which he meant that they should be segregated. He was still drawing applause when he denounced busing in campaign speeches more than a decade later.

In a letter to voters in Osterberger's district, Duke pledged to stand up to black legislators. "The politicians who are enslaved by the black block [sic] vote fight hard for the minority position in taxes, law enforcement, school policies, etc. while the rest of the legislators limply wring their hands and bury their heads in the sand, scared to death that if they do anything significant in behalf of the interests and ideals of the White majority, that they will be called racist or incur the disfavor of the powerful political forces and the media," he said. "I'm not wringing my hands or burying my head in the sand. I'm openly talking about what most politicians are afraid to even whisper about. . . . On November 1, let us . . . SEND THEM A MESSAGE."

He touted himself as the leader of the antibusing fight across the nation and the recipient of "35 awards from patriotic movements all over America including: an honorary doctorate from Los Angeles Christian University, the Patrick Henry Award for Patriotism [and the] Proclamation of Freedom Award from the Anti-Communist Federation." He said proudly that Governor Wallace had made him an honorary colonel in the Alabama State Militia. Demonstrating his willingness to trim his sails for political gain, Duke did not mention his current Klan and previous Nazi activities.

Osterberger followed the standard practice of a well-known incumbent facing an offbeat challenger by ignoring Duke. He declined to appear on a local television debate with his challenger. Jumping at the chance to get free exposure, Duke showed up anyway and maligned an empty chair labeled "Ken Osterberger." The publicity boosted Duke's candidacy.

Osterberger was forced to step up his campaigning and take a strong stand against busing and gun control. Five days before the election, he bought an ad in the Baton Rouge *Morning Advocate* that took a jab at Duke, although it did not mention him by name. "Don't be hoodwinked," the ad told voters. They weren't. Osterberger won, compiling 22,287 votes, or 66 percent, to Duke's 11,079, or 33 percent. Duke declared victory anyway. "Over 11,000 people went to the polls and voted for my ideals," he said. "The movement has just started. We've just begun. This is not the ignorant redneck from the hills voting for me. The voters are just about ready for us."

Duke spent $16,200 on his campaign, according to a report he filed after the election. This included $4,800 of his own money and a $1,000 loan from his father. Duke said that Klansmen provided most of his contributions, although, because he was required to list only donors who contributed $500 or more, he identified only one contributor. Duke spent most of his campaign money on television, radio, and newspaper advertising.

With the election over, Duke again turned his attention to the Klan. But he had suffered a setback during the campaign when Bill Wilkinson, his organizer in Livingston Parish, abandoned the Knights of the Ku Klux Klan to become imperial wizard of his own Klan, which he called the Invisible Empire, Knights of the Ku Klux Klan. Wilkinson later said he broke with Duke following the rally in Walker because Duke had pocketed the $5,000 that had been raised. Duke denied the charge, saying that the rally raised only $600— and that all the money went into the Klan's coffers. Whichever version is correct, it was probably inevitable that the two men would split up. Both were smart and aggressive and had egos too big to allow them to take a back seat to anyone else. Duke regularly sniped at Wilkinson afterward, calling him "practically an illiterate, a man who has never read anything."

Duke suffered many defections over the years, but none caused him more problems than Wilkinson's. Within months of leaving Duke, Wilkinson was showing that he, too, could win the media's fancy. Whereas Duke played down the Klan's violent image, Wilkinson played it up—and grabbed headlines when he and his Klansmen openly carried guns at public rallies. "Get ready for the coming race war," Wilkinson would declare. He also liked to say, "These guns ain't for shooting rabbits." By the late 1970s, with longtime Klan leaders Robert Shelton and James Venable in decline, Wilkinson emerged as Duke's top rival. Dashing any hopes Duke had for remaking the image of the Ku Klux Klan, Wilkinson would play a major role in Duke's decision to quit the Klan altogether in 1980 and form the National Association for the Advancement of White People.

Following his defeat in the state senate election from Baton Rouge, Duke returned to the New Orleans area for good. He moved to the house at 3603 Cypress Street in suburban Metairie that he had bought in May 1975 for $20,500. A white frame structure in a middle-class neighborhood, the house had served as the rectory for the Highland Baptist Church next door.

Duke ended 1975 with another quick foray to Boston to exploit white anger at Judge Garrity's busing plan. Black and white students at South Boston High School fought for two days in a row in early December. Duke immediately flew to Boston to try to join a demonstration organized by the city's most vocal antibusing group, Restore Our Alienated Rights. Protesters stalled dozens of cars on highways leading into the city, which brought the morning traffic to a near-standstill. Duke played no role in the traffic tie-up, but he took credit anyway. "This was just a test to see what could be done," he told reporters. "We'll just have a lot more of it on a lot larger scale." But Duke did not return to Boston for the antibusing protests that followed.

His next major media event was to occur in Metairie. The date was September 11, 1976. The occasion was a four-day joint convention of the Knights of the Ku Klux Klan and the International Patriotic Conference.

It was early afternoon when David Duke burst through the front doors of the International American Motor Inn in Metairie and headed for an unmarked police car in the hotel parking lot. Striding at a fast clip, Duke was setting in motion a chain of events that would nearly land him in jail, destroy his carefully cultivated image of nonviolence, and bankrupt his Klan. Following Duke out of the hotel were Jim Warner, his Louisiana grand dragon, and about 80 people attending the convention. About 300 people had come to the event, including some from overseas.

Since 9:00 A.M., when the delegates had begun their meeting in the Chateau Room on the 16th floor, Klansmen had been complaining that detectives from the Jefferson Parish Sheriff's Office were taking photographs of them as they entered and exited from the hotel. One Klansman had screamed "White Power!" at the detectives from his hotel balcony while another had given them the finger. Aware of the Ku Klux Klan's reputation for violence, the sheriff's department had been keeping Duke under surveillance for several years. But on this day, they were maintaining an especially close watch because two of the men attending the convention were John Taylor and Wolfgang Droege, leaders of a Canadian neo-Nazi group called the Western

Guard. Canadian police had notified New Orleans authorities that they believed the Western Guard had been involved in recent bombings in Canada.

At about 1:15 P.M., as the Klan meeting was ending, Warner announced that those who did not want their pictures taken should exit through the hotel's back entrance. Those who wanted to openly stand up for their rights, he added, should join him and Duke downstairs. A few minutes later, they were heading out the front doors and left toward the unmarked police car. Inside sat detectives Larry Babin and Danny Samrow. As Klansmen crowded in behind him, Duke, his face contorted in rage, began shouting at Babin and Samrow. "Who do you people think you are? Why are you harassing us by taking our pictures? You must work for the FBI, that Communist organization within the government. All of the FBI agents are Communist spies."

The detectives, following instructions not to speak with demonstrators, kept silent. Duke was not deterred. "Jews run the country!" he ranted. "Jews run the FBI, and you're working for Jews! You are Communists yourselves!" The Klansmen, eighty strong and pressing up against the police car, began to clap and cheer. One man in a Klan uniform darted up to Babin and blew a shrill whistle in his ear. This delighted the Klansmen, who yelled and clapped louder. Duke shouted, "You Commie Jews! Get out of here! We don't want you here!"

Louis Beam, Duke's Texas grand dragon and a Vietnam War veteran, joined the fray. Furious at a recent decision by the United States government to admit large numbers of Vietnamese refugees, he seemed to want a scapegoat for his rage. "I fought for this country during the war," Beam shouted. "I don't have to be harassed by people I fought for. I killed a lot of them bastards for this country. Then this country brings 125,000 of those slopehead son-of-a-bitches over here!"

The crowd cheered again and began chanting, "White power! White power!"

"Do you want us to turn the car over?" one man yelled to Duke. The Klan grand wizard laughed and raised a clenched fist.

"They are nigger lovers!" another man yelled at the detectives.

A third man shouted: "They must belong to Jews Anonymous!"

A second police car was idling on the other side of the hotel. Detectives Pete Cicero and Richard Cantin could not see Babin and Samrow's car. But when they heard the shouting, they decided to find out what was happening. Cicero put the car in gear and sped through the parking lot.

He parked about forty yards from the first police cruiser. Duke and Warner spied Cicero and Cantin. "Here they are!" they yelled. "Let's get them."

"White power! White power!" the Klansmen chanted as they surrounded the second car.

Cicero, worried that the crowd was getting out of control, contacted police headquarters and yelled into his microphone that he needed a marked police unit at the hotel immediately. Duke and Warner leaned on Cicero's open window and turned their invective on him. "You are a Jew!" Duke shouted. "You work for the FBI, who are Commie spies. They are Commie traitors, and you are, too! You have no right to be here. We rented this facility, you didn't."

The other Klansmen cheered.

Glaring at Cicero, Warner joined in. "You Commie Jew bastard!" he yelled. "I hate you. You can't destroy what we have already! You will die trying!" Enraged, Warner reached through Cicero's open window with his right hand and grabbed his collar. Warner began pulling the detective toward him as the crowd, howling in delight, began to beat and rock the police car.

Cicero reached up and snatched Warner's hand from his collar. The detective immediately flipped on his microphone. "We have a riot situation here!" he yelled. "We have a 'signal red' situation here."

Cicero and Cantin tried to push open their doors, fearful that the mob was going to overturn their car. The crowd held Cantin's door shut. Cicero was able to open his, but Warner slammed it against the detective's ankle. Yelping in pain, Cicero scrambled back into the car. He and Cantin tried to get out a second time, and this time they made it only to be shoved up against the police car. One woman kicked Cicero, but when he tried to handcuff her, the crowd wrested her away.

Samrow, meanwhile, had been blocked by the crowd from seeing what was happening to his two colleagues. He began pushing his way over to them. Upon reaching their car, he grabbed their police radio and repeated the signal red warning to headquarters. Almost immediately, another police car arrived, sirens flashing, and still another burst into the parking lot seconds later.

The Klansmen stepped back, screaming, "White power! White power!" But they would not leave the parking lot. Circling the police officers, they continued their chant. By now a dozen police cars had come screeching into the hotel parking lot, and a police helicopter was hovering overhead. The officers decided to form a line and walk toward the jeering crowd. "Disperse immediately or face arrest," a police loudspeaker warned. The sight of the advancing blue line in riot gear was too much for the Klansmen. They began running into the hotel. As officers walked toward Duke to arrest him, he, too, slipped through the front doors and disappeared into the hotel.

The officers decided that it was better to arrest Duke later. Pursuing him into the hotel could provoke a violent confrontation. They did have three Klansmen in custody, charged with resisting arrest. When Samrow and Cicero walked back to their police cars, they noticed that the antenna had been broken off. Pasted on the cars were bumper stickers. "Bus judges to mental hospitals," read one. Another said: "If you want integration, buy a zebra." The detectives were in no hurry to arrest Duke partly because they knew where he would be that night: first at a Klan rally and then at a cross-burning ceremony, both in St. Bernard Parish, which abutted New Orleans. A judge signed three arrest warrants. One charged Duke with inciting a riot, and the others charged Jim Warner with inciting a riot and simple battery against Cicero.

The rally was at the St. Bernard Civic Center. After the auditorium filled, a parade of Klan speakers addressed the throng. When it was Duke's turn, he strolled onto the stage in a white suit. "This afternoon," he began, "I wasn't quite sure I was going to be here. But I'm here, not in jail." The crowd cheered. Duke recited his usual litany of complaints against Jews, integration, the welfare system, and affirmative action programs. He then described the events at the International American Motor Inn that afternoon.

"They wanted to charge me with inciting to riot," he said as the crowd laughed. "And, looking back on it, I think I should have incited a riot!"

"Yeaaa, Dave!" one man called out.

"Give 'em hell, Dave!" another yelled.

"Are they [the police] down at the N-double-A-C-P meeting?" Duke asked.

"Noooooo," the audience replied.

"The N-double-A-C-P is run by 15 Communists and one . . . ," he hesitated, " . . . black, nigger, whatever you want to call him."

"Nigger!" the crowd shouted, egging him on. "Nigger!"

The meeting soon broke up. It was time for the cross burning. A caravan of cars snaked through St. Bernard Parish until it came to a clearing where a tall wooden cross had been built. Robed in white, a torch in his left hand, Duke led the ceremony for dozens of Klansmen. He walked solemnly to the cross and laid his torch at its base. Other Klansmen followed suit. Standing back in a circle, they extended their left arms in a stiff salute and chanted, "White power! White power!" As the cross burned, turning the sky orange, Duke preached, "By lighting it, we are not destroying the cross. We are illuminating it. Showing the way to the white world. May we be victorious in this struggle for our race and our freedom! White power!"

Police watched quietly from a distance. They arrested Duke and Warner while the Klan leaders were driving home. It was the first time Duke had been arrested since 1972. He and Warner spent the night in a Jefferson Parish jail, but they were released on bail the next day, just in time to join a march in New Orleans. Duke initially put on a brave face about his arrest, insisting that he was the victim of police harassment and that either the charges would be dropped or he would be found not guilty. But Jefferson Parish's district attorney, John Mamoulides, was intent on trying Duke. Mamoulides charged Duke with inciting to riot and refusing to disperse. He charged Warner with both these crimes and simple battery against Detective Cicero—all misdemeanor offenses.

The trial began May 23, 1977, and lasted four days. A six-person jury in the Jefferson Parish Twenty-fourth Judicial District Court heard Samrow, Cicero, and Detective Babin recount the parking lot incident. Eddie Selby, a New Orleans Police Department undercover agent who had infiltrated the Klan, corroborated their testimony. Several Klansmen, Duke, and Warner took the stand to declare that only twenty Klansmen had been in the parking lot—not eighty, as the officers had testified—and that there had been no riot. Duke in his testimony said he had actually been helping the police get Klansmen out of the parking lot when the police overreacted.

After six hours of deliberation on May 27, the jury found Duke and Warner guilty of inciting a riot and Duke guilty of refusing to disperse. But the jury acquitted Warner of battery against Cicero and refusing to disperse. A week later, Judge Patrick Carr fined Duke $250 ($125 for each charge) and sentenced him to three months in jail for each offense (six months in all). Carr also sentenced Warner to three months in jail and fined him $150.

The guilty verdict and prospect of jail deeply distressed Duke. But he and Warner remained free by immediately appealing their convictions to the Louisiana Supreme Court. Their appeal argued that the judge had allowed Shirley Wimberly, the assistant district attorney who prosecuted the case, to ask irrelevant questions about their political beliefs in an attempt to prejudice the jury against them.

Duke saw his whole career riding on the appeal. He feared that being found guilty of inciting a riot would undo the carefully constructed nonviolent image he had been trying to create of himself and the Klan. "If I get convicted of this crime," Duke testified during the trial, "I might as well forget about trying to reach people legally, because every time I go on radio or television, they'd say, 'What do you mean you're legal? You've been convicted of inciting to riot.' What do I say to that?" Duke also feared that he would be thrown into jail with a group of hardened black criminals who would pummel him. To defend himself in case he had to serve time, he began a rigorous weight-lifting program that soon added bulk to what had been a slender frame.

Duke got good news three months later on September 5 when the Louisiana Supreme Court overturned his and Warner's convictions. The state high court agreed that Judge Carr had improperly allowed the prosecution to ask the defendants about their political views, leading the jury to judge them for their beliefs rather than for their conduct at the International American Motor Inn. But Duke's jubilation was short-lived. On May 24, 1979, eight months after the Louisiana Supreme Court had overturned his conviction, the prosecution announced that it would retry him on the charge of inciting a riot. Duke, who had just declared his candidacy for president of the United States, blasted the decision, saying authorities were harassing him to thwart his electoral ambitions.

Wimberly, the Jefferson Parish assistant district attorney, denied Duke's charge. "We didn't even know he was running for president," Wimberly said. Indeed, Duke was not a serious candidate, and at twenty-eight, he was seven years too young to be eligible to take office even in the extremely improbable event that he won.

Threatened again with the prospect of jail, Duke wasted no time in hitting up supporters for a legal defense fund. He sent out an "Emergency Appeal" to supporters on the same day that authorities announced that they would retry him. He wrote, "My campaign for President has obviously led the enemies of this Movement to grasp at straws in an attempt to discredit me, financially break me and incarcerate me. . . . I don't need to tell you what those blacks in the 90 percent black jail I'd be in would do to the leader of the Ku Klux Klan. I need your help and I need it now, today. I've tried to give my all for this cause and I believe I've accomplished a great deal for the White race and the Klan." He signed the letter, "Yours in White Fraternity." The response from the faithful was underwhelming.

On August 16, five days before his retrial began, a distressed Duke dashed off another appeal to his Klan membership. This time he pulled out all the stops. "One person wrote to me and insulted me for daring to ask for financial help in this court fight," he wrote. "I have the feeling that a few more that didn't write also resented the asking for help, and others thinking that this was just one more right-wing appeal, helped very little. Reading the insulting letter, I got a lump in my throat so taut that I inhaled sharply. I thought about the countless TV and radio shows and debates where the enemies of our kind were soundly defeated, thus causing me to incur the hatred and the wrath of the most powerful and brutal enemies of the White race. I thought of the hundreds of marches, demonstrations, rallys [sic] and programs that I completed where the Communists had screamed for and promised my blood, but where nevertheless I did my duty. I thought about the rumors and the character assassination I had endured for daring to be effective for my race. The group that Jesus branded 'the fathers of the lie'—those same agents that smeared Joe McCarthy, Lindbergh, General George Brown and MacArthur, were hard at work accusing me of every falsehood and evil perceived by society. Don't worry that some of the following terms are contradictory, but I've been accused of being a Nazi, a Communist, a Jew, a FBI and/or CIA agent, a homosexual, whoremonger, pornographer, money monger and ruthless fanatic. I expect those kinds of smears from the Jews, but to be repeated by people who are supposed to be on our side is almost too much to bear. The most common method of smear is the 'he's in it for the money' argument. Well, I'd like to know where in Hades it is. I'd like to see some of the SOB's who repeat a rotten Jewish smear like that come down here and live with me, work with me, travel with me and fight with me."

Duke went on to make one last desperate plea in the letter. "This final appeal for funds is in effect a serious question posed to all of you," he wrote. "Do you want me to resign as Grand Wizard of the Knights of the Ku Klux Klan? I have fought hard for you, and I can't help feeling many of you are not really backing me up. . . . We are $5,000.00 behind right now, and we must have help right now from those who have not helped all they can. I am serious about possibly resigning. I think I can put up with the slanders and the dangers, but not with supposed patriots who don't help like they could and should. We are in a life and death struggle, not only in this case, but indeed for the very survival of our White race and its beautiful culture. I am willing to breach the barriers, but not by myself. I have always been willing to storm the barricades of the enemy, but I am not willing to throw myself on the bayonets of the enemy in a meaningless sacrifice. I will let this appeal make the decision for me. If this appeal falls short, I will resign as Grand Wizard. I have done all that I can." Duke signed the letter, "In the Deepest Sincerity."

This time his Klan members came through. One elderly woman donated $1,000. Klansmen in Florida held a bakesale and picnic that raised $220. Several Alabama Klansmen borrowed $5,000 that they contributed to his defense. In all, Duke received nearly $10,000. His second trial, which began on August 21, 1979, had a new judge, Thomas C. Wicker, and no jury. This time Duke was tried alone because the prosecution had allowed Jim Warner to plead guilty in July to the lesser offense of disturbing the peace. Warner was given a three-month suspended sentence and fined $100.

No dramatic new information emerged during the second trial. On August

23, a half hour after the trial ended, Wicker pronounced Duke guilty of inciting a riot. Duke was still fearful that he would have to go to jail. But on November 28, Wicker gave him a six-month suspended sentence, placed him on probation for a year and fined him $500. Wicker said Duke did not deserve jail because this was his first conviction, no one was hurt in the riot and no property was damaged. It was an anticlimactic end to Duke's toughest ordeal.

CHAPTER FOUR

PROPAGANDA FOR THE CAUSE

David Duke's 1976 arrest and his trials in 1977 and 1979 consumed much of his time and attention during those years. But he still managed to carry out a number of activities that won massive publicity and in the process helped revitalize the Klan. One of the strategies that Duke believed Jews were employing to weaken the white race was to encourage blacks to have more and more children. But Duke's anxieties were not limited to concern that blacks might be outbreeding whites and thus reducing the white majority in the United States. He also fretted over the large number of illegal aliens crossing the Mexican border. To him, Latin Americans were just as much of a plague as blacks.

"Every new immigrant adds to our crime problems, our welfare rolls and unemployment of American citizens," he said in a 1982 interview. "In two or three years, the majority in our most-populous state—California—is expected to be non-white. That's incredible. It is said that whites will eventually become a minority in Texas. New Mexico is literally becoming a *new* Mexico. We are being invaded in the Southwest as if a foreign army were coming over the border. The Mexican immigrants in these states are of the lowest social strata. Their future political impact as voters will be tremendous. They will certainly strengthen the leftist power block. They're going to vote for legislation that will take more and more hard-earned money away from the productive middle class in the form of taxes and social programs. They're going to vote for weak law enforcement, as every minority group has done in this country. Because they're on a lower rung of the ladder, they're going to be voting for more welfare. This massive immigration will change the face of American politics.

"The massive birthrate among minorities is getting out of hand," he went on. "The Mexican birthrate in this country is five times that of white people. The black birthrate is four times larger. America will become a Third World nation if these trends continue. Unless we slow down and cut off immigration by beefing up border control and encourage welfare recipients to have fewer kids, the white population in America will be swamped."

Duke's plan for stemming the flow of illegal aliens into the United States called for sealing the border. "I'd make the Mexican-American border almost like a Maginot Line," he said, referring to a system of heavy fortifications that France built on its eastern border before World War II. He said he would prohibit businesses from hiring illegal aliens, round up all the illegal aliens, and deport them. He laid out his plan on October 16, 1977, as he and Tom Metzger, his California grand dragon, toured the San Ysidro Port of Entry near San Diego. As a group of protesters chanted "Death to the Klan," Duke also told reporters that 500–1,000 Klansmen would undertake a Klan Border Watch stretching from San Diego to Brownsville, Texas.

Once again Duke was trying to fool the media, and once again he succeeded. Southern California radio stations broadcast news of the impending Klan Border Watch around the clock in the days leading up to the event, and television stations covered it extensively. The impending patrol provoked so much indignation in Mexico that reporters asked about little else when California governor Edmund G. (Jerry) Brown, Jr., made a brief visit to Baja California. The publicity prompted San Diego mayor Pete Wilson and California senator Alan Cranston to ask United States Attorney General Griffin Bell to prohibit the Klan patrol. When the night of the much-anticipated Klan Border Watch finally arrived on October 25, the media were in a feeding frenzy. About forty newsmen converged on the appointed site near the town of Dulzura in rural San Diego County. They far outnumbered the force Duke could muster: seven Klansmen in three old sedans that featured hand-painted "Klan Border Watch" signs taped on the doors.

It was a comical evening. The newspaper reporters, photographers, and television cameramen spent the night under a full moon, trying to avoid crashing their cars into each other and the Klansmen riding in the three sedans. When he was not giving interviews, Duke was talking into a citizens-band radio on which he purported to be relaying illegal alien sightings to federal government border agents. Throughout the night, Duke claimed that hundreds of Klansmen had turned out and that they were responsible for the arrest of thousands of illegal aliens. Most of the media reported this as the gospel truth.

What the media—with few exceptions—did not report was that border patrol officials said it was a normal night. They had arrested 400 illegal aliens, 11 fewer than the night before and 4 more than the night before that. There was no evidence that the Klan was responsible for even a single arrest. Duke claimed that Klan spotters had telephoned the border patrol to report groups of 4, 11, and 15 illegal aliens slipping into the United States. But Robert McCord, chief assistant of the Chula Vista Border Patrol sector, said that the largest number of illegal aliens reported by a telephone tipster that night was a group of 10.

One reporter who did catch on to Duke's fraud and reported it as simply a media event was Frank del Olmo of the *Los Angeles Times*. He spent most of the night monitoring CB channels and heard nothing except Duke talking to his friends in the two other Klan cars. Del Olmo reported that there were but 8 Klansmen, not the 1,000 that Duke claimed. "Many of my colleagues in the news media," del Olmo wrote later, "swallowed Duke's self-promotion hook, line and sinker."

Another reporter who was disgusted at how easily Duke had manipulated the media was Lou Cannon of the *Washington Post*. "The media hype alarmed and insulted Mexicans, who under President Jose Lopez Portillo and American-born Baja Gov. [Roberto] de la Madrid are seriously addressing the issue of illegal border crossings," Cannon wrote in a column two weeks after the Klan Border Watch. "It also provoked a coalition of radical groups into a counterdemonstration that could have resulted in violence. And it reinforced the belief that the press can be taken in by a publicity stunt at the expense of serious examination of a difficult and complicated issue. Duke's claim of his intended border watch was worth at most a couple of paragraphs on the basis of his original press conference. Reporters and editors should have questioned his estimate of 1,000 Klan border watchers in [California] where the KKK is virtually non-existent. Instead, they gave the bedsheet brigade a free ride."

While Duke was establishing himself as the undisputed Klan leader, he was facing a renewed challenge in the South from Bill Wilkinson, who had left Duke's Knights of the Ku Klux Klan to form his own Klan in 1975. Duke came to despise Wilkinson. Wilkinson had made off with a copy of Duke's secret membership list and a large quantity of Duke's literature. Wilkinson had so little shame, Duke thought, that he even reprinted the literature in his own newspaper, the *Klansman*, which itself was a carbon copy of Duke's. Worse yet, after forming his own Klan, Wilkinson had become a direct competitor. He talked tough and liked to be photographed carrying guns, which threatened the nonviolent image of the Klan that Duke was carefully trying to craft.

Duke was looking for the chance to one-up Wilkinson, and he got it in early 1978. Duke noticed that after Wilkinson had announced plans to recruit Klansmen in Great Britain, two English newspapers had promptly dispatched reporters to visit Wilkinson at his home in Denham Springs. Both papers carried front-page stories about Wilkinson, calling him *the* Imperial Wizard of the Ku Klux Klan. Wilkinson had shown that the British press was ripe for manipulation. For all the British reporters knew, Duke did not even exist. This possibility did not sit well with Duke. Wilkinson had yet to leave for England, so Duke moved quickly. He flew to New York City and obtained a seat on Laker Airlines, a no-frills carrier. He arrived in London on March 2 for what would be his most intensive effort to take the Klan beyond United States borders.

Duke had been banned from England—as were all Klansmen—under the country's 1974 Race Relations Act, which forbade any speeches or activity that might incite racial hatred. But because he was not singled out on no-entry lists by name, he was able to slip through customs with a tourist visa. Duke gleefully attributed his successful entry to his choosing to pass through a customs station manned by a black agent, who, he said, was naturally inept. "Upon arrival at Gatewick [*sic*] airport, I noted a number of non-White passport checkers," he wrote later. "I headed for the dumbest looking and most lathargic [*sic*] black and patted him on the back and said, 'How are you doing, man'? Woosh, my passport was stamped with the entry visa quicker than I could say Aunt Jemima." British authorities soon regretted his entry.

Duke's arrival coincided with a Conservative party campaign to limit the influx of "coloureds"—nonwhite immigrants mainly from Asia and the West Indies. Tory leader Margaret Thatcher said they threatened to "swamp" the "particular British character." Thatcher and other Tory leaders suggested that the Labour government establish quotas limiting nonwhite immigration into England. An uproar followed as Labourites branded the plan racist. Duke could not have chosen a better time to come.

Almost as soon as he arrived, he called the London bureau of the Associated Press and a number of British newspapers. "Klan Chief Sneaks In," reported the front-page headline in the *Daily Mirror*. In the article, Duke crowed that he had been able to slip into the country and demanded that the government impose the immigration limits. He also promised to hold clandestine cross-burning rallies and recruit hundreds of people into his Klan. His statements won banner coverage in newspapers throughout England—tabloid and serious dailies alike—and landed him twenty minutes on the BBC's top-rated show. On March 6, his fourth day in England, he won more headlines by urging Ku Klux Klan members in Britain to watch ports for illegal nonwhite immigrants trying to sneak into the country—a take-off on his Klan Border Watch.

Duke's comments—and his mere presence—outraged leftists in Britain, which added to his notoriety. "This man must be found and sent home," demanded John Lee, a Labour Party member of the House of Commons. "He is clearly an undesirable." Home Secretary Merlyn Rees, who oversaw England's internal affairs, initially shrugged off calls for expelling Duke, saying he wasn't important. "I don't intend to use the powers I have to crack a nut," Rees said. But as Duke continued to star in the British media, pressure on Rees mounted. The staunchly conservative *Daily Express* bellowed in a front-page headline: "GET HIM OUT OF HERE!" Rees relented and signed an order to deport Duke immediately.

But ordering Duke home was one thing. Finding him was quite another. Over the next week, he played cat and mouse with British authorities, making sure that the press publicized his antics. Newspapers gleefully described his ability to make Scotland Yard look like the Keystone Cops. Duke took great pleasure in tweaking authorities, who had ordered policemen to memorize his face. He arranged to be photographed in front of Scotland Yard and the Home Office. Outside the Tower of London, he sported his Klan robe alongside one of the colorfully garbed Beefeaters. Not one policeman recognized him. The police thought they had cornered him one night at a farmhouse in Warwickshire County, where a cross-burning ceremony was planned. But sympathizers tipped Duke off, and he stayed away. The police also thought they were going to nab him at a London hotel. But as two policemen charged up one escalator, Duke scampered down another and disappeared into the street. "The whole thing is turning into a comedy," one left-wing activist complained.

On March 13, Duke set up yet another clandestine interview, this time at the Fox and Geese pub in northwest London, with Robert McGowan, a reporter for the *Daily Express*. During the interview, McGowan excused himself and made a telephone call. He called Scotland Yard and, in the finest tradition of British tabloids, gave them Duke's location. But even then the police couldn't get things right. When a plainclothes policeman showed up, he served the deportation order on McGowan, who was about the same age and build as Duke—and, like Duke, had a mustache. Amid the confusion, Duke darted out of the pub and ran down a dark alley. But there was no escape.

He was carted off, shouting, "God Bless Britain" and "God Save the Queen," all of which McGowan reported in his front-page exclusive the following morning.

"GOT YOU!" read the *Daily Express* headline.

Duke was angry when he learned that McGowan had double-crossed him. But he knew he couldn't play hide-and-seek forever. Besides, he had wrung about as much publicity as he could out of being a fugitive. He had made headlines not only in Britain but also throughout the United States. Duke didn't leave Britain immediately but exercised his right to remain there for two more weeks while he appealed the deportation order. The media had lost interest in him, however. He returned to the United States on March 30, four weeks after he had arrived.

To celebrate his trip, he published a special twenty-four-page issue of the *Crusader*, filled with articles from British newspapers detailing his escapades. The *Crusader* hailed his success in typically adoring fashion. "It is interesting to think that a racialist leader could have the charisma and intelligence to become a folk hero in Britain," the newspaper said. "His visit had an impact on Britain that may ultimately be the turning point in her fight to preserve her racial heritage. Duke left the left in Britain awed and sputtering and the racialist forces inspired and encouraged."

To top it off, he had trumped Wilkinson, who did not arrive in England until March 11, nine days after Duke. Moreover, Wilkinson captured little media attention. Because Wilkinson—unlike Duke—had been forbidden by name to enter England, when police seized him on March 21 they threw him in jail for four days before deporting him. "Man, it's rough over there," Wilkinson told an interviewer in the United States three weeks later. "They treat us like terrorists, like murderers or worse."

The feuding between Duke and Wilkinson continued as soon as both had returned to the United States. "He had nobody [in England]," Wilkinson said of Duke. "All he would do was leave his safe house, go downtown and start hitting the phone booths to call the news media. His one cross burning was a couple of sticks stuck up in a field. He lit it and ran." Duke dismissed Wilkinson's comments. "He follows me around like a shadow," he said. "Everything he knows he learned from me." Duke's trip to England not only generated publicity and one-upped Wilkinson but also strengthened his ties with British white-rights advocates. He met with members of several British extremist organizations, including the League of St. George and the better known National Front, which Duke admired for its efforts to preserve and strengthen "the Anglo-Saxon bloodstock." (The *Crusader*, in detailing Duke's exploits in England, featured an advertisement for the League of St. George's publication, *League Review*.)

Unlike Klan leaders such as Robert Shelton, who believed the Klan was both the end and the means, Duke saw the Klan as only a means to an end: smashing the power of Jews and asserting white supremacy. Duke had begun with the National Socialist White People's party and moved to the Klan only when he became convinced that Americans would never tolerate an open identification with Nazism. He also joined the Klan because he realized that its notorious legacy guaranteed coverage by the media. And while he was serving as grand wizard of the Knights of the Ku Klux Klan, he maintained his ties to other white supremacist leaders who did not belong to the Klan.

"Instead of emphasizing the Klan's unique philosophical approach to the race question and the Jewish question, Duke saw himself and his Klan as part of the broader extremist movement," Boston University doctoral student Evelyn Rich wrote in a dissertation on the Klan. "It was simply one of many vehicles which could help turn his vision of America into a reality. Thus when more traditional Klan leaders like Shelton criticized Duke for what they perceived as his Nazification of the Klan and his lax attitude towards the ritualistic aspects of the Klan, they were also criticizing Duke for his lack of commitment to the idea of the Klan. The view of Duke as a charlatan did not stem from his lack of belief in the 'cause,' but came about because he did not see the Klan and the cause [as] one."

Duke did not limit his goals to reestablishing a segregated society in the United States, as did most Klansmen. He intended to create a movement of whites throughout the world linked by a conviction that they had to save their race. This explained in part why he went to England.

When he was arrested in 1976, Duke was sponsoring not only a national convention of the Knights of the Ku Klux Klan but also the International Patriotic Conference with delegates from Canada, England, and Germany.

Duke championed the white minority government's effort to retain power in Rhodesia. When President Gerald Ford visited New Orleans aboard a steamboat in 1976, Duke and his followers placed a huge sign on the bank of the Mississippi River. It read:

> Long Live Rhodesia.
> Down with Kissinger.
> KKK.

As part of Duke's broader goals, the *Crusader* in 1978 decried the death of "100 White men, women and children, many of whom were raped and mutilated," in Kolwezi, a small mining town in Zaire. "Kolwezi: Portrait of Terror," read the banner front-page headline.

Duke's trip to England was not his first foray to Europe. In 1976, he attended an annual neo-Nazi rally at Diksmuide, Belgium, hosted by the Flemish Militant Order. Its leaders had fought alongside the Germans during World War II. Duke attended the rally with Jim Warner, a grand dragon in his Klan, and Ed Fields and J. B. Stoner, the leaders of the National States Rights party, an anti-Semitic group.

Duke also made several trips to Canada to try to establish a Klan and white supremacist movement there. He first visited Canada in March 1971 as head of the White Youth Alliance at LSU. He established ties with leaders of the country's nascent neo-Nazi group, the Western Guard, some of whose members eventually fell under his sway and revived the Klan in Canada. John Ross Taylor, James Alexander McQuirter, and Wolfgang Droege, three of the Western Guard's leaders, attended Duke's 1976 International Patriotic Conference in Metairie.

The following year, Duke repaid the visit by hopping across the border to Toronto while on a trip to Buffalo. In Toronto, he made the usual round of radio and television talk shows. "Canada is ripe for the Klan to come out of the closet," Duke said. "Canada is the last bastion of the white race on this planet, but we're going to lose the battle unless something is done. A few years ago, when I came to Toronto, Montreal and Vancouver, the cities were refreshingly different from those in the States. But when I look at them today, they have become dirty, overridden by non-whites."

Duke's message hit a chord with some Canadians, and requests for information on the Klan poured into the Western Guard's office in Toronto. Droege and McQuirter were impressed and decided to forsake their organization to create an official Canadian realm of the Knights of the Ku Klux Klan. The Canadian Klan went public in January 1978, garnering headlines at its first appearance. McQuirter, who had just graduated from high school, idolized Duke. "Many times you have right-wing leaders who were misfits or inarticulate people that people can't identify with," McQuirter recounted. "David Duke wasn't like that. He was a good speaker. He discussed issues at the level of the common man. He was young, a college graduate and good looking."

Duke, who toured British Columbia in April 1978, helped devise the Canadian Klan's political platform. "Our plans for Canada are simple," Duke said in a 1979 interview. "We are 100 percent for stopping the non-white immigration into Canada. And then we believe that the government should pay to send the blacks back to their own countries." In interviews, McQuirter parroted Duke almost word for word. Duke returned to British Columbia for another organizing tour on March 30, 1980. By now, however, Canadian authorities were tired of him. As he was leaving a Vancouver radio talk show on April 1, Duke was arrested and charged with entering the country illegally for having failed to note his 1979 conviction at customs. After a hearing, an immigration board ordered Duke out of the country, ruling that he was offensive to Canadian standards.

The Canadian Klan ended up attracting several thousand members and winning substantial media coverage. But Canadians were too tolerant on racial matters to pay the group much heed. By 1982, both Droege and McQuirter had been sentenced to jail for their involvement in a harebrained scheme to invade the Caribbean island of Dominica a year before with a group of Klansmen. In 1983, McQuirter ran afoul of the law again. He was convicted of plotting to murder a Klan underling and sentenced to eight years in prison. He was to serve this sentence after completing a two-year term for plotting to overthrow Dominica. The Canadian Klan limped along for several years before finally dying out.

Duke also tried to establish a Klan presence in Australia. He gained a foothold there in 1978 with a Klan chapter organized by a police officer in the city of Darwin. But when Australian authorities denied Duke the visa he needed to enter the country, the Australian Klan fell apart. Duke's attempts to expand the Klan overseas had all ended in failure.

Although Duke traveled to other countries in the late 1970s trying to build a worldwide network of racialists, he spent most of his time in the United States, trying to make a name for his Klan. He succeeded. The Anti-Defamation League, which closely monitors extremist groups, said that Duke, who founded the Knights of the Ku Klux Klan in 1973, had built his membership to about 1,000 by early 1978. By November 1979, he had increased his membership to 1,500–2,000 and had extended the Klan's reach beyond the South by establishing Klaverns in California, Massachusetts, New Jersey, New York, Illinois, and Hawaii. He also had another 10,000 followers who did not formally belong to the Klan.

The growth of Duke's Klan spearheaded an increase in overall Klan membership. The ADL said membership in the many different Klans rose from 6,500 in 1975 to 10,500 in 1979, reversing a decade-long decline. Nonmember supporters, the ADL added, jumped from 30,000–40,000 in 1978 to 75,000–100,000 in 1979. The ADL credited Duke with much of the Klan's overall growth. "If any one man can be deemed responsible for the Klan's resurgence, he is 27-year-old Grand Wizard David Ernest Duke," reported the *Los Angeles Herald Examiner* in a 1978 four-part series on the Klan. "Duke—an articulate, media-hip Louisianan who prefers a finely tailored business suit to a loose-fitting robe—has taken a dying hate group and tried to turn it into a mainstream 'movement of love' every bit as respectable as the Elks, Masons or Rotarians."

Duke's Klan would have grown faster, but his top aides kept quitting and denouncing him publicly, taking a share of his membership with them. In 1975, Bill Wilkinson abandoned Duke to start his own Klan, just after organizing the biggest Klan rally in years, a gathering in Walker, Louisiana, that drew 2,700. Wilkinson claimed that Duke had pocketed $5,000 that had been donated to the Klan at the rally.

In late 1976, Jerry Dutton, whom Duke had chosen to replace him in name—but not in power—as grand wizard just a few months before, resigned and joined forces with Wilkinson in a campaign to undermine Duke. Dutton had come to Louisiana at the invitation of James Warner, who had been active with Dutton in protests against the civil rights movement in the early 1960s in Birmingham. When Dutton left Duke's Klan, he published a pamphlet entitled, *The Truth About David Duke*. The pamphlet, which Dutton sent to reporters and other Klansmen, described Duke as a money-hungry egomaniac. Dutton said Duke had only 300 members, not the thousands he claimed, and kept his Klan going only because he bamboozled the media into reporting that he headed a large, vigorous organization. "It is now time to expose him for what he is—a liar," Dutton wrote.

In 1979, Duke's top assistant, Karl Hand, quit and denounced him in a single-spaced, five-page letter. A second-generation Klansman from Buffalo, Hand had moved to New Orleans in mid-1978 to assume the position of national organizer of the Knights of the Ku Klux Klan. In time, he developed an intense hatred for Duke and even had visions of killing him. Hand in the early 1990s was serving time in a Louisiana penitentiary for attempted second-degree murder in an incident that involved neither Duke nor the Klan. Hand's December 1979 resignation letter was similar to Dutton's and charged Duke with selling out the Klan for his own self-interest and greed. "I am tired," Hand wrote Duke, "of seeing you hurt, abuse, use and deceive good white people in the name of the Klan."

Hand was particularly angered by Duke's reluctance to go forward with a Klan rally in the posh seaside town of Barnegat, New Jersey, in August 1979. It had been organized by a seventeen-year-old named Aaron Morrison at his parents' house with their permission. Because it was unlikely territory for the Klan, plans for the rally had been reported in the press beforehand and several dozen people had promised to show up to protest. Hand, who came to Barnegat to stay with the Morrisons several days before the rally, said that Duke had tried to cancel the event four days beforehand because of growing opposition. Duke, Hand charged, was more concerned with his personal safety than with winning an important victory for the Klan.

On the day of the rally, Hand added, Duke tried to avoid showing up by getting his driver to stop so that they could go swimming. "Only by the threat of being shown up," Hand wrote, "did you decide to go." The *Crusader*, though, gave a glowing report of Duke's performance at the rally, which was attended by about twenty Klansmen and dozens of protesters.

"After the rally, Mr. Duke instructed the Klansmen to file in before him, thus defying the Reds in the finest fashion," the *Crusader* reported. "No leader should ask his men to do that which he himself is afraid to do. David Duke is a true leader."

In his resignation letter, Hand also accused Duke of softening his rhetoric against Jews in order to win more public support. "Are we to sacrifice our most sacred principle for the benefit of the anti-white media and establishment forces?" Hand wrote. "If so, then we are not Klansmen, for honor is more important to the true Klansmen than social and/or media acceptability." Like Dutton, Hand thought Duke was an egomaniac. As he tried to carve out a new image for the Klan, Hand said, Duke was making himself Exhibit A. In nearly every interview, Duke claimed that he had an IQ of 173. At every opportunity, he would demonstrate the success of his weight-lifting program by doing twenty-five one-handed pushups. For one article, Duke even had himself photographed without a shirt while doing pull-ups. Hand hated this sort of gimmick.

Just before Hand quit, Duke's California grand dragon, Tom Metzger, also resigned and took most of the California members with him to start the California Knights of the Ku Klux Klan. Like Hand, Metzger grew disenchanted with Duke's willingness to soften his words and actions in public. There was no mention in the *Crusader* of Metzger's leaving nor of Hand's or Dutton's. Each of them as Klansmen had been lionized regularly as white heroes, but when they resigned they disappeared into a black hole.

The final straw for Metzger came at the 1979 Klan National Leadership meeting that Duke organized in Metairie. Duke had promised the Klansmen a big surprise at the end of the event. When the curtain on the stage rose for the finale, they got their surprise—Duke, shirtless and in shorts, was lifting weights to show his rippling muscles. "We couldn't believe the egotism," said Metzger. "It was all some people could do to avoid laughing." Metzger was also disgusted at Duke's authorship of two books, *African Atto* and *Finders-Keepers*. "I'll never forgive him for writing those books," Metzger said years later.

African Atto was a seventy-page manual that purported to teach street-fighting techniques to blacks in preparation for a coming race war with whites. Written under the pseudonym Mohammed X in 1973, the book was salted with misspellings and bad punctuation. In *African Atto*—which was supposedly a translation of "African Attack"—Mohammed X prescribed a series of punches and kicks for blacks to learn that would kill or effectively render their white oppressors helpless. The techniques, which the author said he had learned while visting a tribe in Nigeria, were described as innate to the soul of blacks. "*African Atto* can only be effectively used by black people," Mohammed X wrote. "Just as whites can't 'soul dance' as well as our people, so they can never use this skill as well either." The manual advised the black fighter to yell "Hootoo!" when striking the white enemy to demoralize him and to rid one's body of "bad air." It also advised, "When you attack Whitey, be sure that you racially insult and psychologically attack him in addition to your physical account." Yelling "BLACK POWER!" was an especially good tactic when fighting white opponents, the book advised.

An ad for the book was headlined, "When was the last time whitey called you NIGGER?" It showed a black man knocking down a white attacker with a foot to his face. "African Atto will show you the way to BLACK POWER!" It was Jerry Dutton who disclosed that Duke had written *African Atto*. Dutton provided documentation from the Library of Congress that *African Atto* was copyrighted in the name of C. E. Hardin, the maiden name of Duke's wife, Chloe.

Duke was reluctant to admit authorship of *African Atto* when confronted by a reporter in 1978. He said only that it was written by "some people associated with me." Duke explained that the book, which was to be sold through the mail, had been written to allow the Klan to compile a list of the radical blacks who purchased it. "I believe very strongly that America is headed for a racial conflict," he said. "What the book essentially did was get us the names of the most radical blacks in the United States, so that when the time comes we will know where they are." In later years, however, Duke admitted that he had written *African Atto*.

Finders-Keepers was just as unlikely a book to be authored by the grand wizard of the Knights of the Ku Klux Klan. Written in 1976 by "Dorothy Vanderbilt" and "James Konrad," the 177-page book advised women "how to find, attract and keep the man you want." The book had eleven chapters, with titles such as "There Is a Man for You," "Where to Find Your Lover," "Dieting and Your Love-Life," and "The Cosmetic Surgery Alternative." Most of the advice was similar to that given in any number of women's magazines. But chapter 10, "Toward a More Fulfilling Sex-Life," stood out. "Sex has come out from under the covers in the Western world," the chapter began. And while this development has helped teach women how to have orgasms and men how to give them, the book went on, "for women over forty, there has been quite a change in their lifetime which many just don't know how to take. This book suggests they take it lying down, standing up or really any way they care to." Women who want a "romantic, sexually aggressive man" have to be a "sexual being" first, the book advised. "When you are around other people, do you ever expose a part of your body to him that only he can see? This kind of sexual teasing can really turn a man on."

The book further advised, "You have got to love sex. Not just sex with love, not just sex at certain times, but the idea of it, the doing of it, the anticipation of it. You must love sex for its own sake." There was advice on things not to do. "There is no quicker way to transform a man's proud erection into limp rejection than by making a comment belittling his manhood even if you are joking," the book noted. Similarly, "Don't ever mention a word about other men! He wants you to have him in your mind to the point of blotting out other people, especially other men."

The chapter then gave technical advice on the need to strengthen vaginal muscles through certain kinds of exercises—"they will certainly add to your ability to be 'attractive' to a man." Next came a ringing endorsement of oral sex. "Sooner or later, if you truly want to drive your man wild in bed, you should bring him to climax by fellatio. He will love you for it. To him it's more than just a beautiful sensation, it's really an expression of caring and concern and pure loving intimacy on your part. You may be like some women, disgusted or afraid of the thought of semen in your mouth, but apparently a majority of modern women occasionally fellate their men to climax and enjoy the experience. Many actually develop a taste for it. That's quite a bedtime snack. At least it's low on calories." The chapter ended by encouraging couples to engage in anal sex and advised women, "Do sleep with a married man as long as you can accept that nothing too serious will ever come of it."

Duke tried to keep his authorship of *Finders-Keepers* secret. But Dutton, who served as Duke's top aide when he wrote the book, disclosed Duke's role. Dutton said that Duke had pieced together the book with passages from self-help books and women's magazines.

One piece of Dutton's evidence came from a questionnaire at the end of *Finders-Keepers* that sought information on women's sexual habits. ("Which best describes your sexual nature? Old Fashioned? Moderate? Affectionate? Swinger? Very Free?") Women were asked to send details on themselves and their sexual desires—along with a photo—to the Togetherness Foundation. Dutton pointed out that the foundation's post office box in Washington, D.C., was the same as that of a company called "Patriot Advertising," which Duke's father operated.

Duke chose the name "Dorothy Vanderbilt," Dutton said, because it sounded sophisticated. "James Konrad" came from the first and middle names of his friend James K. Warner. Warner, who had not given Duke permission to use his name, was furious.

When questions about the book resurfaced during Duke's 1990 Senate campaign, he said he had only had a hand in the book and had had nothing to do with the chapter on sex. He said the book had been written because a female friend of his had committed suicide over problems with men and that the book was meant to spare other women a similar fate. Dutton, however, in a 1989 interview, said Duke was the sole author. Duke wrote *Finders-Keepers*, Dutton said, because he thought it would be a best-seller, making him rich and solving the Klan's chronic financial problems. But the book flopped. "I don't know that he sold hardly any," Dutton said. "It was a dismal failure. It was too hard-core for the right wing and too soft-core for perverts."

Another matter that concerned Dutton, Hand, and Metzger when they left the Knights of the Ku Klux Klan was Duke's womanizing. Duke had been married to Chloe since 1972, and they had two daughters. Erika Lindsay (her middle name came from James Lindsay, Duke's mentor, who had been murdered in June 1975), was born on August 30, 1975; Kristin Chloe, on June 24, 1977. Duke had wanted a son, but he made do, occasionally dressing Erika in a tiny Klan robe. In time he came to see his daughters' healthy appearance as an affirmation of the superiority of the white race and said he hoped his children looked like him. To the dismay of intimates, however, he favored Erika, who was blonde and had his features. When they were with him, he would put his arm around a beaming Erika while Kristin, who looked more like Chloe, would stand apart, looking on uncomfortably. But Duke was an absent father, usually away on his Klan travels, even on the day Erika was born. Raising their two girls was left to Chloe.

While Chloe was busy with Erika and Kristin, Duke was frequently pursuing other women—so avidly that it embarrassed former Klansmen. "He feels like he has to conquer every woman who comes near him," says Dutton. In their resignation letters, both Metzger and Hand said they were tired of having to cover up for Duke. "You don't seem to care what anyone else thinks or feels, just so long as you can satisfy your ego, by publicly chasing and displaying everything in skirts," Hand wrote. "You are a married man with two children, and there are many Klanspeople who view your behavior as contradictory to Klannish principles. . . . I appealed to you a hundred times, for the movement's sake, to be discreet if you couldn't be moral."

In a later letter denouncing Duke, Hand said that Duke called local organizers before arriving for rallies to ask them to fix him up with a woman. "We had many a good man quit," Hand wrote, "as a result of David's 'organizational tours.'" Duke's womanizing was not reported publicly until August 1991 by *Spy* magazine in an article entitled, "Behavior Unbecoming of a Racist." *Spy* reported that Nancy Manning, a prostitute, had spent the night with Duke in 1978 while he was visiting his Colorado organizer, Fred Wilkins, who lived in a Denver suburb. Duke denied the charge.

Chloe Duke had won admiration among Klan members for her behind-the-scenes work for her husband. For a time, she kept the Klan's books and organized Duke's schedule while raising their children. Hand and other Klansmen were sure she knew of his extramarital affairs. Hand said he thought she dismissed them as she did many of her husband's foibles. "Chloe worked hard and long for the Klan," Hand wrote, "sacrificing beyond belief and defending David from every accusation regardless of the validity."

In August 1979, Chloe and Duke separated (four-and-a-half years later they got divorced). One version holds that she left him because she had tired of his absence, his womanizing and the strain of living under the death threats he received. Another version holds that he simply asked her to leave. Chloe has never spoken publicly about her private life with Duke.

That same August, Duke resumed his political career by qualifying for the state Senate. He had run for the state Senate in Baton Rouge four years before—the last time statewide elections were held—and had lost with one-third of the vote. This time he was running for a seat in his home district of Metairie. The favorite was Joseph Tiemann, the incumbent. Two other men entered the race: Robert Namer, a businessman, and Robert Clarke, an attorney. When Duke qualified for the race on August 7, he was about to go on trial a second time on the 1976 charge of incitement to riot. The trial resulted in his conviction sixteen days later. Duke was nervous because he faced a possible sentence of up to six months in jail, which would, of course, wreck his political career. Hoping to avoid jail, he decided to continue his campaign anyway. The verdict—a suspended sentence—was not handed down until after the campaign had ended.

Duke's 1979 race was similar to the one in 1975: he challenged another incumbent, he ran as a conservative Democrat, and he campaigned on virtually the same issues. And as in 1975, he downplayed his Klan affiliation, preferring to call himself a white-rights advocate. In 1979, his "Program of Courage" pledged to:

* stop reverse discrimination against white people in employment, promotions, scholarships and union admittance.

* cut welfare benefits, require all able-bodied welfare recipients to work and give financial incentives to welfare mothers to have fewer children.

* reduce taxes and cut government spending.

* fight busing and forced integration of public schools, while "textbooks should be chosen that reflect the high traditions of our people and nation and not debase our heritage or make saints of those like Malcom [sic] X and Martin L. King."

* fight crime by instituting mandatory penalties for people convicted of violent crimes.

As he had four years before, Duke canvassed door to door, handed out leaflets at busy intersections, and attended every campaign forum. His campaign staff consisted of Klansmen.

Throughout his career, Duke had focused on hot-button issues that would generate coverage from newspapers, television, and radio. But his magic act had worn off on the New Orleans media, and his campaign failed to generate much publicity. The biggest news during the race came when Namer, a Jewish businessman, claimed that his office had been ransacked and—a week later—that his home had been firebombed. Suspicion naturally fell on Duke and the Klan. He denied any involvement and suggested that it was a "dirty political trick" cooked up by Namer and his "Zionist" friends to discredit him. Policemen who investigated the incidents privately agreed with Duke, noting that Namer had a reputation for unorthodox behavior.

Duke impressed observers with his appearances at campaign forums, but it was not enough. Senator Tiemann won the October 27 open primary outright. The vote totals were:

Tiemann	21,329	57 percent
Duke	9,897	26 percent
Namer	4,635	12 percent
Clarke	1,824	5 percent

Duke was disappointed. But he felt he had won a victory over Jews by winning twice as many votes as Namer. Duke spent $18,632 on the campaign, according to a report he filed after the election—about $2,000 more than he spent in 1975. About one-third of the money he raised in 1979— $6,697—came from his own pocket or, more likely, from Klan coffers. In 1979, as in 1975, he spent most of his campaign money on media advertising and did not disclose any individual contributors, apparently because no one gave more than $500, the minimum amount requiring disclosure.

As he had four years before, Duke in 1979 put a positive spin on his defeat. In a letter sent to Klansmen, Duke made the outlandish claim that from his percentage of the vote, "we can deduce that at least one-fourth of the White people in America look with favor on the KKK." Duke may have seen himself advancing, but Klansmen were growing disenchanted with him. His failed campaign contributed to the decision by Karl Hand and Tom Metzger, two of his top officials, to quit the Knights of the Ku Klux Klan.

In his resignation letter, Hand criticized Duke's decision to downplay his Klan affiliation during the campaign and complained that the single campaign television advertisement "reeked to high heaven with egotism." The ad showed Duke in a tank top and shorts "so tight that they split down the back," Hand wrote. He added that he had dissuaded Duke from running another television ad by threatening to resign. In the second ad, Duke was to be shown lifting weights. "What do these cheap displays have to do with our principles?" Hand wrote in his resignation letter a month after the campaign ended. "Nothing! Your contention that they showed you were human does not hold up under scrutiny. If you wanted that effect, why not show you playing golf, instead of those lewd and suggestive displays?" Metzger complained that most of Duke's campaign money came from the Klan. "That in itself is not wrong," Metzger wrote in his resignation letter, "but no leader was ever consulted that I know of."

While Duke was campaigning for the Metairie state senate seat, he was also ostensibly running for president. He had announced his candidacy with a huge "DUKE FOR PRESIDENT" headline on the front page of the February 1979 *Crusader*. At twenty-eight, the article said, he planned to "take up where George Wallace left off."

While he was seven years younger than the minimum age of thirty-five required to be president, "he can still enter some primaries in the same fashion as black leader Julian Bond did in a previous election," the article said. "What he hopes to accomplish is the acquisition of a large number of votes and delegates to the Democratic Party Convention, which would increase public awareness of the problems facing America's White people.

"Additionally, the course of the campaign will provide a sounding board for the vital issues facing America, including the illegal alien immigration problem, anti-White discrimination, the high taxes and inflation caused by massive minority welfare programs, forced integration and foreign policy, including the pro-Zionist, anti-American and oil Mideast policy now being pursued by the government." The article concluded: "One thing seems certain. Before 1980 is over, [President] Jimmy Carter, [Massachusetts Sen.] Ted Kennedy, [California Gov.] Jerry Brown, or perhaps all three, will trail David Duke in one or more primaries for the Democratic nomination for the Presidency of the United States."

Instead, Duke's campaign never amounted to anything. He campaigned briefly in only a few states and generated little news coverage. Few people were willing to take an underage racist seriously as a presidential candidate. The March 1980 *Crusader* carried a small announcement that Duke had canceled plans to seek the Democratic nomination for president. Always looking for a scapegoat, he blamed his exit on states having passed "minimum entry age laws specifically designed to keep me off the ballot."

CHAPTER FIVE

A PROPHET WITHOUT AN AUDIENCE

While making his aborted bid for president in late 1979 and early 1980, David Duke was secretly making plans to leave the Klan. Since founding the Knights of the Ku Klux Klan in 1973, he had sought to change the image of a Klansman from that of a potbellied redneck who beat up blacks for sport to that of an educated man or woman concerned less with hating blacks than with advancing his own race and building a political movement of like-minded people. Duke regularly announced that the Klan was rising again, but this was just media hype. He was never able to instill his racialist beliefs in more than a few thousand people. Particularly disappointing was the failure of large numbers of whites to grasp that a Jewish conspiracy was making them second-class citizens in their own country. As James Warner said in explaining why he left the Klan, "People attracted to the Klan were just nigger haters. They were not intelligent and could not be educated to anything other than nigger hating. They couldn't get into the Masons, the Elks or other fraternal orders so they joined the Klan. It was a temporary fix for their lives and they soon dropped out. They had no grasp on Jews and could not be made to grasp it."

At the same time, Bill Wilkinson was eclipsing Duke within the Klan. Racist whites found Wilkinson's gun-toting, tough-guy image more appealing than Duke's nonviolent ballot-box approach. "Duke is a man of words, and we need a man of action," said Willard Oliver, explaining in March 1980 why he and the majority of Duke's followers in northern Alabama—where he had his largest concentration of members—were switching from Duke's Klan to Wilkinson's. "We need a leader who will get out in the streets with us. Duke is more of a media spokesman." Duke realized that he was losing ground to his rival. He regularly railed against Wilkinson, remembers Karl Hand, charging that Wilkinson was undoing the good that Duke had done for the Klan.

By 1980, the Anti-Defamation League confirmed, Wilkinson's Klan had more members than Duke's. "The most notable aspect of the Klan's growth over the past year," the ADL said in 1979, "has been its accompaniment by an increase in lawlessness and violence, due largely to the fact that the organization which has grown fastest, Bill Wilkinson's Invisible Empire, is the most militant and violence-prone of the existing Klans." A series of widely reported incidents involving Klan groups other than Duke's kept reminding the public that, no matter what Duke said, the Klan was still a violent, racist organization. Duke repeatedly tried to point out that it was not his Klan engaging in the violence, but the public did not make this distinction.

In the summer of 1978, Klansmen attacked a group of blacks in Tupelo, Mississippi, who were protesting reports that a white policeman had beaten a black suspect. Shortly afterward, a similar demonstration by blacks in Okolona, Mississippi, ended when Wilkinson's Klansmen arrived and a shootout occurred. One white man was wounded and a black leader's car was hit. In May 1979, a group of blacks marking the first anniversary of the arrest of a retarded black man charged with raping three white women held a march in Decatur, Alabama. More than 100 Klansmen showed up, and a brawl ensued that left three blacks and two Klansmen injured. The worst was yet to come. On November 3, 1979, a confrontation in Greensboro, North Carolina, between Klansmen and members of the Communist Workers party ended in a shootout that left five CWP members dead and nine people wounded. Television crews filmed the shootout and broadcast the bloody incident nationwide.

With the Klan irretrievably linked with violence, Duke cast about for a way to promote white-rights ideals without the Klan's baggage. He decided to leave the Knights of the Ku Klux Klan and form a new group. He would call it the National Association for the Advancement of White People, a name that alluded to the National Association for the Advancement of Colored People, the nation's best-known civil rights organization. The name was not original. A Cincinnati white supremacist had organized a NAAWP in the 1960s, but it was inactive by the time Duke took the name for his own group. On December 20, 1979, Duke incorporated the NAAWP as a nonprofit group and applied two months later for tax-exempt status with the IRS.

As the founder and leader of the Knights of the Ku Klux Klan, Duke could not simply abandon the group. Just quitting would seem too opportunistic. He had to bow out gracefully, either by turning it over to one of his state grand dragons or by agreeing to merge it with another Klan group. He chose the second option. In January 1980, he called Bill Wilkinson and said he wanted to discuss something that could be "mutually profitable for both of us," according to Wilkinson's later account. Several months passed, however, before Duke called his hated rival again. He asked that they meet. The location would be Middendorf's, a popular fried seafood restaurant in Manchac, a small fishing community halfway between Duke's home in Metairie and Wilkinson's in Denham Springs. There Duke outlined his plan: he would sell his members' names and addresses to Wilkinson and would agree to resign from the Klan for at least ten years. In return, Wilkinson would pay him $35,000. Duke would use this as seed money to start the NAAWP. Knowing that turning over his membership list to an outsider was one of the worst offenses he could commit as grand wizard, Duke demanded that the deal be kept secret. Wilkinson had to agree not to reveal the transaction to anybody. He had to pay Duke in cash. And they would not record the contract at a courthouse where it could be found and be made public.

Wilkinson was noncommittal at the meeting. But within a few days he had hatched a plan to expose Duke's scheme publicly. If he could prove that Duke had tried to sell his secret membership list, Wilkinson figured, he could destroy his rival. Wilkinson called Duke and agreed to the deal. He asked Duke to meet him at midnight on July 20, at a secluded farmhouse near Cullman, Alabama. Wilkinson carefully laid the trap. He wanted to make sure that independent sources would be able to verify Duke's sell-out, so he called Bob Dunnavant, a free-lance reporter for Nashville's daily newspaper, the *Tennessean*, whom he trusted. He also called Don Lefler, a reporter from WHNT-TV in Huntsville, and told him to bring along a cameraman. Wilkinson did not reveal his plan but guaranteed them a good story. Dunnavant, Lefler, and the cameraman, Keith Lowhorne, reached the farmhouse at about 11:00 P.M. When they arrived, they discovered that Wilkinson had already posted khaki-clad Klansmen toting semiautomatic rifles to stand guard. This made them nervous, and they wondered if Wilkinson wasn't setting them up. But their fear dissipated when the guards explained Wilkinson's plan. Dunnavant put a microphone in the farmhouse hooked up to a tape recorder outside.

Wilkinson and Roger Handley, his Alabama grand dragon, drove up first. Duke and Don Black, his Alabama grand dragon, followed a few minutes later. As the latter pair pulled up, Dunnavant, Lowhorne, and Lefler hid in a chickenhouse behind the farmhouse. The four Klansmen exchanged greetings and then went inside. The reporters then sneaked around the farmhouse and positioned themselves outside the window of the room in which the Klansmen were meeting. Lowhorne, who was close enough to see inside but could not be seen, began rolling his film.

Wilkinson read the proposed contract aloud. The conditions called for Duke to endorse Wilkinson as "clearly the most effective and capable leader of the

Ku Klux Klan"; for Duke to agree to resign from the Klan by August 15 and agree not to set up any organization using the Klan name for at least ten years; and for Wilkinson to agree not to take part or be connected financially with any white-rights organization other than the Klan for at least ten years. Both Duke and Black agreed to the contract. Duke then handed over a brown paper bag filled with file cards that contained his members' names.

Wilkinson was now supposed to give Duke the $35,000. But he said he had no money to hand over. Instead, he told Duke that he had secretly videotaped the meeting. "I'm sorry that we had to do this . . . ," he said. "I'm really surprised that this ever could take place, because I can't believe you would go through with it—taking money to sell your endorsement and quit the Klan." Duke's jaw dropped in astonishment. He snatched back the bag of membership file cards, and he and Black hustled out the door—only to be met by the reporters. Lowhorne switched on his kleig lights and caught their faces frozen in shock. Not only had Wilkinson burned them but the media had caught them. Dunnavant and Lefler shouted questions at Duke and Black, but they brushed the reporters off. They jumped in their car and roared off.

It was a humiliating setback for Duke, especially since Wilkinson's ploy was reported nationwide. "[Duke] was going to sell his people out," Wilkinson gloated. Duke denied the charge, but since the incident had been witnessed and recorded by reporters, no one believed him. Other Klan leaders called Duke a traitor for breaking his Klan oath to keep his membership secret.

Three days after the farmhouse setup, Duke announced that he was leaving the Klan to form the NAAWP. "I'm resigning because I don't think the Klan can succeed at this point," Duke said, "because of its violent image and because of people like Bill Wilkinson. He's low and dishonorable. And people see Wilkinson and believe all Klansmen are like that—bad and violent. All the good in the world I have done and could do doesn't make any difference because most people don't differentiate between Klans. They think we're all like that, and that's disgusting."

Duke's seven-year effort to reshape the Klan's image had failed. But he attempted to portray his leaving the Klan not as a personal defeat but as an organizational defeat.

In an attempt at damage control, he dashed off a resignation letter to his Klan members. After detailing his efforts to promote "White victory" since he was fourteen years old, Duke echoed James Warner's words as he wrote, "The bottom line is that we simply haven't grown fast enough and have not reached enough of the quality people we need to succeed. Although millions of good, solid Americans agree with our basic principles, a number of factors have destroyed the ability of our organization to attract and recruit them. Some factors are the media's fault, some are the fault of those who call themselves Klansmen but are simply weirdos or nuts looking for publicity or violence." He added: "The Hollywood image of the Klan, which is purposefully concocted to hurt the cause, is actually an attraction to a number of shadier elements who actually like the violent, Mafia-type image and think the Klan is really that way. As a result, a number of people apply simply because they want to be 'tough' or because they 'hate niggers,' but they don't have an inkling of what we're really fighting for. . . . Even though I feel I have been as successful as possible in my media debates, too many of them were centered around whether or not the Klan committed such-and-such an atrocity, or whether we were anti-Catholic, violent, illegal, etc. Precious little time has been spent on the vital issues of integration, anti-white discrimination, Zionism, welfare and non-white immigration."

Duke wasted no time trying to put the Klan behind him. Along with the resignation letter, he enclosed the inaugural issue of the NAAWP's newspaper, the *NAAWP News*. "I believe you will find it the most interesting and informative White rights paper in America," he wrote. "I hope that many of you will see the potential of this Movement to garner massive support from America's White majority. I would like to personally invite you to join the NAAWP." He concluded the letter by promising never to "publicly denigrate the Ku Klux Klan or its legitimate leaders." He signed the letter, "Yours for White Victory!"

Don Black had planned to follow Duke into the NAAWP, and in fact was prepared to sign a contract at the meeting with Wilkinson promising, like Duke, to remain out of the Klan for at least ten years. But the fiasco with Wilkinson prompted Black to agree to succeed Duke as grand wizard of the Knights of the Ku Klux Klan. Louis Beam, the Texas grand dragon, succeeded Black as second in command. Five years later, Duke in an interview called the attempted sale "a very stupid maneuver." He also admitted that he had attempted to carry out the transaction even though he suspected that Wilkinson was an FBI informant. In retrospect, Duke got out of the Klan at a good time. The Klan's latest resurgence was fading.

With Duke's departure, Wilkinson became its undisputed leader. But in August 1981, the *Tennessean*, which had been aggressively covering the Klan for a year, revealed that Wilkinson had indeed been an FBI informant since 1974. Wilkinson insisted that he had given only basic details to the FBI—such as when and where he would hold a rally—and had not released secret information about his Klan. He added that he had not been paid by the

FBI and had received no favors for the information he provided. Nevertheless, he had violated his Klan's bylaws, which prohibited talking with the FBI or other plainclothes police agents. Other Klan leaders, including Don Black, denounced him.

With his membership down sharply, Wilkinson in 1983 declared the Invisible Empire, Knights of the Ku Klux Klan, bankrupt and filed for protection under federal bankruptcy laws. A year later, he resigned as imperial wizard and withdrew completely from the Klan. By 1989, he was running a small hotel outside the United States and living quietly. When he was tracked down, he at first denied his identity. Then, after admitting that he had been the Klan imperial wizard, he said he had ended his racist activities and was building a new life. He asked that the location of his new home not be disclosed to avoid possible harassment or deportation.

The Knights of the Ku Klux Klan, Duke's old group, also faded in the 1980s. Many members followed Duke into the NAAWP, leaving Don Black, Duke's successor, doomed to failure. The Knights of the Ku Klux Klan made a splash once with a 1982 rally in Washington, D.C., that ended with blacks rioting. But soon after, Black began a two-year jail term for joining the conspiracy to overthrow the government of Dominica, a Caribbean island. Two veteran Klansmen, first Stanley McCollum and then Thom Robb, succeeded him. But by 1990, the Knights of the Ku Klux Klan had only a few hundred members.

Also contributing to the Klan's decline during the 1980s was the Southern Poverty Law Center. Its aggressive attorney, Morris Dees, began filing lawsuits at every opportunity against Klansmen who had participated in violence against blacks. Dees and the SPLC were devastatingly effective. They dug up evidence for state and federal prosecutors that helped convict more than twenty-five Klansmen on charges ranging from civil right violations to murder. They also forced Klan groups to divert scarce funds from organizing to defending their members.

In 1987, Dees and the Southern Poverty Law Center dealt organized racism a mortal blow. They won a $7 million judgment that put out of business Robert Shelton's United Klans of America, which a decade earlier had been the biggest Klan faction. A jury held the UKA liable for the 1981 murder of a black teenager that had been committed in Mobile, Alabama, by two of its members.

The presidency of Ronald Reagan also hurt the Klan. The most conservative United States president in at least fifty years, Reagan on many issues advocated the same views as did nonviolent Klan members. Reagan talked tough on crime, called for cutting liberal social programs that benefited blacks and spoke of the need to return to traditional—i.e., white—values. Non-violent Klansmen unhappy with the group's ineffectiveness pinned their hopes on Reagan and drifted out of the Klan.

With the Klan disintegrating, violent white extremists who thought Reagan was too moderate left the Klan and formed The Order and Posse Comitatus. The members of The Order, in particular, realized that the kind of society they had been seeking would never exist without a violent revolution that would overthrow the United States government. For two years, members of The Order robbed banks and murdered law enforcement officials. But the group was finally broken in the mid-1980s, when the FBI captured or killed virtually all of its important members. Robert Mathews, The Order's leader, burned to death in December 1984 when a house where he was hiding caught fire from illuminating flares fired by FBI agents.

By 1990, the Klan existed in little more than name. Klanwatch, the intelligence arm of the Southern Poverty Law Center, estimated the Klan's membership nationwide that year at 5,000, half the level in 1981. Klan rallies turned out only a handful of people, and the group's activities won only occasional mention in the media. But while the Klan may have died in the 1980s, white supremacist organizations had not. Like Duke, many Klan leaders had left the Klan but continued their activities under other labels.

The non-Klan anti-Semitic groups active in the 1980s included William Pierce's National Alliance, Ed Fields's National States Rights party, Willis Carto's Liberty Lobby, James Warner's New Christian Crusade church, and Tom Metzger's White Aryan Resistance. David Duke, the head of his own non-Klan group, the NAAWP, retained close ties with these men throughout the decade.

Like David Duke's Klan, the NAAWP was dedicated to fighting for white rights. But Duke decided that his new group had to be different, at least stylistically, if it was to grow into a political force. He organized the NAAWP along more traditional lines than the Klan. He jettisoned the secret Klan oaths, the mysterious rituals, and the cross-burning ceremonies. He discarded his robe. He called himself president of the group, not grand wizard. He installed a board of directors. The board, he liked to boast, included two retired admirals and one retired army general. (He was bragging that retired Admiral Ira McMillian was on the board even after McMillian had died in 1987.)

But the National Association for the Advancement of White People was simply the Klan without sheets. Its aim was the same as the Knights of the Ku Klux Klan: to protect the purity of the white race from what Duke called "mongrelization." Not only were Duke's goals the same, but the people who worked for him in the Klan—Ethel Segui, James McArthur, Ray Leahart, and Sandra Bergeron and her husband, Eddie—simply switched over to the NAAWP. As before, they worked out of the basement in Duke's Cypress Street home in Metairie. "My basic ideology, as far as what I believe about race, about the Jewish question, is the same," Duke said in a 1985 interview. "My difference is in my tactics and organization."

Duke, though, retained ties to friendly Klansmen, most notably Don Black. When Black was sent to prison for the Dominica invasion, he continued as grand wizard, and Duke was supposed to quietly fill in to keep the group going. He did little more, however, than oversee the mailing a few times of the KKK's renamed newspaper, *White Patriot*, to NAAWP members. Duke also spoke at the Klan's 1982 National Leadership Conference at Stone Mountain, Georgia. It was to be his last formal involvement with the Klan.

Duke portrayed the NAAWP as a white civil rights group—the white counterpart of the NAACP. In the first issue of the *NAAWP News*, he wrote that leaders of the NAACP try "to instill racial pride in their children, preserve black culture and fight for black rights. The problem is that they are also working for the destruction of white rights in their promotion of anti-white discrimination, busing, resentment and hatred against whites and a never-ending myriad of programs designed to take more and more money away from the productive elements of society and give it to the unproductive."

Every issue of the *NAAWP News* featured a full-page statement entitled "NAAWP vs. NAACP" that denigrated the respected civil-rights group while setting forth the NAAWP's ideals. The theme was the same one that Duke had espoused in the Klan: the government, backed by a propaganda campaign waged through the Jewish-controlled media, was systematically discriminating against white people. The main two programs behind this strategy, the statement said, were affirmative action and the busing of white children to black schools. "If it is appropriate to punish whites today because a small number practiced slavery over a hundred years ago," the statement said, "why shouldn't blacks be punished for their ancestors' practice of slavery, brutality and oppression in Africa for at least the last ten thousand years? . . . no people have contributed more to the well-being of all the people of the earth than the Caucasian. In the creation and spreading of the concepts of freedom and democratic principles, education, the arts, medicine, technology and science, whites have played an indispensable role. One for which our children should certainly not be punished."

Critics who said the NAAWP promoted hatred were guilty of a double standard, Duke declared. "If the NAACP pushes for black civil rights, black interests and attempts to instill black pride in their children—and then advocates discrimination against whites—the mass media and government refer to it as love and brotherhood. If a white dares to defend white civil rights, white interests and attempts to instill white pride in his children—and opposes racial discrimination against anyone—it's often called hate and bigotry. It should be readily apparent that the real hatred rests with the minority-racists." Having concluded that his followers could not grasp why Jews posed a grave threat to whites, Duke shifted the NAAWP's focus to the menace he saw from blacks and Hispanics. Like the *Crusader*, *NAAWP News* articles railed against race mixing and warned that the influx of Latin American immigrants into the United States was like a foreign invasion.

Throughout the 1980s, but especially in the NAAWP's early years, Duke missed no opportunity to portray blacks as lazy, dishonest, and violent. The *NAAWP News* noted every incident of racial violence in the country precipitated by a black and every instance of political corruption involving a black—and ignored corruption by white politicians and attacks by whites against blacks.

The early issues of the *NAAWP News* were reports of gloom and doom. Headlines from the fourth issue included: "Supreme Court Decision Grants Privileged Status to Blacks," "The White Race: An Endangered Species?" "Blacks Riot in Philadelphia," "Black & White Gays 'Together' in SF," and "One Million Illegal Aliens in Los Angeles." Few institutions were immune to the black peril. Several articles said the American military was in a shambles because blacks were being admitted in large numbers. Another article was headlined "Professional Boxing: How Blacks Ruined a Once-Great Sport."

Duke particularly disliked the legacy of the slain civil rights leader, the Reverend Martin Luther King, Jr. In 1983, he sent a letter to all 100 senators opposing the proposed national holiday marking King's birth. "He was a Communist sympathizer," Duke wrote in the *NAAWP News*, "a person revered by only a small percentage of Americans, a man who was elected to no political office and whose policies were opposed by the vast majority of Americans, a man whose personal integrity was in the gutter, a man whose record is so damning that the government agreed to hold it in secret for 50 years." Duke was still railing against King and calling him a Communist in the early 1990s.

Duke's heroes were men like Allan Bakke, who had sued the University of California at Davis Medical School in the late 1970s because minority applicants who scored lower on entrance exams were admitted under a quota system in an attempt to boost the number of minority doctors. Bakke, who won his lawsuit in a landmark Supreme Court ruling and was admitted to the medical school, was frequently profiled in the *NAAWP News*.

So was Bernhard Goetz, a white man who was arrested after shooting four black teenagers on a New York City subway car in 1984. Goetz claimed that he acted in self-defense because the four were about to mug him. A 1987 trial acquitted him of attempted murder, to Duke's delight. A third hero was aviator Charles Lindbergh, whom Duke praised for having tried to prevent the United States from preparing for war against Nazi Germany.

A fourth hero was Turkish dictator Kemal Ataturk. An article in the *NAAWP News* applauded Ataturk for expelling foreigners from Turkey and for hanging a Jewish financial expert. "The odds are that every nation will have one or more dictators during its existence," said the article, which was reprinted from the anti-Semitic journal *Instauration*. "Even England had its Cromwell. When it is America's time to go totalitarian, we should pray that we get a Kemal, who was more aware than any other great public figure of modern times that national resurrection depends first and foremost on the distillation process of racial separation."

The *NAAWP News* showed that Duke continued to abhor interracial marriages. The December 1984 issue called for a boycott of Tyne Daly, star of the television series "Cagney and Lacey," because she was married to a black man. "There's nothing glamorous about selling out your race, either, Ms. Daly," the article read. "Let's hope our readers can show a little courage, too—by turning off the set whenever your face appears on it."

The same issue of the *NAAWP News* reprinted an article from *Instauration* outlining a plan to carve up the United States by ethnic group. The plan called for forcibly resettling blacks and whites in designated territories. An accompanying map showed that most of the United States would be reserved for whites. But a swath of land running from San Diego to Texas would be reserved for Hispanics. The area would be named Alta California, and a twenty-mile buffer zone would be established to "separate the U.S. from its new southern neighbor," said the text accompanying the map. "To stop the creeping Mexican invasion once and for all, anyone who crossed into this buffer zone without permission from both countries will be shot on sight." A chunk of land carved from New Mexico and Colorado would be reserved for Native Americans and named Navashona. "Although the land is not rich or fertile," the article said, "it already supports a considerable number of Indians and whites, so there is no reason why Indians, including those from the big cities and eastern reservations, will not have enough elbow room, once the whites have decamped."

West Israel would include all of Long Island and Manhattan. "Jews from the Bronx, Westchester and other New York suburbs will only have a short move to their new country," the article said, "as will those from Boston, Philadelphia and Washington, D.C." A small area surrounding New York City would serve as the homeland for "various other Unassimilable Minorities, such as the Puerto Ricans, Southern Italians, Greeks and immigrants from the eastern and southern Mediterranean littoral." The homeland for blacks would be called New Africa and would stretch east along the Gulf Coast from Louisiana to include most of Florida. "Almost 12,000,000 Negroes will have to be transported from northern urban centers and millions of southern Negroes will have to be regrouped within the designated area," the article said. "Whites, particularly in that part of New Africa divested from the Deep South, will probably not give up their homes peacefully. In Florida, however, where hardly anyone has roots, population transfers will be easier." The bit of Florida that would not be given to New Africa was to include Miami, Miami Beach, and Dade County. It would be called New Cuba. "Only Negroes, Jews and a few aged Majority members," the article said, "will have to vacate."

To complete the resettlement plan, French Canadians would get a slice of land along the northern border, and the Hawaiian Islands would become East Mongolia, a preserve for Chinese, Japanese, and Filipinos. "If all this sounds impractical, we ask our readers to think of the alternatives," the article said. "If the races are not separated soon, the Majority will have to fight for survival or go completely under." Duke did not write this article but it reflected his thinking, and the *NAAWP News* printed articles like it throughout the 1980s that called for dividing up the United States by race as the solution to what the newspaper labeled the "racial quagmire." Ideas like these, of course, did not fit the norm for a civil rights organization. But many of the NAAWP's other activities did.

Just as he looked to the NAACP in choosing the name of his organization, Duke attempted to imitate the civil rights group's pressure tactics. At various times in the 1980s, he called for a boycott of Coca-Cola because the company had agreed to demands by the Reverend Jesse Jackson that it hire more blacks. Duke wrote letters to major corporations to complain about one practice or another involving race. And he visited Washington, D.C., to lobby Congress. But none of his tactics had any impact. Worse, he received virtually no press coverage. In leaving the Klan, he had freed himself of the Klan's baggage, but he had also lost his media drawing card. He could no longer manipulate the media into giving him the kind of nationwide coverage he had won with his Klan Border Watch or in his TV interviews with Tom

Snyder, Phil Donahue, and others. Not only did reporters stop trooping to his home to write yet another story about the "young, articulate and handsome leader," but he also received few invitations to speak at college campuses and give interviews on radio talk shows. For Duke politically, losing media attention was like being deprived of oxygen.

He had appeared on at least a half dozen national television shows while in the Klan. But he appeared on only one program between the time he left the Klan in 1980 until 1987. It was CNN's "Crossfire" program, in April 1985. The show was an uncomfortable thirty minutes for Duke. He was of course thrilled to be on national television again. But with the FBI rounding up the last members of The Order at the time, "Crossfire" wanted Duke to talk about the group, which had sought to overthrow the United States government. Duke was caught in a dilemma: after years of crafting a nonviolent reputation, he did not want to appear to be condoning murders and bank robberies committed by The Order. But he also did not want to repudiate the group and alienate his supporters in the extremist movement.

To seek advice on how to respond, he drove to the suburban Washington, D.C., headquarters of William Pierce, the head of the neo-Nazi National Alliance and author of *The Turner Diaries*. The novel had served as the model for The Order's activities. Duke thought Pierce was a brilliant thinker and had reprinted many of his articles in the *Crusader* and the *NAAWP News*. When they met, however, Pierce gave him unwelcome advice: Duke should stand by The Order.

Duke chose instead to steer a middle course. He decided to answer questions on "Crossfire" by quoting from a letter that Robert Mathews, The Order's leader, had drafted shortly before his fiery death four months before. In the passage Duke read, Mathews spoke of his fear that his son, a blond, blue-eyed Aryan, would grow up to become a stranger in his own land, outnumbered and isolated by nonwhites. The excerpt allowed Duke to dodge the matter of violence. It also placed him on familiar territory by allowing him to guide the conversation toward the theme of whites as a dispossessed majority who were quickly losing their rights because of reverse racism. After the show, Duke could not stop worrying about whether his compromise answer had offended Pierce. He visited his patron the next day. Ironically, however, Pierce had forgotten to watch the show and had no comment on his appearance.

Duke disappeared not only from the airwaves as president of the NAAWP but also from newspapers and magazines. For example, while Duke had appeared in dozens of articles in the *Times-Picayune* as a Klansman in the 1970s, he did not appear once in the paper from 1981 to 1987. As president of the NAAWP, Duke was featured only three times in national publications through 1987. Two of them were not exactly reputable publications: *Hustler* and *Gallery*. They printed question-and-answer sessions with Duke, interviews that he did not want known in 1990 and 1991 when he ran as a profamily candidate, first for the Senate and then for governor. *Southern Magazine* also profiled him in 1987.

But the profile chagrined and angered Duke because it portrayed him as a down-and-out racist who was "quick to accept free dinner invitations to restaurants where he will order the most expensive items on the menu." The piece focused on his personal life and said his major dilemma was deciding between two women he was dating. One had what he described as "great breasts," while the other had a long, thin body. The article was headlined, "The Duke of Deception: Does white power advocate David Duke believe his own act anymore?"

In February 1987, Duke went to Howard Beach, New York, to try to exploit its much-publicized racial incident. A gang of whites had been arrested after attacking three blacks, one of whom had died while fleeing. But the trip only showed how far he had faded into obscurity. The morning after his arrival, he sat on a bed in his cheap motel calling reporter after reporter to announce that he would hold a press conference in front of the Howard Beach pizza parlor where the attack had occurred. However, only a few half-interested reporters showed up to hear Duke denounce the prosecution of the whites. When they asked him what right he as an outsider had to speak out on Howard Beach, he said that local residents had invited him and that he had met with them. Duke, however, had come on his own initiative and had not met with anyone.

Duke then drove to Manhattan to seek a meeting with Mayor Ed Koch. Shivering in the cold, he went to a bank of pay telephones outside city hall and called the mayor. No one in Koch's office would talk to him. But it seemed that all was not lost. A *New York Post* reporter recognized Duke and began interviewing him about his visit. Duke eagerly explained the NAAWP's purpose and, with the reporter in tow, walked to the front doors of city hall. A security guard barred Duke from the building.

The following morning, Duke bought every New York newspaper to look for news about himself. He was bitterly disappointed to find nothing but the *New York Post* article. And that piece left him fuming. "All Dressed Up, Nowhere to Go," read the headline recounting his failed day.

Duke was less eager for publicity on another occasion, a bizarre mission involving several of his friends that sought to overthrow the democratically elected government of Dominica. Part of the Lesser Antilles, Dominica is a small Caribbean island 2,000 miles southeast of New Orleans that had won its independence from Great Britain two years earlier. But a powerful hurricane had destroyed most of the island's banana crop. Amid domestic unrest and protest, Patrick John, Dominica's first prime minister, had been forced to resign. In July 1980, Eugenia Charles was elected as John's successor.

Almost all of the ten mercenaries who were to carry out the coup attempt, code-named Operation Red Dog, were members of Ku Klux Klan factions or neo-Nazi groups. They planned to sail for ten days on a fifty-seven-foot charter boat named the *Manana*, drop anchor just off the coast, and then put ashore in a rubber raft a few miles north of the capital. With local collaborators, they would capture the armory and the police station. Resistance would be minimal, the mercenaries figured, since the army had been disbanded, leaving only a poorly trained police force of 300. Within a few hours of landing, Dominica and its 80,000 black residents would be under their control, and they could begin to reap a promised economic harvest. The mercenaries had plotted with Patrick John to install him as president and depose Charles. John in return was to give them concessions to export lumber and operate a casino. (Unbeknownst to the mercenaries, John was planning to have them killed once he had returned to power.)

Duke might have been among the mercenaries but for one thing: having narrowly avoided a jail sentence two years earlier, he was not about to involve himself directly in so risky a venture. Besides, he had an aversion to violence. Duke had been one of the first people asked to participate in the invasion by Michael Perdue, the thirty-two-year-old ringleader. Perdue, a high school dropout whose dreams for a glorious military career were dashed by a one-year prison stint for petty theft at the age of nineteen, met with Duke on December 31, 1980, on a fourth-floor apartment balcony in the French Quarter. They talked for an hour, with Duke agreeing to help Perdue find a charter boat owner who would carry the mercenaries to Dominica.

Duke also agreed to help Perdue find recruits for the venture. One man to whom Duke referred Perdue was Donald Andrews, a veteran white supremacist in Canada. But Andrews decided not to participate. Duke also referred Perdue to Wolfgang Droege, who like Andrews had become impressed with Duke when he was grand wizard of the Knights of the Ku Klux Klan. Droege, younger and more adventurous than Andrews, agreed to join the Dominica invasion team. In time, he formulated plans to operate a cocaine-processing laboratory on the island. It is not clear whether Duke knew of this scheme. Duke also put Perdue in touch with several men who provided financing for the coup, Perdue testified later. One was J. W. Kirkpatrick, a Memphis attorney who committed suicide shortly after Perdue testified that Kirkpatrick had given him $10,000.

Duke held subsequent meetings with Perdue at his home and at New Orleans hotels. Also attending the meetings were two close friends who had agreed to be mercenaries, Danny Hawkins and Don Black, who had succeeded Duke as grand wizard of the Knights of the Ku Klux Klan. Duke, like Black, hoped that by taking over Dominica, the white supremacist movement could earn millions of dollars exporting lumber and operating the casino. By April 27, 1981, the plans for Operation Red Dog were set. Perdue had rounded up nine other mercenaries, purchased a trunkload of weapons, and hired a boat to take them to Dominica.

At 10:00 P.M. on April 27, two cars holding the ten men pulled up to Fort Pike State Monument, an isolated park thirty-one miles east of central New Orleans on a narrow spit of land dividing Lake Pontchartrain from the Gulf of Mexico. As they approached the monument, they were met by John Osburg and Lloyd Grafton, deckhands on the charter boat. Osburg and Grafton quickly took charge, telling the mercenaries to load their equipment into a waiting van. The arsenal was potent: thirty-three guns, twenty sticks of dynamite, twenty blasting caps, and 5,000 bullets. Also included were fatigues, several Radio Shack walkie-talkies, a Confederate flag, a Nazi flag, a bottle of liquor, and a copy of *Soldier of Fortune* magazine. Osburg and Grafton directed the men to climb into the windowless back of a rented truck. They locked the door and made a short drive across a bridge to a marina, where the charter boat was supposed to be.

Waiting instead were forty heavily armed SWAT team agents. The charter boat captain had tipped off federal law enforcement officials of the invasion plans weeks before. When Osburg and Grafton, who were undercover agents with the federal Bureau of Alcohol, Tobacco, and Firearms, pulled up, Operation Red Dog turned into what the press would dub the Bayou of Pigs. A blaze of floodlights illuminated the truck. "We have a SWAT team surrounding you," boomed a voice on a bullhorn to the men inside the truck. "You're not going to Dominica. You're going to jail." The stunned mercenaries offered no resistance.

Duke was sitting at home that evening, nervously waiting for word that the voyage had begun without a hitch. But when he received a phone call informing him that Don Black and the others had been arrested, he grew pale and visibly distraught. Fearful that police were about to show up on his doorstep with an arrest warrant, he immediately sent home a friend who was visiting him. Duke was not arrested, but he was called to testify before a grand jury shortly afterward. He never actually appeared because he said he would refuse to answer questions by taking the Fifth Amendment. It was a smart move. Federal authorities wanted to indict him but did not have quite enough information and were hoping he would incriminate himself. Duke escaped indictment.

Seven of the ten mercenaries pleaded guilty to violating the Neutrality Act by admitting to having planned to invade a friendly nation. Don Black and Danny Hawkins chose to go to trial and were convicted on two counts of conspiracy and violating the Neutrality Act. The other mercenary was acquitted. The federal government also tried two of the men fingered by Perdue as financiers. But the two men—James C. White and L. E. Matthews—were acquitted.

Duke sweated out both trials in fear that he would be implicated and face charges. One night during the second trial, he kept nervously asking a friend who had attended that day's hearing: "Was I mentioned? Was I brought up?" His name did come up at times, but the government never elicited enough information to bring charges.

Duke kept a low public profile during the trials. He did not comment about the botched raid until 1983, two years later, when the United States invaded the Caribbean island of Grenada to oust a leftist government. The Grenada invasion vindicated the Dominica operation, Duke said, because the mercenaries were attempting to root out Communism in the Caribbean, first in Dominica and then in Grenada. "Mr. Black's forces were to join up with the Dominican army and high-ranking police to restore John to power to stop the expansion of Communism in the Windward Islands," Duke said in an interview. "After Dominica was secured, it was planned to use Dominica as a base from which to eventually liberate Grenada from Cuban and Soviet rule." This was an outrageous claim. Not only was Eugenia Charles, Dominica's prime minister, not a Communist, but she was also a staunch ally of the Reagan administration who provided crucial support for the invasion of Grenada. Lindsay Larson, the assistant United States attorney who prosecuted the Dominica plotters, immediately questioned Duke's statements. "They weren't out for God and country, they were out to make money," Larson said. "Their defense that they were out to stem the flow of Communism was a big sham."

The invasion of Dominica was only one of many schemes that Duke pursued in the 1980s as he desperately sought a way to gain respectability for the white supremacist movement. These were difficult years for him as he sank into obscurity with the NAAWP. But Duke did not give up his belief that he was destined to become the savior of the white race—if only he could find the right formula.

By the mid-1980s, he thought he had found that formula. For years, Duke had believed that the key to Jewish control of the white majority was using television as a propaganda tool. Through television, Duke believed, Jews brainwashed the white majority into accepting integration, which brought crime into their neighborhoods, lowered the educational level of their schools, and led to interracial marriages.

In the mid-1980s, he developed a plan to circumvent what he held to be the power of the "Jewish-controlled" networks: Duke would record what he dubbed "fireside chats" and sell them to the masses he believed were hungering for the "white" viewpoint. He thought this could spawn a "white" revolution that would overthrow the Jews. "Television is the most powerful communication on earth," Duke wrote in the December 1984 issue of the *NAAWP News*. "Since it became widespread thirty years ago, it has promoted every anti-white policy and program imaginable. In the '50s and '60s, it was the primary battering ram used to destroy White opposition to integration of education, since then it has unceasingly fostered black hatred and resentment of white people and white self-hate and guilt. It has spurred on massive black breeding programs kindly referred to as 'welfare,' unleashed the minority criminal, brought on the most intensive government-sponsored racial discrimination in American history: affirmative action, opened our borders to the scum of the earth as shown by the recent Cuban boatlift and promoted racial intermarriage."

"Blacks are always portrayed on TV as intelligent and good students," Duke added, "so even after whites actually go to school with blacks and experience them firsthand, some still cling to their TV image, rationalizing that the blacks they go to school with must not be normal blacks but 'exceptions.' How could the racially conscious white person compete against such a powerful force penetrating every American's home? Yes, we have had the Truth, the Truth that is so vital to the preservation of our rights, our heritage and way-of-life, and even the continued existence of our people on this planet. But the truth just couldn't compete against the tidal wave of propaganda surging into our homes."

"Until recently," Duke added, "only the major networks could use the almost magical appliance called television. With millions of Americans buying VCRs, all that is changing. With video cameras and recording equipment we can put our most powerful weapon: the Truth, on television!" People would pass around his videotapes "much like the patriotic newspapers spread before the American Revolution of 1776." In time, Duke imagined creating an alternative network that would promote "white" values. "The final step will be to do our own dramatic and comedy programming," he wrote. The videotape venture, he concluded, was "the most important project in the NAAWP's history and, indeed, in the entire White Racialist Movement since WWII." Duke got so engrossed in his fantasy that by the middle of the decade, he neglected the *NAAWP News*. Published eight times a year initially, the newspaper appeared only half as often in the mid-1980s.

But Duke failed to fulfill his dream. His followers did not share his excitement, and by 1987 they had given him enough money to produce only two videotapes. One was called *Race: A Time for Truth*. The other was *The Truth About the Holocaust*. (He sold each for thirty dollars.) There was to be no "white" revolution through videotapes. A year before Duke announced the videotape venture, he had embarked on another bizarre scheme that he thought would pave the way to "white victory": a series of "white leadership training" seminars that would create higher racial consciousness among white activists.

Duke had always been frustrated that so few whites had grasped what he called "the truth": the understanding that reasserting white supremacist values was the key to establishing a higher civilization and culture. At the same time, he could not help but notice how cult figures like Werner Erhard and the Indian guru Bagwan Sri Rajneesh had succeeded not only in winning large numbers of followers but also in instilling in them an almost slavish devotion. Duke took Erhard's est seminar in late 1981.

Erhard had founded est in 1971, only several years after quitting jobs as a car and encyclopedia salesman and changing his name from Jack Rosenberg. Est had quickly moved to the forefront of the human potential movement as Erhard combined ideas from Zen Buddhism, Scientology, and some of the alternative psychotherapy and self-motivation techniques developed in the 1950s and 1960s. During weekend sessions, trainers harangued seminar participants, trying to break down their emotional defenses and accept the est credo. Trainers told seminar participants to "take charge of your lives" and "create space for your lives to work." No one could leave the room during a seminar, even to go to the bathroom.

Many people thought est was a silly rip-off. Duke was not among them. He became a disciple, taking seminars of est and its successor, The Forum, into the late 1980s. He shied away from talking about the seminars publicly but privately urged his close friends to take them. And he began developing plans for his own est program. Instead of empowering people to help themselves, his program would empower them to become white supremacist activists.

When Duke hired Tom Wilson, a recent graduate from Murray State University in Kentucky, to be editor of the *NAAWP News* in November

1981, his first assignment was to have Wilson take est. Wilson took notes and typed them up for Duke to show what he had learned. But Duke was unsatisfied and had Wilson take est a second time. In early 1983, Duke was ready for his first "white leadership training seminar." It was held in Palm Springs, California, which had an active NAAWP membership under a local construction worker named Tom Crist. Crist acted as Duke's chief assistant during the seminar.

The seminar lasted fifteen hours. Borrowing from est, Duke forbade anyone to leave the room, even to go to the bathroom. Like est trainers, he berated the forty participants, urging them to overcome any lingering tolerance they might have for nonwhite people. The *NAAWP News* recorded Duke's harangue. "You wonder why the white race is dying?" he shouted. "Why many of our women are raped by minority savages? Why our children are denied their educational birthright? Why our nation lies prostrate before a brown swarm of locusts devouring our jobs, our paychecks, our neighborhoods, our culture and even our genetic heritage? It's all because of the fact that you and people like you can't keep commitments and are willing to lie to themselves and others instead of facing the hard truth."

Afterward, Duke was excited about his latest program. "If new members can be motivated and trained in skills of recruitment," he wrote, "we can explode in an almost fission-like growth. In all my years of activity and study, I believe this program holds the most promise of any I have ever engaged in." But like the videotape venture, Duke's quest to instill an estlike fervor among whites died a quiet death. While a good salesman, he was no Werner Erhard. He could not recruit enough people to take the course or find the money to finance it. Duke, though, did not lose faith in the human potential movement. He took the six-day program of The Forum, which Erhard created in 1984 after dissolving est, and he attended additional Forum seminars. But he did not attempt to resurrect the white leadership training program.

In the mid-1980s, Duke was left to flounder, a prophet without an audience. He had run unsuccessfully for the state senate in 1975 and 1979. But in 1983, Louisiana's next legislative election year, Duke realized his star had fallen so far that he did not bother running for office. He did not even vote in any of the nine local, state, and federal elections held between the 1984 presidential election and the November 1987 Louisiana general election. With nothing else to do in the mid-1980s, he played golf every day at New Orleans' City Park. He had learned the game from his mother, who had played avidly. He particularly liked to play with a group of men known as the

Dawnbusters. (They got their name because they teed off before the sun came up.)

With his free time, Duke also delved deeply into a favorite pursuit, the casino game of craps. He bought how-to books and worked out strategies on a computer program devised by a friend. Duke liked craps both because it was a high-adrenaline game—crowds of people stand around the table cheering the players on as they toss the dice—and because it offered the best odds. With the strategies he had learned, and by being disciplined enough to follow them, Duke calculated that on average he would lose only half a cent for every dollar he gambled. In the mid-1980s, Duke began flying frequently to Las Vegas. He always went to Binion's Horseshoe Hotel, which gamblers said offered among the best odds of any casino. He became such a high roller that the Horseshoe sent a limousine to fetch him at the airport and gave him free food, tickets to shows, and a free room.

Duke would go for a weekend at a time and stay up most of the night playing craps feverishly. He often took Gwen Udell, his live-in girlfriend. Sometimes, Udell says, he lost several thousand dollars—but she also remembers nights when he had built his winnings up to $10,000 on the table. He had an even more successful trip one night in February 1986, recalls Evelyn Rich, a Boston University student who interviewed Duke as part of her doctoral thesis on the Klan. In conducting her research, she traveled throughout the country with Duke, including an overnight trip to Las Vegas following a conference in Los Angeles. Duke had ostensibly gone to Las Vegas to attend a conference of the Duck People, an offbeat economic group. But he spent all his time gambling.

Rich tired of the gambling and went to bed at 10:00 P.M. But at about 3:00 A.M., Duke pounded on her door and woke her up. "Look at how much money I've won," he shouted excitedly, throwing a pile of chips on her bed. They counted them. He had won $17,000. But Duke was not through. He dashed downstairs and played until after the sun came up. At one point, he was up $21,000—but then he dropped to $15,000 before quitting. Still, it was a banner evening. Federal tax laws required casinos to report winnings of more than $5,000. To avoid the law, Duke had Rich and James K. Warner, who was also on the trip, each cash $5,000 of his chips.

Duke did not want his passion for gambling to become widely known. He never discussed it publicly and tried to dodge questions when asked about it during the 1990 Senate election. "Well, first off, you know, I don't, you know, I don't, I, anybody who comes and stays at a hotel in Las Vegas gets picked up [by the hotel]," he said, stumbling for the right answer. He then said he had occasionally gone to Las Vegas but only as a side trip on a visit to the Grand Canyon. "I go hiking in the desert a lot," he said. When pressed for more information, Duke said he could not recall how often he had gone to Las Vegas or how much he had wagered. "I wasn't a high-roller," he said several times. In 1991, he described his gambling activities differently but no more accurately. "I stayed at a place in Las Vegas," he told Ted Koppel on "Nightline," "a sawdust-on-the-floor kind of place in Las Vegas that cost $21 a night. And I had the air fare paid by the programs that I've gone on out there."

While Duke seemed to have faded into obscurity in the mid-1980s, he still nursed dreams of revitalizing his political career. As a preliminary step one morning in 1987, he had Udell take him to the clinic of Dr. Calvin Johnson, the most expensive plastic surgeon in New Orleans. Duke planned to have his nose reduced. But he agreed to Johnson's suggestion that he also have a chin implant "to even out his profile," he explained to Udell as she drove him home afterward. The surgery cost him an estimated $5,000.

"He came back with a black-and-blue face," remembers Udell. "He told the people on his staff that he had a medical problem that had to be corrected. He told me that he was going to be in the public eye so he needed to look nice."

In subsequent months, Udell says, Duke had two operations known as chemical peels, to remove the crow's feet from around his eyes. The chemical peels literally burned off the skin and made his face look badly sunburned for several days. Duke also dyed the gray out of his mustache he wore for years before he shaved it off in early 1989. By 1990 and 1991, he was dying his hair. It was dark blond. Sometimes it had gray in it, and sometimes it didn't.

As with his gambling, Duke was reluctant to discuss his plastic surgery. When asked about it in August 1990, he admitted to the nose job, saying it was needed to ease a breathing problem that had resulted from having his nose broken three times over the years. He denied having had a chin implant. He said he could not recall whether he had had chemical peels but added: "I wouldn't be embarrassed about anything I've done for my health and well-being, and I certainly don't think anybody in this country should be." But clearly it was a touchy subject. When Michael Kinsley asked him during the 1991 gubernatorial campaign on CNN's "Crossfire" why he could not remember having had the chemical peels, Duke, who rarely got ruffled under intense questioning, blew up. "That's the kind of question a worm like you would ask," Duke shot back. When Kinsley persisted with the question, Duke said, "You look like you could use a little plastic surgery yourself."

As David Duke dropped out of the news, his followers steadily drifted away. By the mid-1980s, membership in the NAAWP had fallen to about 1,000. This meant not only that Duke's views reached fewer people but that less money came in. A drop in revenue, of course, concerned Duke as president of the NAAWP, but it also hit him right in the pocketbook. Duke had lived off the white supremacy movement as a professional racist since graduating from LSU in 1974. Until his 1989 election as a state legislator, which was a part-time position, he had never held a regular job.

When he was in the Ku Klux Klan, Duke paid his bills from proceeds of racist literature he sold through the Patriot Bookstore near his home in Metairie and by mail through a company he owned called Patriot Press. Every issue of the *Crusader* offered items from Patriot Press that no good Klansman could do without: "top-quality" Klan T-shirts (five dollars), Klan robe and hood (twenty-eight dollars), "an exquisite handmade" Klan ring (thirty dollars), a "studio quality" color photograph of Duke (four dollars), and a cassette tape of his "outstanding" 1974 appearance on the "Tomorrow" show (five dollars). For those more prone to violence, there were "self-defense and survival" books: *Boobytraps, Field Fortifications, Chemical Magic, Chemistry of Powder and Explosives.*

Duke also earned as much as $1,000 per speech speaking at a few colleges a year while in the Klan. To enhance his respectability, he marketed himself under a separate company he called Yardley Enterprises. He chose the name, he said, because it sounded "Ivy League." In 1980, he said his earnings for the previous year had been only $1,000. He added that he drew "a little under $10,000" in travel expenses. The biggest source of his income—the Knights of the Ku Klux Klan—was taking in $60,000 to $100,000 a year. Initiation fees were $15 and annual dues were $30 for the 1,000 to 2,000 members of his Klan. Unless Duke was living on less than $20 a week, he was siphoning off Klan income for personal use.

Jerry Dutton, who was grand wizard of the Knights of the Ku Klux Klan during the latter half of 1976, said Duke used Klan funds to purchase and refurbish his Metairie home, purchased for $20,500 in 1975. Dutton sent copies of checks to reporters that Duke had written on the Klan bookstore's account for the down payment of his home and for flooring and plumbing payments. Duke denied Dutton's charges at the time and said the funds were his. But he told the *Clearwater Sun* newspaper in 1979 that he had used Klan funds for the repairs of his home because the Klan used 2,000 feet of it for office space.

On at least two occasions, local Klan leaders accused Duke of pocketing Klan money. Bill Wilkinson said Duke failed to turn over to the Klan the

$5,000 collected at the 1975 rally in Walker, Louisiana. The dispute caused Wilkinson to drop out of Duke's Klan and start his own.

Jack Gregory, Duke's grand dragon in Florida, said Duke refused to account for collections from a series of Florida rallies in 1979 where the average take was $500. Gregory denounced Duke, who denied the charge and banished Gregory from the Knights of the Ku Klux Klan. "David Duke is nothing but a con artist," Gregory told the *Clearwater Sun*. "Our members were pouring in money to the organization, and we never saw any of it. When I asked Duke where our money was going, I was thrown out of the Klan. Yeah, he tells everyone he doesn't make anything from the Klan—that he's doing it for the cause. But that's the biggest lie there is."

Exactly how much money Duke got while in the Klan is not known, but he did not live opulently. In 1980, he was driving a seven-year-old Montego, and his Metairie home was a modest two-story, white clapboard structure in a working-class neighborhood. Duke's prized possession was a grand piano in his small living room whose apparent purpose was to burnish his reputation as a new breed of Klan leader. He could not play it well.

Leaving the Klan for the NAAWP in 1980 did not improve Duke's personal finances. He continued to live in the same house, using the downstairs as the NAAWP's office. He continued to buy his suits at Kmart and J C Penney and complained about not having enough money. He told *Gallery* in 1985 that he had bought the suit he was wearing on sale at J C Penney for eighty-seven dollars. "I watch my pennies," he said. "I guess it's my Scotch blood."

Friends say that Duke watched his pennies so closely that he would save money by making his daughters share a hamburger at a restaurant or make them drink water rather than milk or juice. When he took his friend Donna Randall to the Western Sizzler steak house in Metairie, he would order the most expensive steak and then go from table to table asking for money. "I'm David Duke, and I'm the head of the NAAWP," he would say. "Can you make a donation?" Randall says Duke would use the money he was given to pay the bill, and if there was anything left over, he would pocket it.

Exactly how he made a living in the 1980s is not entirely clear, and Duke has been less than forthcoming when asked about it, other than to say he sacrificed financial gain to fight for his political goals. For years, he claimed to make a living as a free-lance author writing under a pseudonym about ecology and the environment. Duke said he used a pseudonym because he was too controversial to write under his own name. He refused to identify the publications. People close to Duke in the 1980s, however, say that they never saw him do any freelance writing.

Duke also said he received "honorariums" but did not pay himself a salary for being president of the NAAWP. He declined to identify who had paid him honorariums. "I have no savings other than an IRA, no summer home, no boat, and no valuable possessions other than my piano," Duke said in 1990. "What little money I have earned has been through very hard work."

In 1989, I was able to identify two companies Duke secretly owned. In line with a pattern from his Klan days, the revenue for both companies came from his followers. One company came to light in 1989 when a Republican Party activist named Beth Rickey, who was to become Duke's biggest nemesis in the party, bought several books from Duke's legislative district office, which was in the basement of his home. The books were essential to any literate Nazi's library: Hitler's *Mein Kampf*; *Imperium*, which had been written by a Nazi apologist and dedicated to Hitler; *The Turner Diaries*, written by neo-Nazi propagandist William Pierce; and *Did Six Million Really Die?* which claimed that the Holocaust was a hoax. When Rickey went public, Duke admitted owning the bookselling operation, Americana Books.

Duke tried to dismiss the notion that he was a purveyor of Nazi propaganda. He claimed he was operating a bookstore just like thousands of other people in the United States. "I've sold a wide range of books," he said. "I also sold the Bible, but that doesn't make me one of the 12 disciples." The *NAAWP News*, where Americana Books advertised, calls Duke's claims into question. Issue 49 of the *NAAWP News*, for example, which was published in December 1987, offered sixty-five titles under the heading "Suppressed Books"—which by definition meant they could not be found in any bookstore. Each of the sixty-five books was either racist or anti-Semitic. The Bible was not listed.

Along with Duke's two favorite books, *The Dispossessed Majority* (four dollars) and *Race and Reason* (five dollars), Americana Books also offered *Jews Must Live* (five dollars, "a Jew reveals shady business practices of Jews"); *War, War, War* (four dollars, "the Jewish origin of wars well-documented"); *The Truth About Rhodesia* (one dollar, "how white Rhodesia was undermined by Communism and liberalism"); and *Pearl Harbor* (six dollars, "the most comprehensive [book] on Roosevelt's treason at Pearl Harbor"). The NAAWP also advertised Americana Books videotapes featuring speeches by George Lincoln Rockwell and Duke. One videotape was "Duke speaks at U. of Montana": "In the face of well-organized opposition, David Duke, through the power of his presence and his eloquence, wins the audience over to a basic racial understanding."

The other company Duke set up secretly was Business Consultant & Enterprises, or BC&E, a sole proprietorship he had formed in 1978. He did not file incorporation papers with the Louisiana secretary of state and did not discuss the company publicly. The tip-off that BC&E existed and was tied to Duke came in the tax returns of the NAAWP, which by law, because the NAAWP was a nonprofit group, had to be made available to the public.

The NAAWP's returns showed that the group paid $119,625—or 28 percent of its revenue—to BC&E from 1983 to 1988 for "mailing list maintenance." The tax returns also indicated that BC&E was owned by one of the NAAWP's directors. The only person listed as a director in each of the six years was Duke. When in August 1989 I called to ask whether he owned BC&E, he became agitated and inarticulate.

"Well, you know, it's obviously a company," he began. "It's just, you know, again, there's really nothing, there's really nothing implied. There's nothing, you know. Again, I'm not commenting about any of the finances of the organization." When I asked again whether he owned BC&E, he said, "You're welcome to talk to my, you know, to my attorney, about any of this material, you know. And he, he can talk to, you know, you about my financial matters. I don't discuss my financial matters with you. You know, why should I?"

I asked Duke to explain what services BC&E provided. "It's none of your business, to tell you the truth," he replied. "It's not any of your business. We, we, we apply and we, we, we, we fulfill all . . ." I broke in to ask again what services BC&E provided. "I'll explain any—you know, you know, you know, that's, you know, you can make whatever assumptions you want, you know," he said. "That's not really the point, you know, I mean. That's not really the point at all."

I could not get him to admit that he owned BC&E, but I still had enough information to write an article revealing the tie between Duke and BC&E and the payments to the company. The day the article appeared, Duke tried to contain the damage by calling a press conference to blast me and the *Times-Picayune*. But amid the denunciations, he admitted that he owned BC&E. That day and in subsequent interviews, Duke explained that BC&E was paid for maintaining the NAAWP's mailing list on its computers and copying videotapes for Americana Books orders.

My initial article also disclosed that Duke had paid his Populist party presidential campaign an additional $2,000 for videotapes and that Duke's Democratic presidential campaign had paid BC&E $19,900 to rent space in his Metairie home—well above the prevailing market rate, an analysis showed. Duke rebutted this point, saying that the rental rate was fair. He insisted that the Democratic presidential campaign used 87 percent of the house. This was obviously an inflated number, since it meant that the Democratic presidential campaign rented every part of his house but his bedroom and included the space taken up by the NAAWP.

In sum, BC&E—i.e., Duke—from 1983 to 1988 received $141,000 from the NAAWP and Duke's presidential campaigns. He dismissed questions about the cozy but apparently legal financial arrangement, saying BC&E had received only about $20,000 per year on average. But for four of those years from 1984 to 1987 he did not file state income taxes, claiming that he had earned below the $12,000 adjusted gross income minimum required to file (meaning he had not earned $12,000 before expenses were taken out). He also said he had owed no taxes for those years. When asked during the 1991 gubernatorial campaign why he had not filed the tax returns, Duke said it was because he had had a bad time financially. "I didn't make much money for a while in my life," he told Ted Koppel on "Nightline." But the NAAWP tax returns showed that in three of the four years, BC&E received more than $12,000, and in the fourth year (1985) it received $11,700, just below the minimum. Since Duke was declaring BC&E's income on his individual tax return, he was required to file in three of the years and almost certainly the fourth, since he had other sources of income. In 1987, according to a report he filed as a presidential candidate, he earned $33,000 from BC&E alone.

During the same years in which Duke was claiming not to have earned $12,000, he was a high roller at the Horseshoe in Las Vegas. When Koppel repeatedly asked him to explain this discrepancy, Duke kept dodging the question. "I've gone out to the West Coast, usually for media appearances, which were paid for by the programs, you know, and I've been to Las Vegas before," he said. "I've never had a gambling debt." Not only was Duke gambling extensively while claiming to earn less than $12,000 a year in the mid-1980s, but he was also heavily playing the stock market, according to his broker, Charles Safford, who occasionally accompanied Duke to Las Vegas. Safford, who worked at Paine Webber, said Duke taught himself how to invest in the options market in less than a year and became an addict of financial news services on cable TV. "David knew more about the stock market than most brokers at Paine Webber," Safford said. He declined to say how much Duke invested or whether he made money. He did say that Duke made "large investments" and that Duke was a "model customer" because he "accepted his losses without complaint." Duke has dismissed questions about his stock market activity, saying he invested only a small amount of money and made a small gain.

Duke faced more questions about his finances in 1991 when I disclosed that he had failed to pay property taxes on his Metairie home in 1987, 1989, and 1990. (In 1990, his home was assessed at $106,700.) As a result, he owed

$2,857.17 to Jefferson Parish: $2,396.13 in assessed taxes, $317.77 in interest, $1.67 for notices sent to him, $135 in processing costs, and $6.60 for the costs of advertising his failure to make the payments. (Duke had earlier incurred an additional $38.68 in interest costs by paying his 1986 and 1988 property taxes late.) When first contacted about the outstanding property taxes for 1987, 1989, and 1990, Duke at first said he had paid the taxes but then changed course and said he would pay what he owed. He made good on this promise several days later. "There's nothing illegal or immoral about waiting to pay," said Duke, "I was going to pay the money. It's not like anybody was cheated out of anything." He added that paying his taxes late benefited Jefferson Parish because he was required to pay the $461.04 in extra charges. "My parish makes more money this way," he said.

CHAPTER SIX

WHITE SUPREMACY, HITLER, AND THE HOLOCAUST

One afternoon in the summer of 1986, David Duke boarded a train in Salzburg, Austria, headed for the town of Linz, two hours away. He had been studying German in Salzburg for a couple of months, and now, with his willowy, blonde girlfriend, Gwen Udell, visiting for a week, he wanted to see a place of intense interest to him: the Mauthausen concentration camp. The Linz train station was about six miles from Mauthausen. Duke, a tightwad, would have preferred to walk and save money. But it was getting late in the afternoon, so he agreed to pay for a taxi to take them there. The couple arrived just as the guard was about to close the tall gates. Duke persuaded him to let them spend fifteen minutes inside.

The Nazis opened Mauthausen in 1938, shortly after taking over Austria. Initially, it housed criminal offenders and prisoners of war. The first trainloads of Jews began arriving in 1941. Mauthausen was not a death camp like Auschwitz or Dachau, where the Nazis killed Jews in an assembly-line-like fashion. But before May 1945, when American troops liberated Mauthausen, 38,120 Jews died there, most in the final two years of the war. "They shot prisoners and made many work so hard that they dropped to death," remembers Maurice Bauman, a Jew from Poland who was sent there in December 1944. "They gave us soap made from the flesh of humans. They were great killers at Mauthausen."

Most visitors to concentration camps are quiet and contemplative as they view the horrors of Nazi extermination. Not Duke. That summer day, he was bubbling over with enthusiasm and could not stop talking as he played tour guide for Udell. "David would say, 'This could not possibly have been a gas chamber because it was too small,'" Udell remembered four years later, shaking her head in embarrassment that she had believed him then. "In another place, he would say, 'This wasn't really a gas chamber, it was just used to de-lice people.' We went through the concentration camp, and he would refute everything the historians had put in there. He said that the ovens could not have been used to cremate that many corpses per day because it takes so many hours to cremate a human corpse." As they rushed through the concentration camp, Duke was willing to concede that some Jews may have died there. "Obviously, there's disease in war, famine and whatnot," Duke told Udell. "Some people did die, yes. But there was no official order to kill Jews."

As they left the concentration camp, Duke noticed a memorial noting the Mauthausen death toll from 1943 to 1945. "And so David of course calculated in his head that that would have been x number of people a day," Udell recalls. "With Zyklon B, the gas they supposedly used to kill the Jews, he said that that type of gas leaves very much of a residue, and that they would have had to air out the chamber after gassing one room of people for a day or hours before the guards could even go in there and clear the bodies out." Thus Duke sought to refute the facts of history. The art memorializing victims at Mauthausen also disgusted Duke. "Typical Jewish art," he said, disdainfully. "It's modern, abstract crap." Duke, like Hitler, preferred the classical art and architecture he had seen in Salzburg's museums. Duke's kooky views on the Holocaust were the fruits of wide reading in anti-Semitic literature, a pastime that, like golf, est, and playing craps, had come to dominate Duke's life as his star waned in the 1980s. His hatred of Jews would finally reach a level of such irrationality that he would insist that the Talmud spoke approvingly of sex with children.

As early as his Klan days, Duke had begun reading such books as *The Six Million Reconsidered* that doubted the existence of the Holocaust. He liked this book so much that he began publishing columns by William Grimstad, its author, in his Klan newspaper, the *Crusader*.

In 1980, in one of the last issues of the *Crusader*, Duke had expressed doubt about the Holocaust. In his article, he said the real holocaust was Stalin's extermination "of our Christian brethren in Communist Russia. Solzhenitsyn in Gulag II shows photographs of the six top administrators of the Soviet death camps where tens of millions of Christians were murdered. All six were Jews." But it was not until several years later that he fully developed his belief that the Holocaust had not occurred.

An obscure group called the Institute for Historical Review played a key role in convincing Duke—and other members of the racialist movement— that the Holocaust was a fabrication. The IHR was founded in 1979 by Willis Carto, the shadowy leader of the Liberty Lobby whom the Anti-Defamation League considered perhaps the country's most dangerous anti-Semite. Just as the Identity movement attempted to give a religious justification for anti-

Semitism, the IHR sought to give it an intellectual defense. Operating under the guise of scholarship, the IHR held annual conventions and published so-called "revisionist" books through Carto's Noontide Press that denied the Nazi genocide. Along with Grimstad's book, Noontide Press also published such works as *Anne Frank's Diary: A Hoax*, by Ditleib Felderer; *The Auschwitz Myth: A Judge Looks at the Evidence*, by Wilhelm Staeglich; and *The Rumor of Auschwitz*, by Robert Faurisson.

The IHR gave Carto many headaches. A fire on July 4, 1984, at the institute's offices in Torrance, a suburb of Los Angeles, destroyed 90 percent of its book and tape inventory. Duke and other extremists blamed Jewish saboteurs. But the cause of the fire was never determined. More problems arose when an IHR official attempted to win publicity by offering $50,000 to anyone who could prove that the Nazis operated gas chambers to exterminate Jews at Auschwitz. The offer succeeded in winning news coverage for the IHR, but it also drew a response from Melvin Mermelstein, a tenacious Jewish businessman from California. Born in Czechoslovakia, Mermelstein had spent time in both the Auschwitz and Birkenau concentration camps. His parents, a brother, and two sisters had perished at the hands of the Nazis. At his last meeting with his father at the camp, Mermelstein said in a 1988 interview, "He told [my brother and me] to separate, and whichever one survived, don't forget to tell what happened." A blue tattoo on his wrist reading A-4685 served as a permanent reminder of his stay at Auschwitz.

When Mermelstein stepped forward in 1980, Carto tried to rescind the offer. But Mermelstein sued for libel and breach of contract after a bulletin allegedly published by the defendants called him "one of those cosmic numbers of extermination survivors who by some stroke of luck and with plenty of pecuniary stealth have survived." In 1985, a California court ordered the IHR to pay Mermelstein the $50,000 reward and another $40,000 for the pain and suffering that the offer had caused. The judge also ordered the IHR to write Mermelstein a formal apology and acknowledge that Jews had indeed been gassed at Auschwitz. The IHR complied with the order but continued its activities.

David Duke attended the IHR's annual conference in 1983 and again in 1986. Evelyn Rich attended the 1986 conference as part of her research on the Klan, and Duke insisted that she meet Carto. "David had a very high opinion of Willis Carto," says Rich. "He couldn't praise him enough." Throughout the three-day conference, which was held in Culver City, California, Rich was struck by Duke's stature among the attendees. "Everybody wanted to meet David," she remembers.

Many extremists, however, mistrusted Duke. Tom Metzger, for one, was not glad to see him. Metzger, whom Duke had recruited into the Klan in 1975, thought Duke was immoral because of his womanizing and his authorship of *Finders-Keepers*. Metzger, an uncompromising neo-Nazi, had also criticized Duke for downplaying the Klan while running for the Louisiana senate in 1979, the year that Metzger broke with him. Metzger also detested Duke's inflated ego, and he began to grow irritated when Duke butted in as Evelyn Rich interviewed him one evening during the conference. When the interview ended, Metzger stood up, looked at Duke and said, "I've got to go, some of us are working men."

"What do you mean by that?" Duke asked.

"I have to get up in the morning, I don't live off the cause," said Metzger, a television repairman.

"Look, Tom," Duke said, "What's the point in this? Let's let bygones be bygones."

Metzger sneered at him. When Duke offered his hand, Metzger refused to take it. "You're lucky I let you sit in the same room with me," Metzger snapped and stalked off.

When he was under close scrutiny in 1990 and 1991 while running for senator and then governor, Duke dropped his anti-Semitic rhetoric, offering vague answers when asked his views on the Holocaust. He still stopped short of denouncing the Nazis for the Holocaust. Instead, he condemned "any atrocities" that had been committed and then quickly segued on to another subject. Duke discussed the Holocaust far more readily and openly in the mid-1980s, however, when the media had no interest in him. He laid out his views in a three-hour interview with Evelyn Rich at Metairie's La Quinta Motor Inn on March 18, 1985.

Duke insisted that the Holocaust was a hoax trumped up by Jews to win support for creating the state of Israel following World War II. "You might say for sure that Israel could not have been created except for the six million theory," Duke told Rich. "It's that strong. . . . 'Oh, these Jews were killed by the millions, we've got to give them a homeland.' So we all closed our eyes to the tens of thousands of Arabs that were murdered, the massive amounts of [Jewish] terrorism and atrocities that took place and the forcible expulsion of a million and a half [Arab] people from their homeland."

Why did Hitler round up Jews and put them in concentration camps? "The same reason we had [with] the Japanese, except that the Germans had a lot better reason than [the United States did with] the Japanese," he told Rich. "They felt they needed to round the Jews up, put them in these areas, and that way they'd have more security." In an interview a year later with Rich, Duke added, "He [Hitler] wanted to ultimately resettle them."

Did the Nazis have a planned extermination policy? "You can't find one written order to one commander at any of these camps which says, 'Exterminate the Jews,'" Duke said. "None. And you know the Nazis were sticklers for orders and making sure everything was clear." What about the gas chambers? "All of the camps had gas chambers, Zyklon B, for the disinfection of clothes, to kill lice so Jews wouldn't die . . . ," Duke said. "The so-called eyewitness accounts are . . . full of holes. Like they say, 'They [the Nazis] sprinkled Zyklon B up to the ceilings in this big room, and there's 2,000 Jews and they all die.' You sprinkle some stuff, and you're going to die yourself." What about the corpses stacked like cordwood? "Doctored photographs and everything," he told Rich.

What about the testimony of the concentration camp survivors? "The fact that they survived themselves is a tremendous argument for the fact that extermination didn't take place," Duke said. "Did you ever notice how many survivors they have? . . . Every time you turn, 15,000 survivors meet here, 400 survivors [have a] convention there. I mean, did you ever notice? The Nazis were sure inefficient, weren't they? Boy! Boy! Boy!"

Duke wasn't through. He told Rich about Ditleib Felderer, author of *Anne Frank's Diary: A Hoax*, whom Duke had met at an IHR conference. "He's an expert on the Holocaust, and he refutes it entirely," Duke said. "He's a real funny little guy. . . . He goes to all the camps and he takes pictures. . . . He says [that] at Auschwitz he got off the beaten track and he went in one of these big buildings by the railway line. . . . He wanted to see what was going on. So he crawled through one of the vents and . . . he took pictures. . . . They don't take the guided tour there. And he said after you got in this building, it's obvious why they don't send the guided tourists through there. Because you know what they have in there? Gas chambers— disinfection chambers where they used to disinfect the clothes. . . . Anybody that actually goes in there and starts investigating—I mean the whole thing comes down like a house of cards because it's just bullshit."

Duke grew excited. "He [Felderer] went to Treblinka in Poland . . . where almost nobody goes," Duke said. "So he says, 'Well, let's check out a few things'. . . . In the tour of the camp, they say . . . the Nazis planted trees there . . . to cover up their crimes, so the evidence of the Jewish bodies and everything wouldn't be found because there'd be a forest there." Duke said Felderer visited a tree chronologist in Sweden who told him he could determine the age of the trees by screwing a little instrument into one and counting the tree rings. So Felderer returned to Treblinka with the instrument, Duke said. "He goes in this area where all these Nazis planted trees to cover the bodies, and he screws it through the tree, and . . . he finds out these trees are 75, 80 years old," Duke said, with a laugh. "The whole thing is ludicrous when you really start thinking about it."

Duke then added some thoughts of his own on Auschwitz. "You know, they had a soccer field at Auschwitz. They had a swimming pool at Auschwitz. They had an orchestra at Auschwitz. . . . The band was for the prisoners' enjoyment, pleasure." He added: "I'm sure it was horrible at Auschwitz in the last six months of the war when the railways were disrupted and bombings took place and the Germans had a long retreat from the Russians. There was terrible disorder and decay; and at a camp that size, you're going to have a lot of starvation. You're going to have a lot of hunger. You're going to have a lot of disease. They had Zyklon B because of the problems with lice and cholera and epidemics. And I'm sure they were very terrible times for all the people. I'm sure there was a lot of human suffering in those camps. But I don't think the human suffering was qualitatively or quantitatively any greater than what the Germans went under or many people all through history have gone under."

Rich told Duke that his account of the Holocaust as a hoax was frightening. "That's why I'm in this fight," he replied. "It *is* frightening. It's like a nightmare. It's like you're living in a nightmare. It's like you're on the *Titanic*, and you see this big iceberg, and you're trying to warn all the passengers and the crew . . . about this iceberg up there, and the ship of state's sailing right into it." Nevertheless, Duke took a pragmatic approach and downplayed his views. "I don't talk about the Holocaust much . . . , because it's a non-productive thing for me," he explained. "People wouldn't believe it. It's too fantastic. . . . It's like saying the world's flat."

Rich was getting exhausted listening to Duke's strange theories. But Duke was entranced and was still going strong. There was more Duke wanted to blame on Jews.

"In the last 60 to 70 years, we've gone from a majority world and a majority culture into an increasingly Jewish minoritization of our culture," he said. "And I don't like it. Every time they've gotten into things, things have become more materialistic and less spiritual—make the fast buck, making something cheap plastic that disintegrates upon using it twice, instead of something that lasts. . . . Just build a house and put some cheap crap into it, and if the walls fall down later after you sell it and make a profit, forget it."

Duke described other ways that Jews made money. "When the government's going to build a base somewhere . . . , they get this information ahead of time . . . , like they know the government's going to grant a contract to General Dynamics. They pass it on to their Jewish brothers. Their Jewish brothers go in there and buy up a couple of million shares. The stock goes up $30 or $40 million. . . . This Jew knows where the government is going to open up a military base. . . . He goes in there, tells his friends. They go buy up a whole bunch of property, vast acres. They pay $100 an acre. The base is opened in two years. They sell out, maybe for $15,000 to $20,000 an acre. . . . They [have] raped the country economically." The Jews even had President Reagan under their thumb, Duke said. "He's been working for Jews all his life, especially Jewish studio heads," Duke said. "And now he knows—he toes the line really well."

Duke repeated his long-held claim that Jews used the media to brainwash non-Jewish whites into thinking alien thoughts on virtually any subject. "In the media, the Jews [are portrayed] as the most kind, trustworthy, loyal, friendly—regular Boy Scouts," Duke told Rich. "They're magnificent doctors, just educators and fighters for truth and justice. . . . And they told us who was the most brilliant man of all time: Einstein—when [German scientist] Max Planck makes Einstein look like a pauper as far as modern physics theory [goes]. . . . Barbra Streisand is [portrayed as] the greatest singer of our age. There are plenty of Gentile singers who look better than her, sing better than her. But they're not Jews."

Duke noted that many people say he is full of hate because of his anti-Jewish views. But, he protested, *he* was the one filled with a sense of humanity—while it is *Jews* who are sick. "I want a society of beauty, culture, art, literature, music," Duke told Rich. "I want to see the reduction of the crime rate. I want to see a clean society—clean up the pollution. . . . I want to see a greater sense of honesty between people, and I want to see mankind growing up on the evolutionary ladder, becoming better and stronger, more able, more fit, healthier. And I'm supposed to be a bad guy. These Jews who run things, who are producing this mental illness—teenage suicide. Just read the modern novelists . . . , all these Jewish sicknesses in there. Of course, that's nothing new. The Talmud's full of it. The Talmud's full of things like sex with boys and girls."

Duke revealed that his ideal country was Nazi Germany, although he reassured Rich that he favored a more democratic form of government. "I believe in more civil liberties than they did," he said. "However, I do realize that they were in a specific time historically, a difficult period, tremendous numbers of Communists in the country and civil unrest. They probably had to take certain types of measures which I wouldn't take."

He added, "But as far as their attitudes are concerned, founding a really fantastic educational system and promoting the best and having very vigorous physical fitness and having a real sense of unity with nature and believing in non-pollution and relocating factories to the countryside and creating a whole community around nature walks . . .—I think I would agree," he added. "The idea of pursuing scientific excellence as they did so much during that period, being very literate people—that's another good example of the Holocaust being inconsistent, because I think it was inconsistent with the German people during that period. Germany had one of the lowest crime rates in the world, per capita. . . . They had a greater sense of gaiety, national purpose and unity and true brotherhood among their people probably than any nation's ever had."

The 1986 trip by Duke and his girlfriend Gwen Udell to the Mauthausen concentration camp also included a quick tour of Germany by train. Duke was in his element. He loved speaking German—he eventually became semi-fluent—and especially loved having the opportunity to talk about his hero: Adolf Hitler. "Hitler was his idol," says Udell. "David thought he was the greatest man who ever lived. It was a constant conversation."

Duke tried to strike up conversation about the Nazi leader with anyone sharing their train compartment. He particularly liked to talk with people who had lived under the Third Reich. "He would just ask them questions about Hitler, and the way it was when Hitler was in power, and what did they believe as far as race was concerned," Udell remembers. "Every time he was relating to me what they said . . . , he always made it sound like, 'Yes, they were Nazis, and they believe it should be the way it was before 1945'. . . . He would always interpret their answer so that they would agree with him, with his beliefs."

Udell could not speak German well enough to know whether Duke was interpreting correctly. But as she watched the Germans discuss Hitler and the Third Reich with Duke, she thought he was not telling her the truth—because they always looked at Duke as if he were strange. "I always got the impression that these people thought he was a nut," she says with an embarrassed laugh. Udell remembers one train conversation about Hitler in particular. It turned out that the computer scientist with whom Duke began talking despised the Nazi leader. A heated argument ensued. When the computer scientist had left their compartment, Duke was fuming and repeatedly told Udell that the man was badly misinformed.

Admiration of Hitler was nothing new for Duke. In his introductory German class at LSU fifteen years before, the professor, James Hintze, had asked why he was taking the course. "To read the works of the greatest genius that ever lived!" Duke said.

"Well, Herr Duke, who might that be?" Professor Hintze eagerly asked. "Goethe? Schopenhauer? Kant? Nietzsche?"

"Adolf Hitler," Duke replied.

One day in the spring of 1974, while in his final semester at LSU, Duke heard a lecture on the Third Reich by a history graduate student named Reinhard Dearing. Dearing had grown up in Germany and had interviewed top aides to Hitler and Himmler for his studies. Afterward, Duke went to Dearing's office. "He thought I was a kindred spirit," Dearing said in 1991, as he recalled the encounter. "He asked if I had read *Mein Kampf*. I said, 'Yes.'"

"Don't you think it was one of the finest books ever written?" Duke asked.

"No," Dearing replied, a bit taken aback. "Hitler intended to go through with what he wrote about."

"Apparently you don't agree with Hitler," Duke said.

"No," Dearing said. "He caused the near destruction of my country."

Duke was dumbfounded. "I can't believe a German would feel that way," he said.

Duke paused and regrouped. "Couldn't *Mein Kampf* be compared to some of Shakespeare's great works?" he asked.

Dearing found the notion so absurd that he started laughing. "Do you speak German?" he asked.

"No," Duke replied.

"I didn't think so," Dearing said. "It was written in coarse, lower middle-class German."

Duke looked at Dearing and shook his head in disgust. "It's obvious they don't make Germans like they used to," he said and stomped out.

Duke may have felt free to discuss Hitler in Germany a decade later, but he was more circumspect in talking about the Nazi leader while in the United States. One occasion when he felt he could reveal his true feelings came at the wedding of a German friend of Gwen Udell's. Duke did not want to go because he was horrified that the German woman was marrying an Italian, a "lower race," in Duke's opinion. But he brightened at the reception afterward when he met the bride's grandmother. She had come from Germany and did not speak English. "When the ceremony was over, there's David, off with this poor little old lady who obviously did not want to talk about Hitler, bending her ear, trying to talk to her in broken German about Hitler," Udell says. "David was asking her, 'Aren't you a good Nazi? What do you believe in?' He related to me what she was saying to him," Udell says. "Of course he told me that she told him, 'Oh, yes, yes, we believed in Hitler. Yes, Hitler was a good man.' That was David's interpretation. But she didn't want to talk to him for very long."

His Metairie home was one place where Duke could be himself. He had swastika rings and armbands lying around and often wore T-shirts with the letters *SS* printed on them—the initials for Hitler's special police, who were in charge of rounding up Jews and operating the concentration camps. When he was watching television and World War II movies or when sitcoms like "Hogan's Heroes" came on, Duke railed against them for portraying Germans as bad guys or buffoons.

At home every April 20 until the late 1980s, he quietly celebrated Hitler's birthday. "David would call a few close friends and let them know that tonight was Hitler's birthday and that he wanted them to come over and have a few beers and chips to celebrate," Udell says. Duke would always give a toast to Hitler. "It wasn't like a wild party where people got drunk or anything like that," Udell says. "But it was always festive, beer, everybody having a good time." Sometimes Duke would spring for a cake. When asked in 1990 about the Hitler birthday parties, Duke denied they had occurred. "Hitler's never showed up at my house for any birthday parties," he said, trying to deflect the question with a joke.

Duke began living with Udell in 1980, a few months after he separated from Chloe. Following the separation, Chloe moved back to her hometown, West Palm Beach, Florida, with Erika and Kristin. She and Duke were divorced on January 31, 1984. It was an amicable divorce; the reason given was incompatibility. Both parents were assigned responsibility for raising their daughters, although the girls would live with Chloe and visit their father only infrequently until their high school years, when Erika went to live with Duke and Kristin with a friend's family nearby. Divorce records show that Duke agreed to pay Chloe $100 a month for child support during the first year after the divorce and $12.50 per month more in each succeeding year.

In 1988, Chloe remarried. Her new husband was Don Black, who had first met Duke at a meeting of the National Socialist White People's Party in 1970 and had been Alabama grand dragon in his Klan. According to Ralph Forbes, Duke was aghast when he learned that his best friend was going to marry his ex-wife. When he expressed his shock to his friend Ralph Forbes, Forbes counseled, "Remember, David, she's not your wife any more." Forbes, who had been a lieutenant in the American Nazi party under George Lincoln Rockwell before becoming a minister in the anti-Semitic Identity religion, presided over the ceremony in West Palm Beach. Duke was the best man. He, Chloe, and Black agreed that this would provide a sort of blessing for the union to Erika and Kristin. But many guests at the wedding felt uncomfortable at the arrangement and sniped at Duke behind his back during the reception afterward. In 1989, Chloe and Black had a son, whom they named

Derrick. Duke was upset, friends say. His ex-wife and best friend had a son, and he did not.

By then Gwen Udell, Duke's most serious girlfriend after the breakup of his marriage, had left him. Duke and Udell lived together from 1980 to 1987. She fit the Aryan profile that Duke yearned for. A decade younger than Duke, she is blonde, a shade under six feet. She was extremely fit from exercising religiously nearly every day. She looks back with wonder at her years with him, wonder that she could have lived with someone who harbored such malignant thoughts. It's hard to imagine her with Duke. She is warm-hearted, thoughtful, and intelligent. In 1990, when first quoted by name in the *Times-Picayune*, she went around to fellow employees and her black friends who had not known she had been Duke's girlfriend. She wanted them to know that she did not share his feelings toward Jews and blacks, though anybody associated with her would have already realized that.

They met when Udell was an undergraduate at the University of New Orleans. She found Duke charming and seductive, adventurous and worldly. She always had serious reservations about him, and in time her friends began telling her to leave him. But Duke repeatedly warned her that people would demean him because they were jealous and that she should ignore them. Young and innocent, she yielded to his instructions. Uninterested in politics, she turned a deaf ear to his complaints of blacks and Jews. She concentrated on her studies instead. "I was naive and I was stupid," Udell says, shaking her head at the memory of their relationship. "I was brainwashed, I was definitely brainwashed. I should have been more aware of what was going on. And I was concerned with getting my degree."

Fearful that blacks were literally outbreeding whites, Duke wanted her to have many babies, six in fact. He told her that he wanted to ensure that all six would be boys. "He wanted me to go to the doctor," Udell says. "He said there was some process whereby they could separate his sperm through artificial insemination so we would have six boys." She refused, and he was left with Erika and Kristin, the daughters from his marriage. Like his idol, Adolf Hitler, Duke was obsessed with the idea of creating a white master race even if it meant employing eugenics and abortion to eliminate imperfect fetuses.

Race mixing, of course, was anathema to Duke, convinced as he was that blacks are innately less intelligent and more prone to violence than whites. He also opposed government efforts to force integration, believing that the races preferred to live apart, and he said that whites descended from Europe had created the United States and made it a great nation. In the political context in which he has gained greatest visibility—the American South—Duke's racism has seemed to play out along black-white lines. The truth of the matter is that Duke subscribes to a much more intricate species of racism, one that borrows more from Hitler than Jim Crow.

"National Socialists view the world as a patchwork of distinct racial nations, each nationality imbued with a particular 'spiritual unity,' with specific moral, physical and intellectual qualities," wrote Lance Hill, a Tulane doctoral student, in a 1990 analysis of Duke's views on race. At the time, Hill was executive director of the Louisiana Coalition Against Racism and Nazism, which was formed in 1989 to oppose Duke. "For National Socialists, nation and race are identical," added Hill. "National qualities such as culture and intelligence are not the product of environment nor can they be absorbed by mere contact between nations. National qualities are immutable, imbedded in race, thus making it impossible for 'inferior' nations to rise to the same cultural level as the Aryans. National Socialists argue that the existence of the superior Aryans is threatened by lesser races, including Slavs, Czechs, Poles, blacks and Jews. In its final, developed stage, National Socialism proposes to elevate the Aryans to their rightful ascendant position by purifying the Aryan race, while subjugating or exterminating the inferior races."

David Duke had gotten his start in politics as a teenager with the National Socialist White People's party, the successor to the American Nazi party. And while he ended his formal ties to the Nazis in the early 1970s to form the Knights of the Ku Klux Klan, Nazi race doctrine continued to provide the foundation for his political beliefs into the 1990s. Like Hitler, Duke believed that genetics determine a person's place and outcome in life. "I do believe that there are genetic differences between the races and that they profoundly affect culture," he told Abby Kaplan, a Tulane student who interviewed him in November 1989. "I believe that in fact nationality comes from genes."

Consequently, as Hitler also contended, people of different ethnic backgrounds could not be assimilated into a national culture. "Both argue that genetic inferiority limits the ability of ethnic groups to absorb 'superior culture,'" wrote Hill. "For Duke, America is not a melting pot in which new immigrants assimilate American culture and make their own contribution. Instead, in Duke's eyes, Africans, Hispanics, Jews and even some Europeans (like southern Italians) pollute the gene pool and destroy American culture."

Even in the late 1980s, while trying to portray himself as divorced from his extremist past, Duke continued to express agreement with biological determinism, the heart of National Socialist race theory.

"I realized that the white species of humanity, that segment responsible for most of the world's great civilizations, was in grave danger of extinction," Duke told the anti-Semitic publication *Instauration* in December 1988, in explaining the development of his racial awareness. "And I came to understand that the most crucial element in the well-being of any society was, ultimately, the biological quality of the people who compose it. I learned that, once the gene pool was damaged, all hope and promise for the future would be lost irretrievably."

Duke was restating three basic premises of Nazi race doctrine, wrote Hill: "First, that people of North European descent are the sole producers of great culture. Second, that this cultural superiority is the product of biology. Natural resources, climate, geography, technology, politics and economics are all minor influences in the development of a people. Race determines history. Civilization derives from the genetic composition of a people. Race sets absolute limits on the advance of some people. Racial distinctions are so influential that, as Duke wrote in a 1986 letter accompanying an issue of the *NAAWP News*, they can lead 'one people to go to the moon while another lives in the mud.'"

Duke at times had to update Hitler's theories. Nazis regarded the Aryan as a physically superior being, a notion destroyed by Jesse Owens in the 1936 Olympics when he won four gold medals while Hitler sat in the stands glowering. Duke had a ready answer for Owens's feats and the dominance of blacks later in basketball and track and field: whites are superior to blacks in strength, endurance, and sports that require intelligence, he said, while blacks excel in sports like track that most reward pure physical ability. Duke liked to note that the top sixteen finishers in the 100-meter race at the 1988 Olympics were black. "There's something genetic," he said, "which gives them an advantage in that particular contest." As evidence that blacks are hopelessly ill suited to modern society, Duke cited FBI statistics showing that blacks commit more violent crimes than whites on a per capita basis. The need for affirmative action programs to help blacks advance, Duke said, also showed that they could not compete on their own.

These beliefs explain Duke's contention that the child of an interracial marriage would be less likely to be a productive citizen than a child of white parents. "If general mixing is allowed, there is always degeneration in the population," he wrote in a 1986 *NAAWP News* editorial headlined "Why I Oppose Race Mixing." One solution Duke has advocated to keep the white race pure is dividing the United States into separate racial nations and ending immigration from the Third World. He has generally said he favors a voluntary separation. But in 1984, the *NAAWP News* reprinted the article from *Instauration* that called for the forcible resettlement of people by race.

Duke has gone even further and embraced the Nazi vision of government eugenics to produce a master race. A 1984 *NAAWP News* editorial called for a government loan program to encourage white couples to have more children, a plan first conceived in 1933 by the Nazi government. The flip side of this plan was to have government programs that would induce non-Aryans to have fewer children. "I see nothing wrong with encouraging unproductive people to have fewer children, economically, and encouraging the most productive people to have children," he said in 1989. "And I think that adds beauty to the whole society, and quality and excellence to all society."

Hitler had articulated the same philosophy sixty-four years earlier. "It [the Nazi state]," he said, "must see to it that only the healthy beget children; that there is only one disgrace; despite one's own sickness and deficiencies, to bring children into the world . . . , and conversely it must be considered reprehensible to withhold children from the state."

While Duke during his 1990 and 1991 political campaigns tried to dismiss these ideas as follies abandoned in his youth, in fact he was still referring to them throughout the 1980s. In 1989, he told Kaplan that he favored a government program to provide low-interest loans to the top 10 percent of college graduates as an inducement to produce elite children. Conversely, he favored voluntary sterilization programs for welfare recipients, another idea borrowed from Hitler. "Why in the world would it be a sin or somehow evil," he asked Evelyn Rich in 1985, "to encourage welfare cases to have fewer children, encourage them to be sterilized or encourage them to have birth control and maybe give them economic incentives to do so?"

A little bit earlier in the interview, Rich had asked whether Duke was talking about genetic engineering—improving society through selective breeding. "Of course," Duke replied. "In terms of a higher humanity. Well, not only genetic engineering, but just promoting the best strains, the best individuals. In fact, most of them [welfare recipients] are too stupid to do anything else but have kids. That's the only way in life they can really entertain themselves, is through sex. They can't entertain themselves very well through intellectual pursuits and so society already has a program, and I say simply reverse that. It's not very hard. All the government needs to do is simply give certain incentives . . . , for those on welfare, for instance, not to have children."

Throughout the 1970s and 1980s Duke also regularly praised William Shockley, who won a Nobel Prize for inventing the transistor and in later years became fascinated with genetic theories of white superiority. "Like a modern day Galileo, Shockley chose truth," the *NAAWP News* wrote in 1982. "Using sophisticated procedures of quantum mechanics applied to sociological data, Shockley clearly demonstrated that heredity was the primary determinant of intelligence and that the intelligence level of blacks was 15 to 20 percent lower than that of whites. This marked difference in intelligence between blacks and whites results in only one in six Negroes being as intelligent as the average white, and in six times as many blacks per capita being mentally retarded than whites. Dr. Shockley also clearly proved that blacks were on the whole becoming even less intelligent because the welfare system low-I.Q. blacks were reproducing much faster than more intelligent ones. He saw the same thing taking place in most societies." Duke mourned Shockley's death in 1989. Shockley was, the *NAAWP News* eulogized, "among the great men of our time."

Duke also lionized Robert K. Graham, a wealthy businessman who in 1979 founded the Repository for Germinal Choice, "a sperm bank like no other in the world," as the *NAAWP News* described it. Graham's sperm bank sought to produce better humans by freezing sperm from geniuses to inseminate bright women. The *NAAWP News* hailed it as "a simple, beautiful idea." To Duke's disgust, conservative columnist George Will blasted the genius sperm bank. "To Will, the filthiest child rapist and murderer is somehow sanctified," the *NAAWP News* wrote, "because he can squirm under the fence as a 'man' and no doubt in Will's scheme of things, next to a productive, caring human being or even an earthshaker like Shockley, that child killer is equal in the eyes of God. To the true white men and women of the West, life alone is not sacred, but productive, beautiful, quality life is the most sacred thing on earth. Those who promote the scum of the species over the cream of the crop are the agents of the threatening darkness. Those like Shockley and Graham who promote the finest genetic elements of mankind are the true angels of Nature and her God."

Duke looked to genetics to solve a trend that terrified him: minorities propagating at a much faster rate than whites. "Society has a very strong birth control against the most creative, the most productive, the most talented, because in general in society, they have the fewest children," he told Evelyn Rich. "Whereas your lowest elements, the way society is constructed, are encouraged—more welfare payments for the more children they have." He told *Hustler* magazine: "Welfare recipients produce kids like they were coming off an assembly line."

Clearly, Duke's belief that many humans were "scum" and not worth nurturing was miles removed from the Christian underpinning of the right-to-life movement. But Duke's belief in eugenics caused him to oppose abortion. He was prolife not because he believed in the sanctity of the human being, as do Evangelical Christians, but because he thought banning abortions would produce more white babies and fewer minority ones. Whites, he said, choose to have abortions—while minorities do not. Duke did favor exceptions where the pregnancy resulted from rape or incest. He also favored abortions as a tool for weeding out imperfect babies, in yet another Nazi-inspired plan.

"It's not human life that's so valuable," Duke told Rich, "it's good human life, productive human life, beautiful human life. . . . There's nothing wrong with aborting a fetus when we know that that fetus is going to be deformed. Why bring all that pain into the world? Why let that individual suffer? As they do suffer, aren't we really creating something that will lessen the beauty and the quality of the human race?"

As Duke began his constant campaigns for elective office in the late 1980s, he downplayed his more overtly racist views. But it seems likely that Duke was only biding his time, waiting for the day when he could return to his racist agenda in a position of political legitimacy. A three-way exchange in 1986 between Duke, Rich, and Joe Fields, a National Socialist party member, supports this view. "I think that most people aren't ever going to come over until things get tough—we have a depression, and people start losing their homes," Fields said, speculating on the prospects for a Nazi takeover in the United States.

"I think that's a very defeatist philosophy," Duke replied.

"No, I look forward to it happening," Fields said.

"I think it's defeatist because you have no guarantee of that happening," Duke said. "This government—it might take decades to bring it down."

"I think it's very close to crumbling," Fields said.

"Joe, I've heard so many people say that."

"I give it 10 years at the most."

"If I had a nickel for every person who told me that in the last 15 years of fighting, I'd be rich," Duke said. "You know, right now, the government, the economy, has never really been stronger. It's growing. Sure we have debt, but we've always had debt. I don't think we have any guarantee. But here's the thing: We've got the truth. We've got absolute truth."

"Yeah, but who cares? The average guy doesn't care who's got the truth, just as long as he's got a TV, and enough to eat and a roof over . . ."

"The way I look at it," Duke interrupted, "we've got truth on our side and we're the majority—that is, white people . . ."

"It doesn't take that many people, though, to start something rolling," Fields said, warming to the idea. "Hitler started with seven men."

"Right, that's why I'm trying to say to you—"

"And most people didn't want to have anything to do with him."

"Right," Duke said. "And don't you think it can happen right now, if we put the right package together? Don't you think that there are millions of Americans that are alienated and are looking for something . . . to believe in?"

Evelyn Rich broke in. "And Guru Duke will come along," she said with a laugh.

"Not necessarily me—somebody," he said. He paused and then spoke as if he had had a revelation: "My God! I might have to do it because nobody else might come along to do it."

David Duke's political comeback began in an appropriate setting: all-white Forsyth County, Georgia. There on a cold winter day in January 1987, he led a march against integration that, because of the widespread press coverage he received, reestablished him among racist and anti-Semitic leaders as the nation's foremost spokesman of the white supremacist movement. This experience encouraged him to carry out his plan later that year to run for president. Forsyth County is north of Atlanta and had had no black residents, legend had it, since 1912, when three blacks were arrested for the rape and murder of a nineteen-year-old white woman. Angry whites shot one of the blacks to death in jail and evicted the other 1,000 black residents of the county. (The two other black men arrested for the crime went to trial, were convicted, and were hanged.)

Black residents of Atlanta for years had resented Forsyth County. On January 17, 1987, Atlanta City Councilman Hosea Williams, a lieutenant of Dr. Martin Luther King's and a veteran of the civil rights movement, held a march with seventy-five other activists to focus attention on Forsyth County's continued all-white status. The march was held in Cumming, the county seat. About 400 Klansmen and sympathizers showed up to greet Williams and the civil rights marchers. It was not a friendly greeting. The whites held up "Nigger Go Home" signs and threw rocks and bottles at the seventy-five marchers. This display of open racism made headlines across the country.

Williams vowed to return to Forsyth County immediately and called for a large turnout to condemn the racism. In response a group of white racists organized a countermarch, to be led by Mississippi attorney Richard Barrett. Extremist leader Ed Fields of Atlanta thought the looming racial showdown was made to order for David Duke and invited him to come to Forsyth County. Duke leaped at the chance to join the fray.

The second march was scheduled for January 24, a week after the first one. The prospect of racial conflict prompted reporters from major newspapers and the national television networks to descend on Cumming. With Duke at the head of their column, the white racists turned out 1,000 demonstrators. They arrived at the courthouse square in Cumming first. Duke, wearing a "Keep Forsyth White" button, gave one of the speeches. If blacks were allowed to enter the county, he told the crowd, crime would increase. He urged them, however, to obey the law to avoid discrediting their movement.

An hour later, as Duke and his longtime friend Don Black were engaged in a shouting match with a black man, they were arrested and charged with reckless conduct and blocking the highway. As he was led away, Duke yelled, "White victory! White victory!" He protested that he had not violated any laws, that the authorities had arrested him simply because he was one of the countermarchers' leaders.

Meanwhile, more than 100 buses were ferrying the civil rights demonstrators from Atlanta to Cumming. When the column began marching on Old Buford Road toward the courthouse square, they were 20,000 strong and were led by veterans of the civil rights movement, including King's widow, Coretta Scott King, Atlanta Mayor Andrew Young, and Benjamin Hooks, the head of the NAACP. It was the largest civil rights march in years. Georgia authorities made sure that there was no violence. A curtain of state troopers and National Guardsmen headed the civil rights column. Standing shoulder to shoulder along the parade route to act as a human shield between the marchers and the white protesters were more than 1,000 National Guardsmen wearing combat helmets, camouflage, and bulletproof vests.

As the marchers neared the courthouse square, the white protesters began waving Confederate flags and shouting racial epithets. "We hate you, we hate you," the white protestors chanted." The civil rights marchers stared back but remained silent to avoid provocation. "We did not come to Forsyth County to scare you to death," Joseph Lowery, president of the Southern Christian Leadership Conference told the crowd after it had reached the courthouse square. "We came to Forsyth to challenge you to live a life of decency."

Afterward, Duke complained that he and Black had been held incommunicado for five hours in a holding pen topped by barbed wire as they shivered in the cold. Nevertheless, Duke was ecstatic at the day's events. Before being arrested, he had been interviewed not only by reporters from Atlanta newspapers, radio talk shows, and television stations but also by the national media. For the first time since he became president of the NAAWP in 1980, he was in the news again. "Victory in Forsyth County," read the headline in the *NAAWP News.* "The truth is that the Forsyth County march and rally was an opening foray in a long struggle for the freedom of our people," an article said. "It is great to see that as time goes on, more and more White people are beginning to stand up."

Duke and Barrett tried to continue exploiting the white anger. But when the civil rights marchers made no effort to return, the heated passions cooled. The whites held a rally in an empty chickenhouse outside Cumming on February 22. Only 125 people showed up to hear Duke and Barrett denounce blacks and the police. Duke and Barrett soon had a falling out over money, and the white unity movement in Forsyth County collapsed. The dispute centered on the sixty-two white marchers other than Duke and Black who had been arrested during the January 24 march. Barrett attempted to raise money to defend them under the auspices of a group he had founded called the Forsyth County Defense League. But without telling Barrett, Duke had begun raising money for his own defense, using a nearly identical name, that of the Forsyth County Defense Fund. Further confusing matters, the post office box for Duke's Defense Fund was 884, while the Defense League post office box number was 664.

Duke mailed a three-page appeal to all Forsyth County residents and to his NAAWP membership, seeking donations for his own defense. The letter was signed by Mark Watts, one of the organizers of the January 24 counter-march. Dozens of people sent money to Duke, thinking they were helping with the defense of all those arrested, not just him. They did not realize that Duke's Defense Fund was different from the Defense League. When the money they had sent in to help the sixty-two whites who were also arrested did not materialize, they began asking where it had gone. Barrett had to tell them that it had gone to Duke—and not to the sixty-two whites who had also been arrested. Questions about the finances tore apart the Defense League. Barrett called Duke to ask for an accounting of the money he had raised, but Duke refused to give one.

In the meantime, Mark Watts told Barrett and Jerry Lord, a founder of the Forsyth County Defense League, that he had not in fact signed Duke's Defense Fund letter. Had Duke forged the letter? When I put this question to him by phone in 1989, he paused a long time. I asked him again. He paused again, before finally saying, "Whatever letters were sent were authorized."

"Authorized by whom?" I asked.

"Authorized by whomever," he replied. "If Mark Watts signed it, he signed it. Or he gave permission for that letter."

"Did he give permission to you?" I asked.

"I wasn't specifically in that aspect of it," he said. "It was one of our people on our staff."

This did not ring true. It looked like Duke's writing style. In addition, Duke was always careful to make sure he handled NAAWP money matters.

"Did any of that money go to actually help the people who had been arrested in Forsyth County?" I asked.

"Absolutely," Duke replied. "We had four people, in fact, who were helped specifically—the leaders of the march."

"Which people received money from the Forsyth County Defense Fund?" I asked.

"That's none of your business, all right? I don't even want to talk to you anymore. OK?"

He hung up.

Mark Watts, an itinerant plumber who had had several brushes with the law, did not complain publicly about Duke's action. I tried to contact him several times through an intermediary, but he declined to talk to me. The intermediary told me that Watts wanted to put the dispute behind him and did not want to damage Duke's political career because he sympathized with Duke's views. In a subsequent interview, Duke told me that all of the money he raised from the Defense Fund letter went for mailing costs and his legal fees, which he said alone totaled about $8,000. That figure seems exaggerated since Duke never went to trial. On June 22, 1987, he pleaded no contest to a misdemeanor charge of obstructing a roadway. He was fined $55 and received a one-year suspended jail sentence. Duke also agreed not to return to Forsyth County or to participate in demonstrations there for a year.

He was glad to put the episode behind him because by then he was a Democratic candidate for president. After his aborted bid in 1980 when he was twenty-nine, Duke was now old enough to be a candidate in the 1988 election. It was to be his first campaign since he ran for the Louisiana state senate in 1979. He was returning to the strategy that by running for political office, he could exploit the media's fascination with extremists to win widespread publicity.

Duke began his presidential campaign in 1987, knowing that he could count on his fellow travelers to provide a base of support. Forsyth County had reminded leaders of the white supremacist movement that Duke was their best spokesman. The fund-raising dispute may also have reminded them that they could not trust him. But he was still their best alternative to mainstream Democratic and Republican candidates.

Leaders of the white supremacist movement gathered at the Atlanta Marriott Hotel in suburban Marietta on June 8, 1987, in a private campaign kickoff. It was like a reunion for many of them, a chance to reminisce about past battles against "niggers" and the Zionist Occupational Government. There was a feeling of camaraderie in the room, a feeling that they may not have the numbers yet but they were bound to win because right was on their side. Duke fueled this feeling with a call to arms for whites to take back America. Duke was running on a right-wing populist platform that mixed the antiblack appeal of his Louisiana Senate campaigns with a broader, anti-Semitic and antiestablishment attack.

As before, Duke opposed affirmative action programs and forced busing. As before, he demanded that welfare recipients work for their benefits. He called for laws encouraging them to have fewer children. Duke also described himself as a protectionist and urged the abolition of the Internal Revenue Service and the preservation of family farms. He favored a constitutional amendment requiring the election of all judges, including Supreme Court justices. He called for the United States to stand "with our white brothers and sisters in South Africa" and for stricter measures against the immigration of nonwhites. He attacked "the forces of international finance" and the Israeli lobby, which "has so much power and influence over our Congress and national media in the United States."

Duke announced his candidacy publicly on the steps of Georgia's state capitol the next day, June 9. He had chosen Atlanta because it was to host the 1988 Democratic National Convention and because it was where he was best known following the Forsyth County marches. Duke boldly predicted that he would win 600 delegates to the convention and painted himself as the Reverend Jesse Jackson's biggest opponent in an attempt to give himself more credibility. "The Democrats will be tweedly-dee and tweedly-dumb," Duke said. "I can confront the issues where other Democrats aren't going to because they are afraid to offend Jackson. I'll be the only one articulating the issues that are important to the Democratic Party."

While Jackson had the Rainbow Coalition, Duke said, he had what he called the Sunshine Coalition. "If Jesse Jackson can speak for the Rainbow Coalition," he asked, "why can't we of European descent have a Sunshine Coalition?" A small crowd of reporters turned out to take down his words, but his announcement won little play in the next day's newspapers across the country.

That night, however, millions of Americans saw Duke discuss his candidacy on CNN's "Crossfire" show. Duke gave himself a typically glowing review. "The show was a tremendous success according to all who saw it," the NAAWP News reported. "During the half-hour interview, Mr. Duke was able to work in the tale about how Jessie [sic] Jackson, who, when once a waiter, spat on the food he served to white people." Following Duke's announcement in Atlanta, Paul Kirk, chairman of the Democratic National Committee, denounced him as part of the "kook fringe" and asked state party officers to use all legal methods to block him from their state ballots. Duke seized on this move to win a bit more media coverage. He showed up the next day at DNC headquarters in Washington to demand a meeting with Kirk. He was thrown out of the building, as he had expected. Waiting for him on the sidewalk was a group of reporters he had notified beforehand. The next day's papers carried articles on Duke's fight with Kirk.

Duke's next move was to hire a campaign manager. His choice was Ralph Forbes, an ideological soulmate. A forty-seven-year-old Identity minister, Forbes had met Duke in 1967 at the National Socialist White People's party headquarters in Arlington, Virginia. Forbes had been a disciple of George Lincoln Rockwell, the leader of the American Nazi party until his assassination in 1967. Forbes had joined the party in 1959 and rose to become commander of its western division before leaving in 1967 to found an Identity ministry that he called the Sword of Christ. In succeeding years, he sold viciously anti-Semitic books and tapes and ran for political office several times in Arkansas. Like Duke, Forbes believed that the Holocaust was a myth.

But while they were ideological bedfellows, Forbes and Duke had starkly different temperaments. Forbes was the father of eleven children (a twelfth had died). He had been married for twenty-eight years and was living on a homestead in rural London, Arkansas. He was bothered that Duke had been divorced and that he did not spend more time with his two daughters when they visited from Florida. When Forbes was working at the presidential campaign headquarters, which was in the basement of Duke's home, he felt uneasy when Duke introduced his latest female conquest.

Forbes was dedicated to his job. He worked 100 hours a week and slept on the floor of the campaign headquarters. Duke, too, worked hard during the day but, knowing that he was engaged in a quixotic struggle, liked to continue leading what he called "a balanced life." "We'd go somewhere and he'd be talking about LSU football," Forbes recalls, "and I wanted to be talking about how we could win in Alabama." Duke thought that Forbes was working too hard and that he needed to shed twenty pounds. He dragged Forbes along to the gym where he exercised, but Forbes soon stopped going, to Duke's disappointment.

Forbes hated to ride in a car with Duke because Duke insisted on listening to loud rock music. Forbes claimed that the music hurt his ears. But Forbes found another trait of Duke's endearing: his extreme concern for his calico cat, Mini. Whenever Mini scrambled outside his home, Duke made everyone stop work to catch her. Mini had been declawed, and Duke feared that she could not fend for herself outside of his home. "It was the most important thing in the world [to grab her]," says Forbes. "I thought it was sort of cute."

To mount his presidential campaign, Duke relied on the NAAWP and fellow right-wing extremists. He drafted the NAAWP's three staffers to do clerical work and paid $500 to the NAAWP to rent its list of subscribers for a direct mailing. He also rented mailing lists from Willis Carto's Liberty Lobby, ran ads in Carto's weekly newspaper, the *Spotlight*, and paid Howard Allen Enterprises, the publisher of the anti-Semitic journal *Instauration*, several thousand dollars for campaign work.

Duke also turned to two men who had worked for the Liberty Lobby—Robert Hoy and Travis McCoy—to help his campaign. McCoy had the key job of ensuring that Duke qualified under a complex formula for federal matching funds. The Federal Election Commission would match every dollar contributed to the Duke presidential campaign if Duke raised at least $5,000 in contributions of $250 or less in each of twenty states. By qualifying for matching funds, Duke could double his campaign treasury and thus greatly expand his message. But McCoy botched the job, and Forbes fired him. Forbes then tried to put the campaign finances in order to qualify for the matching funds. But it was too late for FEC deadlines. Duke would have to campaign with the small amount of contributions he received. Whatever chance he had of winning any delegates had disappeared.

Duke was not having much success anyway. The Democratic party was ignoring him, and he could not find a way to recapture the media coverage that had won him stardom in the Klan. One of the few times he received media attention came in December 1987 when he ambushed presidential candidate Jack Kemp, a Republican congressman from Buffalo, during a campaign stop in New Hampshire. As Kemp was ending a press conference, Duke began demanding loudly to know when Kemp would oppose affirmative action programs. Kemp yelled back that he was not a racist. The incident was covered in a brief Associated Press dispatch.

Duke was thwarted in his efforts to be invited to the televised debates of the Democratic candidates. He was especially angry at being shut out of the November 2, 1987, debate at Tulane University in New Orleans, which was only five miles from his home. Duke filed a lawsuit against the debate sponsor, the Democratic Leadership Council, three days before the event, demanding that he be included and that he be awarded $1 million in damages for an alleged conspiracy to violate his free speech rights. On the day of the debate, Duke and Forbes were at the federal courthouse when a judge refused to issue an injunction allowing him to participate.

After the ruling, they sought out Steve Cannizaro, the *Times-Picayune's* court reporter, to make a statement. Cannizaro interviewed Duke and Forbes for a few minutes and then, as he was preparing to leave, heard them discussing how they were going to get to Tulane for the debate—where Duke planned to seek more coverage from reporters. "Duke was looking through his wallet, and I could hear him saying that he only had a dollar or two," Cannizaro remembers. "Forbes then told Duke that he didn't have any money. I started laughing and thought to myself: this joker wants to run for president, and he and his campaign manager don't even have enough money between them for cab fare."

Duke had no better success when he tried to participate in the January 24, 1988, debate at the University of New Hampshire in Durham. Duke and Forbes again filed suit to be allowed to participate, and again they failed. Duke then decided to show up at the debate site and demand to be included. Evelyn Rich, who had met up with Duke in Boston to do more interviews for her doctoral dissertation on the Klan, drove him and Forbes to the event. As they arrived, Duke demanded that Rich park in a roped-off area near the auditorium and tell the policemen that Duke was one of the debate participants. Rich refused. "David, they'll tow my car if I park here," she said. Duke insisted. "Just tell them that you're driving David Duke," he said. She refused again and found the nearest parking spot, which was far from the auditorium. Duke was still determined to try to gain admittance to the debate. Once inside, he and Forbes planned to cause a ruckus and refuse to stop until he had a spot on the candidates' panel.

Duke marched up to the auditorium door and demanded entry. The guard turned him away. He began handing out leaflets, keeping one eye peeled until he spotted a reporter and cameraman. He approached them. "Hi, I'm David Duke," he said. "I'm running for president, too. Why don't you interview me?" The reporter was from MTV and obliged him. As the interview ended, it was nearly time for the debate to begin. With others who could not gain admittance to the auditorium, Duke, Forbes, and Rich trooped over to a school cafeteria where the debate was being shown on a big-screen television.

Duke fidgeted throughout the debate and kept sniping at the debate sponsors and the seven Democratic hopefuls. When the event ended, he and Forbes were unsure what to do—until they heard that one of the candidates, Representative Richard Gephardt of Missouri, was hosting a reception at a local motel. They rushed over because Duke thought he might get himself photographed with Gephardt and have the photo appear in a newspaper. But as they arrived at the motel, Gephardt was walking out the door. "Hi," Duke said as he shook Gephardt's hand. "I'm David Duke." Gephardt looked at him blankly and moved on, leaving Duke standing alone. "Nobody knew who he was," Rich said, "or cared about him."

Another candidate might have bowed out of the campaign, but not Duke, who had suffered rejection thoughout his life. Still to come was the March 8 Louisiana Democratic primary and a last chance to win delegates to the party convention in Atlanta. Duke poured most of his remaining funds into media advertising for the Louisiana primary, spending $30,000 to produce and broadcast a thirty-minute television commercial and another $2,000 in newspaper ads to promote it. "For the first time in their lives, people heard the voice of someone who was running for president who was speaking the truth, powerfully, intelligently, with courage and conviction," the *NAAWP News* gushed in describing the television ad.

Boosted by it, Duke won 23,390 votes in the Louisiana Democratic primary, 3.8 percent of the total. As in his previous electoral defeats, Duke claimed victory. He received more votes in Louisiana than Illinois Senator Paul Simon and former Arizona Governor Bruce Babbitt, the *NAAWP News* wrote. This statement ignored, however, the fact that Babbitt had withdrawn from the race and that Simon had skipped Louisiana and the other Super Tuesday primaries. The *NAAWP News* also failed to note that Jesse Jackson, whom Duke had painted as his chief rival, won the Louisiana primary.

Duke was on firmer ground when he criticized the *Times-Picayune* for not even mentioning him in a preelection supplement and in the news accounts of the primary election results. As he pointed out in the *NAAWP News*, the *Times-Picayune* listed the vote totals in metropolitan New Orleans parishes for Simon, Babbitt, Gephardt, former Colorado Senator Gary Hart and Tennessee Senator Al Gore—while putting his vote total in the "other" category—even though he beat each of the better-known candidates in at least one of the New Orleans-area parishes.

With the *Times-Picayune* owned by the Jewish Newhouse family, Duke had a ready reason for the paper's decision to ignore him. "A perfect illustration of how America's Zionist controlled media suppresses truth is the reporting of the election done by the *Times-Picayune*," the *NAAWP News* wrote. "If David Duke can beat the biggest Democratic candidates with no coverage, how would he have done if he was given fair treatment? In all likelihood, he would be heading toward the convention with the most delegates of any Democratic candidate; instead, the nation continues to sink under the ponderous weight of the liberal/minority/international finance coalition." New Orleans television stations had also failed to mention him, but he did not try to explain why.

Duke's presidential campaign as a Democrat was a colossal failure. He raised only $260,000, a fraction of what he needed to mount a serious campaign. He was ignored as a fringe candidate and won none of the 600 Democratic Convention delegates he had predicted. His "chief rival," Jesse Jackson, won 1,218.5 delegates and finished second only to the Democratic nominee, Massachusetts Governor Michael Dukakis.

But Duke's odyssey in 1988 was not over. The right-wing extremist Populist party wanted him to be its presidential candidate in the November general election. Immediately after the Louisiana primary, he flew to Cincinnati, where the Populist party was holding its nominating convention.

Founded in 1984, the Populist party was the electoral vehicle for the extremist Right and a haven for neo-Nazis and former Klansmen. Willis Carto was its founder and guiding light. Its first chairman was Robert Weems, who had been active with the anti-Semitic National States Rights party.

The state chairman for the Populist party in Ohio was Van Loman, who had been a Klansmen for twenty years before taking off his white sheets in 1985. Don Black, who had succeeded Duke as grand wizard of the Knights of the Ku Klux Klan, joined the party after serving time for the Dominica invasion. Ralph Forbes became the Arkansas party chairman.

The Populist party had fielded candidates in 1984 with Bob Richards, an Olympic gold medalist in the pole vault during the 1950s, as its presidential candidate, and Maureen Salaman, a Liberty Lobby activist, as its vice-presidential candidate. On the ballot in only fourteen states, the Populists generated little attention and won but 66,000 votes.

In 1988, Carto wanted to field candidates again, but Richards was not an option, since he had broken with the party by denouncing it as anti-Semitic. For a time it looked as if former Idaho Republican Representative George Hansen would head the party's ticket. Hansen, who had served a fifteen-month federal prison sentence for failing to disclose loans and silver commodities profits, had given the keynote speech at the Populist party's 1987 national convention. Duke also gave a speech, and with his appeal to racial resentment, he was greeted more enthusiastically than Hansen. Hansen had made a pro-Jewish statement that upset many of the Populists. He and the Populists obviously were not a good match, and he eventually told them to find another presidential candidate. Many party members began lobbying for Duke. Other party members, however, favored Bo Gritz, a Vietnam War hero whom party officials touted as the model for Sylvester Stallone's Rambo character.

Duke was not enthusiastic about being the party's nominee. Unlike his Democratic candidacy where he thought he could turn the establishment on its ear by winning a chunk of delegates, he was under no illusions about the Populist party candidacy. He knew the media would ignore him as a third-party candidate. But he decided to go to Cincinnati anyway. He had nothing else to do. Besides, he felt at home with the Populists ideologically. Their leaders were a who's who of the extremist Right.

The nomination was set for March 13, a Sunday. The day before, party leaders held a series of meetings to decide between Duke and Gritz. These meetings lasted into the wee hours of Sunday morning. While Gritz button-holed a dozen party chiefs making the choice, Duke was absent. He was selected to be the nominee, however. While Gritz was a political neophyte, Duke was a polished speaker. Party activists had known him for years and liked his racist and anti-Semitic views.

But when it came time on Sunday to bestow the nomination on Duke, he still could not be found. Everyone began wondering where their candidate was. They delayed the day's proceedings an hour but then had to press ahead, since many people had planes to catch that afternoon. Only after Gritz, who had been selected as the party's vice-presidential nominee, had begun giving his acceptance speech did Duke turn up. He had been holed up with a blonde woman he had met the night before in the hotel lounge. As he introduced her around, party members grumbled about his lack of morals and wondered whether they should have given the presidential endorsement to Gritz.

After he and Duke had given their acceptance speeches, Gritz met with Duke. The meeting did not go well. Gritz came away convinced that he did not want to be on the ticket with David Duke. "He'd change his speech from audience to audience," Gritz said. The Populist party scrambled to find a replacement. He was Floyd Parker, an unknown doctor from New Mexico. The presidential campaign was run by Don Wassall, the Populist party's executive director, from his office in Ford City, Pennsylvania. It was a shoestring operation. The Populist campaign rented the Liberty Lobby's membership list for $9,389 and hit the members up for donations. But the campaign raised and spent a paltry $136,000. Duke and Parker qualified on only twelve ballots for the November election.

Duke hopscotched around the country visiting these states. He delivered the same right-wing populist message as when he was a Democratic presidential candidate. And the media continued to ignore him (as it did the other third-party candidates). The high point of Duke's Populist campaign came on October 25 when he broadcast a thirty-minute television ad in Louisiana and on two cable superstations that reached millions of voters nationwide. The ad showed Duke and an attractive young woman sitting in a studio as she tossed him softball questions.

Q. "Mr. Duke, how does it feel running for president and being classified as a racist?"

Duke: "Well, I think I don't see any racist here. I mean, Jesse Jackson's not here with us in the studio. I think it's very interesting that when a person is white and they believe in equal rights for everybody in this country that then they're called a racist. George Bush and Mike Dukakis . . . are now endorsing so-called affirmative action, which is nothing more than blatant discrimination against better-qualified white people in hiring, promotions, scholarships, college admissions, union admittance. . . . So what we've got going on right now is massive racism being exercised against white people in America, and I'm called a racist because I believe in equal rights for everyone. I think that's quite hypocritical."

The ad was vintage Duke and was, of course, sprinkled with anti-Semitic venom. "I can tell you the Zionists have long ago bought George Bush and Mike Dukakis," he said at one point. "We need an America First policy in foreign policy."

On election day, November 8, Duke received 48,267 votes, or 0.05 percent of the 91.5 million cast. He spent election night at a party hosted by a group of New Orleans lawyers he did not know. They had decided to invite an assortment of odd characters to enliven the evening, and Duke had nowhere else to go. When he realized at the party that he had been invited as an object of ridicule, he was hurt. The presidential campaign that was supposed to lift him out of obscurity had not. At thirty-eight years old, his political career seemed over, his dreams for achieving widespread popular support as the spokesman for the dispossessed majority seemed dashed. The best he could hope for, it seemed, was a continuation of life on the fringe.

CHAPTER SEVEN

THE REPRESENTATIVE
FROM METAIRIE

The Metry Bar and Cafe is in the heart of the New Orleans suburb of Metairie and features twelve bar stools, one pool table, and a forty-something bar maid named Dee. Budweiser on tap is one dollar, hot garlic links are two dollars, and the red beans and rice are free during Monday Night Football. The patrons are working class and white. So when David Duke arrived unannounced at the Metry cafe just after 9:00 P.M. on December 21, 1988, clutching a batch of campaign flyers, the two dozen customers knew who he was and why he was there. They stood and applauded for Duke, a candidate for a just-vacated seat in the Louisiana House of Representatives.

Duke's ignominious defeat in the November 8 presidential election had not meant the end of his political career after all. A month earlier, Chuck Cusimano, the representative for Louisiana House District 81, had won election to a Jefferson Parish judgeship. A special election was to be held to fill the seat. This was the stroke of luck that Duke had dreamed of for years. The district was tailor-made for him: 99.6 percent white and extremely conservative. And many of the residents knew Duke because its boundaries were part of the state senate district in which he had campaigned nearly a decade before.

But even before he could begin his campaign, Duke faced a potentially crippling problem: Louisiana law required candidates to have lived in their districts for at least a year. Duke's home on Cypress Street was two blocks outside the boundary. But this was too good an opportunity for a technicality to stop him. On November 22, he visited the Jefferson Parish registrar of voters and quietly changed his address in Metairie to 1161 Lake Street, Apartment 323, a residence within the district.

To have any chance of winning, Duke needed a succession of events to break his way. The first was in the actual timing of the election. After Cusimano vacated the seat, two local attorneys, Jay Zainey and David Vitter, appeared to be the immediate front-runners. But both needed to have the election held as late as possible, Zainey so he could finish a big trial and have time to get organized and Vitter so he could have lived long enough in the district to qualify for the one-year residency rule. It was up to Governor Buddy Roemer to set the date of the special election. Under Louisiana's unique election law, there would be a single primary in which all candidates, regardless of party affiliation, would compete. The top two finishers, again regardless of party, would meet in a runoff four weeks later, if the top vote-getter did not win a majority.

The other prospective District 81 candidates, naturally, wanted to hold the election as soon as possible to keep out Zainey and Vitter. One of the other candidates was John Treen, and he had a well-placed supporter in Jim Donelon, a state representative from another district in Metairie. Donelon was close friends with Tom Casey, Roemer's executive counsel, and asked Casey to have the governor schedule the primary on January 21, 1989—too early for Zainey and Vitter. Donelon told Casey that of the prospective candidates, Treen would be Roemer's biggest ally. Donelon got his answer a few days later when he saw Roemer at a New Orleans Chamber of Commerce luncheon. "Jim, we'll call that election when you want," Roemer told him. Zainey and Vitter, who would win the seat in 1991, were knocked out.

A few days later, Sam Altobello, Jefferson Parish's registrar of voters for eighteen years, was eating Chinese food for lunch at the Elmwood Food Court near his office when a friend stopped by with the latest political rumor: David Duke was going to run for the District 81 seat. As he remembered Duke's recent visit to change his address, Altobello nodded knowingly. Back at his office, Altobello pulled the returns from the 1979 state senate race. While Duke had lost, Altobello saw that he had run strongly in the District 81 precincts. "This boy's got a chance," Altobello said to himself. When Duke became the seventh and final person to qualify for the seat on December 2, few people shared Altobello's view. The political establishment in Jefferson Parish thought Duke was a kook who couldn't be elected dog catcher. When Duke appeared at a political function in Jefferson Parish during the 1988 presidential campaign, local politicians kept an eye on him—but only to make sure that if he came near them, no photographer was there to snap a picture.

The conventional view was that the race for District 81 was a contest between two Republican party stalwarts, Treen and Delton Charles. Treen was well known in the district as a longtime party activist whose younger brother, David, had been elected in 1979 as Louisiana's first Republican governor since

Reconstruction. Charles had served on the parish school board until he resigned to run for the District 81 seat.

In qualifying for the race, Duke had switched not only his address but also his party registration from Democrat to Republican. So when the Jefferson Parish Republican party scheduled a closed meeting on December 5 to decide its endorsement, party leaders felt compelled to invite Duke along with the four other Republican candidates. Each spoke that night, but one among them stood out for his polished style and strong message: Duke. Afterward, the state party chairman, Billy Nungesser, clapped him on the back and said, "David, you gave the best speech of the evening." Duke also made a favorable impression the next night when he spoke at a public campaign forum sponsored by a local group, the Alliance for Good Government, even though Treen won its endorsement. "You know, I think like he thinks," one woman confided to Altobello after listening to Duke. "But I'm in the closet about it."

When he began his presidential campaign in 1987, Duke had had his face resculpted. When he began the District 81 race, he not only became a Republican but also dropped the anti-Semitic attacks that had played a central role just weeks before during the presidential campaign. But Duke did not make himself over completely. His platform for the District 81 seat featured many of the same racially tinged issues as his presidential campaign: he opposed affirmative action and minority set-aside quota programs, opposed new taxes, called for changing the welfare system to require welfare recipients to work for their benefits, wanted to reduce the illegitimate welfare birthrate, and demanded tougher penalties for criminals.

Duke, though, added one key position to his District 81 platform: opposition to reducing Louisiana's homestead exemption. This was smart politics. The $75,000 homestead exemption was a sacred cow in Louisiana politics because it allowed all but the wealthiest homeowners to escape paying property taxes. Governor Roemer, who was elected on a reform platform in 1987, was taking on the sacred cow. Backed by business groups, which along with wealthy homeowners paid the bulk of property taxes, Roemer was lobbying the state legislature to lower the $75,000 exemption and thus shift the tax burden to middle-income homeowners.

But in trying to reduce the homestead exemption, Roemer was taking on Jefferson Parish's most powerful politician: Lawrence A. Chehardy. Chehardy had been Jefferson Parish's assessor and had won a huge following as the state's most staunch defender of the homestead exemption. Neil Curran, a campaign adviser to Treen in the District 81 race, remembers seeing shoppers mob Chehardy when he visited a local supermarket in Metairie. "People reached for his hand," Curran says, "and looked like they were ready to kneel before him and thank him for protecting their homestead exemption."

In 1989, Chehardy was no longer Jefferson Parish's assessor. His son, Lawrence E. Chehardy, had replaced him. "Big Lawrence," as the father was known, had made sure that "Little Lawrence" at age twenty-two succeeded him in the type of adroit political maneuver that made him Jefferson Parish's most powerful politician. In 1975, Big Lawrence qualified for the assessor's election as usual, and no one dared challenge him. But minutes before the filing deadline, Little Lawrence also qualified. His father then withdrew, which allowed Little Lawrence to win unopposed. Little Lawrence won every succeeding election by steadfastly defending the homestead exemption. Big Lawrence, who was elected to a parish judgeship, continued to wield enormous influence behind the scenes. Duke's opposition to reducing the homestead exemption would discourage the Chehardys from opposing him forcefully.

Duke was elated at the positive response he got at the Republican party meeting on December 5 and at the campaign forum the next night. But after the campaign forum, he told Sandy Emerson, chairman of the Jefferson Parish Republican party and a Treen campaign adviser, "Sandy, I know John will make it into the runoff and would make a good legislator. If you want, I'll come out and support him." When Emerson told Duke that he was about as popular among Treen supporters as a skunk, Duke said, "Maybe I could do it under the table." Emerson told him politely that the Treen camp would discuss the matter during the runoff.

After years in the political wilderness and after having suffered his latest—and most humiliating—political defeat just a month before, Duke began the District 81 race expecting to lose. "David didn't have a positive attitude at the beginning," recalled Debbie Thomas, who was one of Duke's initial campaign aides.

Thomas had been reluctant to talk to Duke when a friend tried to recruit her to be an office manager for his young campaign. She didn't know much about Duke but had heard that he was surrounded by crazed followers. When she walked into his basement office around Christmas 1988, she was hardly reassured. The basement was damp and cold, cluttered with boxes and papers. Old army blankets were strung up against the windows, and Duke used a small gas heater to warm the room. "I'm scared," she told Howie Farrell, Duke's campaign manager. "I'm afraid there are Satanic altars upstairs." Farrell laughed and said she should meet with Duke before making up her mind. She spoke with Duke for several hours, as he laid out his views on the issues and outlined his philosophy of life. Thomas was reassured enough to agree to make some phone calls for him. After she made the last of the calls, she turned toward Duke and said, "I think you're a winner, I think you can win this." He was shocked.

Any one of Duke's opponents could have knocked him out of the race even before he got his campaign off the ground. Election law allowed anyone within ten days of qualifying to challenge candidates' claims that they had lived in the district for a year. Duke had qualified on December 2. As the December 12 deadline loomed, Duke grew nervous. It would take only a quick check to see that he had changed his address to within the district only two weeks before qualifying. But the deadline came and went. No one was taking Duke seriously. Probably the best chance to prevent his election had passed.

Much of Jefferson Parish had been swampland until the 1950s when Interstate 10 was extended to New Orleans and the push to the suburbs began. This process accelerated during the 1960s as whites fled New Orleans in the wake of desegregation rulings. By 1989, New Orleans had gone from a white majority to a 60 percent black majority. Jefferson Parish, meanwhile, had grown to 485,000 residents, only 15,000 fewer than New Orleans, and was 87 percent white. Many Jefferson Parish residents simply did not want to be around blacks. Sheriff Harry Lee, a 300-pound Chinese-American, directed his deputies in 1986 to stop black people in white neighborhoods or any blacks in "rinky dink cars." While Lee was criticized in New Orleans and was forced to rescind the directive, many people in Jefferson Parish cheered him on, and he was reelected the following year in a landslide.

District 81, bounded by New Orleans to the east and Lake Pontchartrain to the north and bisected by Interstate 10, had the largest concentration of whites of any Jefferson Parish legislative district. But while it may have been homogeneous racially, it was divided into three distinct areas economically. Alongside the Metairie Country Club were white-pillared mansions on tree-shaded lanes in an area known as Old Metairie. Across Interstate 10 were working-class bungalows in an area known as Bucktown that had been a fishing village before urban sprawl. The third area in District 81 was on both sides of Interstate 10 and featured 1960s brick houses on low-level land that tended to flood in heavy rains.

Politically, the district had grown increasingly Republican over the past decade. But by 1989, about 55 percent of the district's registered voters were still Democrats. They were Reagan Democrats, however. Reagan won the district overwhelmingly both in 1980 and in 1984, and George Bush did nearly as well in 1988. Cusimano, who represented the district for three terms until being elevated to a judgeship in 1988, was a Democrat turned Republican. District 81 was fertile territory for Duke not only because of residents' views on race but also because of his antiestablishment candidacy. With the oil bust in Louisiana, many of District 81's middle- and lower-income white residents had lost their jobs or seen their income drop. Democrats in the district, especially, were hungry for a candidate willing to shake up the status quo.

Duke kicked off his campaign on December 10 with a rally at the Lion's Club on Metairie Road. The turnout was enthusiastic but small. He had three campaign volunteers. Two of them were former New Orleans policemen, Howie Farrell and Kenny Knight, and the third was a court stenographer and sometime girlfriend, Donna Randall. "We gave ourselves fancy titles—Howie was campaign chairman, Kenny was campaign manager—to make it seem like there were a lot of us," Randall recalls. The odds were long against Duke, but he was game. After all, he had nothing else to do.

Duke spent the next month of his campaign going door to door in the district. This was a smart strategy for any legislative candidate in Louisiana, where the personal touch was still very important. But it was especially important for Duke. He had to make a good personal impression early on with voters both to reverse a negative opinion among those who had heard bad things about him and to inoculate those who knew little about him but could be swayed against him when his racist and anti-Semitic activities were revealed.

Washington Post reporter David Maraniss saw the success of this strategy when he walked with Duke one day during the runoff election. "In a white clapboard house at the corner of Ridgewood and Stroelitz," Maraniss wrote, "lives Earline Pickett, 72, the wife of a retired oil engineer. When Duke came to her door during the campaign, she said, it ranked with the most thrilling moments of her life. 'He's honest, and he's not trying to hide any of his past,' she said. 'He's been open about it, and he just makes you like him. I liked him from way back. That affirmative action, he wants to get rid of it. I think if blacks are not qualified for anything, why should they be given a better chance?'

"Working in the garden of her big gray house on William David Parkway is Sue Wegmann, a teacher who looks and talks like the quintessential baby boomer, concerned about the education of her two children and the quality of the social and cultural life in her community. At first, she declined to discuss her feelings about Duke, saying: 'I can't say it out loud. I also teach'. . . . Eventually, Wegmann revealed that she voted for him [in the primary] and was thinking of doing it again, fully aware of his role in the Klan and the NAAWP. 'I'm more interested in what he'll do than what he's done in the past,' she said. . . . 'It wouldn't influence me one bit what he did in the past.' Wegmann said Duke appealed to her on the issues, too. She cited his opposition to affirmative action and minority set-aside programs and his promise to crack down on what he calls welfare abuse. 'If they are willing to work for it, like us, then they deserve it,' she said. 'But the ones who sit out on their front porch and don't try, that aggravates us.'"

Another typical part of legislative campaigns was putting up candidate yard signs. But signs were especially important to Duke not only to increase his name recognition but, more important, to make him seem more credible. He knew that the more yards that displayed his blue-and-white signs, the more that people would feel comfortable voting for him. He and his dedicated core of campaign volunteers aggressively sought permission to plant yard signs and also put up signs on vacant property. As December wore on, hundreds of Duke yard signs sprouted throughout the district. And the ranks of his volunteers swelled.

As 1989 began, Duke's opponents still were not taking him seriously. Sure, he may be winning the yard sign war, they said, but that only showed he had a core of committed supporters. The latest poll showed him with only 7 percent of the vote, they noted. Treen led with 20 percent, and Delton Charles followed with 13 percent.

Finally, two weeks before the January 21 primary, Charles began to note Duke's looming shadow. Duke may not have been a factor in the polls, but he had too many yard signs to be ignored, Charles thought. Charles ordered up a campaign mailer that emphasized Duke's Klan past. But Charles's advisers argued that he would make the runoff with Treen and that the mailer would only alienate Duke's supporters, whose backing they would need to defeat Treen. Charles killed the proposed mailer. A chance to perhaps fatally wound Duke had passed.

Meanwhile, events in New Orleans were playing into Duke's hands. The city was suffering a record-setting murder a day. Almost all the crime was black on black and resulted from crack drug wars within New Orleans's public housing projects. But the daily headlines in the *Times-Picayune* and reports on local television reminded District 81 residents that only the narrow Seventeenth Street Canal separated them from the crime-filled city they had fled. It also made them receptive to Duke's racially charged message.

On January 16, what was perhaps the climactic moment during the primary campaign occurred. During a parade commemorating the birthday of Dr. Martin Luther King, Jr., on Canal Street in New Orleans, a pack of black hoodlums began punching and kicking pedestrians. Police moved in and restored order, but a local television camera crew captured scenes of white women huddled in fear during the blacks' rampage. The images sent a jolt through whites in the New Orleans area, including residents of District 81. Canal Street, which for years had been the prime shopping thoroughfare in New Orleans, was not even safe in broad daylight.

Even before the incident, Duke had been playing on the racial fears of District 81 residents by blaming the crime spree in New Orleans on welfare and had been warning that the underclass was growing more threatening. Now with the January 16 melee, Duke had a single event that galvanized those fears. Delton Charles, who was watching the news that evening with his wife, Jacquelyn, recognized its effect immediately. "I think we're going to have some trouble with this," he told her. "This is all we need." A poll taken immediately afterward confirmed Charles's fears: Duke had gained ground and was now second behind John Treen.

At the beginning of January, registrar Sam Altobello had predicted a 25 percent turnout of the district's 21,298 registered voters, a typical figure for a special legislative election. But by January 20, the day before the primary, he was predicting a 40 percent turnout. In fact, it was 54 percent. Treen campaign adviser Sandy Emerson was attending an inaugural ball for President Bush in Washington, D.C., on the night of the primary. Normally, Emerson would have been caught up in the revelry. But as she watched Bush's campaign manager, Lee Atwater, celebrate Bush's victory by playing guitar on the ballroom stage, she kept thinking to herself: "I've got to get to a phone and find out what happened in the District 81 election."

The ballroom was so packed that Emerson, dressed in a long gown, could barely move. Finally, she spied a policeman, and he led her to a bank of pay telephones. She called the Treen headquarters.

"Sandy you won't believe this," a dejected Treen told her. "I'm in the runoff but with David Duke, and he ran first."

"You're kidding," she replied. "It can't be."

"I'm not kidding," Treen said. "You better believe it."

Emerson rushed back to the ballroom to tell her friends from Louisiana. They could not believe that Duke had run first either, and they kept asking her if she was sure that she had really talked to Treen.

Jim Donelon, Treen's campaign coordinator, was clad in a tuxedo and serving as master of ceremonies for the Atlas Mardi Gras supper dance in New Orleans that evening. About 8:20 P.M., he ducked away to call Treen for election returns.

"We made the runoff," Treen told him. "But guess what? Duke ran first by a mile."

"Hold on," Donelon advised him. "You're going on a four-week ride like you've never been on before."

Duke led with 33 percent, while Treen trailed with 19 percent. The two would square off in the February 18 runoff. Charles was third with 17 percent, while the other four candidates split the remaining 31 percent.

Duke's candidacy had increased interest in the January 21 primary, both within and outside District 81. But his first-place primary finish changed the stakes dramatically. Over the next twenty-eight days, the once quiet special election in Metairie would become the most closely followed state legislative campaign in memory. President Bush and former President Reagan would weigh in, reporters from throughout the United States and overseas would camp out in Metairie, and David Duke—who only weeks before had run for president in obscurity—would launch his political star.

When Jim Donelon went to bed on the night of the primary, he thought Treen was in good shape. Duke had run first, but he was such an extremist candidate that anyone who would support him already had, Donelon figured.

The next morning, he read the precinct breakdown of the election returns. As he showered, he mulled over the results and realized he had been too optimistic the night before: Delton Charles had run strong in the areas where blue-collar Democrats lived. "Those voters are Duke-prone," Donelon said to himself. That morning, Treen and his top advisers met at campaign head-quarters at the Metairie Village Shopping Center on Metairie Road. After a heated discussion, they settled on a campaign strategy for the runoff: attack Duke at every opportunity as a dangerous extremist and emphasize his neo-Nazi activities. "People knew he'd been a Klansman, but that's all," Neil Curran, a campaign adviser, recalled two years later.

Lance Hill and Beth Rickey, two Tulane University graduate students researching Duke's past for the Treen campaign, stepped up their work. "We decided to bludgeon him with negative media," Curran says, "and treat him like a disease—no debates. It's very hard to look at Duke, listen to him and think he's a radical Nazi anti-Christ. He looks too charming. And appearing with him gives him credibility." When Curran visited the campaign office the next day, however, Treen told him offhandedly that he had agreed to appear at a campaign forum that week with Duke. Curran blew up.

"John, we agreed to no debates," Curran reminded him.

"It's not a debate, it's a forum," Treen explained. "And I've already agreed to go."

"John, you can't go," Curran said.

"Don't worry," Treen said. "I can handle him."

Of the five other candidates Duke could have faced, he could not have chosen a better opponent than Treen. The silver-haired Treen, who turned sixty-three during the campaign, was haughty and stubborn. His campaign advisers implored him to get out and knock on doors. But he preferred to remain at his headquarters, especially when reporters from *Time* magazine, the *New York Times*, and other out-of-state newspapers sought interviews.

At the same time, Treen was weighed down with political baggage. He had managed to offend nearly all of Jefferson Parish's important politicians for one reason or another in recent years, so they were in no rush to help him defeat Duke. Most significantly, Treen had earned Big Lawrence Chehardy's enmity by coauthoring a 1986 letter sent to Henson Moore, a Republican congressman running for the Senate. The letter denounced Chehardy and warned Moore against seeking his support for his candidacy. Moore not only ignored the advice but read the letter to Chehardy. Sheriff Harry Lee summed it up best when he assessed the two candidates. The runoff election, Lee said, was "a choice between a bigot and an asshole."

The first campaign forum with Treen and Duke came five days after the primary. It was held at the Old Metairie Public Library, and as Curran had feared, Duke emerged the winner. Duke's loyalists arrived early and took most of the 120 seats, so he appeared to have more support when he was cheered more enthusiastically. Duke, who had honed his speaking style during hundreds of radio and TV appearances dating to the 1974 "Tomorrow" show, also simply looked and sounded better than Treen, who tended to pontificate.

C. B. Forgotston, a business lobbyist and Treen campaign adviser, was among the crowd of people outside the packed forum at the library, unable to get in. As he was standing there, he spied a former classmate from LSU pull up to drop off a library book.

"What's going on?" the friend asked.

"There's a debate between Treen and Duke," Forgotston explained. "I'm with the campaign."

"Yeah, I voted for him."

Forgotston assumed he meant Treen. After all, the friend was a nice guy from a good background and was college educated. But something the friend added caused Forgotston to quickly interject a question.

"You mean, you voted for Treen. Right?"

"No, I voted for Duke."

"You're kidding," a dumbfounded Forgotston said.

"No. The guy knocked on my door and I liked what he had to say. I'm not going to put up a yard sign or anything like that. But I'm going to vote for him again."

As the friend drove off, Forgotston got a sinking feeling in his stomach.

"From then on, I knew we were in trouble," he says. "He was the kind of guy we needed on our side to win."

For many people, the Treen-Duke race was a choice between good and evil. One of the people who cast the election in this light was New Orleans Archbishop Philip Hannan, who for years had worked to improve the lot of blacks in New Orleans. At seventy-five, due to retire four days before the election, Hannan felt that a Duke victory represented everything he had fought against in his lifetime. He resolved to speak out publicly, knowing that his words carried great weight in the heavily Catholic area. But Hannan's position in the church put him in a difficult position. He believed strongly that the church should not endorse candidates in a political race, but he thought he had to take a moral stand against Duke. Hannan's solution was not to endorse Treen but to write a statement and ask his parish priests in District 81 to read it during services on January 29. The message was clear: "The election will determine the convictions of the voters of the district about the basic dignity of persons, the recognition of human rights of every person, the equality of races made by Divine Providence." Hannan was not the only influential Catholic leader in New Orleans to warn against Duke. The Reverend James Carter, president of Loyola University in New Orleans, mailed 783 letters to Loyola alumni living in or near District 81. Carter did not mention Duke by name but attacked the NAAWP.

Treen got another boost shortly after the primary when florist Roger Villere, who had finished fifth, attorney Ron Courtade, who had finished sixth, and engineering consultant Bobby Savoie, who had finished last, endorsed him. Villere and Savoie, in particular, did not need much persuading—Duke spooked both of them. Villere felt he had been followed in the final days of the primary campaign by cars with out-of-state licenses, and he had received obscene phone calls from women in the middle of the night. He suspected Duke was behind both ploys. Duke also seemed to appear mysteriously whenever Villere was talking with a group of people. During the final two weeks of the primary, Villere would not walk door to door unless accompanied by an off-duty sheriff's deputy, who was a friend. Savoie also thought he was being watched and followed during the primary campaign by Duke supporters.

Duke visited Savoie at home several days after the primary to try to win his backing. They talked for three hours. During the first part of the discussion, Duke laid out standard political arguments in explaining why he was the best candidate. But the more they talked, the more Duke veered into topics that made Savoie uneasy. Duke told Savoie that the bone structure and skull of black people were more apelike than those of whites and that this helped explain why blacks were intellectually inferior to whites but better suited for manual labor. Duke also laid out his theories of how American Jews used money and the power of the media to control the United States on behalf of Israel. "You know those people who give you a shiver down your spine," Savoie said as he recalled the conversation a few weeks later. "David is one of those people."

While Villere, Savoie, and Courtade backed Treen, Delton Charles and the fourth place candidate, bingo hall operator Budd Olister, stayed neutral. The Treen campaign suspected that both were acting on orders of their political patrons. The Chehardys had backed Charles in the primary, while Sheriff Lee had endorsed Olister and, getting word from his deputies of Duke's popularity, did not want to offend his supporters. Not only did the Chehardys dislike Treen for writing the 1986 letter denouncing Big Lawrence, but Treen was unwilling to take the pledge to defend the homestead exemption at all costs. Treen said that he was willing to let Louisiana voters reduce the homestead exemption if they voted in favor of it in a referendum election. Meanwhile, the small Jewish population in not only District 81 but the entire metropolitan New Orleans area was aghast at the prospect of a Duke victory. The Jews were contributing heavily to Treen's campaign and began pressuring Little Lawrence, with whom they had close ties, to endorse Treen.

Just after returning from a ski vacation in Colorado, Little Lawrence agreed to meet with Treen. It was a week before the runoff election. Before Treen left for Chehardy's townhouse, Neil Curran beseeched him to switch his position on the homestead exemption and to promise to defend it. "Your position could cost you the election," Curran advised. Treen was unmoved. "I'm not going to kiss his ass," he said as he left. Chehardy endorsed Treen the next day. Not only was it less than the ringing endorsement the Treen camp hoped for, but it was given in such grudging terms that it may have hurt Treen. "It was the most damaging endorsement that I've ever seen given for a candidate," Treen says. "It said he had to support me only because my opponent was a monster."

Jews had been helping Treen quietly, not wanting to become an issue in the campaign. They lost their anonymity three weeks before the runoff when Mordechai Levy thrust himself into the campaign uninvited. Levy was head of the Jewish Defense Organization, a New York-based Jewish-rights group that trains members in self-defense and advanced weaponry. On January 24, Levy announced he was coming to New Orleans to oppose Duke. Levy vowed to "meet force with force" and said, "We will do everything we can to destroy the David Duke campaign. If anyone brings about bloodshed, it's the foolish people who voted for someone who wants to put me in a gas chamber." The incendiary statement incensed local rabbis, who immediately distanced themselves from Levy, fearful that he was playing into Duke's hands. Jane Buchsbaum, a local Jewish leader, called Levy and begged him not to come. He refused her request.

When Levy arrived two weeks later, television cameras met him at the New Orleans airport, and local news stations played up his visit to the dismay of not only Jewish leaders but the Treen campaign as well. Over the next four days, Levy spoke at sparsely attended events, but local news stations repeatedly broadcast his fierce denunciations of Duke. This gave Duke a nightly forum to profess his horror of racism and anti-Semitism and to re-state his political platform. Next to Levy, he looked and sounded like a level-headed moderate.

Television was especially important for Duke. His crisp sound bites came across particularly well on local news stations, which were now broadcasting stories on the campaign virtually every night. TV reporters invariably asked Duke about his Klan past, but having heard the question so many times before, he had a ready answer and then quickly segued into a sound bite on a hot-button issue. The TV reporters, who rarely had the time or the incli-nation to do the necessary research, were unprepared to ask follow-up ques-tions that would elicit more than a canned response. As a result, Duke used TV to get his message out to voters. He went on TV at every opportunity, doing dozens of local and national media interviews during the runoff. To supplement the free exposure, he also taped a thirty-minute television ad that, like the spot in the presidential election, featured Duke answering friendly questions from an attractive woman.

In the meeting the Treen campaign held the day after the primary, a con-sensus emerged that Duke's first place finish and the intense interest this was already sparking was too much for a team assembled to handle what was supposed to be a quiet little special election. So they decided to ask for reinforcements in the form of three staffers from the Republican National Committee. The RNC was eager to help: defeating Duke would help dimin-ish charges that the party was racist, a charge most recently provoked by the Willie Horton television ad during the 1988 presidential campaign.

Treen's advisers knew they had to downplay the role of the RNC to avoid accusations that they were letting outsiders influence the election. When RNC Chairman Lee Atwater proposed a trip to New Orleans to blast Duke, the Treen campaign demurred. But Treen's advisers nevertheless made a fateful decision: to wheel in the two biggest guns in the Republican party, Ronald Reagan and George Bush. Reagan, who had stepped down as presi-dent two weeks before, cut a radio ad "for my good friend John Treen."

Reagan did not mention Duke but instead extolled Treen's "good reputation" and his defense of the "traditional values and principles which you and I cherish."

Bush weighed in with a letter to residents in the district. He cited Treen's "strong sense of compassion for others and an abiding faith in the future of America."

The involvement of two presidents in a local legislative campaign was unprecedented and created a backlash, which Duke fed by portraying himself as the honest man taking on the powers that be. "It has to be political favors being called in," he told voters. "It's like the establishment is closing the ranks to prevent an independent from coming through." Dan Beck, one of the RNC staffers, could feel the backlash set in during the final days of the campaign. "When I went to little cafes," he said, "I could hear people parroting Duke."

Treen media consultant Neil Curran, acting on the strategy devised at the meeting the day after the primary, had spent long hours preparing two four-page tabloid pamphlets. They were mailed to all households in District 81 in the final days of the campaign. "The Unmasking of David Duke," they were entitled. Using information dug up by Lance Hill and Beth Rickey, the mailers featured photos of Duke at Klan meetings and during the 1970 protest against William Kunstler where he wore a swastika and a Nazi uniform. The mailers also included numerous racist and anti-Semitic statements made by Duke over the years and the map the *NAAWP News* published in 1984 that divided the country by ethnic group.

Curran was excited when the mailers went out, confident that Duke's own words would sink him. They did not. Duke's strategy of looking and sounding respectable had already had too strong an impact. "People didn't believe the tabloids," says Curran. "They said: 'It can't be true. It must be a smear campaign.'" Meanwhile, Duke and his supporters were quietly carrying out a smear campaign of their own. Treen's older brother, Paul, was emotionally disturbed and had once been accused of molesting a child. In the final days of the campaign, Duke supporters warned voters against Treen "the child molester." The Treen campaign quickly got word of what was happening and discussed whether to call a press conference to rebut the rumors. But John and David Treen squelched the idea. Their elderly mother was unaware of the accusation against their brother, and they feared she would hear about it if they aired it publicly in issuing denials.

On the Thursday and Friday before the Saturday runoff, Treen could feel the tide running against him. He blames the child molester rumor. "People began refusing to shake my hand," he says. "One guy glared at me and said,

'I'd never vote for someone like you.' Another said: 'I won't vote for a man with your record.'"

In December when Duke announced to supporters that he planned to run for the vacated District 81 seat, he wrote that "winning this election could break the dike and set loose a flood of White activism and political involvement. It would be a proverbial 'shot heard round the world.'"

Now in the final days before the February 18 runoff, as he realized that he might fulfill this prophecy, he stepped up his already-feverish pace. Subsisting on three or four hours of sleep a night and a handful of Vitamin C pills, he continued to campaign throughout the district. When he walked in Mardi Gras parades in Jefferson Parish, parade goers stuffed his pockets with hundreds of dollars of cash. Meanwhile, the pair of black loafers Duke had been wearing since the beginning of the campaign were falling apart, but he insisted on continuing to wear what he called his "lucky shoes." On the night before the election, his staff had to glue the sole with Elmer's Glue and cover the glue with black shoe polish.

Duke spent much of election day at the district's busiest intersection, Bonnabel and Veterans Memorial Boulevards. Standing on a median strip along with dozens of sign-waving supporters, he exhorted passing drivers to vote for him. A smaller contingent of Treen supporters waved signs and tried, less successfully, to drum up enthusiasm for their candidate.

Treen's inner circle felt that the higher the turnout, the better their chances of winning, since Duke's voters were believed to be more committed. If turnout was 75 percent, they felt, they would win the election. Turnout, in fact, was 78 percent—double the percentage in a normal Louisiana House election.

After the polls closed at 8:00 P.M., Duke went to the First Parish Court in Metairie to watch the election returns come in. For a time it looked like he was going to lose. Campaign manager Howie Farrell took him outside at one point to prepare him to accept the defeat. But shortly after they came back in, the tide turned in their favor. By 9:00 P.M., Duke was leading by 299 votes. Only one of the thirty-four precincts was missing. Duke thought he had won. But he waited restlessly by the computer to be sure. Finally, the numbers popped up onto the screen. Treen had won the precinct—but by only seventy-two votes. The final result was:

| Duke | 8,459 | 50.7 percent |
| Treen | 8,232 | 49.3 percent |

The shot heard round the world was fired. After years of defeats and ostracization, Duke could claim legitimacy as a state representative. Duke ran down the courthouse hallway, madly punching his father's phone number into a portable phone. "Dad, I won!" he shouted.

He jumped into a limousine and headed for the Lions Club Hall on Metairie Road, scene of his runoff-night party. The turnout had been small for the primary-night party. But this evening, not only was the Lions Club packed with people, but hundreds more spilled into the parking lot. Word spread in the hall that Duke had defeated Treen, but the news was too good to be entirely believed. When Duke arrived at the hall, he stood before a microphone, smiled, and announced the outcome.

"I just talked to the clerk of court," Duke said, as the crowd waited expectantly. "And we won." Thunderous cheers shook the building. Duke made his way outside and climbed atop the trunk of a sheriff's squad car. As a light mist fell, the yells and whistles of support grew louder and louder. Smiling broadly, he pumped his fists in the air and gave thumbs up. "Duke! Duke! Duke!" the crowd chanted.

Two weeks later, Duke was in Chicago to speak at the Populist party's annual meeting. As the party's standard-bearer in November, Duke before the Metairie runoff victory had agreed to attend the convention. But after defeating Treen, he tried to opt out. Duke had been elected as a Republican and wanted to distance himself from the Populists and from his own racist and anti-Semitic activities. But Populist party leaders pressured him to come to Chicago, noting that they had been his longtime friends and had contributed thousands of dollars to his state legislative campaign. They also warned that Duke risked censure among his supporters in the white supremacy movement if he immediately turned his back on the Populists.

Duke was in a difficult position. He was no longer just the leader of the white supremacists but a rising political star. His election had been front-page news across the country and won him appearances on the national morning talk shows, CNN's "Crossfire" and ABC's "Nightline." But instead of washing away questions about his past, his election only intensified them. At a press conference the day after his victory, he faced such a barrage of questions about previous anti-Semitic statements that he cut short the session. His extremist activities had also prompted a move to prevent him from being seated in the Louisiana House of Representatives on the grounds that he had not fulfilled the state Constitution requirement to have lived in the district for a year. But on a 69–33 vote, the house agreed to seat him after an influential Democratic legislator advised his colleagues not to thwart the will of District 81 voters. That night as he walked into a Baton Rouge restaurant, the crowd stood up and applauded. Duke agreed to go to Chicago.

One of the people attending the Populist Convention was Beth Rickey, who had investigated Duke's background for Treen's campaign. Rickey, however, was attending the convention incognito in an attempt to confirm her suspicions that Duke had not changed as he claimed. Rickey had to survive several nervewracking moments in passing herself off as a member of the Populist party to gain entrance. A guard at the door blocked her, asking whether she was a reporter.

She denied it indignantly. When a second guard eyed her suspiciously, she threw him off by acting like she knew him.

"How are you?" she gushed. "Haven't seen you in a while." The guard, confused and too embarrassed to admit that he didn't know her, let her pass.

But Rickey had another anxious moment. As she walked into the meeting room at the Bismarck Hotel in Chicago, the tape recorder tucked into the skirt hidden underneath her coat was beginning to slip. If it fell to the floor, she might be discovered after all. She reached the nearest chair just in time to secure the tape recorder.

Rickey grew nervous as she scanned the 150 people at the Populist party convention. To her right was a group of skinheads, conspicuous with their shaved heads and black boots. To her left was a man wearing what appeared to be a brownshirt uniform. At the podium, the speaker was ranting and raving about the Japanese when he suddenly stopped to say he had been informed that infiltrators from the Anti-Defamation League, the Populists' sworn enemy, were in the room. As Rickey sat uneasily, the speaker pointed to the skinheads and said they would take care of any ADL spies. The tension was broken when Duke came to the podium. The Populists stood and applauded, greeting him like a returning hero. "We all did it!" Duke greeted the cheering throng.

He may have run as a Republican, but he still viewed the Populists as his comrades in arms. "We have started something in a small little race in Louisiana," he said. "If I can do it, with the political machine against me now, with my character savaged for weeks on end to every resident in my district, if I can beat the president of the United States, a former president of the United States, if I can overcome the organized religious leaders in the area, if we can overcome tremendous spending by the opposition, ladies and gentlemen, you can do the same thing. . . . And the reason why I chose to work with the Republican party in this election was because that's where so many of our people are. . . . But let me tell you something, ladies and gentlemen, I am a Republican, but I am and always will be a Populist Republican."

Duke had barred reporters from his speech, not wanting them to capture his continuing embrace with the white supremacist Populists. Instead, he held a press conference in a separate room afterward. Reporters asked Duke several questions about the Populists, but he deflected the queries by concentrating on his victorious race in Louisiana as a Republican. It appeared that Duke's apprehension about appearing with the Populists was unfounded. But then disaster struck.

To provide security for the meeting, the Populists had recruited a group of Klansmen, who in turn had sought the help of Art Jones. Jones, a Chicago resident, was the no-holds-barred vice chairman of the American Nazi party. As he ushered Duke into the press conference room, a photographer snapped a picture of them shaking hands. Chicago television reporter Michael Kirsch had been tipped off about Jones. As the press conference was ending, Kirsch pointed to Jones and asked Duke why he was associating with a Nazi. As Duke fumbled for an answer, Jones shoved Kirsch and shouted, "You creep!" In the tumult, Duke was hustled out of the room. But the damage had been done. Not only was the incident carried on Chicago television but the photograph of Jones and Duke shaking hands went out over the Associated Press wire along with a news story.

Duke immediately sought to contain the fallout. When the house met two days later, he told his colleagues that he had not known Jones but had been the victim of a "smear" campaign by the media to discredit him. Jones in a later interview confirmed that the two had not met, although he said he thought that Duke knew of him since Jones had long been active in the Nazi party. Either way, the incident reminded legislators and the public of Duke's extremist activities—activities that he was trying to get them to forget. Rickey a week later gave reporters the tape of Duke's Chicago speech, which prompted additional news reports that Duke was still cozy with the Populists.

During the Metairie campaign, Duke's powerful message had overwhelmed questions about his racism and anti-Semitism. Now, to put the Jones incident behind him, Duke had to shift attention from his extremist activities to his issues. Luck was on his side. Duke had been elected as Governor Buddy Roemer convened a special legislative session to consider his tax-restructuring proposal that would shift the tax burden from corporations to middle-income people. The legislature on March 7 approved the measure. But to become law, it required the approval of Louisiana voters. The election was set for April 29. Duke had his hot-button issue.

Over the next month, Roemer stumped the state for the tax plan, warning that failure to approve the measure would force cuts in teacher pay, in health care for the poor, and in spending for state universities. He was backed by the state's major newspapers, largest corporations, and biggest civic groups. Duke took the lead in opposing the tax plan. He dogged Roemer throughout the state, portraying himself as the defender of the little guy who was paying too much in taxes—while the government wasted money and large corporations escaped taxation. When Duke at one rally asked the crowd if they wanted to pay more taxes, they shouted "no!" When he bashed Jim Bob Moffett, a Roemer backer who headed the Fortune 500 company Freeport-McMoRan, Incorporated, calling him "Jim God Profit," the crowd hooted and hollered.

The crowds for Duke were small at first but grew steadily larger as election day neared. He drew four times as many people as Roemer when both spoke in Shreveport on April 21. On election day, eight days later, the measure was defeated 55 percent to 45 percent. It was a big victory for the newly elected state legislator. Not only had Duke helped torpedo the measure, but he had gained credibility as an effective spokesman of the overburdened taxpayer. His antitax campaign also laid the foundation for a statewide movement of supporters.

The initiative campaign showed Duke at his best—on the campaign stump, tapping into whites' frustration by denouncing special interests and a government that he said was concerned more with helping undeserving people on welfare than with the "hard-working, taxpaying middle-class." As a legislator in actually trying to put his ideas into law, however, he was far less successful. When Duke was elected, he knew nothing about being a legislator—the process in which bills were considered in committee hearings, the rules for debate on the House floor, that he would receive money for overhead and to hire a legislative assistant. Worried that he would be taken advantage of, his staff made him watch "Mr. Smith Goes to Washington"—a popular 1930s movie about a freshman congressman who successfully takes on the entrenched interests.

Duke did not even know his way around the state capitol. Aide Debbie Thomas during his first week in Baton Rouge had to pin his schedule to the inside of his suit jacket. When Duke got lost, he would call her. With a map of the capitol in hand, she would tell Duke how to get to his next meeting: "David, go down that hallway, turn right . . ."

Thomas also made Duke buy new clothes. He owned only two polyester jackets and several pairs of pants—cheap-looking attire that his staff abhorred. After years of living on the fringe, Duke had so much to learn, Thomas thought.

During his first legislative session, Duke introduced nine bills. All aimed at reducing government benefits to convicted drug users or repealing programs he considered anti-white. Duke's bills sought to:

* raise penalties on drug offenders who lived in public housing projects
* repeal affirmative action programs; repeal minority set-aside programs
* require drug testing of teenage drivers license applicants
* require drug testing for recipients of welfare and Medicaid.

Duke's bills had strong surface appeal. Who wanted to have their tax dollars go to drug users? If discrimination against blacks was wrong, was it not equally wrong against whites? If firemen and policemen have to be tested for drugs, why not welfare recipients? Duke repeatedly emphasized these themes. Of the nine bills that he introduced, four were approved by a house committee, the first of four steps before a bill was adopted by the legislature. But all four were killed on the house floor or by the senate.

Conservative legislators had proposed bills like Duke's in previous years. But measures like repealing affirmative action had usually been defeated without much fuss. When Duke introduced his bills in 1989, his notoriety ensured them a much greater hearing and put pressure on legislators representing overwhelmingly white-majority districts to go along with Duke. But his notoriety was a double-edged sword. Some lawmakers voted against his bills, even if they favored them, because they were jealous of the publicity that the newly elected legislator received. Other potential supporters opposed his measures because of his racist and anti-Semitic activities.

But more important, every time that Duke made headway, an incident occurred that reminded legislators of his extremist activities. In March, there was the Populist party convention and Art Jones. Then, in June, Duke was confronted by a Holocaust survivor in the state capitol in Baton Rouge at an exhibit entitled, "The Courage to Remember: The Holocaust, 1933–45." The exhibit, sponsored by the Simon Wiesenthal Center, was mounted in the capitol rotunda, which adjoins the chamber of the house of representatives. The gruesome photographs had been placed there because of Duke's election.

Duke undoubtedly knew that the exhibit could mean trouble for him, but having argued for years that the Holocaust was a myth, he could not stay away. As a crowd gathered to hear a speech opening the exhibit, he left the house chamber and circled the reporters and cameramen recording the event. Anne Levy, a small woman who had come to the capitol from New Orleans for the event, saw him out of the corner of her eye. The image of the tall, blond man holding his hands behind his back and inspecting the photos triggered an unwanted memory: the way that German officers had stood when they watched Jews standing in lines during World War II. Levy had lived in the Warsaw Ghetto and had survived the Nazi genocide by going into hiding with her mother, father, and sister. But both her father's and mother's parents and most of their brothers and sisters had perished at the hands of the Nazis. Levy walked up to Duke. "What are you doing here?" she demanded. "I thought you said this never happened."

Duke stared ahead at the photographs without replying. "I thought you said this never happened," she repeated. Without looking at her, he said, "I never said it never happened, I just said it was exaggerated."

"Get out of here!" Levy said angrily. Duke turned and walked quickly into the house chamber. He did not return to the exhibit. But word quickly spread of the incident. A day later, he became embroiled in another controversy, this time courtesy of Beth Rickey. She and Lance Hill, a Tulane doctoral student who had researched Duke's background for the Treen campaign, had wondered whether Duke was still selling racist and Nazi books after his election. Duke sold most of the books by mail through the *NAAWP News*, but visitors to the NAAWP's office in his basement could also purchase books there. Hill and Rickey hatched a plan. Rickey would visit Duke's legislative office, which was also in his basement, and ask to buy books offered on the *NAAWP News* "Suppressed Books" list. No one in Duke's office knew what she looked like.

Over a three-day period in May, Rickey and a private detective bought *The Turner Diaries, Mein Kampf, The Myth of the Six Million, Imperium, The New Mythology of Equality*, and a cassette of American Nazi commander George Lincoln Rockwell in a debate with an NAACP official. On June 7, she held a press conference in the state capitol to reveal that Duke was still selling racist and Nazi books. "Duke has not changed his stripes," Rickey said. When Duke emerged from a committee meeting room shortly afterward, New Orleans television reporter Robyn Ekings waved one of the books in his face and, with the camera rolling, asked, "Are you selling this out of your legislative office?"

Duke froze. "Who gave you that book?" he asked excitedly. Ekings pointed to Rickey.

"What are you trying to do to me?" he shouted. "You're treating me like Salman Rushdie!"

He hurried away, with camera crews and reporters in hot pursuit until he reached the floor of the house of representatives, which is off limits for the press. When he had a chance to formulate a response shortly afterward, Duke said that he had recently stopped ordering the books and that Rickey had simply purchased a few of the ones remaining in stock. "I don't want to handle books of a controversial nature anymore," he said. "I want to get rid of anything that distracts from my agenda."

Rickey had wounded Duke. "Everybody went, 'Well, that proves he hasn't changed his colors,'" said Republican state representative Quentin Dastugue, who represented a Metairie district adjoining Duke's. Beth Rickey had emerged as Duke's most vociferous critic. And in an extraordinary effort over the next four months, Duke would try to win her over to his racial theories with a barrage of late-night phone calls and luncheon dates. Rickey said later of her time with Duke that she thought she was living in "the twilight zone."

Rickey was an unlikely person to become Duke's biggest nemesis. She was an academic, not an activist, and had never sought the spotlight before. A dyed-in-the-wool Republican from Lafayette, Rickey cried when President Richard Nixon resigned in 1974 and was an alternate delegate for Ronald Reagan at both the 1980 and 1984 Republican party national conventions. She had not complained when first Reagan and then George Bush carried out campaign tactics branded racist by critics, such as Bush's use of black rapist Willie Horton during 1988 to portray Michael Dukakis as soft on crime. In 1989, she was thirty-two, pursuing her doctorate at Tulane and a member of the Republican state central committee representing a portion of New Orleans.

But while Rickey condoned the Republicans' race-tinged campaign strategies, she could not accept a former Klansman and neo-Nazi in her party. Her family history may explain why. Her great-grandfather had been sheriff of St. Helena Parish in the late 1800s and had once held off a mob of Klan supporters wanting to lynch a black man accused of raping a white woman. Her great-grandfather had his twelve-year-old son hide the black man under a bale of hay and transport him by wagon in the middle of the night to the next parish so that he could receive a fair trial. To Rickey, the Klan was not the upholder of southern tradition, as Duke believed, but a terrorist organization. Rickey also had a special dislike of Nazis. Her father had served under General Patton during World War II and had helped liberate a concentration camp. Before he died when she was ten, he told her stories of the concentration camp victims, whose only crime, he emphasized to her, was to be Jewish. These stories left an indelible imprint on her, as David Duke was to find out.

Immediately after Duke's election, Lee Atwater, the chairman of the Republican National Committee, denounced him as a racist and anti-Semite and said Duke would receive no assistance from the RNC. But confronting Duke was a tricky proposition for the Republican party. The GOP had built a conservative presidential majority over the past generation in large part by playing the race card. This conservative majority was built on disaffected middle-class and working-class whites—particularly in the South—who had been Democrats. It was Alabama governor George Wallace who showed Republicans how to win over these whites. In the 1968 presidential election, Wallace played on the feelings of whites who saw themselves as victims and being displaced by both the black struggle for civil rights and by social upheaval. Wallace told whites that a Democratic establishment comprised of unelected judges, the liberal media, elitist professors, and faceless government bureaucrats wanted to raise their taxes, coddle dangerous criminals, and force their children to ride buses to attend schools far away from home.

Richard Nixon also pursued a race strategy in the 1968 campaign, but he staked out more of a middle ground. Nixon realized that a growing majority of whites now opposed withholding from blacks the right to vote, attend public schools and live where they wanted solely because of their skin color. So Nixon endorsed racial equality, but he—like Wallace—attacked the way the government and the courts enforced civil rights statutes. In 1968, Nixon and Wallace won a combined 57 percent of the vote. Pitted against a liberal Democrat in 1972, Senator George McGovern, Nixon strengthened the Republicans' hold on discontented whites and swept to victory.

After Watergate and the election of Jimmy Carter, a southern Democrat, in 1976, the Republicans pieced together their conservative majority again in 1980 behind Ronald Reagan and his antigovernment, antiwelfare, antiliberal, law-and-order candidacy. There were explosive forces nationally behind Reagan's strong showing: incomes were stagnating, the number of manufacturing jobs was declining, welfare rolls were rising, crime was skyrocketing, drug use was climbing, the number of illegitimate babies was soaring, taxes were rising because inflation pushed people into higher tax brackets. Middle-class whites, in particular, were paying more taxes for a government that they felt was providing less in return.

At the same time, the government was aggressively pursuing programs like affirmative action and minority set-asides, which sought to redress a history of discrimination by giving preferences to blacks. "The most aggressive efforts to provide jobs for blacks were directed at the most besieged white Democratic constituencies: the building-trades unions and police and fire departments," wrote Thomas Byrne Edsall and Mary Edsall in a May 1991 *Atlantic Monthly* article. "White men working as carpenters, plumbers, sheet-metal workers, iron workers, steamfitters, cops and firemen became the focus of the anti-discrimination drive waged by the Civil Rights Division of the Justice Department."

So while whites continued to support the principle of racial equality, they were turning on affirmative action and minority set-asides, believing that these programs put them at an unfair disadvantage during a time when it was increasingly difficult to find good jobs at good wages. By a 62 to 38 percent margin, whites in one 1980 poll said the "government should just let everyone get ahead on his own" rather than guarantee employment. (Blacks split in the opposite direction by a 70–30 margin, believing that it was the responsibility of government to provide jobs.)

In 1988, George Bush used a potent race symbol of his own to help defeat Massachusetts governor Michael Dukakis: a black convicted murderer named Willie Horton who raped a white woman while on a Massachusetts furlough program. "Republican strategists correctly perceived that the furlough of Willie Horton epitomized an evolution of the far-reaching rights movement and of post-war liberalism, an evolution that was resented and disapproved of by significant numbers of voters who saw crime as existing on a continuum with other social and moral problems aggravated by liberalism," the Edsalls wrote in their 1991 book, *Chain Reaction: The Impact of Race, Rights, and Taxes on American Politics*, from which the *Atlantic Monthly* article was excerpted.

So while Lee Atwater in 1989 attacked Duke because of his Klan past, Louisiana Republicans, whose neighbors and white constituents liked Duke's right-wing populist message, were more ambivalent about him. All but three of the eighteen Republican members of the state house voted to seat him after his election in February 1989, and Louisiana party leaders dismissed suggestions that they prohibit him from joining the Republican legislative caucus. State representative Emile (Peppi) Bruneau, chairman of the caucus, helped Duke shape his bills and taught him parliamentary procedure. When asked why he was helping Duke, Bruneau said that Duke was no different from anyone else and that he tried to help all Republican lawmakers. After Duke was elected, the caucus newsletter featured a photograph and short profile of him that omitted his Klan past, saying only, "He ran on a conservative platform." Duke would repeatedly point to the newsletter profile and his good standing in the Republican caucus to blunt charges that he was an extremist. "I'm an accepted member of the Republican legislative caucus," he would say. "They vote for my bills."

Billy Nungesser, chairman of the Louisiana Republican party, denounced Duke after his election as "rotten to the core." But he refused to freeze Duke out of the party. Nungesser said that he had not seen Duke endorse racism or anti-Semitism since switching to the Republican party. "I don't think it's the role of the Republican Party to repudiate Duke for things he did as a Democrat," Nungesser said. He also said he feared that attacking Duke would give him undue publicity.

Beth Rickey dismissed that fear. In researching Duke for the Treen campaign, she not only came to appreciate his intense hatred for Jews and blacks but also saw how effectively he won media attention. She thought the Louisiana Republican party had to take a stand and formally disassociate itself from him. "We have a moral responsibility to speak out," Rickey said. "We have a Nazi in our midst. If Duke is not confronted, he'll go on and gain legitimacy. He is blurring the line between racists and conservatives. David Duke has no place in the Republican Party."

In late May, just after she began buying the white supremacist books from his legislative office, Rickey submitted a motion to Nungesser for the upcoming meeting of the 140-member Republican state central committee, calling for the body to investigate Duke. Nungesser immediately called her, said he would squash the motion, and added that it would just give Duke publicity.

Rickey responded that she might still go ahead with her motion. But under pressure from Nungesser and other state Republican leaders, some of whom liked Duke because they thought he would prompt Democrats to change parties, she backed down at the June 3 meeting in the chamber of the house of representatives. Reporters on hand to cover the potential fight were left with no story. But it was a memorable day for Rickey because she met Duke for the first time.

Duke had gotten word that Rickey was pushing the motion to investigate him, so he attended the Republican state central committee meeting even though he was not a member. He was just learning about Rickey. Only two days before, he had asked in an interview whether she was white or black. When Duke came up to her in the house chamber, Rickey was sitting with John Treen. When Treen refused to shake his hand, they got in a heated discussion. "You're a lying, character-assassinating son of a bitch," Treen told him as Rickey hurried off. A few minutes later, Duke hurried after her. "Hi, I'm David Duke," he said when he reached her. Rickey was holding a copy of *Mein Kampf* in her right hand and had to shift the book to her other hand to shake Duke's. "You know, I never had seen Art Jones before in my life," he said, not stopping to engage in pleasantries first.

"Then what were you doing at a convention where Nazis were hanging out?" she asked.

Before Duke could reply, the party meeting began, and Rickey moved to her seat. When the next free moment came, he sat down next to her and picked up where he had left off. Talking quickly, he laid out his theories on race, confident that in exposing her to his ideas, he would win her acceptance.

"You really believe all this, don't you?" Rickey asked at one point.

"Oh, yes, it's a religion for me," he said.

Duke's initial attempt to neutralize Rickey failed. Four days later she held the press conference to publicize his bookselling activities. But Duke did not give up on her.

Two weeks later, he called Rickey at home late at night. They spent three hours on the phone, with Duke doing most of the talking. He started slowly but soon became enthralled with his ideas as he talked about India and its caste system, his love of nature, the value of "genius" sperm banks, how Iceland has a superior culture and his admiration for an obscure scientist who had proof that whites were superior to blacks. Duke's fervor can mesmerize his listeners, and at the end of the conversation, Rickey to her horror found her resolve against him weakening.

Duke pressed his advantage with more late-night phone calls, talking for hours on end. On one occasion, Rickey, exhausted, fell asleep for several minutes while he was talking. She awoke with a start, but he kept on going, much as he had done with his friend Mike Wells more than twenty years before. Rickey wondered if she had judged him too harshly. She sought out Lance Hill for what she called "a reality check." In a long conversation, Hill recited a litany of reasons why Duke was evil. Rickey felt reassured.

Duke's attempt to court Rickey had its lighter moments. One day when she went out with Duke and his two daughters, she had to stop and buy gas. She went to her usual place, the Shell station on St. Charles Avenue in New Orleans. As she pulled in, she saw several of the black employees she knew. "David, would you please stay in the car," she said. "I don't want people to know I'm with you." Duke laughed and got out. Rickey hid her face in embarrassment. "It looked like a family outing," she recalls with a laugh, "me and David in the front seat and his daughters in the back." As they drove off, he put a soul station on the radio. "Oh, negro music," he said. Rickey rolled her eyes. They drove to Cooter Brown's, a bar that Duke liked because it offered beers from all over the world. When he ordered a South African beer, Rickey burst out laughing. "What's so funny?" he demanded, not realizing the irony.

Duke lost his advantage with Rickey several weeks later when they had lunch at Ming Palace restaurant in Metairie. As they ate, he propped a copy of *The Six Million Reconsidered* on the table. "Rudolf Hess was a great man," he said, "because of his loyalty to Hitler and because of his attempts at peacemaking. He should have received the Nobel Peace Prize for his flight to England. One of the great travesties of justice was his imprisonment in Spandau Prison."

Rickey began to get uneasy.

"And Dr. Mengele," Duke said, referring to the Nazi who had performed experiments on humans at concentration camps.

"Oh, you like *him*, too?" she asked.

Duke leaned close. "Beth," he said, "he had a Ph.D.! Do you think he would have jeopardized his career by performing experiments on people with so many witnesses around? Come on!"

Duke outlined Mengele's research on twins and then began railing against the "injustices" done to Adolf Eichmann, the concentration camp superintendent captured in South America in 1960. Auschwitz, he added, was operated not to kill Jews but to provide cheap labor. The stench in the air, he said, came from the manufacture of rubber, not from corpses.

On a napkin, he drew a map of the Mauthausen concentration camp he had visited in 1986 with Gwen Udell. Repeating what he had told Udell, he said there were no extermination showers at Mauthausen, that the showers were used to kill lice infesting the Jews.

"What about all the bodies?" Rickey protested.

Most of the people died of typhus and starvation, he explained, adding that disease and deprivation always occurred during war. Besides, he said, repeating what he had told Evelyn Rich four years before, many of the photographs of corpses were doctored.

"You see, Beth," he said, "the extermination camps were a myth concocted by Hollywood to help create the state of Israel." When she asked why Hollywood would invent such a story, he replied, "Because they are controlled by the Jews!"

As he continued eating his Chinese food, he said there was no "Final Solution" to kill Jews. Instead, he said, Hitler wanted to segregate Jews from the rest of society, much as the United States had interned Japanese during World War II. "Jews were enemies of the state because they supported Communism," he said.

"Oh, come on, David," Rickey said. "You don't believe all of this."

"Beth, don't you think that transporting the Jews to Poland and other far away locales would be stupid if Hitler wanted to kill them? Why would he transport these people all over the place, make a big deal out of it if they were going to be killed? They were just going to labor camps." Duke had gone too far with Rickey. Too excited to hold back from discussing his most repulsive thoughts, he snapped her back into reality. "This is too bizarre," Rickey thought to herself. "I've got to get out of here." She cut short the lunch and refused his entreaties after that.

In September, a month later, when Neil Curran, who was also a member of the Republican state central committee, decided to try to have the committee censure Duke, Rickey agreed to help him. In a final phone conversation five days before the September 23 meeting, Duke warned her that he would no longer consider her a friend if she backed the censure motion. But Duke's effort to woo her had failed. In the days before the meeting, it appeared likely that the committee would adopt a motion to either censure Duke or call for a Republican investigation of him. But Nungesser and other party leaders met and secretly decided to block Curran and Rickey. They decided that the best strategy was to ignore Duke—to avoid antagonizing his supporters. Meeting in the capitol's house of representatives, the state central committee killed Curran and Rickey's motion, 115–25.

As reporters crowded around Duke afterward, he called the committee's vote an endorsement. "To censure me would be an action against their own constituencies," he said. "I'm accepted by the Republican delegation." Rickey was furious. "The Republican Party did not want to stand up and be counted on this," she angrily told reporters. "The party is thinking that if they don't say anything, the problem will go away. But it won't." She shook her head. "It's clear that we have a problem in our midst," she said. "I've been surprised over the past six months at the tacit support for Duke."

As she left the chamber of the house of representatives, state central committee members berated her for bringing up the censure motion. One man followed her out to her car, accusing her of challenging Duke to win publicity and make money. Rickey tried to ignore him but finally stopped and turned toward him.

"I don't like Nazis," she shouted. "I especially don't like them running around in the Republican party. If you have a problem with that, then I suggest that there is something seriously wrong with you and the other 114 members of the state central committee who voted to ignore this matter."

The man pulled up short as Rickey got into her car. "Now wait a minute," he sputtered. "I never said I liked Nazis."

CHAPTER EIGHT

THE SENATE CAMPAIGN

David Duke fiddled with a sheaf of papers as he stood in the Napoleon Room at the Quality Inn on Tulane Avenue in New Orleans. It was December 4, 1989, and he was announcing his candidacy for the United States Senate against a three-term Democrat, J. Bennett Johnston. About ten reporters, photographers, and television cameramen turned out to record the event.

Duke, now thirty-nine, had campaigned for the Louisiana senate twice, for the presidency—first as a Democrat and then as a Populist—and for the Louisiana house. But in making his announcement for the Senate, he seemed like a political neophyte. He stumbled over words and could not provide a compelling reason for his candidacy. Johnston, Duke emphasized, had led the campaign two years earlier against Robert Bork's nomination to the Supreme Court—hardly an issue that would galvanize Louisiana voters, who cared more about pocketbook issues like jobs and taxes. And when asked to identify his key backers, Duke named his receptionist and a former Jefferson Parish councilman forgotten by voters.

Just about any freshman state legislator running for the Senate would have been in over his head. But Duke, of course, wasn't just any freshman state legislator. How many other freshman had had their election reported on the front page of the *New York Times*? How many of them had appeared on CNN's "Crossfire" and ABC's "Nightline"? And after being elected, how many of them had appeared on the "Phil Donahue Show" and ABC's "Prime Time Live!"?

Duke got off to a shaky start in the Senate campaign because he had not planned to announce his candidacy for another month. But at the beginning of December, he decided to try to win the Louisiana Republican party's endorsement. To do so he had to jump in immediately, because half the delegates to the nominating convention were to be chosen at caucuses statewide on December 9.

While Duke may have been unprepared to begin his candidacy in early December, he had been laying the groundwork for the Senate campaign since his state house election. In his campaign against Governor Buddy Roemer's tax-restructuring proposal, he had built the nucleus of a statewide political organization. And each of his national television appearances had won him thousands of new supporters throughout the country. The "Prime Time Live!" appearance in November 1989 especially helped Duke, although host Sam Donaldson was obviously trying to slice him up. Donaldson aggressively challenged Duke with hostile questions during the twelve-minute interview. When Duke tried to shift the discussion to welfare, Donaldson interrupted him with another tough question. Duke again tried to talk about welfare, and Donaldson cut him off again with another question.

Many people would have cracked under the intense questioning but not Duke. He had had years of practice facing antagonistic interviewers and had found that by remaining unruffled, he could turn the tables and win over television audiences. In the cool medium of television, he remained cool, while Donaldson, overly aggressive, became hot. "You're really not being fair, Mr. Donaldson," Duke repeatedly said calmly, in an appeal to viewers. His ploy worked. Donaldson came across as a bully. Duke, who twice during the interview asked viewers to write him at the state capitol, received thousands of letters from well-wishers throughout the country. Workers in the capitol mailroom were stunned: no Louisiana legislator in memory had received so much mail.

Before beginning the Senate campaign, Duke took several steps to make himself more appealing to voters. He underwent another chemical peel to eliminate the crow's feet that had reappeared around his eyes. As with his previous plastic surgery, he kept this a secret. In a speech soon afterward, he blamed his reddish complexion on a sunburn. But several friends knew that he had not been in the sun recently and teased him about the operation. Duke stalked away in anger. Following the advice of Cheryl Mart, a New Orleans socialite who befriended him, he also discarded his Kmart suits for more expensive tailoring. Mart advised him that if he was going to be in the limelight, he had to look more stylish.

With Mart's help, Duke attempted to gain entrance into upper-crust New Orleans society. In 1989 and 1990, he attended several black-tie charity balls in New Orleans. While he may have been trying to curry favor from wealthy patrons, he probably cared more about rubbing elbows with a set that had scorned him for years. He achieved only limited success. When he attended a fashion benefit for the New Orleans Symphony, his presence prompted whispered complaints among many of the rich benefactors in attendance. "What's that horrible man doing here?" one woman demanded to a friend.

Duke also sought to make inroads within the New Orleans political establishment. Probably no entity was more respected by the political community than Loyola University's Institute of Politics. Many elected officials, journalists, and political activists in metropolitan New Orleans had enrolled in the IOP, a four-month course on state and local politics that met once a week and was taught by Ed Renwick, Louisiana's most respected pollster. So when the IOP held a fund raiser in early November 1989, more than 200 people showed up. Every local elected official had been invited to the large home in an exclusive New Orleans neighborhood except Duke. But the omission did not deter him.

Fifteen minutes before the party was to begin, the doorbell rang. It was Duke and his legislative assistant, Callie O'Pry. "Hi, David," Billy Schultz, a New Orleans political consultant, said uncertainly as he answered the door. Renwick and several other people organizing the party heard Schultz's greeting, turned, and saw Duke. Shocked and dismayed, all hurried off into other rooms. Renwick ended up outside by the swimming pool.

Renwick's assistant, Lucy King, had been in the rear of the house, and when she went to see who had arrived, she found Duke and O'Pry standing alone in the front hallway. "It was hilarious," King recalled. "Nobody wanted to be seen with him, much less talk with him. They all probably figured I'd kick him out." But not wanting to be rude, she let them buy the tickets, which cost fifty dollars per person. As other people arrived, they quickly learned of the uninvited guests. When they poked their heads into the living room to catch a glimpse of Duke, they saw him standing alone with O'Pry near a buffet table. Few people at the party would talk to him.

One person who would was Dutch Morial, who had served from 1978 to 1986 as the first black mayor of New Orleans. Morial was short, feisty, and hated by many whites because he had ruthlessly grabbed power from the white political establishment. Morial was someone who would obviously not like Duke, but he needed Duke's help to add a final prize to a long and illustrious career: he wanted to become Louisiana's first black senator in Washington. If Duke ran against Johnston, Morial figured, Duke would grab a chunk of Johnston's conservative support. If Morial also ran, he could capture Johnston's black and liberal white supporters. Together, they could squeeze Johnston from the sides, finish first and second in the primary, and end up in the runoff against each other. Each was the other's best opponent. The race would be a tossup. Duke liked the idea and urged Morial at the IOP party to join the race. Six weeks later, however, on Christmas Eve, Morial died of a heart attack. The man who could have joined with Duke to end Johnston's political career was eliminated.

Ironically, this was not the first time a politician's death had helped Johnston. He had first been elected to the Senate in 1972 when Allen Ellender, the eighty-one-year-old, seven-term incumbent he was challenging, died three weeks before the primary. Johnston then sailed to victory. Johnston's career had almost taken a very different turn. He had come within a whisker of being elected governor the year before when he built a coalition of conservatives and businessmen to make the Democratic runoff against Edwin Edwards, the candidate of Cajuns, blacks, and organized labor. In the Democratic runoff, Edwards edged Johnston by only 4,518 votes and went on to defeat his Republican opponent for governor.

Johnston, an attorney, ran for governor after one term in the state senate representing Shreveport and one term in the state house. During the early 1960s, as he began his political career, he was a segregationist, defending Shreveport's right to block integration of city bus terminals, airports, and schools. By the time he was elected to the Senate in 1972, he had moved with the times and no longer opposed integration.

Johnston, fifty-seven in 1990, stood a couple of inches below six feet and walked on the balls of his feet, a characteristic reminiscent of the star running back he had been at Byrd High School in Shreveport forty-one years before. One of the senate's most avid tennis players, he spoke in a flat voice with little trace of emotion or of a southern accent. A hair weave covered most of his bald spot. He was a bit stiff in public but could be more relaxed and funny among friends.

Johnston during his eighteen years had built a reputation as a conservative Democrat who voted with business interests but had no compelling world vision. A firmly entrenched Senate insider, he was chairman of the Energy and Natural Resources Committee and chairman of the Appropriation subcommittee on water and development. He was known as a master at getting legislation approved and for protecting Louisiana's oil and gas industries. In return, the oil and gas industries and many other industries with legislation before Johnston's committees contributed heavily to his campaign chest.

Johnston was skilled at using his position to snare federal money for projects throughout Louisiana—for new roads, factories, medical research, water projects, buildings, ports. But as Johnston began his campaign for reelection, Geoff Garin, his pollster, discovered that Louisianians were unimpressed with Johnston. With the state deeply in recession, with the state's unemployment rate higher than the national average for the tenth year in a row, and with many residents—particularly recent college graduates—leaving the state in droves looking for new opportunities, Louisiana voters thought they weren't getting the help they deserved from their elected officials.

A Garin poll in June 1989, sixteen months before the primary, showed that by an 81 to 16 percent margin, Louisiana voters thought the state was in deep trouble. And by a 44 to 37 percent margin, they wanted to elect a fresh face rather than someone with a proven track record. These numbers spelled trouble for Johnston. His biggest strength was his pull in Washington, but with voters' antiincumbent mood, this was also his biggest weakness.

It looked like Republicans might win a Senate seat in Louisiana for the first time. As the race began to take shape, their two most formidable potential candidates were Henson Moore, a former congressman who had nearly been elected to the Senate four years before and was now deputy secretary of energy in the Bush administration, and David Treen, who had been elected in 1979 as Louisiana's first Republican governor since Reconstruction but had been defeated for reelection four years later by Edwin Edwards. Both men, however, declined to challenge Johnston.

Two Republicans who did become candidates were Fox McKeithen, the Louisiana secretary of state whose father had been governor from 1964 to 1972, and Ben Bagert, a state senator from New Orleans. McKeithen, Bagert, and Duke all competed in the Republican caucuses held throughout the state on December 9 to elect 540 delegates to the state GOP convention on January 13. The elected delegates and 257 party regulars who were automatic delegates would select the party's endorsed candidate at the convention.

Bagert, who was far better organized than McKeithen and Duke, won big at the caucuses, capturing 70 percent of the delegates selected that day. And at the state party convention a month later he added the support of enough automatic delegates to be chosen as the party's endorsed nominee, winning 451.5 of the 797 delegates. Duke won only 52 delegates and finished fourth among the four candidates. (State representative Quentin Dastugue had become the fourth candidate just before the convention.)

Winning the endorsement did not preclude other Republicans' running against Johnston in the open primary, but it meant that the state and national party would provide money and volunteers only to Bagert. McKeithen and Dastugue dropped out of the race, but Duke did not. He predicted he would outpoll Bagert and force a runoff with Johnston, because, he said, he was supported by both conservative Republicans and conservative Democrats.

Bagert, forty-six, was an attorney and veteran lawmaker. He had served fifteen years in the state house representing a working-class section of New Orleans and then had won a state senate seat in 1983. A boxer in high school and college, Bagert was known as a street fighter who would push hard—and reach into his bag of tricks if necessary—to kill opponents' bills or get his passed. During his tenure, he had authored legislation establishing a life sentence for heroin dealers and legalizing the death penalty in Louisiana. He was also a strong environmentalist who sponsored legislation that created a trust fund to protect the state's vanishing wetlands.

A supporter of affirmative action and many social programs, Bagert had always won strong support from blacks and campaigned as a moderate. But in the Senate race he shifted to the right and emphasized his antiwelfare and law-and-order views. Describing himself as a "conservative reformer," he opposed new taxes, called for reforming the welfare system, advocated tougher punishment for drug users, and called for a cleaner environment.

As Johnston's campaign manager, Jim Oakes, sized up the race in mid-January, nine months before the October 6 primary, the prospect of facing Ben Bagert and David Duke gave him great confidence. Bagert was unknown outside New Orleans and garnered only 7 percent in a December poll of the Senate candidates. Nor was he popular within the GOP. Bagert had switched from the Democratic party only one year before and was not trusted by the party hierarchy, which thought he was an opportunist. Bagert for the first month of the campaign also faced the threat of being indicted in a New Orleans case alleging that employees for the clerk of city court had worked for his campaign during office hours.

In addition, Oakes believed the Johnston campaign had a silver bullet that would eliminate Bagert if he proved to be a greater threat than expected: they had evidence that Bagert had used his position in the legislature for personal gain. They would release the information to the media if necessary. Oakes, a thirty-four-year-old whiz kid in Louisiana politics who left his position as Johnston's chief of staff in Washington to manage the campaign, was wary of Duke. But like the political leaders at the beginning of the District 81 race, Oakes dismissed Duke's candidacy. Not only would he sink under the weight of his Klan and Nazi past, Oakes figured, but he would be unable to raise the $2 million needed to campaign effectively. Johnston at the beginning of the campaign already had a war chest of $2.5 million.

As Johnston began to gear up for the campaign, Garin in January flew down from Washington to conduct a focus group with voters. By hearing what was on voters' minds, he could provide Johnston with a better road map to follow during the campaign. The focus group was held in Bossier City with a group of twelve white swing voters. Garin moderated the ninety-minute session and began with a few noncommittal questions to loosen them up. "What are you looking for in a senator?" he asked next.

"Someone who will stand up to the NAACP," said one man.

"The NAACP is the most powerful interest group in America," said another man.

"All the benefits go to blacks at the expense of whites," said a woman.

For nearly the rest of the session, the group poured out its hostility toward blacks—or "niggers" as two of the men repeatedly said—and praised Duke as willing to stand up to blacks and the political establishment. When Garin asked if anyone was concerned about Duke's Klan past, no one responded. A few minutes later, when he asked if Duke's Nazi past was of concern, one woman said, "You know, Hitler had some good ideas." As the group filed out, Garin was shaken. A veteran pollster, he had spent more than a decade directing focus groups, particularly when the topic was race. But he had never seen such anger directed at blacks or the political establishment. "This race is going to be tougher than some people think," Garin thought.

A warning shot had been fired across the Johnston campaign's bow, but Johnston's advisers still weren't concerned. Polls showed him crushing Duke. A December head-to-head poll for the *Baton Rouge Morning Advocate*, for example, showed Johnston leading Duke 60 to 23 percent. A full 50 percent of the voters gave Duke an unfavorable rating. Candidates with a 50 percent negative rating did not win elections, Johnston's advisers reminded themselves.

They decided to follow a classic strategy for an incumbent with a big lead. Johnston would spend as much of 1990 as possible campaigning in the state to reestablish contact with voters, speaking at local fairs, courthouses, and factories. Meanwhile, the campaign would spend heavily on television. In both his TV spots and his personal appearances, Johnston would emphasize the numerous projects and grants he had won for Louisiana. At the same time, he would ignore his opponents. If Johnston needed to attack them, he would do so only near the end of the campaign. There was no point, his advisers figured, in attacking Duke or Bagert and giving them free publicity. Nor would they allow Johnston to debate his opponents and give them the opportunity to trip him up. Johnston's advisers knew that their strategy would not excite voters and would undoubtedly be criticized for being unimaginative. But with a big lead, they felt, this approach minimized mistakes and thus ensured victory. And their candidate was not a dynamic campaigner.

Along with competing for delegates at the January 13 Republican state party convention, Duke spent the first part of that month organizing a campaign staff. His campaign manager, as in the District 81 race, would be Howie Farrell. A Vietnam veteran, Farrell had been a New Orleans policeman until he was fired from the force for bullying a citizen in 1972. He later became a medical supplies salesman. A beefy man quick to anger, Farrell became known within the campaign for his hatred of blacks and Jews.

Supervising the campaign's volunteers would be Kenny Knight, who had been one of Duke's key aides during the District 81 race. Knight, like Farrell, had been a New Orleans policeman but was dismissed from the force in 1973 for stealing lumber from a construction site while off duty. He later worked for a trucking company and sold insurance.

To run his Baton Rouge campaign office, Duke turned to Babs Minhinnette Wilson. Wilson, fifty-two, had been a surrogate mother of Duke's since their meeting while he was at LSU. A true believer in the cause of white supremacy, she had been active in Duke's National party in 1971–72 and had then followed him into the Knights of the Ku Klux Klan. Her home was filled with paintings of Confederate generals, and she fervently believed that the South would one day rise again. Wilson, like Duke, believed that Martin Luther King was a communist. To run his Shreveport office, Duke turned to David Touchstone, an attorney. Touchstone, thirty-eight, had met Duke at LSU and for a year had been a member of the Knights of the Ku Klux Klan.

Another top adviser would be Jim McPherson. McPherson, fifty-eight, had once been one of Louisiana's top criminal defense attorneys but had virtually stopped practicing in the mid-1980s to raise three small children after his wife died of cancer. A classmate of Bennett Johnston's at Byrd High School, McPherson had been a liberal during the 1960s, marching with a black armband in a 1969 parade to mark the one-year anniversary of the Reverend Martin Luther King's assassination. He had also been a member of the American Civil Liberties Union and once had represented LSD guru Timothy Leary. McPherson had first met Duke in 1981 when he represented Duke in the Dominica investigation. Over the years, they had remained in touch, with McPherson taking a fatherly interest in Duke and trying to steer him more into the mainstream. McPherson himself was becoming more conservative during the 1980s. He became convinced that social programs like affirmative action and welfare caused blacks to become dependent on government. This attracted him to Duke's candidacy, and he applauded Duke's willingness to speak out on issues that other political leaders would not touch.

A pivotal moment for McPherson came on the day in February 1989 when Duke was sworn into the legislature. As he sat with Duke, he began reading the stack of congratulatory letters sent to Duke from across the country. Letter after letter, McPherson found, contained a heartfelt plea from ordinary Americans asking Duke to right a system they thought had gone wrong. McPherson got emotional as he read their appeals. The hope and faith they placed in Duke coursed through him. "I'm hooked, I'm in with Duke," McPherson thought to himself. McPherson's role during the Senate campaign would be to act as a kind of wise man and troubleshooter.

For his constant companion as he traveled the state, Duke wanted someone who was personable and carried no Klan or Nazi baggage. He hired a twenty-five-year-old Metairie native named Billy Hankins to fill that role. Hankins's grandfather had been a state representative from New Orleans, and he himself wanted to make a career in politics. He saw working for Duke as an opportunity to learn politics from the ground up. He also liked Duke's opposition to affirmative action, minority set-asides, and new taxes. Having Hankins—tall, well-groomed, good-natured, and articulate—by his side helped Duke reinforce the clean-cut conservative image that he was trying to fashion.

Duke's scheduler would be Marc Ellis, a thirty-eight-year-old Vietnam War veteran who had just graduated from the University of Alabama law school. Ellis, whose first wife had been Vietnamese, was attracted to Duke, like Hankins, because of Duke's views on affirmative action and welfare.

Several of Duke's more radical ideological friends also helped out, but they were kept hidden from the press and public. Don Black, Duke's deputy and successor in the Knights of the Ku Klux Klan, helped set up the campaign's computer system. Bernie Davids, who had been arrested for agitating with the American Nazi party in the 1960s, worked in the office. James K. Warner, who had been a lieutenant in the American Nazi party in the 1960s, had been in Duke's Klan in the 1970s, and had later formed his own neo-Nazi group, served as a Duke delegate at the Republican convention.

Duke had assembled an unlikely group to mount a campaign for major political office, a mix of racists, anti-Semites, and more traditional conservatives. Few of them had campaign experience. But then again, this was no traditional campaign. There was no formal campaign structure. Duke made most of the major decisions himself, and his advisers had loosely defined roles. Unlike traditional Senate candidates, for example, Duke had no press secretary. Nor did he have a pollster since the campaign didn't do any polls. It was unheard of for a campaign not to do polls.

There was a simple explanation for the unusual campaign structure: shaped by his life on the fringe and a student of history, Duke deeply believed in destiny and was convinced that he was on a crusade that would land him in the Senate and then the White House and allow him to fulfill his role as the savior of the white race. Who needs an organized campaign structure and polls telling you what voters think when destiny is carrying you toward your appointed goal? Still, after years of being scorned by the public, Duke at the outset could not help but be less than fully convinced that he could win the Senate race.

The campaign's first formal rally was scheduled for January 20 at the Holiday Inn Holidome in Monroe. Duke was nervous that afternoon. "I don't know how many people are going to show up tonight," he told Hankins. "Let's set up 100 chairs." An hour before the rally began, Duke peeked out from behind a curtain into the hall where he was to speak. His eyes widened. "Billy, set up more chairs," he said excitedly. "People are pouring in here. This is incredible." By the time Duke began to speak, 750 people had jammed the Holidome and spilled into the lobby.

Two weeks later he spoke at the Bossier City Civic Center. This time Duke told his northwest Louisiana coordinator, Thomas Cochran, to set up 800 chairs. But when Duke looked through a peephole fifteen minutes before the 7:30 p.m. speech was scheduled to begin, he was dismayed. The crowd numbered only 100. Afraid that the media would demean his candidacy by pointing to the empty chairs, he ordered Cochran to take down most of them. But first Cochran dashed out the front door to see how many more people were arriving. His jaw dropped in amazement. A line of cars several blocks long was streaming into the civic center parking lot. "My God!" Cochran thought. "This guy's going to win." In all, more than 1,000 people packed the hall. "Duke! Duke! Duke!" they chanted throughout the rally.

On and on the road show went as Duke turned out hundreds at each stop: Lake Charles, Baton Rouge, Lafayette, Sulphur, Bastrop, Natchitoches, Opelousas, Shreveport, Ruston, Minden, Homer, Vivian, Houma and so on. Everywhere, the message was the same: the middle class had to reclaim its rights taken away by a liberal-dominated government that was concerned more with helping minorities than whites, more with criminals than with victims, more with the well-to-do than with the overburdened little guy. In an age where most politicians forsook public appearances to campaign in thirty-second television ads, Louisiana hadn't seen anything like Duke's road show in years.

Rallies always followed the same script. Several days beforehand, his campaign would advertise the event in the local newspaper and on the radio. Duke would arrive in town the day of the rally in time to be interviewed live on the 5:00 P.M. news, where he would plug his appearance. Rallies always began with a prayer and the Pledge of Allegiance, which were meant to burnish his conservative message. Duke was then given an introduction. Frequently, it was given by John Rarick, a former congressman who had spoken at Citizens Council meetings in the early 1960s. In his introduction, the archconservative Rarick invariably railed against what he called the four p's in Washington, D.C.: "the perverts, the pinkos and the political prostitutes." Crowds roared with delight.

Duke was running as a right-wing populist, much as he had in the District 81 race. His key issues were racially oriented. He opposed government-sponsored affirmative action and minority set-aside programs. "If it's wrong to discriminate against a black person as a minority," he would say, in a line that always drew applause, "it's just as wrong to discriminate against a white person."

Duke called for the drug testing of welfare recipients and residents of public housing projects, advocated reducing the welfare benefits of women who bear illegitimate children, called for the end of busing to achieve racial equality in public schools, called for the death penalty for drug pushers, and demanded that welfare recipients work for their checks. "The greatest problem we face in this country is the rising welfare class," he said at every stop. He never mentioned blacks, but then, he didn't have to. He was speaking in a code that white people easily understood. To them, welfare recipients, public housing residents, drug users, and illegitimate babies were black.

Duke's supporters mainly lived in the suburbs and rural areas. Writing in the *Atlantic Monthly*, Thomas Byrne Edsall and Mary Edsall described a growing gulf between blacks and whites nationwide, one that helped Duke. "The contact between whites and the black underclass has routinely violated every standard necessary for the breakdown of racial stereotypes," the Edsalls wrote. "Most white contact with the underclass is through personal experience of crime and urban squalor, through such experience related by friends and family, or through the daily reports about crime, drugs and violence which appear on television and in newspapers. The news includes, as well, periodic reports on out-of-wedlock births, welfare fraud, drug-related AIDS, crack babies and inner-city joblessness."

Increasingly identifying blacks with crime, squalor, and government handouts, whites were concluding that blacks were responsible for their own condition and felt that whites could do little to help them. Whites certainly didn't want to pay more taxes for government programs that they didn't think were successful.

Eighty percent of white Louisiana residents opposed preferential hiring of blacks, and 71 percent opposed universities' practice of reserving slots for blacks, one 1990 poll showed. Most white voters in Louisiana—55 percent—believed that the gains blacks received from these programs in jobs and university admissions came at the expense of whites. When asked whether they thought that blacks could be as well off as whites if they tried harder, 73 percent of whites agreed. And when asked whether slavery and discrimination had made it harder for blacks to get ahead, 56 percent of whites disagreed.

Duke went beyond race in his rallies to deliver a broader antiestablishment attack that resonated well in a state that still regards Huey Long as its political godfather more than fifty years after his assassination. Duke denounced companies that polluted the environment, large corporations that didn't pay taxes, and special interests that backed candidates such as Bennett Johnston to win political favors at the expense of ordinary citizens. Duke said he would not accept PAC contributions. The fact that no prominent elected officials backed him, he said, provided further evidence that he would shake up the system.

Duke also campaigned as an economic conservative. He opposed new taxes and said the progressive income tax system should be replaced with a flat tax of 8 to 10 percent. He called for slashing government spending and taking power away from unelected government bureaucrats.

Duke sounded a nationalistic note by bashing the Japanese for buying American companies and calling for higher tariffs on imported goods. He also called for shifting troops from Western Europe to the Mexican border to reduce the flow of illegal immigrants entering the United States. Otherwise, he rarely discussed foreign affairs. To a lesser extent, Duke also campaigned as a cultural conservative. He blasted pornographers, endorsed prayer in public schools, and opposed abortion.

Unlike most challengers, Duke devoted only a small portion of his stump speech to attacking his incumbent opponent. More than anything else, he was pushing his issues. Duke's campaign speeches were a masterpiece of deception. By speaking in racial code, Duke distanced himself from his Klan past. But in reality, although he never mentioned Jews or "niggers" and although he presented himself as a conservative, his views hadn't changed—as becomes clear from a comparison of his campaign statements with the views he expressed to doctoral candidate Evelyn Rich in 1985, when he laid out his belief in eugenics and the principles of National Socialism race doctrine.

Duke opposed affirmative action and minority set-asides because, as he told Rich, he believed that whites were a superior race and would inevitably get the job if blacks were not given a special advantage. He wanted fewer illegitimate babies, because, as he told Rich, he feared that blacks were deliberately procreating to try to outnumber whites. He thought that welfare was evil, as he told Rich, because welfare recipients had nothing to do but breed—and more blacks inevitably meant race mixing, more crime, inferior schools, increased drug use, more people on the welfare.

Left: At age 7, with Dotti; *below:* Duke, age 4, dressed as "Mammie" for Halloween in 1954, with his sister Dotti

Left: An eighth grade yearbook photo. Courtesy *The Times-Picayune; above:* Eleventh grade yearbook photo, Riverside Military Academy. Courtesy *The Times-Picayune.*

A member of the scuba diving team in eleventh grade. Courtesy *The Times-Picayune.*

Duke's parents, Christmas 1990

Challenged by a student at LSU's Free Speech Alley. Courtesy *The Times-Picayune.*

Duke in a 1970 stunt that would haunt him for years. © 1994 Matt Anderson.

With wife Chloe and daughter Erika in 1976

In 1976, with two of his favorite symbols: Klan founder Nathan Bedford Forrest and a Confederate flag. Courtesy Bill Feig.

Right: Duke's 1976 arrest nearly forced him to quit the Klan. Courtesy *The Times-Picayune; below:* Leading a crossburning ceremony. © 1994 Mitchel Osborne.

Left: Duke fooled reporters with his 1977 Klan Border Watch. Courtesy AP/Wide World Photos; *below:* In front of Parliament during his 1978 jaunt in England. Courtesy AP/Wide World Photos.

Leading a Klan rally. Courtesy Nancy Rhoda, *The Tennessean*.

Cultivating his image as a "new" breed of Klansman. Courtesy Nancy Rhoda, *The Tennessean*.

Above: With two of his Klan lieutenants, Don Black, center, and Louis Beam, right. Courtesy Klanwatch; *left:* Duke's 1979 campaign for state senate ended in defeat. Courtesy the author.

Duke recruited Tom Metzger into the Klan, but Metzger later broke with him. Courtesy Nancy Rhoda, *The Tennessean.*

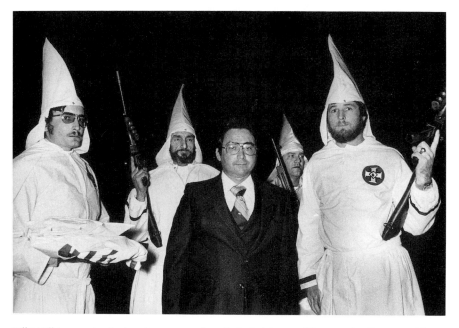

Bill Wilkinson, in dark suit, emerged as Duke's biggest Klan rival. Courtesy Nancy Rhoda, *The Tennessean.*

Above: Duke in 1985 revealed his deepest beliefs in National Social-ism to Ph.D. candidate Evelyn Rich, to his later regret. Courtesy Evelyn Rich; *left:* To burnish his image, Duke liked to play the piano. Courtesy Evelyn Rich.

Duke began his political comeback at a 1987 Forsyth County (Georgia) march. Courtesy Ron Munnerlyn.

Announcing his 1988 presidential candidacy. Courtesy AP/Wide World Photos.

A key leader in the American Nazi Party in 1964, Ralph Forbes managed Duke's 1988 presidential campaign. Courtesy AP/Wide World Photos.

Duke's political future seemed over after the disastrous presidential campaign. Courtesy the author.

Duke gained a second chance when a seat opened up in the Louisiana legislature. Courtesy Eliot Kamenitz.

Of Duke's six opponents, John Treen, at the microphone, was the one he could defeat. Courtesy *The Times-Picayune*.

Sworn into the Louisiana legislature after firing "the shot heard 'round the world." Courtesy Irwin Thompson.

With his victory, Duke was no longer an outsider. Courtesy the author.

Above: Sen. J. Bennett Johnston in 1990 did not take Duke's challenge seriously. Courtesy Ellis V. Lucia, *The Times-Picayune; right:* GOP member Beth Rickey challenged Duke when few Republicans dared to. Courtesy Eliot Kamenitz.

Lance Hill, director of the Louisiana Coalition Against Racism and Nazism, thought the 1990 election was a referendum on hate. Courtesy G. E. Arnold.

Duke on the stump during the 1990 Senate campaign. Courtesy Joe Beaugez.

Buddy Roemer was elected governor in 1987 by promising a "revolution" in the state's politics. Four years later, Duke challenged him. Courtesy Ellis V. Lucia, *The Times-Picayune.*

Above: Duke's opponents in 1991 used every means possible to voice their displeasure. Courtesy Ted Jackson; *left:* Duke supporters reacted angrily to the anti-Duke sign. Courtesy Ted Jackson.

Despite unflattering signs, Duke made a triumphal return to Free Speech Alley five weeks before the primary election. Courtesy James Terry III.

People waited hours to register to vote in the Duke–Edwards election. © 1991 Matt Anderson.

When Edwin Edwards defended welfare to a group of senior citizens, they shouted him down. Courtesy Bryan S. Berteaux, *The Times-Picayune.*

Duke with daughters, Kristen, left, and Erika, right, during the '91 campaign. Courtesy Matt Rose, *The Times-Picayune.*

This page: Reporters, supporters and bodyguards surrounded Duke throughout the runoff campaign. Top photo courtesy Chuck Cook. Bottom photo courtesy Ted Jackson.

Edwards is embraced by his daughter, Anna, after his victory speech. Courtesy Kathy Anderson.

The day after. Courtesy AP/Wide World Photos.

The crowds disappeared during the 1992 presidential campaign. Courtesy AP/Wide World Photos.

His broader message was also rooted in his National Socialist views. He damned pornography because, as he told Rich, he thought Jews spread pornography through their control of Hollywood and the media as a means to debase white society. He opposed abortion, he told Rich, because he thought that only whites—the productive members of society—had abortions, while blacks continued to propagate. He was a protectionist against the Japanese and favored tighter border controls because, as he told Rich, he wanted to keep the United States as white as possible. He blasted large companies because, as he told Rich, he thought they were part of the Jewish financial network that controlled the world. He wanted a clean environment because, as he told Rich, pollution damaged the clean, pure society that he envisioned for the United States and that Nazi Germany had been building.

At his campaign rallies, Duke typically spoke for more than an hour—far longer than most politicians. But few people got up to leave. His message riveted them. "He says in public what we all talk about in private," said Jimbo Hundley, a rice farmer wearing a blue and white Duke T-shirt and a Duke baseball cap who was attending a Duke rally. Duke supporters echoed this thought time and time again throughout the campaign. But Duke's rallies also had a darker side. His supporters were angry, and when Duke pushed hot-button issues like affirmative action and welfare, they thrust their fists in the air, stomped their feet, and chanted his name over and over. In the us-versus-them atmosphere at Duke's rallies, his supporters frequently heckled reporters, especially Jewish reporters. "How does it feel for a Bolshevik like you to be in this kind of crowd?" one man snarled at Adam Nossiter, a stringer for the *New York Times*. "Doesn't it make you want to get on the next Greyhound bus out of town?"

Rallies were important for Duke not only so that he could deliver his views directly to voters but also to establish credibility early on. As word spread of the large crowds, more people felt comfortable telling their friends that they liked what he was saying, that they would vote for Duke. By the spring, volunteers were streaming into Duke's campaign offices throughout the state. And every day, his Metairie headquarters received sacks and sacks of mail from supporters, not only from Louisiana, but from throughout the country.

The rallies were also important for another reason: to raise money. At every rally, about three-fourths of the way through, when he began talking about how Johnston was the political action committee candidate and he was the little guy's candidate, Hankins and campaign volunteers would pass buckets among the audience, something no contemporary politician other than the Reverend Jesse Jackson had done. Up and down the rows of people went the buckets, and by the time the money was counted later, the buckets would always contain at least several thousand dollars. And in an era where political candidates were happy to give away T-shirts and baseball caps, Duke's supporters paid cash for them at his rallies, further filling campaign coffers. Duke would raise $2.4 million during 1990—or about as much as Bennett Johnston raised that year. This was an astonishing feat.

David Duke was running a grass-roots campaign the likes of which Louisiana hadn't seen in years. When he finished his speech at rallies, Duke always ran to the back of the room and planted himself at the exit. He explained why to Billy Hankins: "You have to shake their hand, look them in the eye and thank them for coming. These people read that I'm a Nazi, the anti-Christ, a Klansman. It's important to let these people know I'm a real person." Not only did Duke make sure he shook everybody's hand, but he usually stayed long afterward, talking to supporters, signing autographs. While this was an admirable quality in a politician, in Duke's case it undoubtedly also reflected his desire to soak up the adulation after a lifetime of being a pariah.

For Hankins, who drove Duke throughout the state in his red 1988 Grand Am and coordinated fund raising at rallies, it was a wild ride. As he and Duke sped from event to event across the state, they were stopped for speeding dozens of times. Not once did a state trooper give them a ticket. Instead, many of them asked for autographs or campaign buttons. "Let me tell you something," Hankins recalled later, "those troopers were all for David." Hankins felt like he was on a rock 'n' roll tour, not a political campaign. Duke would put tanning cream on his face and sleep while Hankins drove. When they pulled into a town, Duke would quickly freshen up for interviews and that night's show.

Hankins could always count on Duke to give a great performance. The crowd would go wild, and women would flock around him afterward. Hankins would stand next to Duke as he shook hands at the door, notepad in hand. When an attractive woman shook Duke's hand and gushed over him, he would nod to Hankins, who would then say to her, "You look like a good, enthusiastic supporter. Can I get your phone number?" Still riding an emotional high from that night's rally, Duke and Hankins always wanted to go out afterward. If Duke didn't already have a date lined up, he would ask the woman to join them. If he already had someone, he would call the woman the next night or when he returned for another rally. As the campaign wore on, Jim McPherson grew alarmed at the number of women that Duke was sleeping with. McPherson was also concerned with their age. They never seemed older than twenty-five, and some were as young as eighteen. He counseled Duke to slow down, that he was better off resting and saving his energy for the punishing campaign. "OK, Jim, OK," Duke would tell him.

But then McPherson would get reports that Duke had resumed his conquests. In desperation, McPherson concocted a story that he fed Hankins: the pipefitters union was going to plant drugs on a woman who would offer herself to Duke in a setup. When Hankins told Duke the story, Duke grew worried and promised again to mend his ways. He didn't. He changed his behavior "for about half a day," McPherson said. Duke was as compulsive about womanizing as he was about gambling.

While Duke never mentioned Jews publicly during the campaign, they remained uppermost in his mind. One day on the road, Hankins said to him, "I can understand why you're down on blacks, but I don't understand this Jewish thing. They work hard, they pay taxes."

Duke turned abruptly toward Hankins and switched off the car radio. "Billy, you just don't understand," he said, pounding the dashboard and startling Hankins. "They control the media, the stock market, the retail outlets, they're against Christians."

Hankins stared at Duke dumbfounded. "I didn't quite understand what he was talking about," he recalled later. "It was like I struck a nerve that I had never struck before. I realized that the Jewish issue was more important to him than the black issue."

By April, politicians throughout the state were taking note of the large crowds Duke was drawing. "The Duke phenomenon," they called it, and they invariably discussed the freshman state legislator when they got together. Eight days after Duke drew 600 people to a rally in Crowley, Cecil Picard, the state senator who represented the southwest Louisiana town, was still shaking his head in amazement. "Bennett Johnston couldn't have gotten half of that," Picard said. "Duke is telling people what they want to hear. He has turned out to be an outstanding spokesman for the people no one is speaking for."

State representative Sam Theriot, who represented a rural district in southwest Louisiana, got a dose of the Duke phenomenon when close friends visited him at the legislature one day. Theriot thought he would impress them by taking them to meet Governor Roemer. But no, the friends said, they wanted to meet Duke. When Theriot watched his friends fall over themselves in excitement at meeting Duke, he thought, "He's a celebrity, he's like a messiah."

As Johnston advisers got reports from throughout Louisiana of the large crowds Duke was drawing, they took notice. "You wouldn't believe how many people saw him last night in Winnsboro," campaign press secretary Bob Mann was told one day. "There were 300 people there." Mann thought, "Hell, we'd go to Winnsboro and we couldn't get 20 people." But the Johnston campaign still wasn't worried. Their latest poll, taken in late April, showed that while Duke had gained ground, Johnston had a huge lead. The poll gave Johnston 56 percent, Duke 20 percent, and Bagert 13 percent. Eleven percent were undecided. Head to head, Johnston was clobbering Duke 65–25 percent. Duke's negative rating was still about 50 percent.

In April, Duke was forced to scale back his campaigning when the three-month state legislative session began. He introduced five bills during the 1990 session. They sought to:

* abolish the state's affirmative action and minority set-aside programs
* withdraw entitlement benefits for people convicted of drug offenses
* require first-time drivers to pass drug tests to get a license
* eliminate welfare benefits to recipients convicted of drug offenses
* increase jail sentences for residents of public housing projects who commit crimes involving drugs.

As in 1989, the legislature defeated all of his bills.

But Duke could claim some victories. His attacks on welfare were generating so much publicity—and support from the public—that policymakers were concluding that the welfare system had to be reformed.

Duke also won widespread attention after the house on May 29 approved a watered-down version of his bill to prohibit affirmative action. The votes had been there to defeat the measure. But it was approved on a 66–28 vote when about twenty white members of the Acadiana delegation switched sides. The Acadians were retaliating against three black members who had broken promises to support the preceding bill, which would have created a state lottery. Without the blacks' support, the lottery, which the Acadians badly wanted, was narrowly defeated.

The twenty-member black caucus blasted Duke and the white legislators who supported the bill. "The House vote sends a signal to the nation that it's all right to be racist, all right to be a former member of the Ku Klux Klan, that you can draw on that experience to be a member of this body," said state representative Charles D. Jones, the black caucus chairman. Never missing a chance to get exposure for his message, Duke in turn blasted the black legislators. "I'm being called a racist because my bill prohibits racial discrimination," Duke said, "but they're the true ones who are racists."

Passage of Duke's anti-affirmative action bill embroiled the house in its biggest racial dispute in years. "I've not seen this kind of turmoil before," veteran state representative Joseph Accardo said the next day. "Before there was more good will." Jack Wardlaw, the longtime capital bureau chief of the *Times-Picayune*, recalled a column he had written following Duke's 1989 election: "What real harm can one legislator out of 144 do? Plenty. A clever racist in that position can propose carefully designed amendments that will be difficult for some fellow lawmakers to vote against, given the makeup of their districts. Worse, he can make statements from the floor so outrageous as to tempt Black Caucus members to reply in kind. If any take the bait, the House could be polarized and the atmosphere poisoned—just what the Ku Klux Klan wanted all along."

While some people said the dispute would hurt Duke by reinforcing his reputation as a racist, state representative Randy Roach, a perceptive observer, said Duke's stock would rise with voters. "He is all about driving a wedge and polarizing the Legislature on racial issues," Roach said. "The stronger the racial undercurrent there is, the better off David is in trying to accomplish his legislative and campaign agenda." A Senate committee killed the anti-affirmative action bill four weeks later, but by then Duke had further burnished his standing with the angry white electorate.

By the beginning of July, the huge turnout for Duke's rallies showed he had succeeded in establishing a firm base of support among blue-collar whites. But to force a runoff with Johnston in October, he knew he had to reach better-educated, higher-income whites—the kind of people who didn't generally attend his rallies because they were wary of his extremist activities, although they were receptive to his message.

To reach these people, he turned to a fifty-year-old former professional saxophonist named Rusty Cantelli, who was one of Louisiana's top media consultants. Black jazz musicians and the Reverend Martin Luther King had been Cantelli's heroes as a young man, but he gradually became a conservative and decided that programs like affirmative action and minority set-asides were unfair to whites and demeaning to blacks. Cantelli had first seen Duke in action during campaign forums during the race for District 81, where Cantelli lived. Duke's message impressed him. "He was saying, 'The emperor has no clothes,'" Cantelli recalled several years later. "When I'd ask my friends what they disagreed with him about, they'd laugh nervously. They liked what he had to say but thought it was politically incorrect to be for Duke."

Cantelli, who had many black friends, voted for another candidate in the primary and planned to vote for John Treen in the runoff. But he got angry that Treen's campaign attacked Duke for being a Klansman and Nazi and didn't address the issues Duke was raising. "Here was this guy vainly trying to discuss ideas," Cantelli said, "and the others were saying, 'Nazi! Nazi! Nazi! Racist! Racist! Racist!'" Duke won Cantelli's vote in the runoff.

When he met with Duke in June 1990, they had a long philosophical talk that impressed Cantelli, who relished discussing political and social ideas. "Unlike other politicians," Cantelli said, "he wasn't afraid of ideas, wasn't afraid of vocabulary." Cantelli also liked the way Duke stuck around after his rallies. Other politicians Cantelli knew headed out the door as quickly as possible. "Duke would be the last one to leave," Cantelli said. "He talked with everyone."

Duke wanted to do a thirty-minute television ad as he had done during his presidential and legislative campaigns. As before, Duke didn't think he could lay out his views adequately in conventional thirty- or sixty-second spots. Cantelli agreed. Few politicians could hold voters' attention for thirty minutes, but Cantelli thought Duke could because he had won so much notoriety in the press. "People were asking: 'Who is this guy?'" Cantelli said. "They wanted to see him for themselves."

After watching the previous ads, he told Duke to scrap the talk-show format where Duke answered questions. Duke had to appear alone and read a script from a teleprompter, Cantelli said. He insisted on an additional change. "You have to look directly at the camera," he told Duke. "By doing that, people will feel like you're talking directly to them."

The ad began running in mid-July. It was filmed at a local television studio that Cantelli had fashioned into a comfortable-looking study. Books, paintings, house plants, a lamp, and a fireplace provided a comforting backdrop. Duke looked like one of the characters on the popular television show "L.A. Law," with a conservative dark suit and a fashionable haircut. For thirty minutes, he looked into the camera and offered a compelling argument why people watching at home should vote for him.

Duke laid out his views but, with Cantelli's help, went beyond his stock speech by evoking powerful memories of a simpler, safer time. "I remember when there were no guns or guards in public schools," he said early in the ad, "when the very ideas would have seemed absurd.

"I remember when you could board a city bus, hand the driver a five, and he'd make change.

"I remember when jobs, promotions, admissions and scholarships were awarded to individuals according to merit, and not to racial groups according to quotas.

"I remember when criminals, not homeowners, lived behind bars.

"I remember when names like New York, Miami, New Orleans and Detroit evoked images of promise and prosperity.

"I remember when kids played ball in the streets until bedtime, and their parents didn't worry.

"I remember when the only dope in the neighborhood was that goofy guy down the street.

"I remember when college girls could walk home after evening classes, unescorted and unafraid.

"I remember when no one thought of sex and death at the same time.

"I remember when kids prayed in class every day and were better for it, and so was the nation. If you're older than I am, you'll know what I mean. If you're younger, you don't know what you missed."

Duke's close pulled at the heartstrings of frustrated white voters. "For too long," he said, "we've been afraid to stand up to reverse discrimination, to liberal social engineering, to attempts to belittle and reduce the role of Western Christian culture in American life. We've been afraid of being called 'Uncle Toms,' or 'racists,' or 'insensitive' or any of the stock names that always silence us and send us running for cover.

"Let's not fall for that any more. Let's insist on true equal rights for all. Let's defend and preserve the values and principles that have enabled this nation to endure and thrive.

"We've been silent too long. If I'm elected, others will speak out, too. I need your open support in this race. If you're not registered to vote, do so. I need your vote, and I'm asking for it.

"Don't just send them a message. Send them a senator."

Billy Nungesser, chairman of the state Republican party, was watching the thirty-minute ad at home with his wife Ruth. When it ended, he turned to her and said, "If I didn't know who David Duke was, I'd vote for him. That's as good an ad as I've ever seen. He's appealing to our conservative voters." Not only did Duke innovatively use a thirty-minute ad, but he added another new twist: he asked supporters to make campaign contributions by calling a toll 900 number where they got a recorded message of Duke. Each call would cost ten dollars, with the Duke campaign keeping eight dollars.

The phone lines were swamped that night and every night the ad ran across the state. In the next month, the ads raised $88,000 for Duke, and he was expecting an additional $200,000 before the campaign ended. But South Central Bell in late August pulled the plug on Duke. The company said corporate policy prohibited billing customers for 900 numbers used for political campaigns.

Duke, who was counting on the money to pay for TV ads late in the campaign, was crushed when he got word of South Central Bell's decision. Those ads could decide whether he made the runoff. "How could they do this?" he railed. A man at that night's rally offered Duke his view of what happened. South Central Bell, the man said, had many important issues before the Senate Energy Committee that Johnston chaired and had acted on Johnston's behalf. "It all makes sense," a bitter Duke replied. "The powers that be will be." Duke sued to force South Central Bell to collect the money, but it was to no avail. For his next thirty-minute ad, he had to ask viewers to call an 800 number and make a campaign pledge. This raised less money than a 900 number, where the phone company automatically billed the caller. Not everybody who made a pledge actually contributed the money.

In early August, another poll was released on the Senate race. It showed Johnston maintaining his big lead over Duke. He had 52 percent of the vote, Duke had 24 percent, and Bagert had 7 percent. While leading big, however, Johnston was still not widely popular with voters, many of whom still thought he was out of touch. A television ad listing all the cities Johnston had visited in Louisiana during the past year had helped him but not enough. It was becoming clear to Johnston's advisers that the biggest issue in the race was David Duke. Johnston could brag about all the projects he had brought to Louisiana, but more than anything else, the election was a referendum on Duke.

In early August, the Johnston campaign announced that their candidate would visit all of Louisiana's sixty-four parishes in a caravan over a three-week period. The "Victory Tour," as they called it, would begin rolling August 20. The goal was not only to help Johnston reestablish contact with voters but also to allow him to define the message at each stop. That message would be anti-David Duke. Johnston visited four or five parish courthouses or town squares each day, giving a short, punchy speech at each stop. The crowds were always small, but the size didn't matter. What mattered was that local television and newspaper reporters covered the event, capturing the campaign's desired message that Louisiana's senior senator was back home with voters and that he represented unity, not division.

"This election is about how we can come together, how we can unite rather than be divided," Johnston said in the shadow of the old state capitol in Baton Rouge as he kicked off the Victory Tour. "Blacks and whites, all of us together, must have a common purpose, a common plan. The people of the world and the country are looking at the race in Louisiana in 1990 as a measure of what we are made of, what our values are." The next day, speaking to a group of students at Nicholls State University in Thibodaux, Johnston inadvertently summed up the gist of the election: "I may not be much, but the other side is pretty bad." As he had throughout the campaign, Johnston during the Victory Tour initially adhered to the front-runner strategy of not mentioning Duke by name. But as the tour wore on, he dropped this approach. Johnston's opening attacks on Duke, however, were flat and perfunctory. He still didn't seem to realize that winning this election depended less on how much federal money he had snared for Louisiana in Washington and more on how successfully he painted Duke as the anti-Christ.

Johnston's youngest son, J. Bennett Johnston, Jr., who was traveling on the tour, was getting frustrated with his dad's failure to blast Duke with both guns blazing. A thirty-one-year-old environmental activist in San Francisco, Bennett, Jr., knew that his dad was overburdened with advice on what statistics and facts to use against Duke. So as his dad stepped out of the recreational vehicle to give his speech on September 5 in Farmerville, in northern Louisiana, Bennett Junior handed him a piece of paper. "Racist! Nazi! Bigot! Get mad!" he had written in big bold letters. Senator Johnston studied the piece of paper for several long seconds, stuffed it into his pocket, and after a quick unsmiling glance at his son, marched to the speaking area, barely stopping to greet the waiting local dignitaries.

"The National Association for the Advancement of White People," Johnston thundered, "is the Klan without bedsheets. Did you all read about the sex book he wrote? If I had done one-tenth of what David Duke has done, one-tenth, why they'd ride me out of town on a rail! Why, this man has celebrated Adolf Hitler's birthday every year!"

The crowd was riveted, almost unbelieving at the emotion being expressed by the normally lackluster senator. Bennett Junior was elated. He had never seen his dad so fired up in public before. From then on during the Victory Tour, Johnston attacked Duke forcefully.

With the Victory Tour's success, Johnston's advisers were now ready to unveil what they thought would be the final nail in Duke's coffin: a thirty-second television ad containing footage of Duke leading a Klan rally in the late 1970s. The ad showed Duke raising a stiff left arm in the Klan's "white power" salute as he stood before a burning cross during a nighttime rally. "There's no more truly representative symbol of the white race than the fiery cross," Duke said in the footage. "White victory!" he shouted. To further dramatize the footage, Johnston's media adviser, John Franzen, dubbed in chilling music. "Holy shit!" Bob Mann thought when he saw the ad before it was broadcast. "This is strong stuff. This will finish him off."

It didn't. The ad began blanketing the state's airwaves on September 20. Five days later, a Garin poll showed Duke's support had dropped six points, from 29 to 23 percent. The ad had clearly scared off some voters. But when Garin polled a week later, Duke had rebounded to 27 percent. Whites were too upset with the status quo to kill Duke's candidacy.

As Lance Hill watched the Johnston campaign unfold, he grew more and more frustrated. Hill, the director of the Louisiana Coalition Against Racism and Nazism, thought that Duke was invulnerable on the Klan but that publicizing his less familiar Nazi past could wound him badly. But when the Johnston campaign began attacking Duke, it concentrated its fire on his Klan activities. The coalition had been founded in 1989 by four people who had worked against Duke in the District 81 race: Hill, Beth Rickey, the Reverend James Stovall, a longtime activist based in Baton Rouge, and Lawrence Powell, a Tulane history professor who lived in District 81.

The conventional wisdom following Duke's victory was to ignore him on the ground that attacking him only gave him publicity. But the four disagreed. They thought that Duke was so adept at attracting media coverage that he would fill a political vacuum if not confronted. They were also convinced that Duke's ambition did not end with the state legislature, that he would run for higher office. In late 1989, they decided to form a group and call it the Louisiana Coalition Against Racism and Nazism.

Hill was worried when Duke became a candidate for Senate. He thought the United States was entering an era of political realignment that created fertile terrain for a right-wing populist movement. A prolonged recession in Louisiana's economy had eliminated many jobs, and whites had less money than before because of declining wages. What's more, Hill thought, social chaos in black urban areas exacerbated whites' racist feelings. In the District 81 race, Hill thought, Duke showed he had an effective strategy for popularizing the Far Right's racial program.

Hill grew even more alarmed when he saw the huge crowds Duke got in Monroe and Shreveport in January at the beginning of his campaign. Duke was the only candidate speaking to the anxieties of voters, Hill thought. Johnston, meanwhile, represented business as usual. Hill feared that Duke might be so successful that he would be the catalyst of a full-scale racist resurgence. From his anti-Vietnam organizing during the 1960s, Hill knew how powerful a political movement could become.

The son of a mechanic and a nurse, Hill was thirty-nine in 1990. He had been expelled from the University of Kansas in 1969 for helping take over the football field to protest a ROTC field review. He became a welder. In 1979, he moved to Louisiana, where he initially worked as a labor organizer and then spent five years as a gardener. But he decided he wanted to do research and teach, so in 1987 he began pursuing a doctorate in history at Tulane. His thesis was on the civil rights movement in Louisiana. A huge man with a red beard, standing six feet two inches tall and weighing 300 pounds, Hill was gentle in nature.

Hill despised Duke. The campaign was a referendum on hatred, he decided. But he couldn't help admiring how Duke skillfully carried out his campaign of deception. Hill thought Duke was particularly deft in how he handled his Klan past. In every speech, Duke noted that he had been in the Klan. Duke did this, Hill realized, not only to remind voters of his racial intolerance but also to emphasize that they could count on him to buck the status quo today. After all, a former Klan grand wizard was the ultimate outsider. At the same time, Duke had to calm fears about his Klan past. So after noting his Klan activity, Duke always said he had left the Klan behind. Duke said this, Hill recognized, because he was trying to reach out beyond his racist base to voters who liked his views but cringed at his extremist activities.

Hill was also impressed with how Duke used anecdotes to accent his views— much as President Reagan had done. One of Duke's favorite stories during the Senate campaign involved a doctor in the small town of Vivian. The doctor, Duke said, was visited one day by a thirty-three-year-old mother and her three daughters, aged eighteen, sixteen, and fifteen. The doctor, related Duke, said all the women were pregnant—and the father for all four was the same man. "Oh, my God!" people would gasp, when Duke delivered the kicker. Duke never said the women were black, but Hill knew that's what his audiences thought.

Early on, the leaders of the Louisiana Coalition Against Racism and Nazism decided that their goal wasn't simply defeating Duke at the ballot box— as Johnston and Bagert sought to do—but discrediting his views. "We wanted to defend the principles of equality and justice in the face of Duke's assaults," Hill said. "We wanted to appeal to the moral conscience of voters. That meant that we wouldn't be tied to what was politically expedient— talking about his womanizing or *Finders-Keepers*, for example."

The coalition researched Duke's background throughout the campaign and called press conferences when they found information that painted him as a Nazi or as an extremist. Until the final month of the campaign, when Johnston began his attacks, they served as Duke's opposition. Hill had an enduring faith that the truth was the most powerful weapon against Duke. But during the campaign he became discouraged at how people reacted to news of Duke's Klan or Nazi activities. "Voters' first response to the truth about Duke was defensive," Hill said. "To admit that he was a fraud and a racist was to admit that they were being misled or were bigots. People don't like to admit this. We were holding a mirror up to the electorate and telling them that they and David Duke were one and the same."

Haters called the coalition's New Orleans office day and night. "You're the tools of the Jews," callers would regularly scream. "You're lying about his record," or "You're working for Johnston," others said. Some callers issued death threats. The morning mail brought more anger. One letter was soaked in urine. One envelope contained dead cockroaches. Letter after letter called them "nigger lovers."

The coalition mobilized hundreds of volunteers against Duke and sent anti-Duke mail to voters throughout the state. But their effectiveness was limited. "They [Louisiana voters] felt ashamed to support him," Hill said. "But they were shamed into hiding their opinions, not changing them." To mount the kind of attack needed against Duke, the coalition needed the strong backing of Louisiana's political, civic, and business leaders—but this they could not get, either because Johnston held such a big lead in the polls that they were apathetic or because they didn't want to offend their many white constituents who backed Duke.

The coalition scored its biggest success in making more voters aware of Duke's Nazi activities. When discussing his past, Duke mentioned only the Klan—until his July television ad, when for the first time the coalition's attacks forced him to deny he was a Nazi. From then on, Duke had to repeat the denial of what the coalition's polling showed was a more damaging charge. The coalition also broadcast a humorous anti-Duke ad late in the campaign. But with the group short of money and the Shreveport and Monroe television stations refusing to run it because of a bomb threat, too few voters saw the ad for it to have an impact.

Meanwhile, a month before the primary, Ben Bagert's campaign was on a life support system. Bagert at the beginning of the campaign thought he could become the first Republican senator from Louisiana since Reconstruction. But the media and voters cared only about Duke and Johnston. Bagert was frozen out. By trying to appeal to white voters by attacking welfare and promising to get tough on crime, Bagert hoped to coopt Duke's issues. But instead, as Bennett Johnston midway through the campaign had prophesied of Bagert's effort, "Given a choice between a real racist and a Johnny-come-lately, they'll choose the real racist every time." The National Republican Senatorial Committee promised Bagert $400,000 early on to give his campaign a needed boost but didn't come through with the money. Bagert found himself caught in a catch-22: without a more viable candidacy, traditional Republican donors were reluctant to give him money. But he couldn't become stronger without the money.

Bagert initially ignored Duke except at a state party meeting in March, when he called Duke a "maggot" and likened him to Hitler. Bagert instead concentrated his attacks on Johnston, figuring that he would make the runoff with Johnston and would need Duke's voters then. But by August, trailing badly in third place, Bagert had no option but to assail Duke. He had detested Duke from the time they had a confrontation during a 1976 ceremony in the state house of representatives where a bust of P. B. S. Pinchback, who served as Louisiana's only black governor briefly during Reconstruction, was unveiled. Duke led a companion into the state house who wore minstrel-show blackface and who dragged his knuckles on the ground while wearing a sign that read "Governor Pinchback." Bagert threatened to punch Duke in the nose if he didn't leave.

Combative and feisty by nature, Bagert attacked Duke late in the Senate campaign with relish. During a radio debate on August 16, Bagert knocked Duke off balance. When Duke accused Bagert of pushing for reform of the welfare system during the Senate campaign because he had seen how effectively Duke used the issue, Bagert snapped, "I've been talking about welfare reform since you were goose-stepping around Baton Rouge." Duke, flustered for one of the few times in his political career, had no reply.

Bagert at every chance sought to rattle Duke by calling him by the female pseudonym he used for *Finders-Keepers*. "Hi, Ben," Duke called out to Bagert as he leaned out the window of a recreational vehicle on September 2 in Morgan City. "Hey, Dorothy," Bagert yelled back. "How are you?" Duke's face froze in a smile. Duke responded by canceling remaining campaign forums with Bagert. But two days later, Bagert ambushed him at a political forum in New Orleans where they were supposed to appear at different times. Forced to appear together with Bagert, Duke complained, "You called me a Nazi, a bigot and a maggot the other day."

"I never called you a bigot," Bagert said, as the crowd laughed.

"How about maggot?" Duke asked, falling further into Bagert's trap.

"I did say that we in the Republican Party were turning a maggot into a martyr. But I never called you a Nazi. Everybody knows about your Nazi activities."

Bagert was having fun, but his campaign was dying. On September 13, his top two aides revealed to the *Times-Picayune* that they were quitting his campaign. The aides, Mari Patterson and Fred Myers, both of whom were being paid by the National Republican Senatorial Committee, said Bagert had no chance and that his continued candidacy might pull enough votes away from Johnston to put Duke in the runoff. "Bagert cannot win, and we have to stop Duke in his tracks," Myers said. "If he gets in the runoff, [Democrats will say] we [Republicans] are wearing hoods and sheets. That would be a disaster for the Republican Party."

When confronted that day with his aides' statements, Bagert said he had fired them because they had misappropriated money. He said Patterson and

Myers told him they would publicly reconcile with him if he paid them some of what they were owed. Regardless of who was telling the truth, Bagert was finished. On October 4, two days before the primary, he stood in his backyard and told a press corps that included reporters from across the country that he was pulling out. "By continuing to play on," Bagert said, "I'd be forcing a runoff—a runoff that Louisiana can't stand." Bagert called on his supporters to pull Johnston's lever in the voting booth.

A poll released the day before showed Johnston with 53 percent of the vote, Duke with 26 percent, Bagert with 8 percent and 16 percent undecided. Bagert's supporters were mainstream Republicans who will vote for Johnston, pollster Susan Howell predicted, giving the incumbent more than 60 percent. The race was declared over. "Johnston a virtual shoo-in in primary, analysts say," read the *Times-Picayune* headline for the article on Bagert's withdrawal. Johnston was traveling in a caravan ten miles outside of Bossier City when he got word that Bagert had dropped out. The caravan stopped and Johnston's aides spilled out of their vehicles and whooped with delight. "This guarantees no runoff," Bob Mann thought happily.

Duke was at a TV station in Baton Rouge preparing to give an interview when he got word. His face fell, and his body sagged in defeat. He had been sure he would make the runoff and then beat Johnston a month later. Now all seemed lost. The election was only two days away. Duke sat slumped in a chair, unsure what to do. His aides huddled and came up with a plan: Duke would fly around the state the next day, hitting each of the major media markets, and claim that Bagert had made a back-room political deal with Johnston. Bagert had agreed to pull out in exchange for Johnston's arranging to pay off his $150,000 campaign debt. Duke had no evidence of this, but the claim might just hit home with the frustrated electorate, his advisers thought. Duke agreed, and he spent the election eve denouncing the "back-room" deal.

There were mostly sunny skies throughout Louisiana on election day. Duke voted early at a polling booth near his home in Metairie. Johnston took a chartered jet to Shreveport to vote. During the flight, he pulled out a yellow legal pad and calculated what his winning percentage would be. Garin's final poll a week earlier had given him 55 percent of the vote, so Johnston allocated himself 55 percent of the undecideds. Added to the vote he already had, this would give him 65 percent of the vote overall. Nodding with satisfaction, he sat back in his seat to enjoy the rest of the flight.

But Bennett Johnston and just about every other political expert had misjudged the electorate and misjudged the impact of Bagert's withdrawal. There was a hidden vote: many whites favored Duke but had been ashamed to admit this to pollsters. And Duke's claim that the pullout was a back-room deal rang true with many voters, who saw this as more evidence that the system was awry. Bagert's withdrawal led other fed-up whites to feel that they could vote for Duke as a protest, thinking that they could send a message to Washington without electing him. Meanwhile, blacks with lukewarm feelings about Johnston stayed home, believing that Duke didn't present a serious threat.

Johnston returned to New Orleans for an election-night victory at the Hilton Hotel. But as he watched the returns from his suite, he smiled thinly. He was going to prevail but with 10 percent less than he had expected. He had to rewrite his victory speech.

Duke was winning an astounding 59 percent of the white vote and was clobbering Johnston in white working-class neighborhoods and rural areas. He was running even with him in predominantly white middle-class suburbs. Of Louisiana's sixty-four parishes, Duke had won twenty-five. Winning nearly 100 percent of the black vote saved Johnston.

The final results were:

J. Bennett Johnston	752,902	54 percent
David Duke	607,391	43.5 percent
Nick J. Accardo	21,485	1.5 percent
Larry Crowe	14,335	1 percent

Duke had lost, but supporters at his election night party at the Lions Club in Harahan, a suburb of New Orleans, were euphoric. Duke had done so much better than expected that his supporters felt as if he had won. His fight would continue. Maybe next year he would run for governor.

"This is not the end of this political odyssey," Duke said as the crowd cheered and chanted his name over and over again. "We are going to build a political movement in this country to bring back the political rights of the majority."

The Louisiana Coalition Against Racism and Nazism had rented a ballroom for a victory party at the Sheraton Hotel in New Orleans. As Lance Hill watched the returns come in, he recalled that throughout the campaign he had proclaimed the election as a referendum on hate. As he watched Duke on television declaring victory, he thought to himself: "Hate won."

CHAPTER NINE

THE RACE FROM HELL

As soon as David Duke lost the Senate election to Bennett Johnston in October 1990, his legions of ardent supporters and opponents both asked: Will he run for governor the following year? With his strong showing in defeat, Duke had established himself as a formidable potential challenger to the incumbent governor, Charles (Buddy) Roemer III.

Roemer, however, was unconcerned. He thought Duke had run strongly against Johnston because voters didn't care much who they put in the Senate—they seemed to view it as a job in far-off Washington held by someone they had little contact with—and had used the election to vent their anger by sending a message to Washington. Louisianians, in contrast, cared deeply about who served as their governor, Roemer felt, because the governor directly affected their taxes, their children's schools, their highways, the safety of their streets, and many other things big and small. In Louisiana, the governor is "the Kingfish," a legacy from Huey Long, wielding enormous power to reward friends and punish enemies by offering or withholding government contracts and patronage appointments to powerful state boards.

Early polls comforted Roemer. They showed him with about 35 percent of the vote, Edwin Edwards with 25 percent and Duke 15 percent. Roemer also dismissed Duke's Senate showing—and the fact that Duke in 1991 raised as much money as Johnston—because he thought Johnston was a lackluster candidate. Roemer had no doubts that he would tear Duke apart if Duke entered the governor's race. Roemer was the dragon-slayer, a title bestowed on him after he won election in 1987 by defeating Edwin Edwards—who had served longer as governor than any of his predecessors and had been the state's most powerful governor since Huey Long. Roemer ran first in the October 1987 primary in a five-man field with 33 percent of the vote. Edwards finished second with 28 percent and, at 1:30 A.M. on election night, shocked his supporters by announcing he would not contest the runoff. Suddenly, Buddy Roemer was governor.

A four-term congressman from northwest Louisiana, Roemer had won by promising to take on the sacred cows and shake up the system. "The Roemer Revolution," he called it. He had started the race the longest of long shots, at 1 percent in the polls. But he catapulted ahead of the other four candidates in the final month of the campaign when the state's major newspapers endorsed him, and he aired tough-talking, plainspoken television ads in which he pledged to clean up Louisiana's corrupt politics, improve education, fight crime, cut taxes, eliminate wasteful government spending, and crack down on polluters that had made the state the most befouled in the Union.

"We must free Louisiana from the grip of political corruption," he exhorted. "And that's going to take more than just new faces, new rhetoric or new style. It's going to take a revolution in Louisiana's politics, government, education and economy—and that's what my campaign is all about."

By making his appeal directly to voters through television ads and news stories, Roemer, an evangelical, mesmerizing speaker, eschewed the traditional approach of seeking endorsements from elected officials, local power brokers and the courthouse crowd. He also broke with tradition by refusing to accept cash donations, contributions over $5,000 per donor—at the time there was no dollar limit—and contributions from political action committees.

Roemer was raised on the 2,000-acre Scopena Plantation, ten miles south of Bossier City, by parents who were unusually passionate about educating their five children. "They would pore over books and learn world history before school in the morning, debate issues of the day at the breakfast and supper tables and sweat in the north Louisiana cotton and soybean fields in the afternoon," *Times-Picayune* reporter John McQuaid wrote in a penetrating 1987 profile of Roemer. "There was no television in the house. A green blackboard mounted on a wall in the dining room became the battlefield for regular mealtime debates on anything from foreign policy to physics. . . . The parents raised their children with a mission: They would take their citizenship seriously, and would lend their intelligence to public service. Buddy Roemer, the eldest, undertook the mission with singular zeal."

Valedictorian of Bossier High School's class of 1960, Roemer headed off to Harvard at age sixteen, where he earned an undergraduate degree and a master's degree at the business school. He returned to work for the family business and also formed two banks. He became active in politics in 1971 when his father, Charles Roemer II, managed the campaign of a reform candidate from Acadiana named Edwin Edwards. After winning, Edwards named Charles Roemer the commissioner of administration, the state's most powerful position after the governor.

Buddy Roemer, who managed north Louisiana during the 1971 Edwards campaign, founded a political consulting firm and managed several successful campaigns before winning a seat in the United States House of Representatives in 1980. During his seven years in the House, he earned a reputation as a maverick who repeatedly angered the Democratic leadership by refusing to go along with their programs. "Often wrong, never in doubt," House Speaker Thomas (Tip) O'Neill said of Roemer. Bucking the Democratic leadership played well at home, however, as he was reelected three times without opposition.

As a political consultant, Roemer received government contracts and additional favors from Edwards and other public officials he had helped elect. But as an antiestablishment member of Congress, Roemer grew uncomfortable with Louisiana's political tradition. He also blamed that tradition for ruining his father. Charles Roemer in 1981 was sent to federal prison along with New Orleans Mafia boss Carlos Marcello for conspiring to sell influence in the awarding of state insurance contracts. During the fifteen months Charles Roemer served in a federal prison in Fort Worth, his son often visited him on trips back to his congressional district.

Buddy Roemer, a bantamweight at five feet seven inches and 145 pounds, attacked Louisiana's political system with a vengeance during the 1987 gubernatorial campaign, aiming much of his fire at Edwin Edwards, whom he blamed for his father's troubles. "I want a governor who puts our pocketbook ahead of his," Roemer said repeatedly. He and his group of young, idealistic aides—dubbed the Roemeristas—took office, and for more than a year they won a string of legislative victories that reshaped the state: teacher pay increases, a teacher evaluation program, tougher environmental enforcement, strict limits on campaign financing. To balance the state budget, Roemer sold off government airplanes, cut many popular programs and borrowed $1 billion. He had staved off Louisiana's bankruptcy, and now he moved to his biggest gambit yet—a restructuring of the state tax system that he said would put Louisiana on sound fiscal standing for years. It was put before the voters in April 1989. And with newly elected state representative David Duke leading the charge against it, the measure was defeated.

It was a crushing blow for Roemer and his so-called revolution. His enemies in the legislature counterattacked, calling him arrogant, snide, and sanctimonious. Allies of Edwards, they plotted against Roemer and began derailing his reform measures. The revolution was becoming untracked. But the worst was yet to come for Roemer. One day in September, his wife, Patti, a former state fair queen who had grown to hate the demands of political life, walked out of the governor's mansion with their ten-year-old son, Dakota. Roemer was heartbroken. "It was probably the first time in the governor's life that he felt a little bit out of control," said Danny Walker, a Baptist minister and close family friend who became his spiritual adviser.

Roemer was an unusual elected official. He was a diabetic who needed two shots of insulin a day. He was a loner who didn't like other politicians. He brought books to football games and often failed to return phone calls, which infuriated many people, especially supporters. When he went to his favorite restaurant in Baton Rouge, a Mexican food place called the Superior Bar & Grill, he would barely talk with any of the other patrons and would sit at a table with his back to the crowd. Roemer's media consultant, Raymond Strother, marveled at his behavior. The many politicians Strother had advised would have worked the room, shaking hands with everyone, and would then have sat facing the crowd so that people would come by to visit.

Patti Roemer's leaving reinforced her husband's antisocial manner. Roemer went into a shell. He canceled appointments and sat by the mansion's swimming pool during the day with strict instructions that he not be disturbed. At night he had trouble sleeping. He desperately missed his wife, and all he cared about was winning her back.

In January, Walker organized a three-day inspirational seminar called "Adventures in Attitudes" and invited the governor's top aides and Patti. Early on during the retreat, Walker urged everybody to put a rubber band around their wrist. "From now on and the rest of the seminar, when somebody says a negative thought about himself or puts you down, you go, 'Cancel. Cancel.'" Roemer's aides rolled their eyes in disbelief—and Patti on the second day fled.

Roemer didn't give up. He took ballroom dance lessons, went to therapy, and read self-help books provided by Walker. The most important was a New Age bestseller, *All I Really Needed to Know I Learned in Kindergarten*, by Robert Fulghum. Following Fulghum's prescription, Roemer sought to "honor" everybody by listening attentively, showing them respect, and trying to fulfill their requests. "Honor," read the sign he hung over his office door.

By now legislators, already unhappy with Roemer's disdain for them, were in open revolt. But with Walker's advice, Roemer decided he could win them over with a positive approach borrowed from Fulghum. He unveiled it in April as he gave the opening address for the 1990 legislative session.

Roemer apologized for his "inflexibility and insensitivity." "Please forgive me, if you can," he asked the legislators. He talked about "listening" and "honor" and "sharing." He said: "Let's say goodby to 'me' and hello to 'we'. . . . Let's say goodbye to the negative and welcome the positive." Then he invited the Legislature to "light the campfire . . . I think it's time to gather 'round, hold hands, laugh, share dreams, find common ground, discover our fellowship, refocus our vision, feel the power of the tribal family and start afresh." Twice he referred to Patti as if they were still a couple. Legislators snickered when reporters asked for their reaction afterward. "I think Danny Walkerism has come into play," said state Senator Hank Lauricella. It was, several others legislators said derisively, Roemer's "campfire" speech.

Roemer's problems with the legislature worsened, and by the time the governor's race got under way at the beginning of 1991, legislators throughout the state were bad-mouthing him to their constituents. Still, Roemer and his advisers thought he would easily win reelection. He was a terrific campaigner—few people could give a better speech—and, his aides figured, the field looked weak. The challengers were Louis Lambert, the Democratic chairman of the Public Service Commission, who had faded from view after narrowly losing the 1979 governor's race to David Treen; Aaron Broussard, the can-do Democratic mayor of the New Orleans suburb of Kenner, who was unknown statewide; David Duke, whom the Roemer campaign dismissed because of his Nazi and Klan past; and Edwin Edwards, whom voters had overwhelmingly rejected four years before.

Edwards was the latest in a long line of flamboyant governors from a state that, with its conservative Protestants in the north and its freewheeling, Roman Catholic Cajuns in the South creating a Byzantine political gumbo, seemed to have more in common with a Latin American country than with the rest of the United States. "Every man a king" and "Share the Wealth," Huey Long had shouted during his near-dictatorial reign, when he handed out free textbooks, paved roads, built charity hospitals, and enriched himself and his biggest supporters. Long ruled from 1928 when he was elected governor until he was gunned down in 1935 in the towering state capitol he had just built. Huey's brother, Earl, later served as governor three times and continued the populist tradition, handing out food to the poor that he had just bought at country stores and increasing spending for education and the indigent. In his final term, Earl Long had a mental breakdown, took up with a stripper, and attacked segregationists.

The next great heir of Louisiana's populist tradition was Edwin Edwards, who had been born in a rural part of central Louisiana, the son of a tenant farmer and a midwife. When Edwards was a boy during the Great Depression, his family lived on butter, beans, flour, and other staples from the government. His early hero was President Franklin D. Roosevelt. "I remember when government made it possible for electricity to be brought to my house," he said in a 1991 interview. "I remember when government made it possible for a bus to pick me up and drive me eight miles into town. I remember when government made it possible for me to eat a free, hot lunch at school. I remember when government made books available to me that I otherwise would not have been able to have."

After getting a law degree from LSU, Edwards moved to Crowley, a small town in southwestern Louisiana. With his bayou charm, razor-sharp intelligence, and intuitive understanding of human nature, he built a successful law practice and won a string of elections that took him from the Crowley City Council to the Louisiana Senate to Congress. In 1971, he put together a coalition of blacks, blue-collar workers, and Cajuns to edge Bennett Johnston in the Democratic runoff. Edwards then trounced David Treen, the Republican candidate, in the general election. He was the state's first Cajun governor and the first to have openly courted blacks.

It was a good time to be governor of Louisiana, particularly if you liked to manipulate the levers of power and government, as Edwin Edwards did so artfully. The state's oil-based economy was strong, and he had plenty of money to do what he liked best—spend on new roads, bridges, ports, hospitals, and schools.

Like Huey Long, he was a populist who championed the poor and underprivileged. And like Long, he cut deals to steer work to favored businessmen, who provided the money he needed to run his campaigns. When news articles raised questions about these deals, some of which seemed to benefit Edwards personally, he dismissed the complaints with a wink and a few one-liners. When asked about accepting illegal campaign contributions, he said, "It was illegal for them to give, but not for me to receive." When questioned about his frequent trips to Las Vegas, he admitted that he loved to gamble, and he cracked more jokes. When questioned about tales of his womanizing, as when a book claimed he once made love with six women in a night, Edwards smiled and said, "No, it wasn't that way. He [the author] was gone when the last one came in."

With the state's economy humming, practically everyone laughed along with Edwards, and in 1975, he was overwhelmingly reelected. "I think people realize that public officials are human and that we have our faults, our inadequacies," he explained once, "and if we don't try to be hypocritical or santimonious about it, I think they'll forgive us for it."

State law required Edwards to step down after two terms, and he was succeeded by David Treen, the state's first Republican governor since Reconstruction. When Edwards was eligible to run again in 1983, he challenged Treen, who was running for reelection. Treen was an honest and fair governor but indecisive and an unwilling deal maker. Edwards sliced him apart. Treen, Edwards said, was "so slow it takes him an hour and a half to watch '60 Minutes.'" Edwards was so confident of his election that he said he couldn't lose unless he was caught "in bed with a dead girl or a live boy." He was right. Voters returned him to the governor's mansion with 63 percent of the vote. Although the challenger, he outspent Treen $16 million to $6 million. After the election, Edwards paid off a $4 million campaign debt by filling two 747s with supporters, at $10,000 a head, for a week-long trip to France. On a side trip to Monaco, Edwards won $15,000 shooting craps.

But when he took office in 1984 as Louisiana's first three-term governor, oil prices were dropping, and the state's finances were soon a shambles. Edwards rammed a $730 million tax increase through the state legislature, but it wasn't enough to stem the red ink. He had to cut cherished government programs. The good times were over.

Edwards over the years had been investigated by more than a dozen grand juries but had always escaped indictment—until 1985. A federal court indicted him on charges that he was paid $1.9 million by hospitals while Treen was governor in return for favors when, as expected, he became governor again in 1983. Prosecutors charged that Edwards needed the money to pay off $2 million in gambling debts from Nevada casinos. Casino executives testified that Edwards paid off his debts with suitcases stuffed with cash at the governor's mansion. Edwards attempted to hide his losses, prosecutors added, by gambling under the aliases of T. Wong, T. Lee, B. True and Ed Neff. The high point of the trial came when Edwards took the stand. He denied the allegations, and almost all of the jury believed him. The judge declared a mistrial. Federal authorities decided to prosecute him a second time. This time he was acquitted.

While Edwards had won a legal victory, he was badly damaged politically. With the Oil Bust pushing Louisiana's unemployment rate into double digits and the state nearly bankrupt, voters no longer laughed at Edwards's escapades. When he ran for reelection in 1987, the magic touch was gone, and he conceded to Roemer without even contesting the runoff. Most everybody thought his political career was over.

Edwin Edwards, however, nursed the idea that he could be elected governor again. Even as he dropped out on the night of the 1987 primary, he began plotting to win back the governor's mansion four years later. He would run again for several reasons. One was his belief that Roemer's preachy style would wear thin with voters and that Roemer would be unable to keep his

1987 campaign promises. Edwards knew that every so often Louisiana, like a boozer swearing off alcohol, elected a reform governor but four years later always replaced him with a populist. "Let the good times roll," after all, is the state's motto.

Another reason Edwards would run again was that he loved being the Kingfish. He reveled in the crowds of people who flocked to him wherever he went, asking for help or just wanting to say hello. As governor, Edwards could help his core constituency: the poor, the elderly, minorities. He could also help his friends and, many said, himself financially. There was another basic reason he wanted to defeat Roemer in 1991: beginning with his election to the Crowley City Council in 1954, he had won twenty-two elections in a row before the 1987 loss. He wanted to avenge that defeat and end his forty-year political career as a winner.

Edwards declared his candidacy on February 8. Silver haired, tan, and sixty-three years old—looking like an aging card shark—he defended his own record and promised "to learn from my mistakes." He would be, he said, "a different Edwin Edwards." He added: "I like to believe I've evolved mentally and emotionally. . . . I think I'm a little more serious, and these are serious times. . . . I am going to be very careful about not falling into some of the traps I fell into when I was less experienced."

Edwards also bitterly attacked Roemer. Playing on Roemer's 1987 campaign slogan, he spoke under a banner that read, "I'm the Solution to the Revolution." Roemer, Edwards said, "promised us an ethical, scandal-free government and gave us Danny Walker voodooism."

While he concentrated his fire on Roemer, Edwards got in a few jibes at Duke. "I cannot believe that anybody who has worn a Nazi uniform or a Klan sheet is respectable," he said. "That is too unlike the philosophy of Americans and Louisianians." Privately, he joked that he and Duke were similar in that "we're both wizards under the sheets." Edwards and his wife Elaine had gotten divorced in 1989 after forty years of marriage. He now had a new lady, a twenty-six-year-old LSU nursing student named Candy Picou. She was blonde and slender and looked like a model. "A man is as old as the woman he feels," Edwards joked to a crowd of supporters one night during the campaign.

David Duke had decided during the Senate campaign that his next step politically would be to run for governor if he lost to Johnston. Several of his advisers told him that he was much better suited to be a legislator than an executive, since it was far easier to demand changes than actually try to implement them. His closest adviser, Jim McPherson, told him he should run for reelection in 1991 and for Congress the following year. But as he sat in the legislature, Duke had been impressed with how much power the governor wielded. And throughout the Senate campaign, he constantly ran into people who implored him not to go off to Washington, telling him that they needed him in Baton Rouge, cleaning up the state's problems. There was another reason Duke wanted to run for governor: with his belief in destiny, he thought that his strong showing in the Senate election showed he was on his way to saving the white race and that winning the governorship was the next step.

Duke in January told reporters that he would run for governor, although he didn't make his formal announcement until March. As in the Senate campaign, he would run as a repackaged right-wing, antiestablishment populist, and he would continue to try to distance himself from what he called "youthful intolerance" and "youthful mistakes." As in the Senate election, he would focus on racially based issues, speaking in code. He would oppose affirmative action and minority set-asides, call for the end of forced busing, advocate reducing the welfare benefits of women who bear illegitimate children, and demand that welfare recipients work for their checks. He would not discuss issues involving Jews.

As a gubernatorial candidate, Duke, who turned forty-one on July 1 that year, would stress additional issues to broaden his appeal and to speak more directly about pocketbook issues: opposition to new taxes, opposition to reducing the state's $75,000 homestead exemption, support for a clean environment, the need to cut government spending, opposition to abortion, the need to get tough on crime. He would still hold old-style campaign rallies throughout the state, but he wouldn't need to hold as many—or speak as long—because voters now knew him. Most of his top campaign aides would be the same as in 1990: Jim McPherson, David Touchstone, Babs Wilson, Howie Farrell, and Kenny Knight.

Buddy Roemer at the beginning of 1991, meanwhile, was preoccupied not only with running state government but also with deciding whether to switch political parties. Roemer in Congress had never been comfortable with the Democratic party. Known as one of the Boll Weevils—the group of conservative Democrats who provided crucial backing for President Reagan—he voted with the Reagan administration more often than almost any other Democrat. He had not even attended the 1988 Democratic Convention.

Republican members of the Louisiana delegation for several years had tried to persuade Roemer to switch parties. But it wasn't until a conversation with President George Bush in early 1990 that Roemer began to consider the idea seriously. Roemer and Bush had become friends when Bush was vice president, and they frequently played paddleball in the House gymnasium. The paddleball games continued when Bush was president and Roemer was visiting Washington as governor.

One day Bush told Roemer that he would love to have him join the Republican party. When the idea came from his friend the president, Roemer listened. There were follow-up phone calls from Bush and John Sununu, Bush's chief of staff. "You're a road warrior," Sununu told him. It was heady stuff for Roemer, especially in the last part of 1990, as Bush's popularity soared because of his tough response to Saddam Hussein's invasion of Kuwait.

For months, Roemer kept it hidden that he was considering changing parties, something no sitting governor in American history had ever done. He informed his aides at the beginning of 1991. On January 25, he invited them to the governor's mansion for dinner along with his family, and he asked everyone for their advice. As he went around the table, person after person— his mother, father, and aides alike—advised that switching would hurt him with voters, particularly among blacks. Roemer's polling corroborated their words. He would lose four percentage points running as a Republican. But still dismissing Duke's candidacy, Roemer thought he could withstand the four-point loss. By switching, he figured, he could also keep out one of the major Republicans—most notably, David Treen—who were considering running and who would take away more than four points.

Another consideration in Roemer's mind far outweighed the impact of his switch on the governor's race, but it was something he kept secret. He wanted to run for president in 1996, but he thought he had little chance to win the Democratic nomination. The party's rank-and-file voters, who dominate the primary process, would dismiss him as too independent, he feared. Roemer, however, did like his odds for winning the Republican nomination. He could run as a fiscal conservative and social moderate, a break-the-mold Republican who would reduce spending, hold down taxes, protect the environment and strongly support civil rights. Roemer announced the party switch on March 11 on the front steps of the governor's mansion.

While President Bush very much wanted Roemer to become a Republican, the state GOP chairman, Billy Nungesser, did not. Nungesser thought Roemer was too liberal. But what bothered Nungesser even more was that Roemer had kept him in the dark about the party switch and now seemed to expect to take control of the state party. Nungesser retaliated by speaking bitingly about Roemer to reporters. Shortly afterward, Nungesser met with Roemer at the governor's mansion. A heated argument ensued. "Goddammit, Nungesser," Roemer shouted, "if you don't get into line and cut this shit out, I'm going to kick your fucking ass out of the mansion." Roemer's outburst shocked Billy Rimes, his legislative lobbyist. Rimes had never before heard Roemer curse in front of his mother, who also attended the meeting.

As Nungesser hurried away from the mansion, he resolved to undercut Roemer. And as state party chairman, he had ample opportunity. After Roemer switched, all the potential heavyweight Republican candidates deferred to him except one: Clyde Holloway, a three-term congressman who represented a rural area of central Louisiana. While national Republican leaders urged Holloway to stay out, the party's small but vocal antiabortion wing implored him to run. Comprised mostly of fundamentalist Christians, antiabortionists badly wanted to defeat Roemer because he had vetoed two bills in 1990 that would have prohibited virtually all abortions in Louisiana—three years after he firmly placed himself in the antiabortion camp. Nungesser joined the right-to-lifers in urging Holloway to challenge Roemer. On April 17, Holloway announced his entry into the race.

Nungesser was to create more problems for Roemer. He went ahead and scheduled a state Republican convention in June to endorse a gubernatorial candidate. Roemer wanted the convention canceled, believing that as the incumbent Republican candidate, he should automatically win the party's endorsement. Besides, with a legislative session coming up, he didn't want to spend the time and money needed to woo Republicans and capture the endorsement. The Republican state central committee on May 11 backed Nungesser, however, and agreed to hold the convention on June 15 in Lafayette. Duke and Holloway applauded the decision and said they would contest the endorsement; Roemer said he would not. Two months after becoming a Republican, Roemer seemed like a man without a party.

These developments thrilled David Duke. At the beginning of the race, he thought he would make the runoff against Buddy Roemer. Now he thought Roemer had been so badly damaged that he would face Edwin Edwards. He preferred this prospect because he thought so many voters hated Edwards that given a choice between the two, they would vote for Duke.

On May 18, Holloway and Duke competed in the GOP's statewide caucuses, where 55 percent of the delegates would be chosen for the convention four weeks later at the Lafayette Cajun Dome. Holloway came out on top at the caucuses, winning about 330 of the delegates selected to Duke's 220. Duke could claim victory, however, because he had won nearly ten times as many delegates as at the Senate caucuses eighteen months before. He was becoming more socially acceptable.

And while Holloway won the party endorsement at the state convention on June 15, Duke flexed his muscle when GOP leaders tried to prevent him from addressing the delegates. He sidled up to the back of the stage, side-stepped a guard trying to block him, and dashed up to the microphone, arms aloft in victory. Dozens of his supporters rushed up to the stage, waving placards and chanting his name, "Duke! Duke! Duke!" Nungesser shouted for order, but Duke's supporters continued their noisemaking for ten minutes. They quieted down only when Duke was allowed to speak later in the afternoon. The boisterous Duke demonstration unnerved Neil Curran, a Republican stalwart who had worked for John Treen in the District 81 race. "It's like we're attending a party convention in Germany in the 1930s," he thought, "and Hitler is coming to power."

With the Republican party badly divided between Roemer, Holloway, and Duke, Edwin Edwards's electoral prospects were starting to improve a bit. But they still didn't look good. The first half of 1991 had not been an easy time for the proud man who had dominated the state's politics for a generation. Some friends he called asking for campaign donations told him to stay out, believing that he couldn't beat Roemer in the runoff. Others didn't call him back. Even two of his top campaign aides, Al Donovan and Bob d'Hemecourt, thought he couldn't defeat Roemer.

But Edwards soldiered on, confident that he would prove the skeptics wrong. By late July he had shored up his base in the Democratic party with the withdrawal of Louis Lambert and Aaron Broussard from the race. Both had run out of money. They were soon followed by Kathleen Blanco, a Public Service Commission member and Democrat who had become a candidate in May. With Lambert, Broussard, and Blanco gone, Edwards could corral their supporters.

Holloway, meanwhile, was going nowhere. As with Ben Bagert the year before, the state Republican party endorsement meant little. Holloway could not raise the $2 million needed to wage an effective campaign, and he could only count on his base of support, the state's fundamentalist Christians, who accounted for but 10 percent of the state's voters.

Like Lambert, Broussard, and Blanco, Holloway was discovering that it was a three-man race. Roemer, Duke, and Edwards each enjoyed such a large bloc of support in a highly polarized electorate that no one else could mount a successful challenge. In general, blacks, Cajuns and union workers backed Edwards; businessmen, environmentalists, pro-choice groups, and good-government reformers supported Roemer; and blue-collar whites and disaffected Republicans backed Duke. When the votes were counted on October 19, primary election night, one of the three would be the odd man out. Most political experts thought that man would be Duke. They expected Roemer to run first and Edwards second in the primary, and then Roemer would triumph in the runoff.

Roemer, however, was having more problems. In June, the legislature approved another strict antiabortion bill. Roemer vetoed it. But this time the legislature overrode him—the first time that had ever happened to a Louisiana governor. Roemer ran into more problems when he vetoed a reapportionment bill he had promised the night before to sign, lawmakers called him a liar. Edwards and Duke jumped on these developments, saying Roemer had alienated so many legislators that he could no longer get his measures approved.

Duke, however, was hardly one to argue this point. He was still far more effective at winning publicity than at getting his racially oriented bills passed. He did have better success with the legislature in 1991 than in his two previous years, as fewer legislators wanted to oppose him. The house adopted five of his seven bills, but most were severely watered down by amendments. His most publicized bill, which would have given each woman on welfare $100 a year to have the Norplant birth control device implanted in her arm, was amended to provide instead for distribution of birth control information to welfare recipients. Duke in 1991 did get his first bill through the legislature. It was an innocuous measure prohibiting jurors from accepting payment from movie producers or book publishers seeking an account of the jury's proceedings.

During July and most of August, the campaign rolled on with little drama. With the state's economy still in the doldrums and with Roemer's $5,000-per-contributor limit now state law, none of the candidates yet had the money needed to wage a high-octane television campaign. Where Edwin Edwards raised $16 million in 1983, Edwards, Duke, and Roemer were hoping in 1991 to raise $2 million to $3 million each. There was another reason for the lack of drama during July and most of August: Roemer, the focal point of the race, was not campaigning. While Edwards, Duke, and the minor candidates were appearing at campaign forums across the state, Roemer was spending most of his time in Baton Rouge governing the state. This was a deliberate strategy by Roemer's campaign advisers, who believed that forums simply let his opponents trash him in front of the media. Besides, they knew that the media would stop covering them if he didn't show up.

Roemer finally announced his candidacy on August 27. Cast in the unfamiliar role of the incumbent who presided over state government, Roemer, forty-seven, tried to update the themes of four years before. He portrayed himself as a reformer who had taken on the state's entrenched interests but needed another term to complete the job. "Louisiana is not going back to the days when our children's futures were held hostage to a bankrupt and inadequate state education system," Roemer said. "Louisiana is not going back to the days when the quality of the air we breathed and the water we drank was taken for granted. And Louisiana is not going back to the days when money ruled our politics, when backroom deals determined our policy, and when the interests of our people and our state's future took a back seat to the interests of the politicians and special interest groups."

Roemer simultaneously launched a massive television ad campaign, echoing the themes of his announcement. The campaign began to heat up. There were now fewer than sixty days before the October 19 primary. The betting was still on a Roemer-Edwards runoff. They were now tied with 25–30 percent apiece in the polls, followed by Duke with 15 percent and the rest of the voters undecided or divided among the minor candidates.

With Roemer formally getting in the race on August 27, Duke stepped up his campaigning, making stops over the next two weeks in Vivian, Oak Grove, Chatham, Bossier City, New Orleans, DeQuincy, Maryville, Sugartown, Ragley, Washington, Morgan City, Kenner, and New Orleans again. On September 11, he returned to LSU to speak at Free Speech Alley—where he had gotten his start in politics in 1969 as a skinny sophomore who called himself a Nazi and called for the eradication of Jewish influence in America. In those days, students dismissed Duke as a kook and jeered him off the soapbox. Now, twenty-two years later, with resculpted features and carrying the promise that he was a changed man, Duke would get a far different response.

Hundreds of students packed the alley in front of the LSU Student Union, despite the sweltering September humidity. Dozens more leaned against the union's second-floor balcony. "I'm here because I believe in freedom of speech, ladies and gentlemen," Duke began, fearful perhaps that the students would shout him down as they had during his days at LSU. The crowd buzzed, but no one tried to challenge him. Duke plunged ahead. "I'm likely to be governor of this state next year." The students cheered and whooped with delight— something Duke had not heard at Free Speech Alley before. He paused in surprise and smiled. "The most precious thing you have is your right to freedom," he cried out, picking up steam. "I believe in less government, not only in the Soviet Union but for us right here in Louisiana. I think it's about time people stand up and say things honestly." The students cheered and whooped some more. And so it went.

Black students scattered throughout the crowd of 700 muttered angrily throughout Duke's thirty-minute appearance, forcing him to shout to be heard. One student held a sign behind him that read, "Nose Job Nazi." Another sign read: "No thanks Mr. Duke—we have enough racists in government already!" But the blue-and-white "Duke Governor" signs outnumbered them. And roars of approval repeatedly interrupted Duke. "Amen, I'm tired of spending my tax dollars on them!" a young woman in a fraternity shirt shouted when Duke attacked the "massive welfare underclass that is growing every day." Shannah Smith, a twenty-two-year-old hospital technician standing nearby, shook her head in agreement. "We work so they can have baby after baby," she called out.

"Duke! Duke! Duke!" the students chanted when he attacked affirmative action and race-based college admission policies and promised to "preserve the distinct quality of LSU," a predominantly white university. Duke received a royal homecoming, and it wasn't over when he finished his speech. Students crowded around him as he made his way to the shade of a nearby oak tree. For the next half hour, he signed autographs and answered more questions.

Billy Hankins stood apart from the crowd, shaking his head in dismay. Hankins had been one of Duke's top aides during the Senate campaign, but no longer wanting to be around Duke's extremist friends, he was now working for Clyde Holloway's campaign. He had stopped by LSU because he wondered how students would react to his former boss's performance. "This is ridiculous," Hankins said, as he surveyed the adoring students surrounding Duke. "Look at all these people out here for Duke when Clyde is the better conservative."

Duke pressed on with his offensive. Eight days after his Free Speech Alley appearance, he broadcast his first TV ad of the campaign, a thirty-minute spot. As in the Senate ad the year before, he mixed his traditional race-based pitch with an appeal to fed-up voters wanting safer streets, a healthier economy and a better educational system. In a new approach to disarm his opponents, Duke in the gubernatorial ad suggested that they were the ones guilty of intolerance. After Duke's two teenage daughters briefly appeared at his side, he said, "It's only been the love of my wonderful family and the strength that Christ gives me that enables me to stand tall in spite of the unfair attacks I've weathered. I sometimes wonder about those self-righteous people who speak about loving everyone and then hate me. Those of you who hate me for my past, I ask you honestly: Have you ever hurt a friend or loved one? Have you ever spoken words you'd take back if you could? Have you ever changed your opinion? If you haven't, I guess you can throw the first stone. I ask only that you treat me as you'd have others treat you."

Throughout the ad, Duke portrayed himself as the candidate of change, and he returned to that theme for his close. "I'm the only viable alternative to those tax and spend policies of the past," he said. "I'm the only one with a chance to break through for the principles we share. Please help me make that breakthrough possible for all of us."

As in the Senate ad, Duke flashed an 800 number for viewers to call to make a contribution, and in yet another novel approach, he told them they could call a 900 number to subscribe to the *David Duke Report*. He said the call would cost fifteen dollars. He did not disclose that he owned the *David Duke Report*; he admitted this several days later in an interview. South Central Bell still prohibited candidates from using 900 numbers for contributions, but it did not stop calls for the *David Duke Report*, since Duke pocketed the money as a private business owner. Politics, after all, was how he made a living. Duke's message was hitting home. White Louisianians who had voted for Buddy Roemer four years earlier because they were angry and wanted a change were still angry and were now turning to Duke as the shake-things-up candidate. The polls did not reflect this, as Duke's support remained at 15 percent. But Roemer's twenty-four-year-old daughter, Caroline, saw the awful truth of Duke's strength on September 29 when she rode in the Louisiana Sugar Cane Festival parade in New Iberia. She had been traveling the state for several months as part of a Women for Roemer group that was founded after her father vetoed the abortion bill.

Duke rode directly in front of Caroline Roemer in the parade, perched on the back seat of a convertible. During the first half of the parade, most everybody in the five-deep crowd was white, and they all seemed to be holding Duke signs and chanting his name. When Caroline Roemer passed, they shouted, "Where's Buddy?" "Where's the governor?" Some people shouted, "Go home!"

Caroline Roemer began to get a sinking feeling in her stomach. Duke was so popular, she thought, it was almost cultlike. And with her dad not attending a parade that featured not only Duke but also Edwards, she realized that voters felt ignored by him. "We're in big trouble," she thought to herself. "Dad's advisers need to get out of Baton Rouge, they need to stop reading polls and see how much support Duke has." Caroline Roemer was further unnerved when, near the end of the parade, Duke drove by a large section of black parade-goers. They yelled obscenities and threw bottles, none of which hit Duke. The police moved in and Duke's car sped ahead to avert a possible riot. "What's happening to Louisiana?" she wondered.

When Caroline Roemer got back to the governor's mansion, she ran upstairs to find her father. He was playing poker with Danny Walker and several others. "Hey, how'd it go?" he asked nonchalantly.

"I'm scared, I'm frightened," she said, choking back tears. She described what had happened. "There was not one Buddy Roemer sign. All I saw were David Duke signs. I think you're underestimating him." She turned and hurried from the room.

Buddy Roemer left the card game several minutes later to comfort her. "Was it really that bad?" he asked.

"Yes, it was overwhelming," she said. "I realize now that we have to do something. On the two-hour drive there, I didn't see one Roemer sign."

"But, Caroline, the polls are showing us way ahead."

"I think they're wrong," she responded. "I think people are lying. They won't admit they're voting for Duke. I've been traveling to small towns for three months. I pass a general store and see Duke signs where four years before there were Buddy Roemer signs."

Buddy Roemer shook his head and asked quietly, "How can we stop him? I don't know what to do."

Caroline Roemer was not the first person to implore her father to take on David Duke. Raymond Strother, Roemer's media consultant, had been warning him for weeks that Edwards's vote was solid and that Duke was threatening to take away Roemer's white voters and keep him out of the runoff. Strother, who was staying at the mansion, beat this drum so incessantly that Roemer began ducking him.

When Roemer switched parties in March, he not only joined the GOP but also recruited officials from the Republican National Committee to run his campaign. The campaign manager was Sam Dawson, who had been a disciple of RNC Chairman Lee Atwater in their native South Carolina, and the press secretary was Gordon Hensley, an accomplished spinmeister. Fred Steeper handled the polling.

Strother, fifty-one, had spent the first half of his career in Louisiana before moving to Washington and had produced the tough-talking ads that had helped propel Roemer to the governorship in 1987. He had always worked for Democrats and had agreed to sign on with Roemer in 1991 only because they had been together four years before. But because he was a Democrat, the Republicans were slow to listen to his warnings about Duke. It wasn't until October that Strother convinced Dawson and Steeper that Duke posed a major threat. He got them to agree to hold two focus groups one evening on the so-called West Bank—a section of Jefferson Parish across the Mississippi River from New Orleans—among white, blue-collar swing voters in an attempt to plumb their real attitudes toward Duke.

Strother, Dawson, and Steve Lombardo, Steeper's research director, watched the session from behind a two-way mirror. To get at voters' real feelings about Duke, the Roemer aides had the moderator ask a series of questions about a hypothetical candidate. "What would you think of a candidate who had evaded the draft during the Vietnam War and lied about it later?" he began.

"I can't imagine a man who wouldn't serve his country," one man said.

"What would you think of a candidate who had plastic surgery?" the moderator asked.

"I'd wonder about his sexuality," another man said.

"What would you think of a candidate who hadn't paid his taxes?" the moderator asked.

"I pay my taxes," a woman said, "and I expect a politician to."

"What about a candidate who has never held a job?"

"How can anybody understand our problems if they've never held a job or sweated for a living?" a man asked.

Clearly, this hypothetical candidate would have a snowball's chance in hell of getting elected.

As the first group filed out, Strother told Dawson and Lombardo that he wanted to try something different with the second group to ferret out and gauge more accurately the pro-Duke sentiment. This time the moderator would discuss the hypothetical candidate and then identify him as David Duke. When the second group was asked how they felt about Duke's having evaded the draft, a man leaped to his defense. "Everybody of that generation was trying to evade the draft," he said. "I went to Vietnam, but I would have evaded going there if I could have."

When asked about the plastic surgery, a woman said, "What's wrong with a politician having plastic surgery? Movie stars do it. And politicians, after all, are movie stars."

What about Duke's not paying taxes?

"Only dumb people pay taxes," a woman said. "Politicians and millionaires don't because they're smart. Duke must be smart."

What about his never having held a job?

"He's a politician," one man said. "Politicians don't work."

What about his having been in the Klan?

"It was when he was a kid," a man said. "Kids do crazy things."

What had been unacceptable character flaws in an unidentified candidate were now acceptable when it was revealed to be Duke. In his nearly thirty years in politics, Strother had never seen anything like it. He was shaken and turned to Dawson, "It's over for Buddy," he said.

But perhaps it wasn't. Responses to questions about the impact of a Duke election on the economy provided a glimmer of hope for Strother and Dawson. When the moderator asked the focus group about the fears of many that a Duke election would hurt the state economically, that it would drive away conventions, tourists, and potential business investors, several people agreed. "People will lose jobs," one man said.

Strother met with Roemer the next day. "If you don't do something immediately about David Duke," he said, "you're going to lose. I've just seen the handwriting on the wall in two West Bank focus groups."

"Well, what would you do?" Roemer asked.

If it had been 1987, Strother would have put Roemer in front of a television camera and let him in his plainspoken, evangelical way tell viewers that he didn't want his ten-year-old son—and their children either—to be educated in a state governed by a racist and anti-Semite. But in 1991, test runs of Roemer ads before focus groups had shown that people didn't want to listen to him. Using so-called People Meters, in which focus group viewers used hand-held dials to rate how favorable they felt second by second throughout the commercial, Strother had found that whenever Roemer himself appeared in the ads, the rating declined. Looking at those results, Strother had come to the startling conclusion that viewers thought Roemer was so smart and mesmerizing that they tuned him out to avoid buying into his message. They didn't want to be convinced.

Unable to use Roemer, Strother decided to put together ads with ordinary people warning of how a Duke election would cost the state jobs and business investment. Strother decided to use slightly upscale people in the ads—the kinds of people who would decide whether Duke or Roemer made the runoff. He produced six ads and wanted to flood the airwaves with them. Strother thought Roemer could be saved if every time that viewers turned on the television set, they saw fellow citizens warning that Duke's election would mean economic catastrophe.

Strother screened the ads for Roemer and Danny Walker at the mansion. When he was through, Walker shook his head. "There's nothing to be gained by being negative," he said. "There's nothing to be gained by winning the wrong way. You can't put these on."

Roemer didn't comment but asked Strother to screen them once more. "I know you're upset about David Duke," he told Strother after watching them again. "But having a bunch of yuppies on TV talking about losing their jobs won't hurt David Duke. The numbers don't show it."

"You have to put them on," Strother pleaded. "I can't point to numbers because we can't poll Duke accurately. We need to go after upwardly mobile voters because they're going for Duke."

Roemer cut him short. "We're not going to run them," he said. He wheeled around and left the room.

Strother looked down and frowned. "It's really over now," he thought to himself.

Buddy Roemer's political future hung in the balance, but he couldn't bring himself to do what was necessary to win: launch a full-scale attack against David Duke. One reason was that, still emerging from the throes of a midlife crisis, Roemer seemed tired of being governor. His aides chafed at how little he campaigned. On the final Sunday before the election, he spent the day watching two football games at the mansion. Another reason was that Roemer didn't feel comfortable attacking a candidate personally. He had always prided himself on that.

But most important, Roemer didn't understand racism and couldn't bring himself to believe that the people of Louisiana preferred Duke to him. When Roemer was growing up at the Scopena Plantation, the black farmhands ate at the dinner table and swam in the swimming pool. Such a thing was unheard of in conservative Bossier Parish. Roemer's parents instilled in him unswerving support for racial tolerance, a belief he embraced. Roemer left the room when somebody told a racist joke, and his best friend was a black man. To an intellectual like Roemer, racism just didn't make sense.

He knew that a core group of racists in the state—perhaps 15 percent of the electorate—backed Duke. But he did not think that reasoned, intelligent people could walk into the voting booth and pull the lever of a bigot and anti-Semite. Couldn't they tell that Roemer was working day and night to turn Louisiana around? Couldn't they tell that Duke was nothing but a hater? Couldn't they tell that Duke had nothing to offer but a few slogans and a bunch of vague promises? And didn't the polls reflect this? They showed Duke running a weak third.

Although he was blind to it, Buddy Roemer was on the ropes, and a businessman named Jack Kent was secretly preparing to deliver the knockout blow. Kent owned Marine Shale Processors, a controversial Morgan City company that incinerated hazardous wastes. It was a benign process, Kent held. Roemer's Department of Environmental Quality had a different view and was trying to shut down Marine Shale. The company, DEQ said, emitted dangerous pollutants into the air. Kent decided that he could no longer survive with Buddy Roemer as governor. But he could with Edwin Edwards—or even David Duke. Edwards had been a friend for many years and would never have tried to put him out of business, while Duke was promising to relax DEQ's enforcement of small businesses. Kent decided to attack Roemer in a massive television campaign in the final two weeks before the election.

Deno Seder, one of the country's best negative ad political consultants, was sitting in his Washington office on September 27 when the phone rang. "Stay where you are," an anonymous caller said. "The man with the cheese is on his way to Washington."

"Who's that?" Seder asked.

"Jack Kent," the caller replied and hung up.

Seder was perplexed. "Who's Jack Kent?" he wondered.

Several hours later his phone rang again. This time it was Kent. He had just arrived in Washington on his private jet. "I'm on my way over," Kent said.

They met for several hours and Kent explained what he wanted. "What would $500,000 get me?" he asked.

"Three to five points off of Roemer," Seder replied. That would probably be enough to spell Roemer's political doom. Kent hired him.

Seder was a smart choice. Having spent twenty years in Louisiana before moving to Washington, Seder knew both the state and Buddy Roemer intimately. They had worked as partners on political campaigns in the 1970s, and Seder had served as Roemer's media consultant during his 1980 election to Congress. But eleven years later when Kent offered him the chance to end his old friend's political career, Seder jumped at the opportunity. Seder worked only for Democrats and thought Roemer was fair game as a party-switcher. Besides, Kent was offering him a ton of money.

Seder quickly hired a team of producers and editors and, working nonstop over the next five days, they produced five attack ads. Each had a similar theme: the "Revolution" had failed, and Roemer was just another politician who made promises and couldn't keep them. Seder flew to Louisiana and showed Kent the ads. Kent liked them. "Let's skin him up a little bit," he said. Before he permitted the ads to air, however, Kent decided to try to cut a deal with Roemer. He sent an emissary to meet with P. J. Mills, Roemer's chief of staff, and tell him about the ads. Kent will pull the ads, the emissary told Mills, if Roemer calls DEQ off Marine Shale.

Roemer got angry when Mills outlined Kent's deal. "I didn't become governor to make deals like this with people like Jack Kent," he said. "If he's violating the law, we should do everything we can to make him stop." When Kent got word of Roemer's response, he immediately swung into action, buying nearly all the advertising time on television still available in the two weeks before the primary. And on October 7 he began flooding the airwaves with Seder's missiles.

Sam Dawson got hold of the five ads that day and watched them at Roemer's Baton Rouge campaign headquarters. "Shit!" he exclaimed after screening them. "These are good." A frustrated Dawson could feel Roemer voters sliding into Duke's column. Not many but enough to make the difference. Strother quickly rushed a counterattack on the air that charged Kent's ad was a political payoff for his friend Edwards. But the Roemer campaign couldn't match Kent's firepower.

Duke was rising, Roemer's nightly tracking polls during the final week showed. The final poll, taken on Tuesday night, October 15, showed he now trailed Roemer by ten points with 12 percent of the voters undecided. Edwards led with 31 percent of the vote, Roemer had 30 percent, Duke 20 percent, and Holloway 6 percent. Duke's campaign staffers could feel that he was surging by the intensity of the crowds that turned out to see him in the final week. People stood on the side of the road just to watch him drive by on his way to the next campaign stop.

Without accurate polls to go by, not privy to the realization of Dawson and Strother and skeptical of Duke's oft-repeated claim that he would win, nearly all political pundits were still predicting a Roemer-Edwards runoff. But a few—like Times-Picayune columnist James Gill—were raising the possibility of the unthinkable. If Roemer loses, Gill wrote shortly before the primary, "we will have to decide whether to turn the clock back four years with Edwards, or 100 years with the other guy." Edwards-Duke, he concluded, would be "the gubernatorial runoff from Hell."

The day before the October 19 primary was a Friday, and Roemer spent it campaigning in Jefferson Parish and New Orleans. He was beginning to comprehend Duke's strength. "My greatest nightmare, as a person who loves the state, would be having to choose between Edwin Edwards and David Duke," he told a lunchtime crowd in New Orleans. "I want to ask each of you to call 10 people tonight. If you do that, we cannot lose." Edwards spent the day in his suite at the Monteleone Hotel in New Orleans, calling his political allies to ensure that his supporters turned out to the polls the next day. Duke held a huge rally that Friday night in the New Orleans suburb of Kenner. He was confident that he would fulfill his destiny the following day. "We [in Louisiana] have been last in so many things," he told a cheering throng. "Maybe that's why you're committed to making Louisiana first in something else.

You're committed to letting Louisiana lead the way for millions across this country who think like you do and think like I do. And who are waiting for us to lead the way."

When the initial returns came in Saturday night, Roemer took the lead. Then Duke jumped out front. With one-third of the precincts reporting, Edwards now ran first, Duke second and Roemer third. And that's how it ended. The final returns were:

Edwin Edwards	523,195	33.8 percent
David Duke	491,342	31.7 percent
Buddy Roemer	410,690	26.5 percent
Clyde Holloway	82,683	5.3 percent
Sam Jones	11,847	0.76 percent
Ed Karst	9,663	0.62 percent
Fred Kent	7,385	0.48 percent
Anne Thompson	4,118	0.27 percent
Jim Crowley	4,000	0.26 percent
Albert Powell	2,053	0.13 percent
Ronnie Johnson	1,372	0.09 percent
"Cousin" Ken Lewis	1,006	0.06 percent

Edwards had held onto his base of blacks, blue-collar whites, and Cajuns. Duke, building on his core group of racist adherents, had convinced enough Roemer supporters in rural and suburban areas that he—not Buddy Roemer—would provide the changes they wanted. Once again, he had flown under the pollsters' radar. In four weeks, Louisiana voters would have to choose between Edwin Edwards and David Duke—the runoff from hell.

At the Sheraton hotel in Shreveport, shortly after the final outcome was known, Caroline Roemer walked into her father's suite. She burst into tears. "It's OK, it's OK," Roemer said as he gave her a hug.

"It's not OK," she replied. "We were beaten by David Duke and Edwin Edwards. I feel so humiliated."

"My strategy was wrong," Roemer said ruefully. "I thought we were winning."

You could almost feel a shudder pass through Louisiana on the morning after the October 19 primary. Only Edwin Edwards stood between David Duke and the governor's mansion. And the white people who had accounted for nearly all the votes for Buddy Roemer and Clyde Holloway in the primary—and who would decide the governor's race in four weeks—reviled

Edwards as a corrupt has-been. These whites, who made up about 30 percent of the electorate—were left to ponder: who was less worse, a bigot or a crook? On the day after the primary, a Sunday, it seemed anybody's guess which way they would go. "It's almost too hard a decision," Roemer supporter Marie Sarrat, a Metairie school administrator, said, in a comment echoed by many others.

While a Duke-Edwards runoff paralyzed many people, it immediately energized thousands more. On Monday, October 21, registrars of voters throughout Louisiana reported long lines of people waiting to register. On Tuesday, the final day to register for the November 16 runoff, the lines stretched even longer. People began queuing up on Tuesday throughout the state hours before the registrars of voters offices opened, and the lines remained long throughout the day and into the evening. At New Orleans City Hall, the line snaked through a block-long hallway and spilled out onto a sidewalk. In Jefferson Parish, the line around the Gretna Court House lapped itself by midafternoon, and when the office was supposed to close at 8:00 P.M., more than 2,000 people were still waiting. It took until after midnight for everybody to register. "It was amazing," marveled registrar Sam Altobello. "People waited four and five hours in line to register."

Many people were registering to elect Duke. "Everybody I know is voting for Duke," said James Heckathorn, as he waited in line to register in St. John the Baptist Parish, thirty miles west of New Orleans. "I like what he says. . . . I think people on welfare ought to have to work for it, too." But even more people registered that Monday and Tuesday to vote against Duke. For blacks, in particular, the primary results served as a wake-up call. In neither the 1990 Senate election nor the gubernatorial primary did Duke's candidacy prompt an outpouring of concern among blacks. They viewed him with alarm but didn't get excited, since they didn't think he could win. Besides, many disillusioned blacks said, Duke wasn't much worse than Ronald Reagan or George Bush. In both the Senate and gubernatorial primary elections, the black turn-out was about ten percentage points below the white turnout.

The runoff would be another story as blacks flocked to registrars of voters offices on Tuesday. In Baton Rouge, student leaders at predominantly black Southern University knocked on dormitory doors to remind classmates to register and rented buses to transport them to the registrar of voters office. The Southern University band serenaded the students as they waited in line throughout the afternoon. The Red Cross handed out water. Restaurants donated food and drinks. One person standing in line, twenty-five-year-old

Darryl Robertson, said he had never voted before. "But I don't want to see David Duke become the governor. I don't want to see David Duke become anything because I think David Duke represents racism to the fullest."

Students from Grambling State University, another predominantly black institution, inundated the Lincoln Parish Registrar of Voters office in Ruston. In Alexandria, one of the last people to register was an eighty-seven-year-old man named George Heggin. When Heggin had last tried to register fifty years before, he had been turned away. His skin was the wrong color. What prompted Heggin to register in 1991? Duke, his wife said.

The flood of people registering to vote stunned state officials. "We've never seen anything like it," said Jerry Fowler, the Louisiana Commissioner of Elections. "Everyone wants to be able to vote in this election." In all, 68,335 Louisianians—nearly half of them black—registered to vote on that Monday and Tuesday, a two-day record. The large numbers of blacks registering alarmed Duke and his top advisers, but they still felt confident they would triumph. They had met at his Metairie home on Sunday morning to discuss the four-week runoff campaign. Duke told his advisers that he thought the election would be close but that he would win. Since the Roemer and Holloway voters had backed Republican candidates, Duke figured, they would likely vote for him in the runoff. He was a Republican and Edwards was a Democrat. Besides, he reasoned, the up-for-grabs voters were white, and he had a higher white vote in the primary (40 percent) than Roemer (33 percent) or Edwards (18 percent). Duke also thought that the runoff campaign would be fought over issues, his strength. How could Edwards attack him for his past when Edwards's own past was so tarnished?

Duke did not like strategy sessions—he cared about ideas, not tactics—so he ended the morning meeting without mapping out a plan. He figured that his approach thus far had succeeded; why not continue it? He called a press conference in New Orleans and unveiled what passed for his runoff strategy—praise of Roemer and more promises to shake up the status quo. "I like what Buddy Roemer said. We have to put education first in our state and reform the political process. We have to end the special-interest control of politics." He added: "One person described me as the Boris Yeltsen of American politics. I like that. I'm certainly opposed to the way the establishment has conducted and run our government both in Louisiana and the nation."

Across town that Sunday morning, Edwin Edwards and his top advisers were meeting in suite 1545 of the Monteleone Hotel in the French Quarter. Edwards, too, felt confident. He had gotten 88 percent of the black vote in the primary and expected nearly 100 percent of the black vote against Duke.

If blacks, who comprised 27 percent of the electorate, turned out in large numbers, he could win without a majority of the white vote.

Unlike Duke, Edwards at his meeting formulated a plan to bring the Roemer voters into his fold. It called for getting the backing of Roemer, his top aides, his business supporters, and Republican party leaders. Edwards hit the phones to ask for their support and began promising to continue some of Roemer's reform programs. He proclaimed himself a "new" Edwin Edwards, one who would not cut deals, direct government benefits to friends, or embarrass the state with ribald behavior. "I'm anxious to make things better than they were the last time I was in office," he said. "I don't want to live the rest of my life with a legacy of bad marks I had eight years ago, six years ago."

Edwards got a lucky break later that day that helped formulate his anti-Duke strategy. At the New Orleans Saints–Tampa Bay Buccaneers game at the Louisiana Superdome that afternoon, Raymond Strother, Roemer's media adviser, by chance ran into two of Edwards's top campaign aides, Bill Morgan and Billy Broadhurst. Morgan, a longtime friend of Strother's, produced Edwards's TV ads. Broadhurst, who had become infamous in 1987 for chartering the yacht *Monkey Business* with former Colorado Senator Gary Hart and model Donna Rice in an incident that helped torpedo Hart's presidential aspirations, acted as the campaign's all-purpose troubleshooter. As they watched the game from a luxury suite, Strother told them what the Roemer campaign's extensive research had found: Duke was invulnerable on his Nazi and Klan past, as voters had already decided whether or not this mattered. Duke couldn't be attacked for his failure to pay property taxes or for his opposition to affirmative action or minority set-asides. "But we found that you can hit him on the economic issue," Strother related. "We think you can hit him hard on it, but Roemer just wouldn't do it."

Both Morgan and Broadhurst relayed Strother's advice to Edwards the next day. Edwards passed along this information to key Roemer backers during the next several days as he moved to line up their support. One of the first people he called was David Treen. His campaign polling showed that Treen's endorsement mattered as much to Roemer's supporters as did Roemer's. The longtime titular head of the Louisiana Republican party, Treen had no doubt about whom he would support. There was only one option, he thought. Edwin Edwards had defeated him twice for governor, in 1972 and 1983, and stood for everything Treen opposed. But David Duke was worse, Treen felt. Duke was a moral blot on the Republican party that had to be removed as soon as possible, or the party would forever be branded racist.

Treen and Edwards met on October 27, eight days after the primary. On October 29, Treen called a press conference. "The implications of this election for the future of Louisianians are profound—more so than I can ever recall," he said. "Some have counseled me to stay out of this run-off election, to make no public statement of my views, to remain neutral. . . . While some of what he says touches on issues with which Republicans are concerned, his true agenda is far from ours. His true agenda is repugnant in the extreme. . . . To my Republican friends, therefore, I say: Do not be persuaded in favor of Duke simply because he has adopted the Republican label. David Duke must be defeated. He cannot be defeated by voters staying at home out of disaffection with both of the candidates for governor."

Edwards met with Buddy Roemer the same day that Treen made his announcement. Roemer strongly disliked Duke but feared that Edwards would undo the reforms he had carried out during his term. Several days after the primary, he expressed reservations to his chief of staff, P. J. Mills, about backing Edwards publicly. "If you don't say something about how bad David Duke is," Mills admonished him, "it will hurt your career in the future." On October 31, two days after meeting with Edwards, Roemer called a press conference and announced he would vote for Edwards. "Duke has no chance to help this state," Roemer told reporters. "Edwards has one chance. I pray to God that he takes it."

Meanwhile, independent of the Edwards campaign, businessmen who had backed Roemer were beginning their own anti-Duke efforts. Most of them had done little to defeat Duke in the Senate race except perhaps make a $1,000 campaign contribution to Bennett Johnston. Nobody thought Duke had a chance for Senate. But now that Duke appeared to have even odds of becoming the state's chief executive, the business establishment was rising up against him. It was a decision based on dollars and cents, not morals.

One of the business leaders leading the charge against Duke was Pres Kabacoff, a New Orleans developer who had signed up for the Roemer Revolution in early 1987 when Buddy Roemer stood at 1 percent in the polls. On the night of the 1991 primary, when he saw that Duke had knocked Roemer out of the runoff, "It took me about two seconds to decide: 'I'm going with Edwin Edwards,'" Kabacoff remembered later. "I thought that if Duke won, Louisiana would be set adrift from the Union. The federal government would shut down Louisiana to show it would not work with a Nazi." Kabacoff contributed $5,000 to the Edwards campaign and urged friends and contractors who worked on his development projects to do likewise. Later in the runoff, he appeared in a television ad warning that Duke's election would cost the state thousands of jobs.

It took a day for the election results to sink in with New Orleans businessman David Dixon, another strong Roemer backer. Dixon, an antiques dealer who in the 1960s had spearheaded the drive to get New Orleans a professional football team and get the Louisiana Superdome built, had flown to New York City the day after the primary. As his friends there expressed horror at the thought of a Duke victory, Dixon realized, "This guy ruins our state if he wins. It's almost like Adolf Hitler is running."

When he returned to New Orleans two days later, Dixon began raising money to defeat Duke. He took in $25,000 and planned to give it to an anti-Duke group led by New Orleans attorney Moise Steeg. But when Steeg told him that his group was still getting organized, Dixon decided to act on his own. With an additional $40,000 of his own money, he cut a television ad the next day standing in front of the Superdome. "David Duke's supporters are already claiming that his election would not hurt tourism and convention business in this state," Dixon said. "They're absolutely right. He won't hurt it, he'll eliminate it."

A group of business leaders joined the fray with a press conference on October 25. Noting that the election was big news not only across the country but overseas as well, Jim Bob Moffett, chairman of Freeport-McMoRan, Incorporated, said, "If Duke is governor, national conventions scheduled for Louisiana would be canceled. Sports events would be turned away, businesses would move, top university researchers and professors would leave, and jobs would be lost." Tourist leaders chimed in a week later to say that many groups scheduled to hold conventions in New Orleans had promised since the primary to go elsewhere if Duke were elected.

Duke came under fire on another front—from the *Times-Picayune*, the state's biggest newspaper and the only daily in New Orleans. Some people had criticized the paper for not going all out earlier to defeat Duke, but the editors of the *Times-Picayune* felt that journalistic rules of fairness prevented them from doing that. The primary election result changed their thinking. On the Monday after the primary, the paper's editors met and decided that they would not treat this as a conventional gubernatorial election. Duke was an extraordinary candidate in American history—no other neo-Nazi had come so close to being elected governor of a state—and the situation demanded an extraordinary journalistic response. The paper's editors decided they would launch a no-holds-barred assault against Duke, with hard-hitting news stories and slashing editorial columns. The paper would not omit negative information about Edwin Edwards, with whom the paper had warred for years, nor would the paper puff him up. The *Times-Picayune* in fact reprinted embarrassing testimony from Edwards's 1985 trial. But the paper would devote its resources to exposing Duke's past, not Edwards's.

The paper fired its first shot with an editorial that appeared the day after the primary: "The limelight of the world is on our state, and we are not a pretty sight to behold—by many measures last or near bottom in education, literacy and living standards. And now we have a first: elevating an extremist of the caliber of Mr. Duke to direct contention for the governorship. But the story is not yet played out. The clear-headed people of this state—and we happen to think there are still many—must now muster their resolve to see that on Nov. 16, Mr. Duke is not elected governor. It's time to sober up."

In the days that followed, the paper launched daily bombing raids on Duke, revealing new details of his extremist activities. The paper also published a five-part series of editorials entitled "The Choice of Our Lives" that detailed graphically why Louisiana could not elect Duke. The *Times-Picayune* became such an adversary for Duke that late in the campaign Duke broadcast a television commercial attacking the newspaper. The newspaper's coverage was important not only because it reached about one-third of the state's voters but also because it emboldened newspapers and television stations throughout the state to follow its lead. The *Baton Rouge Morning Advocate* and the *Shreveport Times*, in particular, stepped up their critical coverage of Duke.

Duke was under attack on many fronts, but at the midway point of the runoff, many people still feared he could win. There were too many signs of massive Duke support throughout the state to count him out.

When Duke visited the luxury suites at the Saints game on the day after the October 19 primary—the game at which Strother outlined the Roemer campaign's findings about Duke—men fell over themselves trying to shake his hand. Duke then went in search of more voters. He walked through a tunnel that led to the terrace stands. In between plays, he popped his head out of a portal and waved to the group of fans sitting in that section. Few politicians would have dared do this, because fans at sporting events typically boo them. But when Duke waved a greeting, the Saints fans roared back their approval. He went to another section and got the same rousing response. For the next half hour, he worked his way around the Superdome's stands, eliciting some boos but mostly cheers at each stop. This response did not bode well for Edwards.

There were more signs that Duke might pull off the unthinkable. A stream of Roemer supporters, including elected officials, called David Touchstone, Duke's northwest organizer, to climb aboard the Duke campaign. "The people who have to vote for Edwards for him to win are voting for Duke," reported business lobbyist C. B. Forgotston. "They're educated people, they're not hicks. But they're mad as hell, they're saying, 'Fuck the establishment. Throw the bums out.' That's what Duke stands for."

Duke also seemed to have found an effective way to distance himself from his extremist activities. He had become, he said, a born-again Christian. Yes, he may have been intolerant in the past, he said, but now he was a new man, thanks to Christ. Many people correctly saw this claim as a cynical ploy to win votes. But in a conservative state yearning for a savior, many others bought it. Duke had begun calling himself a Christian during the 1990 United States Senate election. But he played the religion card far more heavily in the gubernatorial runoff, crediting Christ in every speech with helping him overcome his past ways. "I want to thank the force in my life that's really enabled me to stand up through all the smears and the personal attacks and all the dirty politics that Louisiana is famous for," he told one cheering crowd. "I want to thank the influence of my Lord and Saviour Jesus Christ. I could not have gone on and continued to stand tall without the prayers He's answered."

Duke may pull it off and win, thought Lance Hill, executive director of the Louisiana Coalition Against Racism and Nazism, which had continued to dog Duke during the gubernatorial campaign. Hill's sources were reporting that good-government conservatives—the kinds of Roemer supporters that Edwards needed—were backing Duke. As he brooded over this on the bus to work one morning, a woman talking harshly about the election interrupted his thoughts. "They talk about Duke's past," she told a friend, spitting out the words. "Look at Edwin Edwards. Nobody wants to come to a state with a crook in charge."

Hill had an enduring faith in the basic wisdom and decency of the American people. But the anger and hate in the woman's voice scared him. "What if I'm wrong?" Hill thought. "What if this isn't some heroic effort to defeat David Duke? What happens if it's a tragedy?" A poll released on October 29 by Mason-Dixon Opinion Research reinforced Hill's apprehension. Edwards was leading Duke but by only a 46 to 42 percent margin. Mason-Dixon had adjusted the numbers to try to account for the hidden Duke vote, but who could be sure? And the 12 percent of voters who were undecided seemed likely to go with Duke: 58 percent of them viewed Duke as more honest and trustworthy than Edwards, and 70 percent thought Edwards's past was worse than Duke's.

A joint appearance by Duke and Edwards the next day at the annual state convention of the American Association of Retired Persons provided more evidence that Duke might triumph. The welfare system encourages women without husbands to have babies instead of encouraging birth control, Duke told the senior citizens, making a familiar charge. Politicians had learned not to challenge Duke's antiwelfare pitch because it resonated so strongly with voters. But Edwards knew Duke's charge was silly and couldn't resist saying so. A welfare mother with two children receives only $190 a month, and two-thirds of that comes from the federal government, Edwards said. For a third child, she receives an extra eleven dollars a week, he added.

"Can you really in good conscience think that this woman is going to sit around the table and wonder how she can get pregnant again to collect another $11 a week?" Edwards asked.

"YES!" the seniors yelled back.

"He's appealing to your base emotions," Edwards said of Duke, but boos cascading from the crowd drowned him out. Edwards paused and said, with emotion rising in his voice, "Who is going to be next? The disabled? The old? You better think about it."

It was Duke's turn to speak. "The elderly who have contributed all their lives have been forgotten by a welfare system that encourages laziness," he said. "And there is no more important freedom than the freedom to live without fear." The seniors erupted in cheers.

"You have worked, sacrificed and produced all your lives while the welfare system expands because people won't work," Duke added. "Many of the children turn to crime because the system doesn't encourage them to work." The crowd cheered again.

When the sixty-minute forum ended, seniors surrounded Duke to clap him on the back and shake his hand. "Man, we've got Edwards," exulted Duke aide Jim McPherson. "We're going to win."

Edwards, normally unflappable, was rattled. "In my entire career," he told aide Al Donovan as he hurried out a back door, "I've helped people like these seniors by making sure their needs are met. They have no earthly idea what Duke's ulterior motives are. If Duke gets elected, he'll do an about-face and these will be the people he'll hurt the most."

Three days later, Edwards and Duke met in the first of two statewide televised debates. The date was November 2, the runoff's midway point. Duke was nervous beforehand. He knew that Edwards, with his razor-sharp mind and quick wit, had made a career out of cutting up his political opponents. But with his years of experience appearing on television and radio, Duke would prove a formidable debating opponent. Throughout the hour-long event, Edwards seemed tentative and flat, while Duke hammered away at him confidently. "If you like what's been going on over the past 20 years, go ahead and vote for Edwin Edwards," Duke asserted. "You'll get more of the same: more environmental destruction, you'll get lower salaries for teachers, more crime in our streets, our schools will continue to decline. We need change. Please let's make a change in this election—a change to turn Louisiana around."

By the luck of the draw, Edwards gave his closing statement first. Expecting to face Roemer, Edwards was like a fastball hitter who unexpectedly had to face a curveballer. Duke was catching him off stride. Duke was unlike Bennett Johnston, David Treen, or Buddy Roemer, the gubernatorial candidates Edwards had faced before. Edwards in a perfunctory close could come up with nothing better than a promise to bring together the state's divergent factions to solve Louisiana's problems, including a slack economy and a projected $1 billion budget deficit. In his close, Duke went on the attack again. He pulled a sheaf of papers from his coat pocket and said they were a sampling of the hundreds of pardons Edwards had granted to dangerous criminals during his three terms as governor. "Edwin Edwards freed more violent criminals in this state over the last 20 years than all the other governors in this century combined in Louisiana," Duke said. The statement was an exaggeration, but it was dramatic, and because Duke went last, Edwards could not respond.

Arnold Hirsch, chairman of the University of New Orleans history department, scored Duke the debate victor. "Any time Duke is able to stand up in that setting wearing a coat and tie and looking like a major candidate, being treated respectfully and deferentially, it helps his legitimacy and buttresses his argument that he's a mainstream candidate," Hirsch said. "He doesn't look dangerous, he doesn't sound dangerous—what's all the fuss about?" Duke and his aides celebrated after the debate. In two weeks, they told themselves, Duke would be elected governor. They looked ahead expectantly to the second statewide debate, which would be held in four days. Duke would finish Edwards off that night, they thought. The debate, which was held on November 6, would prove to be the pivotal event of the runoff, but it would not turn out as Duke and his aides expected. Edwin Edwards, Louisiana's master politician for the past generation, would see to that.

By now Edwards had tired of Duke's challenge. He thought he should not just win but win big over a former Nazi and Ku Klux Klan grand wizard. Yet his latest tracking poll showed him with 52.7 percent of the vote, enough to win but perhaps only barely if voters were still lying about supporting Duke. Edwards cleared his schedule the afternoon of the debate to prepare. He met at his Baton Rouge home with Billy Broadhurst, his longtime friend and former law partner. They spent a couple of hours discussing key issues and how Duke would likely respond to them and how Edwards ought to respond. They agreed that Edwards had to be more aggressive and forceful than in the first debate. Edwards should focus on Duke's extremist activities, they decided, and portray the election as a moral choice between a longtime public servant and an unqualified candidate who had sown discord all his life. Edwards wouldn't make the same mistake as Bennett Johnston. He would assault Duke's character.

When he and Broadhurst had completed the debate preparation, Edwards excused himself and sat alone for twenty minutes writing on a yellow legal pad. He was working on his closing statement, and he wanted to be sure it packed a wallop. He thought of Duke and said to himself, "This is the time I'm going to show the difference in our lives. I spent my life helping and building, and you spent your life tearing down and burning."

Duke at that moment was driving to an American Legion hall in Uptown New Orleans. His top adviser, Jim McPherson, wanted Duke to take it easy that day and spend the time before the debate preparing and collecting his thoughts. But after winning the first debate, Duke felt overconfident going into the second one. He was spending the day as he had every other since the primary election, campaigning nonstop. It was to be a fateful error.

A dozen anti-Duke protesters were waiting for him outside the American Legion hall. When Duke, McPherson and his two bodyguards pulled up to the curb, the protesters surrounded the car, screamed insults, and cursed him.

"Nazi, Nazi!"

"Klan bastard!"

"Shithead!"

"Fuck you, Duke!"

Duke and his three associates paused for a minute and then pushed their way into the hall. Inside was a small group of elderly men and women. Over the protesters' shouts, which were audible within the building, Duke gave a short speech and asked for their support. He then apologized, saying he had to leave. It was 4:00 P.M.—two hours before the debate was to begin in Baton Rouge, eighty miles away.

They pushed their way through the protesters again and sped off. They had to get to Baton Rouge quickly, or Duke might arrive late for the debate. But the driver, it turned out, didn't know New Orleans well, and they got lost on their way to Interstate 10, which would take them to Baton Rouge. They lost precious minutes. When they found I-10, they got stuck in rush hour traffic. As they crawled toward Baton Rouge, Duke was talking excitedly in the back seat about the hostile reception he had received outside the American Legion hall. He should have been calmly preparing for the debate.

They finally cleared rush hour traffic and sped ninety miles an hour to Baton Rouge. Duke every few minutes anxiously checked his watch to see whether they would arrive before the 6:00 P.M. starting time. The debate was to be held at Louisiana Public Broadcasting. At 5:50, Edwards had already been through makeup and was standing on the set reviewing his notes.

The four journalists on the panel were reviewing their questions. And Duke was on the outskirts of Baton Rouge hurtling at ninety miles an hour toward the television station. He—and everybody at LPB—was wondering whether he would get there on time. The car screeched to a halt at the station. Duke jumped out and rushed through a throng of waiting reporters. It was 5:59—one minute to airtime. He dashed onto the set. As he was miked up, he ran his hand through his unkempt hair. And then the debate began.

Duke's lack of preparation showed immediately. In his opening statement, he was unfocused and rambling. It was downhill from there, as he came up against an aggressive set of reporters and a well-prepared Edwards. Several minutes later, Norman Robinson, a news anchor at WDSU-TV in New Orleans, asked Duke to name his main legislative goals as governor. When Duke instead went into his standard antitax spiel, Robinson interrupted Duke to say he wasn't answering Robinson's question. A short time afterward, another panelist, Richard Baudouin of the *Times of Acadiana*, asked Duke how many jobs he would cut from the government rolls to balance the budget. When Duke went into his government-is-too-big pat answer, Baudouin interrupted him to ask for specifics. Yet another panelist, Jeff Duhe, an LPB correspondent, interrupted Duke after Duke gave a vague answer to the question of what jobs he had held. "This is a job," Duke responded. "This is work."

"Are you saying," Duhe asked, interrupting him again, "you're a politician and you run for office for a living?"

Duke sputtered an answer.

Edwards then jumped in. "The fella never had a job," he said. "Look, this is an important business. There is $9 billion involved and 75,000 employees. These professional politicians who make a living by running for public office and living off of contributions aren't qualified to be governor."

The emotion and intensity of the debate were at a fever pitch. And now Norman Robinson was about to elevate them even higher. Since being asked several days earlier to serve on the panel, Robinson had debated with himself how aggressively he should question Duke. As a news anchor who had to be liked by both blacks and whites, he felt that he should ask bland questions to avoid offending viewers. But as he ruminated, he decided that first and foremost he was a journalist and had been one for nearly nineteen years. He had to ask tough questions. And as a black man, he had to ask Duke a question that would cut to the heart of his racial appeal.

As Robinson, forty, had watched Duke throughout the campaign, he had been reminded of his boyhood in Toomsuba, Mississippi, a town of 500 residents. As a boy, he had watched whites run his uncle out of town and his grandfather off his land. His uncle's offense was hitting a store owner who called him "nigger." Robinson was once beaten with a chain by two white boys because he drank water from their pump.

Duke gave him that same dry taste in his mouth and uneasiness in his gut he had had as a boy who always feared that he might offend white people by what he said, how he looked at them, and how long he stayed in one place. Duke, to Robinson, represented the reemergence of the unbridled, unapologetic, raw hatred of whites he had known as a boy. "We've gone though the Civil War," Robinson thought at one point during the campaign, "the Civil Rights movement, the country has been turned upside down. We're supposed to be in an age of enlightenment, and here we are fighting the same old hurtful politics of the past."

As the hour-long Duke-Edwards debate progressed, Robinson thought again of all these things. He would have one last chance to ask Duke a question. That moment arrived. "Mr. Duke, I have to tell you I am a very concerned citizen," Robinson began. "I am a journalist, but first and foremost I am a concerned citizen. And as a minority who has heard you say some very excoriating and diabolical things about minorities, about blacks, about Jews, about Hispanics, I am scared, sir."

Robinson paused. "I have heard you say Jews deserve to be in the ashbin of history. I've heard you say that horses have contributed more to the building of America than blacks did. Given that kind of past, sir, given that kind of diabolical, evil, vile mentality, convince me, sir, and other minorities like me to entrust their lives and the lives of their children to you."

Duke frowned. He then reached for a pat answer. "Mr. Robinson, I don't think there is a human being on this earth or in this state who hasn't at some time been intolerant in their life." Jesse Jackson, he added, had spit in white people's food while working at a restaurant as a young man.

Robinson broke in. "Sir, we are talking about political, economic genocide. We're not talking about intolerance. We are not talking about spitting on people, sir. As a new-found Christian, a born-again, are you here willing now to apologize to the people, the minorities of this state, whom you have so dastardly insulted sir?"

"Of course I apologize for things I have said that have been intolerant and improper," Duke replied.

Robinson was unsatisfied. "Do you repudiate the Klan? And the neo-Nazis?"

"I do repudiate the Klan and any other racist organization or intolerant organization that exists in this state or this country," Duke said blandly. He then segued into his anti-affirmative action spiel. "There is violence in our streets every day directed at white people as well as the other way around," Duke added.

"As well as against black people?"

"Look, Mr. Robinson, I don't think you are really being fair with me," Duke said testily.

"I don't think you are really being honest, sir," Robinson replied.

Duke campaign aide David Touchstone, watching the debate in Shreveport, exulted at the harsh exchange, convinced that it would prompt undecided whites to vote for Duke. Henry Dillon III, who was organizing a get-out-the-vote effort among blacks in New Orleans, also cheered the Duke-Robinson exchange but for different reasons. "Robinson's stuck a hole in the aura of Duke's invulnerability," he thought. "This is going to motivate a lot of blacks to vote."

The televised debate was now nearly over. Duke made his closing statement. He was defensive and unfocused. It was Edwards's turn. He pulled out the statement he had written that afternoon. "This man has attacked us for 20 years," Edwards said. "Now, all of a sudden, he wants to stop the attacks. While David Duke was burning crosses and scaring people, I was building hospitals to heal them. When he was parading around in a Nazi uniform to intimidate our citizens, I was in a National Guard uniform bringing relief to flood and hurricane victims. When he was selling Nazi hate literature as late as 1989 in his legislative office, I was providing free textbooks for the children of this state. When he was writing porno books, I was signing anti-pornographic legislation."

He paused. "I have been in this business for a long time. I have a record, and he has a record. I suggest to you he has given us 20 years of hate and hurt, and I don't think he has earned the right to ask you to be governor. Let him go back to our communities if he in fact has a new-found religion. And let him spend some time providing some healing and help to overcome what he has done to us for all these years, giving us this reputation in the nation and the rest of the world. Then after he has done community service and served mankind with some help, then let him come back to us 20 years from now when he has matured and truly shown us that he is a different, new man. Maybe at that time we'll think about letting him be governor of our state. But until then, don't let him divide us. Don't let him separate us from the rest of the nation. Don't let him make a mockery of Louisiana. We're too important, and we're too good for that. The people of this state need a governor as good as the people of this state, not someone whose reputation, deserved or not, around the nation is one of hate and division. I don't want my Louisiana to fall into that morass. We went down that road one time a long time ago, and we suffered for it for many decades. We'll not let David Duke take us down that same road again. Not ever."

The debate was over and with it David Duke's chances of being elected governor. His weak showing and Edwards's brilliant closing statement had destroyed his momentum. Louisianians watching on TV throughout the state breathed a sigh of relief. They felt that the barbarians had been repulsed at the gate—but that they could not rest easy because the barbarians might attack again at any moment.

Duke tried to regroup, but he was to come under a withering attack during the final ten days before the November 16 runoff. The anti-Duke movement had raised millions of dollars in the previous two and one-half weeks—the amount of money normally only a popular presidential candidate could raise during such a short period of time—and would ensure that no one could watch television in Louisiana during the election's final ten days without seeing ads warning that the state faced economic catastrophe if Duke was elected. Defeating Duke had become a crusade.

Much of the anti-Duke money had been pouring into the coffers of the Edwards campaign and the Louisiana Democratic party—not just from Louisiana but from throughout the United States. In a year when only three states held elections, the Duke-Edwards race had become front-page news throughout the country and dominated radio talk shows nationwide. The *New York Times* was publishing at least one article a day, as if it were a local race. When Louisianians traveled out of the state, they found that all anybody wanted to talk about was the governor's race.

Duke, meanwhile, was appearing repeatedly on the evening news and national television shows: "Good Morning America," "Nightwatch," "Larry King Live," "Donahue," "Crossfire," "Today." His appearances prompted thousands of people from around the country to contribute to his campaign. But it scared many others, particularly Jews, into thinking that he could win. While Duke's supporters made $5 and $10 contributions, his opponents gave $1,000 or more.

Donald Spector, a professional fund raiser hired by the Louisiana Democratic party to tap into big donors during the runoff, had never seen people make contributions so eagerly. They were frantic at the thought that Duke might win. "There was a feeling of life and death," Spector remembered later. "It wasn't just about winning or losing a race." When Spector called business executives of major companies seeking contributions during normal campaigns, they usually returned the call a couple of days later, and then it was only their secretaries who made the call. When Spector called seeking money for the anti-Duke campaign in 1991, the business executives themselves called him back immediately.

Steven Ross, chairman of Time-Warner, worked feverishly to defeat Duke. Ross, who was dying of cancer, gave the Louisiana Democratic party $25,000, and he wrote letters and called friends, beseeching them to make contributions. Dustin Hoffman sent $25,000; Michelle Pfeiffer gave $1,000. So did Dan Akroyd, Kirstie Alley, James Garner, Norman Lear, and Herb Alpert. Five Democratic senators joined the effort, sending out an appeal for the Louisiana Democratic party. They got back eight boxes worth of letters, in a response rate that was fifteen times higher than normal.

When Edwards visited New York City on November 5, he raised $200,000. "I'll do whatever I can to help," contributors told him throughout the day. Many people felt they had to stop David Duke in Louisiana, or his success would be repeated in New York, Connecticut, and other states. Edwards in the primary had raised $1 million, barely enough to mount a successful campaign. But in the runoff, checks flowed into his campaign at a dizzying rate. Eating lunch at Tujague's restaurant in the French Quarter one day during the runoff, Edwards's friend and adviser Bob d'Hemecourt recalled how at the beginning of the campaign they had been strapped for funds. He asked Edwards: "Do you remember when you personally got on the phone and wanted to know where that $5,000 check enroute from Lafayette was? You needed the money to pay an expense."

"Yeah, I remember," Edwards said with a laugh.

"Well, I have $700,000 in my briefcase that we picked up in the last two days," d'Hemecourt chortled.

During the final ten days of the campaign, Duke was under attack by not only Edwards, businessmen, the Louisiana Coalition Against Racism and Nazism, and the state's newspapers but also the Louisiana Democratic party, which kicked off a massive anti-Duke television campaign on November 8, two days after the second debate. The ads were produced by Deno Seder, who wanted to ensure that he had not helped knock out Buddy Roemer in the primary only to see Louisiana end up with David Duke.

The state Democratic party ads concentrated on the economic angle, but several attacked Duke for his Nazi activities. In the most effective spot, Major General Ansel Stroud, commander of the Louisiana National Guard, stood in full dress uniform in front of an American flag and said, "I joined the army in 1944 to fight against the Nazis. And I'm going to fight the Nazis in this election." Another ad broadcast excerpts from Duke's 1986 taped interview with doctoral candidate Evelyn Rich in which Duke told neo-Nazi Joe Fields it could take decades to bring down the United States government. A third ad, as it showed a photograph of Hitler in stiff-arm salute, told viewers: "Vote for Duke. Create a Fuehrer." Separately, New Orleans businessman David Dixon was running his anti-Duke ad, and Bobby Hebert, the Cajun working-class hero who quarterbacked the New Orleans Saints, cut a thirty-second spot in which, without mentioning Duke by name, he told voters to reject racism.

Altogether, the anti-Duke ads were running virtually around the clock. "It has to be the largest single advertising buy ever in American politics against one person," Raymond Strother said. "There's so much of it. I don't see how he can withstand it." Meanwhile, business owners wrote their employees, warning that a Duke election would spell economic doom. "Vote for Governor Edwin Edwards," the general manager of the New Orleans Hilton wrote his employees. "It may be the most important vote you cast in your lifetime." Anti-Duke bumper stickers sprouted on cars throughout the state. "No Dukes" was the favorite, but other popular ones were "Vote for the Lizard, not the Wizard" and "Vote for the Crook. It's Important." President Bush denounced Duke as a racist and anti-Semite, and national Republican party leaders chimed in.

David Duke was thick-skinned after a lifetime of enduring slings and arrows. But the massive onslaught in the runoff was taking its toll. Usually surefooted on television, Duke stumbled on Sunday, November 10, when he appeared with Edwards for the final time during the campaign, on NBC's "Meet the Press." It was six days before the runoff, and all the world was watching. Timothy Russert, NBC's Washington bureau chief and a panelist on the show, was determined not to let Duke manipulate "Meet the Press" panelists as he had unprepared interviewers on so many other television shows. He researched Duke thoroughly to come up with tough questions that would keep Duke from giving his canned answers.

The show was a verbal slugfest. Duke and Edwards, sitting side by side in a New Orleans television studio, frequently interrupted each other to charge the other with improprieties and to launch spirited defenses. But neither candidate had scored an advantage until Russert late in the show asked Duke to identify the three manufacturing companies with the most employees in Louisiana.

"I couldn't give you their name right off, sir," Duke said, stumbling for words.

"You don't know who the biggest employers in the state of Louisiana are?" Russert asked incredulously.

"Well, I don't have the statistics in front of me," Duke said.

Jim McPherson, sitting a few feet away off camera, was silently imploring Duke to turn the question around and make his points, as he had done time and time again throughout the campaign. "Tell him there aren't enough jobs," McPherson said under his breath. "Tell him that when you're governor, there'll be new industry. Tell him how many jobs Louisiana lost while Edwards was governor." But Duke, worn down by the attacks, came up empty.

Russert followed up with another question. "How many people in your state live below the poverty line?" he asked.

"I don't have the exact numbers in front of me, sir," Duke said, faltering again. "I don't carry around an almanac with me."

"It's 24 percent," a playful Edwards, sitting next to him off camera, whispered, giving the correct answer. Duke looked at him blankly and turned back to the camera but said nothing.

A few minutes later, the show ended. As Edwards and Duke were taking off their microphones, Duke said to Edwards, "Well, a week from now it will be a very close election. Whichever way it goes, I want to stay in touch with you."

"Well, number one," Edwards responded, "it's not going to be a close election. And you can visit me at the mansion anytime you want." A few minutes later, he told reporters, "Heavens to Betsy, if he doesn't know where the jobs in Louisiana are now, how is he going to be more effective in getting the jobs tomorrow or the next day?"

Duke had taken a pounding during the past week, and there would be no letup in the final five days of the campaign. On Monday, November 11, Bob Hawks, a former Tennessee state legislator who had worked for Duke for several months, quit his campaign and charged that Duke's claim of a recent conversion to Christianity was a hoax.

Hawks, a devout Christian, said that while Duke praised Christ in public, in private he never displayed any religious fervor or read the Bible. "I would hear it in his words where he was stage-center, which included talking to the media and from platforms," Hawks said, "but failed to hear it from his daily life." The incident damaged Duke's credibility with a key constituency, Protestant evangelicals. It also reminded them that nine days earlier, he had claimed to belong to the Evangelical Bible Church—only to have to admit the next day that it did not exist. Actually, he explained, he participated in a nondenominational Bible study with a small group of individuals who met in different homes.

Duke had further stumbled when, pressed to identify the moment when he had become a born-again Christian, he said it had happened at age thirteen. If so, he had been an admirer of Hitler and had been a Klan grand wizard after finding Christ, a claim that did not square with many Christians. "It is not possible that someone who found Christ 28 years ago could have burned the cross, could have twisted the cross into a Swastika," Neil Curran, an Evangelical Christian and Republican party activist, told reporters.

On Wednesday, two days after Hawks blasted Duke, Duke suffered a final body blow. Ros Davidson, a Scottish journalist, told the *Times-Picayune* that Duke had said Jews were a plague on the white race during a 1990 interview with her—at a time when he was claiming to no longer hold extremist views. While Duke was normally careful not to display his true anti-Semitic views to reporters, Davidson said she thought he opened up with her because she was Scottish. Because his forebears were from Scotland, he told her, he felt a special affinity for the country. "You know the [Ku Klux Klan] fiery cross is a symbol adopted from Scotland," he told Davidson.

Despite the battering, Duke wasn't giving up. That Wednesday night, his largest crowd yet of the campaign, more than 2,500 people, turned out for a rally in Lafayette, a traditional Edwards stronghold. "On Saturday," Duke shouted, "the silent majority is not going to be silent any longer." Edwards at a New Orleans rally on Thursday night scoffed at that notion. "David Duke says the polls can't tell about his strength because he flies below radar," Edwards said. "Forty-eight hours from now, he's going to crash." His own tracking poll showed him with 59 percent of the vote, up from 51 percent two days before.

Three polls released that week, after attempting to adjust for Duke's hidden vote, showed Edwards leading by seven to ten points. Who was right, Duke with his silent majority or Edwards and the pollsters? "We're all holding our breath for tomorrow's election," a woman told the *Dallas Morning News* on Friday. Duke held the final rally of his long campaign that night at an American Legion hall in the New Orleans suburb of Jefferson. He predicted victory the next day and denounced Edwards and the *Times-Picayune*. Afterward, hundreds of people spilled into the parking lot, not wanting to go home. Neither did Duke. Lit up by the floodlights of half a dozen TV cameras, he stood on the back of a truck, waving to his supporters, who were chanting, "Go to hell, *T-P*, go to hell!" Duke finally left to be interviewed by Ted Koppel on "Nightline." It would be another night when he didn't get much sleep.

Henry Dillon III didn't get any sleep that night. Executive director of the Louisiana Voter Registration/Education Crusade, a nonprofit group based in New Orleans that registered black people to vote, Dillon was exhausted but too excited to rest. For four weeks, since Duke had made the runoff, he had helped organize a get-out-the-vote effort on a scale he had never dreamed possible. And he was not alone in ensuring that blacks turned out in record numbers. Black political organizations in New Orleans and other major cities throughout Louisiana had organized similar drives. The Edwards campaign financed many of these groups, spending hundreds of thousands of dollars to hire workers to knock on doors in the days before the election and turn out voters on election day. Many blacks traditionally worked in get-out-the-vote efforts because of the money they were paid. But money didn't matter in this election. Defeating Duke had become a moral imperative for blacks. Everywhere Henry Dillon went in New Orleans during the four-week runoff, blacks wanted to talk only about the governor's race. "What do I have to do to stop Duke?" they asked him. National black groups, meanwhile, sent thousands of dollars to aid the get-out-the-vote effort.

On election day, November 16, Dillon began deploying his forces before the sun came up. Hundreds of people put up Edwards signs throughout the city. By 6:00 A.M., when the polls opened, they were manning a fleet of vans that would take people without transportation to the polls. Blacks in New Orleans traditionally voted later in the day. But Dillon's workers found this morning that blacks throughout the city were waiting to vote at polling stations when they opened.

"If Duke wins, it'd be just like the '60s," said Jay Jackson, a thirty-three-year-old maintenance man, as he waited to vote at 7:30 A.M. in New Orleans. "Different water fountains, all that stuff. We'd be slaves again."

A little later, Dillon was at his headquarters when a group of students walked in. They wanted to help out. "We don't have any more money to pay you," Dillon said.

"We're not here for money," one woman said. "We just want to know how we can beat Duke."

At 11:00 A.M., a group of drivers sent by Lance Hill to black precincts to take voters to the polls found to their astonishment that there was no one to drive. Everyone had voted. In Baton Rouge, Duke campaign aide David Touchstone saw hundreds of black people displaying red "Stop Duke" signs in their car windows and long lines of black voters at the polls. He shook his head in resignation. "We can't possibly win now," he thought.

This day, blacks would turn out in record numbers: 78.3 percent of registered blacks voted, a rate nearly as high as whites' 79 percent turnout. Overall, the turnout was 78.7 percent, an extraordinarily high rate in an era when only 50 percent of registered Americans voted to elect their presidents. It was the highest rate in a Louisiana election since a 79.3 percent turnout for the 1964 second Democratic primary.

Polls on election day were scheduled to close at 8:00 P.M. People across the state nervously turned on their TV sets to get the results. The election that had weighed on their minds for days and days was now over. At two minutes before 8:00 P.M., a dozen Duke supporters at Mama's Place, a neighborhood bar in Duke's legislative district in Metairie, thought their man was about to make history. "I think it's beautiful that the white people stuck together on this one like the niggers did," said Lois Brondum, "Mama" in the bar's name. "I can't wait for Duke to win. I just can't wait." At seconds past 8:00, Bob Schieffer came on the air for CBS. "Edwin Edwards has won the Louisiana governor's race by a substantial margin," Schieffer said, citing exit polls.

Duke's supporters at Mama's Place fell silent. The crowd of people in Edwards's suite at the Monteleone whooped and hollered. Bob d'Hemecourt shook Edwards's hand. "Congratulations," he said, "you did it again."

Word spread immediately throughout the French Quarter. A brass band materialized from somewhere and led a group of revelers to the Monteleone, playing "When the Saints Go Marching In." The final result was:

| Edwin Edwards | 1,057,031 | 61 percent |
| David Duke | 671,009 | 39 percent |

Duke could run from his past, but he could not hide from it. In the end, truth had won out. Duke was unfit to be governor.

Along with the huge black turnout, the economic issue had proven decisive for Edwards. Exit polls showed that 94 percent of the people who listed losing business as a top concern voted for Edwards. When asked to pick their top two concerns in the election from a list of nine possibilities, 37 percent named business. The economic issue swung Roemer's supporters into Edwards's camp. Three out of every four Roemer supporters voted for Edwards. Edwards won not because voters liked him but because he convinced them that Duke posed a grave threat to their well-being. Nearly half of the people who pulled Edwards's lever did so because they did not want Duke to be governor, exit polls showed. Six in ten voters said they thought Edwards was a crook.

The *Times-Picayune* and the television advertising bombardment overwhelmed Duke in the New Orleans metro area, where one-third of the state's voters lived. Edwards crushed Duke in New Orleans with 87 percent of the vote, and he won a whopping 59 percent vote in conservative Jefferson Parish. Edwards even defeated Duke in his Metairie legislative district with 56 percent of the vote. Duke won only nineteen of Louisiana's sixty-four parishes, with most of them in the rural northeast corner of the state. Duke had not just lost but lost big. Analysts pointed out that he had received a lower percentage of votes than in the Senate race. He was going backwards politically, they said. There were some bright spots for Duke. He had won 55 percent of the white vote, despite the massive negative assault, exit polls showed. He carried 56 percent of the Republican vote and 56 percent of the Cajun vote.

At 9:30 P.M., Edwards went down to the Monteleone grand ballroom to make his victory speech. "Tonight, Louisiana became first," he told a cheering throng, "first to turn back the merchant of hate, the master of deceit. I ask the nation, the national press, I ask all those whose opinions we respect, to write and to say of us that Louisiana rejected the demagogue and renounced irrational fear, dark suspicion, evil bigotry and division and chose a future of hope and trust and love for all of God's children."

An hour later, a subdued Duke conceded before his supporters at the Baton Rouge Hilton. "Right doesn't win every battle, but right always triumphs in the end," he said. "This is just the beginning, not the end." Surrounded by a phalanx of bodyguards, he moved onto the floor to thank his supporters and give interviews to the dozens of reporters covering his election-night party. In one brief interview, he blamed his defeat on "power, money, endorsements, the media and economic blackmail. . . . All the factors working together were too much to overcome."

Two hours later, Duke was still circling the littered ballroom, looking for hands to shake and reporters to talk to. He wasn't ready yet to yield the spotlight.

CHAPTER TEN

THE PRESIDENCY OR BUST

The day after his landslide defeat for governor of Louisiana, David Duke did what he had done throughout the runoff campaign: take to the national airwaves. In appearances on ABC's "This Week with David Brinkley" and "CNN's Newsmaker Sunday," he put on a cheery face and proclaimed that while he may have lost in Louisiana, he had amassed a national following. "We have a national movement right now based on the principles that I'm speaking about," he said on CNN. Asked if he would enter the upcoming presidential primaries, he replied, "I don't have any plans whatsoever to get into those primaries at this time."

The next day, however, Duke called a press conference in New Orleans and announced he was forming an exploratory committee to study whether to challenge President Bush in the Republican primaries. "The least that we could possibly accomplish in this country is to make George Bush adhere to the principles of the party and stop the drifting to the left that we've had so long," Duke told reporters. Duke had not been trying to mislead CNN viewers the day before. At that point, he didn't have plans to seek the presidency. He made the decision to run the next day, shortly before he announced it, and in eschewing planning once again, he did not discuss it with his political advisers beforehand.

On December 4, two and one-half weeks later, Duke formally announced his presidential candidacy at a press conference at the National Press Club in Washington. It was a media zoo, with more than 100 reporters, photographers, and television cameramen present, including the top guns from the *Washington Post*, the *New York Times*, and the three major television networks. Duke stationed guards outside to limit the event to media only, but several hecklers slipped in. "Nazi! Nazi! You're a goddam Nazi!" one woman screamed at him before guards dragged her away. A New York rabbi holding aloft a sign that read, "David Duke—Nazi of the '90s," also got within several feet of Duke before guards hustled him out of the room.

Duke was running as an antiestablishment, right-wing populist once again, as he attacked President Bush for selling out the hard-pressed middle class by raising taxes, signing the civil rights bill days before, and supporting a free-trade agreement with Mexico. Duke called for tough anticrime measures and a reduction in government spending, and he opposed quotas, affirmative action, new taxes and "the welfare illegitimate birth rate." Playing the race card, he twice described Democrats as the party of "Jesse Jackson and Ron Brown," referring to the former Democratic presidential candidate and the chairman of the Democratic National Party, both of whom are black.

Invoking his belief that the country's Western European values were under siege, he complained that "Christian society" was being undermined to the point "where we can't even sing Christmas carols in many of our public schools anymore."

Duke also pushed two other hot-button issues that had concerned him for years, calling for a clampdown on illegal immigration and advocating "fair trade," not "free trade," with Mexico and Japan. In a racial slur, he added: "We must go to the Japanese and say, 'You no buy our rice, we no buy your cars.'" He also called for laws preventing foreigners from owning American businesses and farmland. Duke demanded that American troops be brought home from Europe and said the United States had to move "from a 'New World Order' position to an 'America First' position." But beyond that, he said little about foreign affairs.

Washington Post reporter Thomas B. Edsall, who had analyzed the issue of race more perceptively than anyone else, wrote that Duke was trying to exploit the fundamental restructuring of American presidential politics forced largely by the four bids former Alabama governor George Wallace had made for the White House from 1964 to 1976. "Wallace succeeded to the extent he did—winning five states in the 1968 general election and five states in the 1972 Democratic primaries—by driving a wedge based on race through the heart of the traditional Democratic coalition of blacks and working-class whites," Edsall wrote the day after Duke announced for president. "In the long run, the political lessons Wallace taught were learned best by the Republican Party, and Wallace voters became a principal component of Richard M. Nixon's 'Silent Majority' and the 'Reagan Democrats' who became a major factor in Republican successes in the 1980s. Now Duke . . . will attempt to rally many of those same voters and, if he runs in the general election as an independent, lead them away from the GOP altogether. Just as Wallace channeled anger and resentment among whites against a liberal Democratic elite, Duke is attempting to focus that anger and discord on the establishment wing of the Republican Party as it is epitomized by President Bush." Edsall noted that Duke spoke approvingly of Wallace at his presidential announcement. "Both of us are talking about a lot of the issues that the establishment politicians weren't talking about," Duke said. "He was a courageous man, and I admire him greatly." But while both Duke and Wallace could be termed populists who used race as a wedge issue, there were sharp distinctions between the two. Originally a progressive on racial matters, Wallace became a segregationist because he realized that doing so could get him elected governor, and when he had played that string out in the 1980s, he moved to the Left and courted black votes.

Duke, in sharp contrast, pushed the race issue because, with his political views based on eugenics and National Socialism, he believed that the fate of the United States depended on continuing the white European heritage that had made the country great.

Duke had moderated somewhat by the early 1990s. Where just a few years before he had denounced "niggers" and Jews, he now spoke in racial code and never voluntarily mentioned Jews. He had supported President Bush's nomination of black conservative Clarence Thomas to the Supreme Court in 1991, something he would never have done before. (He disapproved of Thomas's having a white wife, however.) Duke, thanks to his political success, had for the first time in his life had the opportunity to visit country clubs, be invited to parties hosted by respected members of society, wear expensive suits, dine at fine restaurants. This tugged him away from the fringe. But David Duke, fundamentally, remained a white supremacist.

While Duke was running for president on many standard conservative issues, his emphasis on race and maintaining the ethnic and cultural purity of the United States betrayed his continuing belief in National Socialism. As a National Socialist, Duke believed that a nation and its race were identical—so that once the United States began diluting its white, European ethnic heritage with increasing numbers of blacks and people from countries with inferior genes, then the United States was doomed.

As a National Socialist, Duke wanted to stop the illegitimate welfare birth rate, as he told doctoral candidate Evelyn Rich in 1985, because welfare was causing blacks to reproduce in higher numbers than whites. He wanted curbs on immigration to keep out the genetically inferior nonwhites from Latin America. He opposed President Bush's "New World Order" because he thought it had led to the Persian Gulf War, which he had told several interviewers he opposed. He told friends privately he thought Jews had pushed the United States into the war to protect Israel's interests. He opposed handing out condoms in public schools—unless it was to welfare recipients—because he believed that the government should discourage only the lazy and lower members of society, i.e., welfare recipients, from having babies.

There were several reasons on a personal level why Duke was running for president. After campaigning for political office practically nonstop for four years, he couldn't stop now. While he railed against the media, he was reluctant to yield the attention. After a lifetime of rejection, he craved the spotlight and the stamp of importance the media accorded. The media also gave him the outlet he needed to spread his views. Running for office was also how he made his living.

There were some sound political reasons to run for president. Duke was trying to build a mass political movement with himself at its head, and he needed constant exposure to attract new followers. He had already accumulated about 125,000 names on his mailing list. By running for president, he told an aide, he could double the list, which through direct-mail solicitations could provide a steady source of financing for his activities.

Duke figured he could garner tons of attention. In a move accorded to few politicians, Dan Rather had interviewed him live on the CBS News on November 18, the day he announced he was forming the exploratory presidential committee. Not only did his announcement for president on December 4 turn out a huge contingent of reporters, he did twelve interviews that day at NBC's Washington studio with local affiliates from around the country. His announcement for president was very closely followed by 16 percent of Americans, the same percentage that had closely followed Donald Trump's financial troubles and the nomination of David Souter to the Supreme Court in 1990, according to a *Times Mirror* poll. Duke could bank on an extraordinarily high level of name recognition nationwide: 58 percent. He was better known than all the Democratic presidential candidates.

Demonstrating his select status, he was satirized beginning in late December in the political cartoon strip "Doonesbury," which appeared in 1,600 newspapers nationwide every day. The portrayal was unflattering—he appeared as a hovering swastika who reunited with his unscrupulous cousin, the Uncle Duke character—but that he appeared at all attested to his political stardom.

Through the media, Duke thought he could increase his appeal nationwide enough to where he could win a few delegates to the Republican National Convention in Houston and perhaps have his name placed in nomination during prime time. In Houston, the thousands of reporters looking for something to write about would flock to him, giving him even more exposure and respectability.

After the convention, by threatening to run as a third-party candidate in the fall general election, he figured, he could get the White House to agree to stop attacking him. This would free him to run for Congress either against Bob Livingston, who represented suburban New Orleans, or for a seat in northern Louisiana, where he enjoyed his greatest support in the state.

The timing seemed right for Duke, who was now forty-one years old. He was riding a wave of what political analyst Kevin Phillips called "Middle America Radicalism" that also manifested itself in 1991 in the antiestablishment victory of Democratic senator Harris Wofford in Pennsylvania and that in 1992 would sustain the independent presidential campaign of Texas billionaire H. Ross Perot. "The American Dream was collapsing in a cross fire of shrunken home values, eroding real family incomes and shaky pensions," Phillips wrote in his 1993 book *Boiling Point: Democrats, Republicans, and the Decline of Middle-Class Prosperity.*

President Bush was becoming a victim of the Middle America Radicalism as euphoria over the United States victory over Saddam Hussein wore off. A New York Times/CBS News poll in mid-November, three weeks before Duke announced his challenge, showed that Bush's approval rating had dropped sixteen points in the past month, and only one in four voters approved of how he was handling the economy. His low rating on the economy had been unmatched since the days of double-digit inflation under President Jimmy Carter.

Duke's criticism of welfare was a winning issue nationally, as mainstream politicians began mimicking him. President Bush called for ending welfare dependency. California Governor Pete Wilson, blaming an influx of indigents and immigrants for his state's fiscal emergency, proposed sharp reductions in welfare payments, including the Duke proposal of not increasing grants to mothers for additional children. New Jersey Governor Jim Florio in January 1992 signed a bill that denied additional benefits to welfare mothers who had babies after joining the program. Welfare mothers in New Jersey had gotten an additional sixty-four dollars a month for each additional child.

"I'm afraid all this originates with David Duke," said New York Senator Daniel Patrick Moynihan, the leading welfare reform champion in Congress. "He started talking about the 'threat' of people on welfare, and it struck a nerve. When Ronald Reagan used to talk about people buying vodka with Food Stamps, that was one kind of attack on the poor. But when you talk about a threat, it's more ominous."

Many trends and events seemed to be working in Duke's favor. But in deciding to run for president, he was making a fatal error, one that would knock him out of the political spotlight for at least several years and perhaps forever. To begin with, Republican primary rules were stacked against challengers in general and specifically against candidates like Duke who received strong Democratic backing. Most Republican primaries were closed, meaning that they excluded registered Democrats. The impact of this rule can be seen by looking at the Louisiana gubernatorial election, in which 26 percent of the voters identified themselves as Republicans, according to exit polls, although only 16 percent were registered as Republicans. The 10 percent of Democrats who considered themselves Republicans would not be able to vote for Duke in a closed primary.

Selection rules for GOP convention delegates in most states created another built-in disadvantage for Duke, because they required that a challenger win a majority of votes in at least one congressional district to win any delegates. So Duke could make a big splash by winning 40 percent of the vote in a state against Bush, but if he didn't carry any of the state's congressional districts, he would win zero delegates. Furthermore, Republican primary voters tended to be upper middle class or wealthier, the segment of the electorate least favorable to Duke, who did best among younger middle-class voters and those without a high school education.

Another factor weighing against Duke was that while he was widely known, he was also widely reviled. His favorable rating in a January 1992 New York Times–CBS News poll measured a scant 4 percent, while his negative rating was a whopping 72 percent. Even factoring in his hidden vote, which at most doubled his support, he had a mountain to climb.

At the same time, while Duke hoped to be the only Republican challenging Bush, the same wave of middle-class frustration and resentment he was riding had attracted the interest of archconservative commentator Pat Buchanan, a former Nixon and Reagan White House aide who wrote a syndicated column and appeared on "Crossfire" as the regular right-wing panelist. While never endorsing Duke's anti-Semitic or racist activities, Buchanan had been impressed with how effectively Duke had used his core issues. In March 1989, shortly after Duke won the Metairie state house election, Buchanan wrote in his syndicated column, "The way to deal with Mr. Duke is the way the GOP dealt with the far more formidable challenge of George Wallace. Take a hard look at Duke's portfolio of winning issues; and expropriate those not in conflict with GOP principles.

"David Duke did not beat John Treen because he is an ex-wizard of the KKK; he beat him in spite of it; he beat him because he was tougher on taxes, and made an issue of urban crime, the primary source of which *is* the urban underclass; he beat Treen because he lit into set-asides and 'affirmative action' in hiring, scholarships, and promotions on the basis of race, i.e. reverse discrimination against white folks who happen to make up 99 percent of his electorate.

"What Mr. Duke did, after he turned in his robes and signed up with the GOP, was run over and seize terrain vacated by the GOP. David Duke walked into a political vacuum left when Republicans, in the Reagan years, were intimidated by moderates and progressives into shucking off winning social issues so we might be able to pass moral muster with [civil rights leaders] Ben Hooks and Coretta King."

In an October 1991 column, just after Duke had knocked off Buddy Roemer, Buchanan quoted these words again and added: "Both the GOP establishment and conservatives should study how and why white voters, who delivered Louisiana to Reagan and Bush three times, moved in such numbers to David Duke—and devise a strategic plan to win them back. What to do? President Bush might take a hard look at illegal immigration, tell the U.S. Border Patrol to hire some of those vets being mustered out after Desert Storm, veto the Democrats' 'quota bill' and issue an executive order rooting out any and all reverse discrimination in the U.S. government, beginning with the FBI."

Buchanan, who had been mulling a challenge to Bush for months, announced his candidacy for president on December 10, six days after Duke. One of the reasons Buchanan entered the race was to prevent Duke from being the only challenger to Bush from the right, Buchanan's press secretary, Greg Mueller, said later.

To a remarkable extent, Buchanan and Duke on issue after issue—welfare, taxes, racial quotas, immigration, affirmative action, trade, opposition to the Persian Gulf War, and the power of the Jewish lobby—held indistinguishable views. They both called for cuts in welfare benefits, blasted Bush for having broken his promise not to raise taxes, opposed racial quotas, called for beefing up the Mexican border to prevent the influx of illegal aliens, bashed Bush for not reducing federal spending more sharply, called for an "America First" foreign policy, denounced Bush for not being more aggressive in reducing trade barriers in Japan and Europe, and held that Congress was "Israeli-occupied territory," to quote Buchanan, in a phrase that Duke had used for years.

Isolationist, protectionist, antigovernment, Buchanan sounded like a carbon copy of Duke. "If discrimination is wrong when practiced against black men and women, it is wrong when practiced against any man or woman," Buchanan said during the campaign. "I think God made all people good, but if we had to take a million immigrants in, say Zulus, next year, or Englishmen, and put them in Virginia, what group would be easier to assimilate and would cause less problems?" he said in one interview. "Does this First World nation wish to become a Third World country?" he asked on another occasion. "Because that is our destiny if we do not build a sea wall against the waves of immigration rolling over our shores."

Both Duke and Buchanan charged that the other was stealing his lines, and Buchanan, in particular, tried to distance himself from Duke. When a reporter pointed out the similarity of their views at one press conference, Buchanan grew testy and tried to cut him off. Duke for his part welcomed the comparison. "I think Pat Buchanan is a fine candidate," Duke said time and time again. There was another link between Buchanan and Duke. Buchanan had held an unpublicized meeting with two members of the Populist party executive committee in early 1991 to learn more about the party and its titular head, Willis Carto, whom the Anti-Defamation League called the leading anti-Semitic propagandist in the country. Duke, of course, was the Populist party's presidential candidate in 1988, although by 1991 he had forsaken it for the Republican party.

When Duke announced for president, he said he did not have time to compete in the New Hampshire primary on February 18. Instead, he said he would enter later primaries, concentrating his efforts in the South—March 3 in Georgia, March 7 in South Carolina, and the March 10 Super Tuesday cluster of states. This was a fateful mistake.

After his presidential announcement, Buchanan spent the next two months camping out in New Hampshire. In a conservative state wracked by recession, his charges that Bush was out of touch with the little man and that he preferred to solve the problems of Russia while Main Street languished found a wellspring of anti-status quo support. Buchanan won 37 percent of the Republican vote in New Hampshire, a showing trumpeted as a sign of Bush's weakness. "New Hampshire establishes Buchanan as a legitimate contender," said Bill Lacy, a White House political director under the Reagan administration.

Unschooled in the dynamics of a presidential campaign, Duke cheered Buchanan's New Hampshire showing. "This has thrown the race for the Republican nomination wide open," he said. "And I'm going to deliver the coup de grace in the South. . . . He (Bush) is coming into my home ground now, and he's going to be facing a born and bred Southerner. I think Bush is going to have a difficult time with me." Instead, it was Buchanan who had delivered the coup de grace to Duke, as would soon become evident.

Duke had acted rashly in deciding to run for president. Shell-shocked from the intense pounding he had taken in the governor's race, he was exhausted and gun shy about campaigning. Getting in the presidential race so late, he should have hit the campaign trail full time immediately, as Buchanan did. Instead, he stayed at his Metairie home/office doing satellite TV and radio interviews. While this got him some publicity, it was no substitute for visiting the states holding primaries that he planned to enter. Aide Marc Ellis scheduled campaign events for Duke, but he canceled them. "David was burned out," aide Jewel Tardiff recalled. "You can only take so much abuse."

The national Republican party, meanwhile, was showing Duke no quarter. While most of the Louisiana Republican party had remained silent about Duke, President Bush's advisers had decided they would attack him at every opportunity during the presidential campaign. The day Duke announced for president, White House press secretary Marlin Fitzwater said Duke "represents the worst of American politics, stands for bigotry, racism and other qualities that have no place in American life." B. J. Cooper, spokesman for the Republican National Committee, chimed in, "He's not a Republican, he's a charlatan," and added that Duke "will never ever, anytime, anywhere, receive any assistance, support, anything, from us."

Bush's advisers decided also to block Duke from being on the ballot in as many states as possible. They passed along word to the state party chairmen, who waged a relentless fight to keep Duke off wherever possible, especially in crossover states—like Georgia—that allowed Democrats to vote in the Republican party. Each state had its own rules about how candidates qualified on the ballot, and in some states the Republican party could not prevent Duke from being a candidate. But the Republican party succeeded in keeping him off in Georgia, Florida, Wisconsin, and South Dakota, and it forced him to divert precious resources to fighting to get on ballots in these and other states.

With Duke not campaigning, throughout December and into late January, almost all the media coverage he received concerned efforts by the Republican party to keep him off Republican primary ballots. This coverage gave Duke some publicity and won him support from a few voters who thought the Republican party was bullying him. But he won a fraction of the publicity he would have received by campaigning, trailed by a horde of reporters, in New Hampshire, Georgia, Texas, and other states.

As Duke failed to mount a serious campaign during those crucial weeks after his December 4 announcement, he lost the controversy and news coverage he needed to get his faithful contributors to fork over more money. By the end of December he had raised only $59,000, the amount he needed to raise every day.

But beyond his failure to campaign, Duke was having problems with his more ardent supporters. Many of them were angry that he was running for president and refused to send him money. They thought he should run for Congress—a race he could win. By running for president, he confirmed the growing suspicion of many that he was a perpetual candidate who campaigned because it provided his source of income. "He could have won a congressional seat if he had chosen not to run for president," said a disappointed John Powell, a retired automobile dealer in Monroe who had worked in his Senate and gubernatorial campaigns. "He has lost many of those who were with him. They realize that Duke is a perennial candidate and a nonwinner." Others compared him to money-hungry televangelists.

While the national Republicans worked to keep Duke off the March 3 ballot in Georgia—the state that promised him his first best opportunity—they made no effort to block him from the March 7 South Carolina primary. Duke leaped at the chance to campaign there. It would be his first primary. "I can't wait for South Carolina," Duke said in early January. "I guarantee we'll do better in South Carolina than Pat Buchanan will do in New Hampshire. I know the pulse of that state. South Carolina in a lot of ways is a lot like northeast Louisiana, where I won 15 of 20 parishes" in the gubernatorial runoff.

The Republican party had laid a trap for Duke in South Carolina—and he was walking right into it. In South Carolina, the GOP boasted its strongest party apparatus, led by the state's popular Republican governor, Carroll Campbell. Campbell and the Bush campaign had laid a similar trap for the Reverend Pat Robertson in the 1988 Republican presidential primaries that eliminated Robertson as a serious contender.

Duke shrugged off warnings that he was walking into a trap. He thought his message would play well in South Carolina, noting that it was nonunion, Protestant, and conservative—his kinds of voters. But South Carolina was not fertile terrain for his message. Not only was South Carolina's economy humming, but the state had not been friendly to populists. South Carolina was the only state in the Deep South that George Wallace had failed to carry in 1968.

Duke campaigned in South Carolina on January 30–31. Aside from an event in Miami while he was visiting his children over the Christmas holiday, it was his first campaign trip since entering the presidential contest six weeks before. By some measures, the trip went well. Duke won lots of coverage from South Carolina TV stations and drew large crowds throughout the state. But he made no effort to build a campaign network there. As a result, the trip produced little more than a flurry of interest in Duke. Republican operatives in South Carolina could feel the noose tightening around an unsuspecting Duke.

A month later he undertook his second campaign trip as he visited Dallas and Houston. The two rallies he held drew large crowds, but Texas newspapers buried stories about his visit. "Initially, we anticipated that the Duke cancer would grow beyond the borders of Louisiana, but there hasn't been much of a presence here," said Texas political consultant Mark McKinnon. "The sheet has become a shadow."

Pat Buchanan, with his strong showing in New Hampshire, had made Duke irrelevant. By challenging Bush in New Hampshire and scoring better than expected, he had become the Republican protest candidate, the alternative to Bush. And for conservatives upset with the status quo, Buchanan sounded like Duke and carried little of the baggage. "I will always be a David Duke supporter, but come election day, I'm going to cast my ballot for Pat Buchanan," said Kenny Knight, who had been one of Duke's top aides and who was one of the many Duke supporters in Louisiana who defected to Buchanan. "Pat Buchanan has a better chance of winning than David Duke. Let's face it, David Duke is not going to get into the White House." After New Hampshire, a pack of reporters followed Buchanan wherever he went. Meanwhile, with Duke not campaigning, reporters lost interest in him. Peter Applebome, writing in the *New York Times*, said Duke was facing a "political fate worse than death. Indifference."

Duke campaigned for two more days in South Carolina on the eve of the March 7 primary, but even he realized the end was near. "It's been hard," Duke told Applebome in South Carolina. "I don't plan on running for office again for a long time. I'd like to get away from politics for a while." Duke won but 7 percent of the vote in South Carolina. "The results show that Duke is a fringe candidate in the Republican primaries," said Earl Black, chairman of the University of South Carolina's political science department.

Three days later came Super Tuesday, and Duke was on the ballot in Massachusetts, Rhode Island, Louisiana, Oklahoma, Texas, Mississippi, and Tennessee. He had campaigned only briefly in the latter three states. The night before Super Tuesday, he held a final rally at the Pontchartrain Center in Kenner. Six months before, on the eve of the Louisiana gubernatorial primary, Duke had swept into the convention center surrounded by bodyguards and clamoring reporters. Thunderous chants of "Duke! Duke! Duke!" had greeted him, and a six-piece band serenaded him with "Dixie." Ardent admirers in the crowd of 1,000 had engulfed him, trying to shake his hand or pat him on the back. But on the night before Super Tuesday when he ambled into the Pontchartrain Center, a thin crowd of 250 greeted him, and it could muster only a feeble cheer. There were only a handful of reporters, no bodyguards, and a lone woman singing pop tunes to the strains of prerecorded backup music.

At the election-night party at the Pontchartrain Center the following evening, Carole DiFalco, an ABC producer who had been covering Duke, felt as if she was witnessing a Fellini movie. About twenty supporters turned up—equaling the number of reporters there—leaving hundreds of seats empty. DiFalco watched in amazement as Duke worked the room as if he had just won the nomination. He stopped to kiss both babies there. He then gave his stock speech as if he were speaking to a large crowd. When Duke finished and gave interviews to TV reporters, his supporters chanted his name and gathered around to try to hide the emptiness in the room. A man dressed as Elvis attracted as much attention as Duke. "It was just pathetic," DiFalco said afterward of the evening. "It was so humiliating."

Duke cracked double digits in only one of the seven Super Tuesday states where he was on the ballot, Mississippi, and then just barely, with 11 percent of the vote. He could do no better than 9 percent in Louisiana, compared with 27 percent for Buchanan and 62 percent for Bush. Overall, that day he won 5 percent of the Republican vote. "I just finished interring the political career of David Duke in a bayou in Louisiana," an exultant Buchanan said.

Duke did not campaign anymore and won 2 or 3 percent in the remaining states in which his name was on the ballot. On April 22, he threw in the towel before a sparse group of reporters in Washington. He had fallen so far that he ruled out a third-party candidacy in the general election. Still, he could claim credit—and did—for turning welfare, affirmative action, and quotas into issues for national debate. "I feel that I've done what I can," Duke said.

Although Duke was out of the race, his impact continued to be felt on the presidential campaign. Republican presidential candidates in every race since 1968—with the exception of President Ford in 1976—had used race as a wedge issue to drive blue-collar Democrats into the Republican column. But Duke, along with the continued fallout from the 1988 Willie Horton ads and the April 1992 Los Angeles race riots, kept Bush from doing so during the 1992 election. To avoid being linked with Duke, Bush in November 1991 had agreed to sign a civil rights bill before Congress that he had vetoed the year before. This action prevented Bush in 1992 from campaigning against quotas, one of the key GOP racially charged wedge issues.

His presidential campaign a flop, Duke's political career was over. He was deeply disappointed but told friends that the American people weren't quite ready for him and that in the meantime he would find other ways to make his voice heard. He hired Holly Sarre, an agent with the New York Speakers Bureau to market his unwritten autobiography, *Boyhood: Growing Up in the Racially Segregated South*, to arrange debates with Nation of Islam leader Louis Farrakhan or the Reverend Jesse Jackson to be carried on national television, and to set up a college speaking tour. But Sarre found no takers for the book or the lecture series, and Farrakhan and Jackson spurned the debate offer. "He's no longer news," Sarre explained.

Angry at him for fizzling out so quickly, the white supremacy movement, which for years had hailed him as its savior, discarded him. "Today his name doesn't even come up," said a disappointed Van Loman, a white rights leader in Cincinnati. Duke tried his hand at several business ventures, but they fell through. He was briefly a partner in an Irish pub in Metairie, but he sold his share when too few customers materialized. He also peddled a long distance phone service that paid him a commission when he got people to switch to it. In August 1992, Physicians Mutual Insurance Company hired him as an insurance agent, but it quickly rescinded the offer when policyholders complained.

That same month, Duke wrote his followers, asking them to help pay for private guards to protect him from an assassination plot revealed to him by unnamed federal authorities; to finance a legal defense against the state, which charged he had violated campaign finance laws during the gubernatorial election by accepting improper contributions; and to help retire his campaign debt. Noting that he wasn't a candidate for public office, he wrote, "a personal gift is not a campaign contribution, so any gift you make is completely private, not public and not reportable to any agency or entity whatsoever. You can make a personal gift of up to $10,000 without it being reportable to the IRS or paying any 'gift tax.'" He wrote that the money wasn't for him. "I ask this not as a reward for my service to you and our cause," he wrote, "but so that I can continue the struggle that is so necessary to preserve our heritage and rights." But at about the same time, Duke was seen in Monte Carlo pursuing one of his favorite nonpolitical activities, gambling. A New Orleans attorney reported seeing him gamble as much as $500 a roll at the craps table.

Duke made few public appearances and reduced his office staff to longtime aide Glenn Montecino, who helped him with the *David Duke Report*, the eight-page monthly newsletter that Duke had begun to publish after the governor's race. A one-year subscription cost fifty dollars. With little to do, Duke attended weekend gun and trade shows where he peddled his newsletter and baseball caps, T-shirts, and buttons left over from his political campaigns. Katie Nachod, a Tulane University librarian, saw him at the Fall Home Fest at the New Orleans Convention Center on one day of an October weekend. Duke had a booth among the carpeting, home alarms, and bathroom features on display. He was standing alone. Meanwhile, a group of admiring men surrounded a *Playboy* Playmate who was a few feet away signing autographs. "He looked sort of pitiful," Nachod said a few weeks later. "No one was paying attention to him."

Having faced rejection throughout all his life, Duke may have been down but he did not count himself out. He looked for opportunities to make a splash, but few came because he was so discredited politically. One opportunity came in March 1993 when he spoke at a rededication ceremony for the Reconstruction Era white-rights Liberty Monument in New Orleans. When the ceremony turned into a shoving match between his supporters and black protesters, Duke was in the news again.

In April, he was hired to be the morning talk-show host for a low wattage radio station in Covington, across Lake Pontchartrain from New Orleans. "This is a hard thing for me," said the man who hired him, station manager Robert Namer, "because I'm Jewish. But business is business." While Duke was thrilled at the opportunity, the statement by Namer, who ironically had opposed him in the 1979 state senate campaign, undoubtedly confirmed all of his worst fears that Jews were willing to do anything for money. In July, Duke moved to a far bigger radio station managed by Namer. Duke bought two hours of time a day from the new station, which required him to find his own advertisers.

In many ways, being a radio talk-show host seemed the perfect job for Duke. It required little more than showing up for a few hours a day, and he got paid to spout his views. Most of the callers talked his talk—complaining that blacks got special privileges while whites were treated as second-class citizens—and he had plenty of opportunities to join in. Occasionally, Duke let down his guard and permitted his true feelings to show, as when he said one day that God had meant for the races to stay apart by creating different skin colors.

"The show's going great," he told his listeners time and time again and talked excitedly about getting nationally syndicated and becoming the next Rush Limbaugh, the reigning conservative talk-show host. The show would launch his political comeback, Duke thought. "He prepares people," Duke said of Limbaugh. "And everybody has a role to play in this effort. . . . He can take them about half the way, and I can take them almost all the way. And between . . . the two of us, there will be a heck of a change in this country."

To most of the country, David Duke's name had faded into a symbol and a catch phrase for racism and anti-Semitism. Political analysts said he could never win elective office again. But Duke nursed his political ambitions, convinced, he told friends, that the country would continue to spiral out of control. In time, he predicted, people would become so frustrated that they would turn to him for solutions. It could come as soon as the year 2000, when he would be only fifty years old. This time his supporters would hold a voting majority and elect him to Congress and then the White House. Duke thought he still had plenty of time to fulfill his destiny by becoming the savior of the white race.

Notes

Citations of wire services such as the Associated Press frequently lack a page number because copy was taken directly from the wire. The date may be the same day as the event, since the copy does not come from the next day's newspaper.

Issues of the newspaper that Duke published in the Klan, the *Crusader*, and the newspaper he published afterward, the *NAAWP News*, are generally not dated, and I have therefore placed the year of publication in brackets. Many articles from the *Crusader* and the *NAAWP News* have no byline; the same holds true for some newspaper and wire service articles.

Readers interested in original source material may want to visit several libraries with a mother lode of information. The Amistad Research Center at Tulane University has copies of the *Crusader* and the *NAAWP News* as well as the research files of the Louisiana Coalition Against Racism and Nazism. The Political Ephemera Collection at Tulane's Howard-Tilton Memorial Library also houses an extensive collection on Duke, particularly from his years in the Klan and earlier. Evelyn Rich's taped interviews with Duke and with other right-wing extremists can be found there, along with transcripts of the interviews. The Louisiana Collection at the University of New Orleans Earl K. Long Library also has copies of the *Crusader* and the *NAAWP News*. Articles on Duke's activities during his university years may be found in the Hill Memorial Library at Louisiana State University, which has copies of the student paper, the *Daily Reveille*. Among the different watchdog groups, the Anti-Defamation League has the most extensive files on Duke. Journal Graphics in Denver has transcripts of some of Duke's television appearances, 1989–92.

I relied on transcripts at the Howard-Tilton Memorial Library for the interviews Evelyn Rich conducted and for the Burwell Ware interview with Duke, which is housed at Xavier University in New Orleans.

A couple of additional notes: I used one of several techniques for my interviews: long-hand notes, notes typed into a computer and a tape recorder (for which I sometimes transcribed the interview).

Finally, following academic style, when I source an interview conducted in person, I write "interview with author" and note the city in which the interview took place. For phone interviews that I source, I use the notation "personal communication."

EPIGRAPH

Page v: *Populist Observer*, October 1988, p. 10.

PREFACE

Page x, paragraph 2. *Ferguson quotations*: interview with author, New Orleans, April 4, 1989.

Page x, paragraph 4. *Duke quotations and quotation of unidentified man*: author's notes, Metairie, La., April 7, 1989.

Page xi, paragraph 4. *Duke said time after time*: Duke speech, author's notes, Slidell, La., August 1, 1990.

Page xiii, paragraph 2. *Warner quotations*: personal communication, January 11, 1990.

Page xiii, paragraph 3. *Warner quotations*: personal communication, August 23, 1990. *Bernie Davids quotations*: interview with author, Harahan, La., October 6, 1990.

Page xiv, paragraph 2. *Duke called a press conference*: author's notes, Metairie, La., August 8, 1989. *He told me one time*: personal communication, August 21, 1989.

CHAPTER 1. *The Making of a Fanatic*

Page 1, paragraphs 1-3. *Rubin at LSU*: "Rubin Runs . . . Scared," *Nationalist*, vol. 2, no. 1 [1972], p. 14; interview with Evelyn Rich, Metairie, La., March 20, 1985, Evelyn Rich Tapes, Political Ephemera Collection, Howard-Tilton Memorial Library, Tulane University, New Orleans.

Page 2, paragraphs 1-2. *Duke recalled the incident*: Interview with Evelyn Rich, March 20, 1985, p. 12.

Page 2, paragraph 3. *Duke gave himself*: "Rubin Runs . . . Scared," p. 14.

Page 3, paragraph 2. *As David Duke told the story*: interview with Burwell Ware, Metairie, La., records of "A House Divided," Xavier University Archives, Special Collections, New Orleans, March 15, 1984, p. 3; Michael Zatarain, *David Duke: Evolution of a Klansman* (Gretna, La.: Pelican, 1990), pp. 75–78; Patsy Sims, *The Klan* (New York: Stein & Day, 1978), p. 179. *Duke had been given the assignment*: Joanne Harrison, "David Duke: Dixie Divider," *Los Angeles Times*, March 21, 1989, p. 1, pt. 5 (Duke quotation).

Page 3, paragraph 3. *Duke quotation*: Zatarain, *David Duke: Evolution of a Klansman*, p. 78.

Page 4, paragraphs 2–3. *David Hedger Duke's quotations*: personal communications, May 30, 1989, June 6, 1989, July 31, 1991.

Page 4, paragraph 4. *Classmates shunned him*: Mike Wells, interview with author, Baton Rouge, February 5, 1992; Mary Elizabeth Gill, ninth grade teacher, personal communication, February 6, 1992. *Dotti Duke Wilkerson quotation*: personal communication, August 4, 1992.

Page 5, paragraph 3. *Dotti Duke Wilkerson quotations*: Joanne Harrison, "David Duke: Dixie Divider," p. 1, pt. 5.

Page 5, paragraph 4. *Dotti Duke Wilkerson quotations*: personal communication, February 13, 1992 (continued on page 6, paragraph 1).

Page 6, paragraph 2. *"Beaver Cleaver" childhood*: Joanne Harrison, "David Duke: Dixie Divider," p. 1, pt. 5; Zatarain, *David Duke*, pp. 73, 83–84.

Page 6, paragraphs 3–5. *Dotti Duke Wilkerson quotations*: personal communication, February 13, 1992 (continued on page 7, paragraph 1).

Page 7, paragraph 3. *Mike Wells quotation*: interview with author, February 5, 1992.

Page 7, paragraph 4. *Mary Elizabeth Gill quotations*: personal communication, February 6, 1992.

Page 7, paragraph 5. *Mike Wells quotations*: interview with author, February 5, 1992 (continued on page 8, paragraphs 1–2).

Page 8, paragraphs 3–6. *Dorothy Singelmann quotations*: interviews with author, New Orleans, February 11, 1992, August 4, 1992, August 5, 1992.

Page 9, paragraph 2. *David Hedger Duke quotations*: personal communication, July 31, 1991.

Page 9, paragraphs 3–4. *Duke was probably looking for a scapegoat*: Several social psychologists who specialize in abnormal behavior helped me understand (personal communications in 1993) why Duke came to hate Jews. They are: Edward Foulks, a psychiatrist and anthropologist at Tulane University's Medical School; Dwight Heath, a professor of anthropology at Brown University; and Howard Stein, a professor of psychoanalytic behavior and anthropology at the University of Oklahoma.

Page 9, paragraph 5. *Dorothy Singelmann quotations*: interviews with author, February 11, 1992, August 4, 1992, August 5, 1992 (continued on page 10, paragraphs 1–4).

Page 10, paragraph 5. *Duke used to call him often*: Mike Wells, interview with author, February 5, 1992.

Page 10, paragraph 6. *Dotti Duke Wilkerson quotations*: personal communication, February 13, 1992.

Page 11, paragraph 4. *Duke told one interviewer*: Zatarain, *David Duke*, pp. 90–94.

Page 11, paragraph 5. *Spencer Robbins account*: personal communication, January 23, 1992 (continued on page 12, paragraph 1).

Page 12, paragraph 2. *Glenn de Gruy quotations*: personal communications, January 21, 1992, February 4, 1992.

Page 12, paragraph 3. *Duke said he was a corporal*: Zatarain, *David Duke*, p. 93. *But school records show*: Col. William Maginnis, superintendent of Riverside Military Academy, personal communication, February 12, 1992.

Page 12, paragraph 4. *Florence Parker quotations*: interview with author, New Orleans, May 27, 1989.

Page 12, paragraph 5. *Phyllis Wilenzick quotation*: interview with author, New Orleans, June 4, 1989.

Page 13, paragraph 1. *Dorothy Singelmann quotation*: interview with author, August 4, 1992.

Page 13, paragraphs 2–3. *Confidential source*: interview with author, New Orleans, September 20, 1991.

Page 13, paragraph 4. *Chris Champagne quotation*: personal communication, March 20, 1990.

Page 13, paragraph 5. *Vidal Easton quotation*: personal communication, May 27, 1989.

Page 14, paragraphs 2–6. *Jim Beckham quotations*: personal communication, November 24, 1991.

Page 14, paragraph 7. *James Hardy, Jr., quotation*: personal communication, June 7, 1989.

Page 15, paragraph 1. *Duke recalls first Free Speech Alley appearance*: interview with Evelyn Rich, March 20, 1985, p. 9.

Page 15, paragraphs 2–10. *Duke at Free Speech Alley*: Bob Anderson and Roger Tanner, "Jews, Blacks Lambasted at Heated Alley," *Daily Reveille*, November 13, 1969, p. 1.

Page 15, paragraph 11. *He spoke again*: Roger Tanner, "Alley Attacks All, with Vigor," *Daily Reveille*, November 20, 1969, p. 6.

Page 16, paragraph 1. *He said that page 29*: Roger Tanner, "Women's Rules Hit Again at Alley," *Daily Reveille*, December 11, 1969, p. 3.

Page 16, paragraphs 2–4. *Tempers flared the following week*: Roger Tanner, "Tempers, Papers on Fire at Highly Emotional Alley," *Daily Reveille*, December 18, 1969, p. 5.

Page 16, paragraph 6. *He was booed off the soapbox*: Cordelia Condon, "Alley Moves Location, Analyzes Union Rules," *Daily Reveille*, October 15, 1970, p. 1.

Page 16, paragraph 7. *He got into a heated discussion*: Cordelia Condon, "Two Alley Participants Assault Speaker," *Daily Reveille*, December 10, 1970, p. 8 (continued on page 17, paragraph 1).

Page 17, paragraph 1. *Duke's account of the fight*: "WYA Leader Attacked," *Racialist*, February 1, 1971, p. 1.

Page 17, paragraphs 3–4. *Col. Joseph Dale quotation*: personal communication, May 3, 1989.

Page 17, paragraph 5. *The most Duke would concede*: Duke interview with Abby Kaplan, Metairie, La., November 29, 1989, interview published in media resource packet prepared by Louisiana Coalition Against Racism and Nazism, New Orleans, 1990 (continued on page 18, paragraph 1).

Page 18, paragraph 2. *Duke replied*: interview with WSMB Radio, New Orleans, January 5, 1990.

Page 18, paragraphs 3–4. *Duke describes National Socialist beliefs*: David Duke, "Duke on Nazism—His Superior System," *Daily Reveille*, November 19, 1969, p. 2.

Page 18, paragraph 5. *Nazi newsletter applauded Duke*: "LSU Activist Stirs Campus," *White Power*, January-February 1970, p. 8. *The newsletter wrote approvingly*: "Jew Lawyer Picketed in New Orleans," *NS Bulletin*, August 1, 1970.

Page 19, paragraph 1. *Duke passed it off*: Kirk Loggins and Susan Thomas, "David Duke: Klan Media Wizard," *Tennessean*, February 1980, pp. 17–21 (reprint of series).

Page 19, paragraph 4. *Duke appearance at Nazi rally*: "Mall Rally a Smashing Success," *NS Bulletin*, September 1, 1970, p. 3.

Page 20, paragraph 2. *Duke advises against being labeled a Nazi*: interview with Evelyn Rich, Culver City, Ca., February 17, 1986, p. 11, Evelyn Rich Tapes, Political Ephemera Collection, Howard-Tilton Memorial Library, Tulane University, New Orleans.

Page 20, paragraph 3. *Duke announces travel plans: Racialist*, vol. 2, no. 4 [May 1971], p. 4.

CHAPTER 2. *The Racialist Ideal*

Page 21, paragraph 3. *He gave the first full definition*: David Duke, "The White Power Program," *Racialist*, September 1970, p. 1 (continued on page 22, paragraph 1).

Page 22, paragraphs 2–3. *Duke on* The Dispossessed Majority: interview with Evelyn Rich, March 18, 1985, p. 51.

Page 22, paragraph 4. *Duke explained*: Harry Crews, "The Buttondown Terror of David Duke," *Playboy*, February 1980, p. 102.

Page 23, paragraph 1. *On Marano Jews*: "Jew Slave Dealers Brought Slaves to America," *Crusader*, July 1976, p. 1.

Page 23, paragraph 2. *Race mixing meant*: Duke appearance on "Tomorrow" show, NBC, New York, January 7, 1974, transcript.

Page 23, paragraph 3. *Duke wrote*: David Duke, "Why I Oppose Race-Mixing," *NAAWP News*, no. 42 [1986], p. 11. *Jews assiduously kept themselves pure*: Michael Bane, "David Duke: Is the White Race Doomed?" *Hustler*, September 1982, pp. 132, 134.

Page 23, paragraph 4. *Duke favored*: "Jew Gas Shortage to Cause a Depression," *Crusader*, no. 2, Winter 1974, pp. 5–8.

Page 24, paragraphs 1–2. *Duke explains why Jews came to control whites*: interview with Evelyn Rich, March 18, 1985, p. 42.

Page 24, paragraph 2. *Blacks would be relegated*: David Snyder, "The 'Nazi' of LSU . . . Head of the Klan," *States-Item*, May 26, 1975, p. A4.

Page 24, paragraph 3. *Duke quotations*: "David Duke and Talk Shows," *Crusader*, no. 28 [1977], p. 4 (continued on page 24, paragraph 4).

Page 24, paragraph 4. *He added*: interview with Burwell Ware, Xavier University, p. 7.

Page 24, paragraph 5. *Duke on wanting a clean society*: interview with Evelyn Rich, March 18, 1985, p. 47.

Page 25, paragraph 1. *Duke quotation*: Interview with Evelyn Rich, March 18, 1985, p. 41.

Page 25, paragraph 2. *Duke thought blacks and whites*: interview with Evelyn Rich, March 18, 1985, pp. 7–8; interview with Burwell Ware, March 15, 1984, p. 7.

Page 25, paragraph 3. *Duke on the Bible*: David Duke, Response to "Letter of the Month," *NAAWP News*, no. 41 [1986], p. 3; interview with Evelyn Rich, March 18, 1985, pp. 8–9.

Page 25, paragraph 4. *Duke said government policy*: interview with Evelyn Rich, March 18, 1985, pp. 7–8; interview with Burwell Ware, Xavier University, pp. 15–18.

Page 25, paragraph 6. *Duke thinks Statue of Liberty inscription should be rewritten*: Bane, "David Duke: Is the White Race Doomed?" p. 36 (continued on page 26, paragraph 1).

Page 26, paragraph 2. *Duke was a true believer*: interview with Evelyn Rich, March 18, 1985, p. 14.

Page 26, paragraph 4. *Duke on Laos*: Campaign appearance during 1989 legislative campaign, on *David Duke Beats the Odds*, videotape produced by Craig DeMott, Metairie, La., February 1989.

Page 27, paragraphs 3–4. *Charles Green remembers Duke*: personal communications, December 3, 1989, July 29, 1990. *Quotation of the teacher*: anonymous teacher, personal communication, December 6, 1989.

Page 27, paragraph 5. *He told an interviewer*: Zatarain, *David Duke*, p. 161.

Page 27, paragraph 6. *Leon LaShomb quotation*: personal communication, July 30, 1990 (continued on page 28, paragraph 1). *Gene Landry quotation*: personal communication, July 30, 1990; other Air America officials also challenged Duke's claims, including helicopter pilot French Smith (personal communication, July 31, 1990) and Tom Krohn, operations manager at Watty Airfield (personal communication, July 31, 1990).

Page 28, paragraph 3. *Duke was classified*: Selective Service System, classification records, 1950 (year of birth), Selective Service numbers from 151 to 180, sheet no. 6, Washington, D.C. (continued on page 28, paragraphs 4–5).

Page 28, paragraph 4. *When it was revealed*: Tyler Bridges, "Veterans Blast Duke's War-Record Claims," *Times-Picayune*, September 6, 1990, p. B4.

Page 29, paragraph 1. *Eileen Wagenhauser statement*: personal communication, June 19, 1989.

Page 29, paragraph 2. *Duke says he met with right-wingers*: Zatarain, *David Duke*, p. 171. *Duke describes his India visit*: David Duke, "India: My Racial Odyssey," *NAAWP News*, no. 15 [1982], p. 3 (continued on page 30, paragraph 1).

Page 30, paragraph 2. *In a letter to WYA members*: David Duke to White Youth Alliance members and supporters, [October 1971], p. 2.

Page 30, paragraph 3. *The newsletter used a format*: *Nationalist*, March 1972; *Nationalist*, April 1972.

Page 31, paragraph 1. *One advertisement read*: *Nationalist*, April 1972, p. 6. *One issue gushed*: "Meetings Held," *Nationalist*, March 1972, p. 13.

Page 31, paragraphs 2–6. *Duke at his crudest*: *Nationalist*, March 1972, p. 16.

Page 31, paragraph 7. *The April 1972 issue*: *Nationalist*, April 1972, pp. 4–17.

Page 31, paragraphs 9–10. *Jackson Square march*: "Hitlerites Scream for 'White Power' at National Party Rally," *Tulane Hullabaloo*, January 28, 1972, p. 10 (continued on page 32, paragraph 1).

Page 32, paragraph 2. *Duke's account of march*: David Duke, "Editorial," *Nationalist*, March 1972, p. 3.

Page 32, paragraph 3. *Duke's first arrest*: "Four Arrested in 'Bombs' Case," *Times-Picayune*, January 19, 1972.

Page 32, paragraph 4. *Duke on James Lindsay*: interview with Evelyn Rich, March 18, 1985, p. 2.

Page 32, paragraph 5. *Duke was arrested again*: "Police Book 4 on Fraud Count," *Times-Picayune*, June 30, 1972.

Page 33, paragraph 1. *How Duke and Chloe met*: Sims, *The Klan*, p. 206.

Page 33, paragraph 2. *Marilyn Memory quotation*: personal communication, November 26, 1989.

Page 33, paragraph 3. *Ray Leahart*: interview with author, Metairie, La., June 22, 1989.

Page 33, paragraph 4. *Dotti Duke Wilkerson quotations*: personal communication, June 13, 1989.

Page 34, paragraph 1. *Dotti Duke Wilkerson quotation*: personal communication, August 4, 1992.

CHAPTER 3. *Knights of the Ku Klux Klan*

Page 35, paragraphs 1–2. *Duke on how he joined the Klan*: interview with Evelyn Rich, March 18, 1985, pp. 1–2; Zatarain, *David Duke*, p. 100.

Page 35, paragraph 3. *James K. Warner quotation*: interview with Evelyn Rich, October 10, 1987, p. 2, Evelyn Rich Tapes, Political Ephemera Collection, Howard-Tilton Memorial Library, Tulane University.

Page 35, paragraph 4. *Jerry Dutton quotations*: Jerry Dutton, *Setting the Record Straight on David Duke* (Metairie, La.: Jerry Dutton, 1977), pp. 1–2 (continued on page 36, paragraph 1).

Page 36, paragraph 2. *Gregory Durel quotations*: interview with author, Metairie, La., May 24, 1989.

Page 36, paragraphs 3–5. *Background on Klan*: Southern Poverty Law Center, comp., *The Ku Klux Klan: A History of Racism and Violence*, ed. Sara Bullard, 4th ed. (Montgomery, Ala.: Southern Poverty Law Center, 1991); *Hate Groups in America: A Record of Bigotry and Violence*, new rev. ed. (New York: Anti-Defamation League, 1988), pp. 75–86; Evelyn Rich, "Ku Klux Klan Ideology, 1954–1988" (Ph.D. diss., Boston University, 1988)(continued on page 37, paragraphs 1–5, and page 38, paragraph 1).

Page 38, paragraph 2. *Duke idolized Nathan Bedford Forrest*: interview with Evelyn Rich, March 18, 1985, p. 1; David Duke, "The Ku Klux Klan: A Short History," *Crusader*, no. 4, Fall 1974, pp. 13–17; David Duke. "Duke Speaks Out!" *Crusader*, nos. 24 & 25, 1977, p. 10.

Page 38, paragraph 4. *First issue of* Crusader: no. 1, Fall 1973, pp. 3–4, 14.

Page 38, paragraph 5. *Quotations:* Crusader, no. 1, Fall 1973, pp. 15–16.

Page 39, paragraphs 1–2. *Quotation:* Crusader, no. 1, Fall 1973, pp. 15–16.

Page 39, paragraph 5. *Background on Shelton and Venable*: Kirk Loggins and Susan Thomas, "'New' Klan's Driving Force Still Fueled by Racism," *Tennessean*, February

1980, pp. 3–7 (reprint of series); Wayne King, "The Klan Has More Crosses to Bear than Burn," *New York Times*, July 30, 1978, p. E5; Rich, "Ku Klux Klan Ideology, 1954–1988" (continued on page 40, paragraph 1).

Page 40, paragraph 2. *Duke ushered in Nazification of the Klan*: Rich, "Ku Klux Klan Ideology, 1954–1988," pp. 179–223. Quoted passages are from a 1975 one-page letter that Duke sent to *Crusader* subscribers.

Page 40, paragraph 3. *A Klansman who attended*: Gregory Durel, interview with author, May 24, 1989.

Page 40, paragraph 4. *Don Black: Hate Groups in America*, pp. 68–69; Don Black, interview with Evelyn Rich, March 24, 1985, pp. 2–5, Evelyn Rich Tapes, Political Ephemera Collection, Howard-Tilton Memorial Library, Tulane University.

Page 41, paragraph 2. *William Grimstad: Hate Groups in America*, pp. 99–100.

Page 41, paragraph 3. *Tom Metzger: Hate Groups in America*, pp. 128–29.

Page 41, paragraphs 4–5. *James K. Warner: Hate Groups in America*, pp. 168–70; Warner, interview with Evelyn Rich, October 10, 1987, pp. 1–2.

Page 41, paragraph 6. *Background on Identity: Extremism on the Right*, pp. 21–22; Rich, "Ku Klux Klan Ideology, 1954–1988," pp. 209–11; Kirk Loggins and Susan Thomas, "'There Is No Genesis for the Colored or Mongrelized Races,'" *Tennessean*, February 1980, pp. 14–15 (reprint of series)(continued on page 42, paragraphs 1–2).

Page 42, paragraph 5. *Duke believed Christianity was created by Jews*: Karl Hand, "Why Not David Duke?" [1980], Political Ephemera Collection, Howard-Tilton Memorial Library, Tulane University; Gregory Durel, interview with author, Metairie, La., July 18, 1991; Gwen Udell, interview with author, New Orleans, December 10, 1989.

Page 43, paragraph 1. *Letter to his followers*: David Duke, letter accompanying *NAAWP News*, no. 41 [August 1986]. *Duke on Nature*: "Nature Versus Nurture," *NAAWP News*, no. 12 [December 1981], p. 1; interviews with Gwen Udell, July 29, 1990, October 4, 1991.

Page 43, paragraph 2. *New Christian Crusade Church advertisement: Crusader*, no. 1, Fall 1973, p. 19.

Page 43, paragraph 3. *William Pierce quotation*: personal communication, November 5, 1991.

Page 43, paragraph 4. *Description of* The Turner Diaries: *Extremism on the Right*, pp. 144–45.

Page 44, paragraph 2. Turner Diaries *book review*: Nick Camerota, *Crusader*, no. 36 [1978], p. 5. *William Pierce quotation*: personal communication, November 5, 1991.

Page 44, paragraph 3. *Description of Willis Carto: Extremism on the Right*, p. 74.

Page 44, paragraph 4. *David Duke quotation*: Knight News Service, "KKK Breeding New Hate," *San Antonio Light*, June 27, 1976, p. 1 (continued on page 45, paragraph 1).

Page 45, paragraph 2. *Reporter describes Duke's appearance*: Philip Lentz, "David Duke: New Klansman," *Crusader*, no. 37 [February 1979], p. 4 (reprinted from the *Bulletin*).

Page 45, paragraph 3. *Duke says media can't resist him*: "The Klan Tries A New Image," *New South Magazine*, July 1978, p. 54.

Page 45, paragraph 4. *Duke said he was scared*: interview with Evelyn Rich, March 20, 1985, p. 8.

Page 46, paragraphs 1–5. *Source for Tom Snyder and Duke quotations*: audiotape of Duke appearance on "Tomorrow" show, NBC, New York, January 7, 1974.

Page 47, paragraph 1. *A position he soon dropped*: Sims, *The Klan*, p. 183. *Other quotations*: audiotape of "Tomorrow" show, January 7, 1974.

Page 48, paragraph 3. *Account of Boston trip*: Gregory Durel, interview with author, May 24, 1989.

Page 48, paragraphs 3–4. *David Duke quotation*: Associated Press, "Klan Plans Boston Trip 'To Organize,'" *Times-Picayune*, September 18, 1974, p. 2.

Page 48, paragraph 5. *Duke told the cheering crowd*: "Busing into Southie," *Ramparts*, reprinted in *ACTION* (the bimonthly "action report" of the Knights of the Ku Klux Klan), December 15, 1974, p. 3.

Page 49, paragraphs 1–2. *Duke shouted at Durel*: Gregory Durel, interview with author, May 24, 1989.

Page 49, paragraphs 4–5. *Account of Louisiana Taxpayers Association meeting*: Jim Amoss, "No Sheets, Crosses—La. Klan Just Talks," *States-Item*, August 24, 1974, p. A1 (continued on page 50, paragraphs 1–2).

Page 50, paragraph 4. *Duke announced he would send*: Joe Lucia, "'No Violence Tolerated,'" *Times-Picayune*, October 9, 1974, p. 1.

Page 50, paragraph 5. *Reporters and television cameras*: J. Douglas Murphy, "Destrehan Having Business as Usual," *Times-Picayune*, October 10, 1974, p. 1.

Page 50, paragraph 6. *Police officers were disgusted*: Murphy, "Destrehan Having Business as Usual," p. 1.

Page 51, paragraph 2. *Fred O'Sullivan quotation*: personal communication, May 12, 1989.

Page 51, paragraph 3. *Said another former New Orleans policeman*: anonymous former policeman, interview with author, New Orleans, May 11, 1989.

Page 51, paragraph 5. *Duke account of North Carolina speech: ACTION*, no. 12 (January 30, 1975), p. 3 (continued on page 52, paragraphs 1–2).

Page 52, paragraph 3. *"Good Old-Fashioned Humor"*: *Crusader*, no. 8 [December 1975], p. 2.

Page 52, paragraphs 4–6. *Another joke went: Crusader*, no. 9 [January-February 1976], p. 11.

Page 52, paragraph 8. *Bill Wilkinson quotations*: Kirk Loggins and Susan Thomas, "'Get Ready for the Race War,'" *Tennessean*, February 1980, pp. 10–12 (reprint of series).

Page 52, paragraph 9. *Account of Walker rally*: J. Douglas Murphy, "'White Power' Cry at Rally of Klansmen," *Times-Picayune*, April 6, 1975, p. 4 (continued on page 53, paragraphs 1–5).

Page 53, paragraph 7. *Duke on Robert Miles trial*: "Trial Reveals Klansmen Framed," *Crusader*, no. 2, Winter 1974, p. 9 (continued on page 54, paragraph 1).

Page 53, paragraph 8. *Calling de la Beckwith*: "Beckwith: a Patriot," *Crusader*, no. 2, Winter 1974, p. 25.

Page 54, paragraph 2. *Duke on Kathy Ainsworth's death*: "ADL and FBI Set Up Mississippi Murder," *Crusader*, no. 2, Winter 1974, p. 26.

Page 54, paragraph 4. *Duke also leaped to the defense*: "Free the Greensboro 14!" *Crusader*, no. 45 [December 1979], p. 1.

Page 54, paragraph 5. *Two of Duke's Klansmen were arrested*: "Man Sought in Slay Try at Klan Event," *Times-Picayune*, November 27, 1978; Tom Metzger, personal communication, February 7, 1990.

Page 54, paragraph 6. NAAWP News *defends Gerhardts*: Jim McArthur, "Freedom for the Gerhardts!," *NAAWP News*, no. 19 [1982], p. 11.

Page 55, paragraph 1. *Duke quotation*: Kirk Loggins and Susan Thomas, "David Duke: Klan Media Wizard," *Tennessean*, February 1980, p. 18 (reprint of series).

Page 55, paragraphs 2–3. *Account of trial*: Lanny Thomas, "Love Tryst Before Murder—Widow," *States-Item*, March 31, 1976, p. A1; Lanny Thomas, "Still Loved Him, Widow Says," *States-Item*, April 1, 1976, p. A1; Lanny Thomas, "Lindsay Widow Found Innocent," *States-Item*, April 2, 1976, p. A1.

Page 55, paragraph 4. *Duke quotation*: interview with Evelyn Rich, March 18, 1985, p. 2.

Page 55, paragraph 6. *Duke listed himself*: incorporation papers for the Knights of the Ku Klux Klan filed with Louisiana Secretary of State, Baton Rouge, La., August 8, 1975.

Page 56, paragraph 1. *Tom Metzger quotation*: personal communication, April 19, 1989.

Page 56, paragraphs 4–5. *In a letter to voters*: Duke to voters of Louisiana Senate District 16, October 1975.

Page 57, paragraph 2. *Duke declared victory anyway*: Zatarain, *David Duke*, p. 218. *Advertisement: Baton Rouge Morning Advocate*, October 29, 1975, p. 12A.

Page 57, paragraph 4. *Wilkinson later said he broke with Duke*: Loggins and Thomas, "'Get Ready for the Race War,'" pp. 10–12. *Duke regularly sniped*: King, "The Klan Has More Crosses to Bear Than Burn," p. E5.

Page 57, paragraph 5. *Bill Wilkinson quotations*: Loggins and Thomas, "'Get Ready for the Race War,'" pp. 10–12 ("Get Ready"); Rich, "Ku Klux Klan Ideology, 1954–1988," p. 172 ("These guns").

Page 58, paragraph 3. *Duke quotation*: Associated Press, "La. KKK Involved as Boston Antibus Protest Halts Traffic," *Times-Picayune*, December 13, 1975, p. 14.

Page 58, paragraph 5. *Account of riot*: Jefferson Parish Sheriff's Office case report; trial testimony, Twenty-fourth Judicial District Court, Jefferson Parish, May 23, 1977, and May 27, 1977.

Page 59, paragraph 2. *Warner announced: Louisiana v. Duke and Warner*, Twenty-fourth Judicial District Court, Parish of Jefferson, Criminal Docket No. 76–2233, Division J, testimony of Maureen Lindstrom, p. 36, May 23, 1977. *Duke began shouting*: Jefferson Parish Sheriff's Office, case report, Intelligence Division, p. 7.

Page 59, paragraph 3. *Duke was not deterred*: Sheriff's Office, case report, p. 7. *Duke shouted*: ibid.

Page 59, paragraph 4. *Beam shouted*: Sheriff's Office, case report, p. 8.

Page 59, paragraph 5. *The crowd cheered again*: Sheriff's Office, case report, p. 8.

Page 59, paragraph 6. *One man yelled to Duke*: Sheriff's Office, case report, p. 8.

Page 59, paragraph 7. *Another man yelled*: Sheriff's Office, case report, p. 8.

Page 59, paragraph 8. *A third man shouted*: Sheriff's Office, case report, p. 8.

Page 59, paragraph 10. *They yelled*: Sheriff's Office, case report, p. 9.

Page 60, paragraph 1. *The Klansmen chanted*: Pete Cicero, interview with author, Avondale, La., May 1, 1989.

Page 60, paragraph 2. *Duke shouted*: Sheriff's Office, case report, p. 10.

Page 60, paragraph 4. *Warner joined in*: Sheriff's Office, case report, p. 10.

Page 60, paragraph 5. *The detective immediately*: Sheriff's Office, case report, p. 11.

Page 60, paragraph 6. *"Fearful that"*: Sheriff's Office, case report, p. 10.

Page 60, paragraph 8. *The Klansmen stepped back*: Sheriff's Office, case report, p. 12. *A police loudspeaker warned*: Pete Cicero, interview with author, May 1, 1989.

Page 61, paragraphs 2–10. *Account of St. Bernard rally*: Sims, *The Klan*, pp. 197–200.

Page 63, paragraph 3. *Wimberly quotation*: "La. Is Trying to Jail Me, Klan Leader Claims," *States-Item*, June 5, 1979.

Page 63, paragraph 4. *Duke letter*: "Emergency Appeal," May 24, 1979, Political Ephemera Collection, Howard-Tilton Memorial Library, Tulane University. *A distressed Duke dashed off*: "Personal: From David Duke" to Members of the Knights of the Ku Klux Klan, Metairie, La., August 16, 1979, Political Ephemera Collection, Howard-Tilton Memorial Library, Tulane University.

Page 65, paragraph 1. *Wicker statement*: "Suspended Sentence Handed KKK Leader," *States-Item*, November 29, 1979.

CHAPTER 4. *Propaganda for the Cause*

Page 66, paragraphs 2–3. *Duke quotations*: Bane, "David Duke: Is the White Race Doomed?" pp. 36–37 (continued on page 67, paragraphs 1–2).

Page 67, paragraph 2. *Duke laid out his plan*: United Press International, "Klan Leader Egged During Tour," October 16, 1977, reprinted in *Crusader*, no. 27 [1977], p. 2.

Page 68, paragraph 1. *Border patrol official contradicts Duke*: Frank del Olmo, "'Border Watch' by Klan Called a Media Event," *Los Angeles Times*, October 27, 1977, p. 3.

Page 68, paragraph 2. *Del Olmo contradicts Duke*: Frank del Olmo, "Taking on GOP's Unwanted Wizard," *Los Angeles Times*, February 28, 1989, p. 7, pt. 2.

Page 68, paragraph 3. *Another reporter who was disgusted*: Lou Cannon, "The 'Border Patrol' That Wasn't," *Washington Post*, November 8, 1977, p. A19.

Page 68, paragraph 4. *Wilkinson had so little shame*: interview with Evelyn Rich, March 18, 1985, pp. 3–4.

Page 69, paragraph 2. *Duke gleefully attributed*: "Duke Speaks Out! The Ku Klux Klan in Britain," *Crusader*, no. 30 [1978], p. 12.

Page 69, paragraph 3. *Margaret Thatcher quotations*: Walter Isaacson, "No 'Finest Hour' for Britain," *States-Item*, March 21, 1978.

Page 69, paragraph 4. *Duke crowed*: George Fallows and Kevin O'Lone, "Klan Chief Sneaks In," *Daily Mirror*, March 3, 1978, p. 1.

Page 70, paragraph 1. *Merlyn Rees quotation*: Associated Press, "KKK Port Watch Is Urged," *Times-Picayune*, March 7, 1978, sec. 2, p. 4. *John Lee quotation*: Associated Press, "KKK 'Dens' in Britain," *Times-Picayune*, March 5, 1978. Daily Express *headline*: Anthony Collings, "Britain: Klansman at Large," *Newsweek*, March 20, 1978, p. 45.

Page 70, paragraph 2. *One left-wing activist complained*: Associated Press, "Klansman Duke Dodges Bobbies," *States-Item*, March 13, 1978.

Page 70, paragraphs 3–5. *Account of Duke's capture*: Robert McGowan, "GOT YOU!," *Daily Express*, March 14, 1978, p. 1.

Page 71, paragraph 2. *To celebrate his trip*: "Klan Leader Blitzes Britain," *Crusader*, no. 30 [1978], p. 10.

Page 71, paragraph 3. *Wilkinson and Duke quotations*: Bill Crider, Associated Press, "Britain 'Klan Country,' Feuding Wizards Agree," *Times-Picayune*, April 16, 1978, sec. 1, p. 30.

Page 72, paragraph 2. *Evelyn Rich wrote*: Evelyn Rich, "Ku Klux Klan Ideology, 1954–1988," p. 199.

Page 72, paragraphs 5–6. *Duke and his followers*: "Klan Greets Pres. in New Orleans," *Crusader*, October 1976, pp. 6–7.

Page 72, paragraph 7. *As part of Duke's broader goals*: "Kolwezi: Portrait of Terror," *Crusader*, no. 31 [1978], p. 1.

Page 73, paragraph 2. *Duke quotations*: Mark Bonokowski, "Ku Klux Kanada," *Macleans*, April 4, 1977, pp. 70–71.

Page 73, paragraph 3. *Alexander McQuirter quotations*: Julian Sher, *White Hoods: Canada's Ku Klux Klan* (Vancouver: New Star Books, 1983), pp. 91–92.

Page 73, paragraph 4. *Duke quotation*: Sher, *White Hoods: Canada's Ku Klux Klan*, p. 92.

Page 74, paragraph 3. *Klan membership*: *Hate Groups in America*, p. 3.

Page 74, paragraph 4. *Duke responsible for Klan resurgence*: Benjamin Bradlee, Jr., "David Duke Revitalizes Klan," *Los Angeles Herald-Examiner*, reprinted in *Crusader*, no. 29 [1978], p. 10.

Page 75, paragraph 1. *Wilkinson claimed that*: Kirk Loggins and Susan Thomas, "Money—Best-Kept Secret," *Tennessean*, February 1980, pp. 32–35 (reprint of series)(statement on p. 33).

Page 75, paragraph 2. *Jerry Dutton pamphlet*: *The Truth About David Duke* (Metairie, La.: The Truth Forum, 1978), p. 1.

Page 75, paragraph 3. *Karl Hand resignation letter*: Hand to David Duke, December 9, 1979, p. 1, Political Ephemera Collection, Howard-Tilton Memorial Library, Tulane University.

Page 75, paragraph 5. *Glowing account of rally*: "New Jersey Klansman Defies Reds," *Crusader*, no. 43 [September 1978], p. 11 (continued on page 76, paragraph 1).

Page 76, paragraph 2. *Hand also accused*: Hand to Duke, December 9, 1979. *Duke was making himself*: ibid. *Hand hated this sort of gimmick*: ibid.

Page 76, paragraph 4. *Tom Metzger quotations*: personal communication, February 7, 1990.

Page 76, paragraph 5. *Description of* African Atto *and quotations from the book*: Dutton, *The Truth About David Duke*; Ronni Patriquin, "Duke Poses as Black to Pen Book," *Shreveport Journal*, August 14, 1990 (continued on page 77, paragraph 1).

Page 77, paragraph 2. *It was Jerry Dutton*: Dutton, *Setting the Record Straight on David Duke*, p. 11.

Page 77, paragraph 3. *Duke quotations*: Wayne King, "Leader Says Klan, Not Black, Wrote 'Attack' Book," *New York Times*, February 20, 1978, p. 12.

Page 77, paragraph 4. *Quotations from* Finders-Keepers: "Dorothy Vanderbilt" and "James Konrad," *Finders-Keepers* (Arlington: Arlington Place Books, 1976). *"How to find, attract and keep the man you want"*: advertisement for book published in *Photo Screen*, September 1976. *"Sex has come"*: *Finders-Keepers*, p. 107. *"For women over forty"*: ibid., p. 108. *"Romantic, sexually aggressive man"*: p. 110.

Page 78, paragraph 1. *"When you are"*: *Finders-Keepers*, p. 110.

Page 78, paragraph 2. *"You have got to"*: ibid., p. 112. *"There is no quicker way"*: ibid., p. 113. *"Don't ever mention"*: ibid., p. 114.

Page 78, paragraph 3. *"They will certainly add"*: ibid., p. 114. *"Sooner or later"*: ibid., p. 118. *"Do sleep with a married man"*: ibid., p. 124.

Page 78, paragraph 4. *Dutton said that Duke*: personal communication, June 16, 1989.

Page 78, paragraph 5. *"Which best describes"*: ibid., p. 177.

Page 79, paragraph 2. *Duke describes his role in writing* Finders-Keepers: John Elvin, "Author, Author!," *Washington Times*, August 27, 1990, p. A5. *Dutton said Duke was the sole author*: personal communication, November 8, 1989.

Page 79, paragraph 4. *Dutton quotation*: personal communication, November 8, 1989. *Karl Hand letter*: Hand to David Duke, December 9, 1979, p. 3.

Page 79, paragraph 5. *In a later letter*: Karl Hand, "Why Not David Duke?" [1980], p. 3 (open letter, presumably sent to Klan members).

Page 80, paragraph 1. *Duke's womanizing*: Andrea Rider, "Conduct Unbecoming of a Racist," *Spy*, September 1991, p. 38.

Page 80, paragraph 2. *Hand wrote*: Karl Hand, "Why Not David Duke?" p. 3

Page 80, paragraphs 5-7. *David Duke: A Program of Courage* (Metairie, La.: Duke Campaign, 1979), p. 3 (continued on page 81, paragraphs 1-3).

Page 81, paragraph 5. *He denied any involvement*: David Duke to Klan members, "Zionist Claims Home Firebombed!" [October 1979].

Page 81, paragraph 9. *Duke made the outlandish claim*: David Duke to Klan members, [November 1979] (continued on page 82, paragraph 1).

Page 82, paragraph 2. *Karl Hand letter*: Hand to David Duke, December 9, 1979, p. 4. *Tom Metzger letter*: Metzger to David Duke, December 4, 1979, p. 1, Political Ephemera Collection, Howard-Tilton Memorial Library, Tulane University.

Page 82, paragraphs 3–5. *He had announced*: "Duke for President," *Crusader*, no. 37 [February 1979], p. 1.

Page 83, paragraph 1. *Duke had canceled plans*: "Announcement," *Crusader*, no. 48 [March 1980], p. 11.

CHAPTER 5. *A Prophet without an Audience*

Page 84, paragraph 1. *As James Warner said*: interview with Evelyn Rich, October 10, 1987, p. 2.

Page 84, paragraph 2. *Willard Oliver quotation*: Susan Thomas, "Factions Switch in KKK," *Tennessean*, March 28, 1980, p. 1. *Karl Hand quotation*: personal communication, October 9, 1991.

Page 85, paragraph 1. *The ADL said*: quoted in Evelyn Rich, "Ku Klux Klan Ideology, 1954–1988," pp. 257–58.

Page 85, paragraph 4. *Wilkinson's account of deal with Duke*: "Duke Attempts to 'Sell' Klan," *Klansman*, no. 55, July 1980, p. 1 (continued on page 86, paragraph 1).

Page 86, paragraphs 2–3. *Dunnavant and Lowhorne accounts of Duke-Wilkinson meeting*: personal communications, October 8, 1991.

Page 86, paragraph 4. *The conditions called for*: Bob Dunnavant and Susan Thomas, "Wilkinson Won't Buy Rival Klan Unit," *Tennessean*, July 22, 1980, p. 1.

Page 87, paragraph 2. *Wilkinson quotation*: Dunnavant and Thomas, "Wilkinson Won't Buy Rival Klan Unit," p. 1.

Page 87, paragraph 3. *Wilkinson gloated*: Susan Thomas and Bob Dunnavant, "Duke Quitting Klan Following 'Sale' Failure," *Tennessean*, July 27, 1980, p. 1.

Page 87, paragraph 4. *Duke quotations*: Thomas and Dunnavant, "Duke Quitting Klan Following 'Sale' Failure," p. 1.

Page 87, paragraph 6. *Duke resignation letter*: Duke to Knights of the Ku Klux Klan, [July 1980](continued on page 88, paragraphs 1–2).

Page 88, paragraph 3. *Five years later*: interview with Evelyn Rich, March 20, 1985, p. 5.

Page 88, paragraph 4. *Wilkinson revealed to be informant*: Jerry Thompson, Robert Sherborne, and Susan Thomas, "Klan's Wilkinson Secretly Fed Information to FBI," *Tennessean*, August 30, 1981, p. 1.

Page 89, paragraph 2. *He at first denied his identity*: personal communication, August 20, 1989.

Page 90, paragraph 5. *Duke bragged that Admiral McMillian was on the board*: Duke appearance on "David Brudnoy Show," WBZ Radio, Boston, December 2, 1987, Evelyn Rich Tapes, Political Ephemera Collection, Howard-Tilton Memorial Library,

Tulane University; McMillian died on April 22, 1987, according to *Register of Alumni*, U.S. Naval Academy Alumni Association, Inc., 1845–1990.

Page 91, paragraph 1. *Duke quotations*: interview with Evelyn Rich, March 20, 1985, p. 7.

Page 91, paragraph 2. *Duke wrote*: "Equal Rights for Whites? An Open Letter to the Open-minded," *NAAWP News*, no. 1 [1980], p. 1. Two different "intro-edition" issues of the *NAAWP News* were published as the first edition.

Page 91, paragraph 3. *NAAWP vs. NAACP*: "NAAWP vs. NAACP," *NAAWP News*, no. 1 [1980], p. 5. The quoted text was published in subsequent issues as well.

Page 91, paragraph 4. *NAAWP vs. NAACP*: "NAAWP vs. NAACP," *NAAWP News*, no. 1 [1980], p. 5. The quoted text was published in subsequent issues as well.

Page 92, paragraph 1. *NAAWP vs. NAACP*: "NAAWP vs. NAACP," *NAAWP News*, no. 1 [1980], p. 5. The quoted text was published in subsequent issues as well.

Page 92, paragraph 3. *Reports of doom and gloom*: "Blacks Riot in Philadelphia," *NAAWP News*, no. 4 [1980], p. 2. In the same issue: "Supreme Court Decision" (p. 5); "The White Race" (p. 1); "Black & White Gays Together" (p. 2); "One Million Illegal Aliens" (p. 11). *Article on professional boxing*: "Professional Boxing: How Blacks Ruined a Once-Great Sport," *NAAWP News*, no. 10 [1981], p. 12.

Page 92, paragraph 4. *Duke letter*: *NAAWP News*, no. 27 [1983], p. 2. *Duke was still railing*: Duke speech in Plaquemine, La., author's notes, May 9, 1990.

Page 92, paragraph 5. *Bakke profiled*: "Affirmative Action: Massive Racial Discrimination Against Whites," *NAAWP News*, no. 1 [1980], p. 1; Bakke was also profiled in subsequent issues.

Page 93, paragraph 2. *Goetz acquittal delights Duke*: "Goetz Set Free—Not Vigilante," *NAAWP News*, no. 47 [1987], p. 12. *On Lindbergh*: "Prophetic Hero," *NAAWP News*, no. 22 [1983], p. 10; Glenn Montecino, "Profile of an American Enigma," *NAAWP News*, no. 57 [1990], p. 14.

Page 93, paragraph 3. *On Kemal Ataturk*: "Salute to Kemal Ataturk," *NAAWP News*, no. 32 [1985], p. 6 (reprinted from *Instauration*).

Page 93, paragraph 4. *Boycott called for*: "Daly Praises Black Hubby," *NAAWP News*, no. 30 [1984], p. 4.

Page 93, paragraph 5. *Map*: "The National Premise," *NAAWP News*, no. 30 [1984] p. 10 (reprinted from *Instauration*)(continued on page 94, paragraphs 1–2).

Page 94, paragraph 3. *Coca-Cola boycott*: "Coca-Cola's Policies Are Anti-White; Join Our Campaign—Don't Drink Coke!," *NAAWP News*, no. 10 [1981], pp. 8–9. *Duke lobbied*: "NAAWP Lobbies in D.C.," *NAAWP News*, no. 22 [1983], p. 1.

Page 95, paragraphs 2–4. *Account of "Crossfire" appearance and visit with William Pierce*: Rich, "Ku Klux Klan Ideology, 1954–1988," pp. 357–59; Evelyn Rich, personal communication, September 26, 1991.

Page 96, paragraph 2. *The* Southern Magazine *article*: Ralph Forbes, personal communication, September 24, 1991. Southern Magazine *profile*: Pat Jordan, "The Duke of Deception," *Southern Magazine*, October 1987, p. 45.

Page 96, paragraphs 3–4. *Account of Howard Beach trip*: Evelyn Rich, personal communication, September 24, 1991.

Page 96, paragraph 5. New York Post *article*: Mike McAlary, "All Dressed Up, Nowhere to Go," *New York Post*, February 25, 1987, p. 7.

Page 97, paragraph 2. *They planned to sail*: William P. Barrett, "Bayou of Pigs: A Rag-Tag Band of Mercenaries Barely Missed the Boat," *Dallas Times-Herald*, May 10, 1981, p. 1.

Page 97, paragraph 3. *Account of French Quarter meeting*: testimony of Michael Perdue, June 16, 1981, *U.S. v. Norris*, U.S. District Court, New Orleans, Docket No. 81–212, pp. 566–68; Gwen Udell, interview with author, New Orleans, October 4, 1991.

Page 97, paragraph 4. *Duke also agreed to help Perdue*: testimony of Michael Perdue, June 16, 1981, *U.S. v. Norris*, pp. 503–08; testimony of Wolfgang Droege, June 16, 1981, *U.S. v. Norris*, pp. 1073–75, 1095–98, 1145–49. *Duke also put Perdue in touch with Kirkpatrick*: "Alleged Coup Backer Found Shot to Death," *Times-Picayune*, June 22, 1981.

Page 98, paragraph 2. *Duke held subsequent meetings*: Gwen Udell, interview with author, October 4, 1991.

Page 98, paragraphs 3–4. *Account of aborted departure*: Mike Howell, personal communication, September 18, 1991; John Osburg, personal communication, September 23, 1991; Barrett, "Bayou of Pigs," p. 1.

Page 98, paragraph 5. *Duke was sitting at home*: Gwen Udell, interview with author, October 4, 1991.

Page 99, paragraph 3. *He kept nervously asking*: Richard Barrett, personal communication, November 26, 1989.

Page 99, paragraph 4. *Duke quotations*: David McCormick, "Klan's Plan to Send Mercenaries to Grenada Blocked," Associated Press, *Vicksburg Evening Post*, October 28, 1983, p. 5. *Lindsay Larson quotations*: McCormick, "Klan's Plan Blocked," p. 5.

Page 100, paragraphs 2-4. *He developed a plan*: "New Video Tape Program Unveiled," letter to *NAAWP News* subscribers; "NAAWP to Channel Efforts into Video Program," *NAAWP News*, no. 30 [December 1984], p. 1; letter to *NAAWP News* subscribers accompanying no. 30.

Page 100, paragraph 4. *Much like the patriotic newspapers spread before the American Revolution of 1776*: one-page letter that accompanied *NAAWP News*, no. 30 [December 1984]. *The final step will be to do*: *NAAWP News*, no. 30 [December 1984], p. 1.

Page 101, paragraph 1. *He concluded*: "New video tape program unveiled," four-page letter mailed to *NAAWP News* subscribers ten days prior to *NAAWP News*, no. 30 [December 1984], p. 1.

Page 102, paragraph 1. *Duke had Wilson take est*: Wilson, personal communication, May 31, 1989.

Page 102, paragraph 2. *Account of seminar*: "Leadership Training Begun," *NAAWP News*, no. 24 [1983], p. 1.

Page 102, paragraph 3. *Duke wrote*: "Training Program Begun—National Leadership Seminar in August," letter to *NAAWP News* subscribers that accompanied *NAAWP News*, no. 24 [1983].

Page 103, paragraph 3. *Udell says*: interview with author, New Orleans, November 5, 1989. *Evelyn Rich recalls*: personal communication, September 26, 1991.

Page 103, paragraph 4. *To avoid the law*: Evelyn Rich, personal communication, August 23, 1990.

Page 103, paragraph 5. *Duke tried to dodge questions*: interview with author, Metairie, La., August 16, 1990 (continued on page 104, paragraph 1).

Page 104, paragraph 1. *Duke told Ted Koppel*: "Who Is the Real David Duke?," Duke appearance on "Nightline," ABC, New York, November 15, 1991.

Page 104, paragraphs 2–4. *Udell account of Duke's plastic surgery*: interviews with author, December 10, 1989, July 29, 1990.

Page 104, paragraph 5. *Duke was reluctant*: interview with author, August 16, 1990. *Duke blew up*: "Duke It Out with David Duke," Duke appearance on "Crossfire," CNN, Atlanta, October 24, 1991.

Page 105, paragraph 1. *Duke lived off the white supremacy movement*: Tyler Bridges, "The Man Who Would Be Governor: A Close Look at David Duke," *Times-Picayune*, November 3, 1991, p. A1.

Page 105, paragraphs 2–3. *Duke paid his bills*: Loggins and Thomas, "Money—The Best-Kept Klan Secret," pp. 32–33.

Page 105, paragraph 3. *Duke chose the name*: interview with author, August 16, 1990. *Duke describes his earnings*: Loggins and Thomas, "Money—Best-Kept Klan Secret," pp. 32–35.

Page 105, paragraph 4. *Dutton said Duke used Klan funds*: handout prepared by Jerry Dutton (which includes copies of checks written by Duke and his wife Chloe). *Duke said he used Klan funds*: Sid Kirchheimer, "Klan Head Admits Siphoning Funds," *Clearwater Sun*, September 2, 1979, p. 1A.

Page 105, paragraph 5. *Bill Wilkinson said Duke failed to turn over*: Loggins and Thomas, "'Get Ready for the Race War,'" *Tennessean*, February 1980, pp. 10–12 (continued on page 106, paragraph 1).

Page 106, paragraph 2. *Jack Gregory denounced Duke*: Kirchheimer, "Klan Head Admits," p. 1A.

Page 106, paragraph 4. *Duke boasted he bought his suit at J C Penney*: John Bowers, "David Duke: White Supremacy—in Black and White," *Gallery*, February 1986 (interview was conducted six months earlier), p. 28.

Page 106, paragraph 5. *Duke at steak house*: Donna Randall, interview with author, New Orleans, November 27, 1992.

Page 107, paragraph 1. *Duke said*: David Duke, letter to editor, *Gambit*, January 9, 1990.

Page 107, paragraph 2. *Duke admitted owning Americana Books*: author's notes, press conference, August 8, 1989.

Page 107, paragraph 3. *Duke claimed he was operating a bookstore*: Larry Cohler,

"Duke's Smooth Entry into Mainstream Politics," *Long Island Jewish World*, August 11–17, 1989, p. 3. *"Suppressed Books"*: *NAAWP News*, no. 44 [1987], pp. 13, 15 (continued on page 107, paragraph 4).

Page 108, paragraph 2. *Payments to BC&E*: NAAWP tax returns from 1983–88, Internal Revenue Service, Atlanta, Ga. *Duke became agitated*: personal communication, August 2, 1989.

Page 108, paragraph 5. *Duke admitted he owned BC&E*: author's notes, press conference, August 8, 1989.

Page 108, paragraph 6. *Article disclosed payments*: Tyler Bridges, "Firm Tied to Duke Paid by His Party," *Times-Picayune*, August 8, 1989, p. A1. *Duke rebutted this point*: author's notes, press conference, August 8, 1989.

Page 109, paragraph 2. *Duke did not file*: Tyler Bridges, "Duke Didn't File Return '84-'87, Records Show," *Times-Picayune*, March 22, 1990, p. B1; Tyler Bridges, "Duke Files Late State Tax Returns," *Times-Picayune*, March 23, 1990, p. B1. *Duke said he had had a bad time financially*: "Who Is the Real David Duke?," Duke appearance on "Nightline," ABC, November 15, 1991.

Page 109, paragraph 3. *Duke kept dodging the question*: "Who Is the Real David Duke?," Duke appearance on "Nightline," November 15, 1991. *He was also heavily playing*: Charles Safford, interview with author, Kenner, La., July 25, 1990.

Page 109, paragraph 4. *He had failed to pay property taxes*: Tyler Bridges, "Duke Owes 3 Years of Tax on Home," *Times-Picayune*, February 2, 1991, p. A1; Tyler Bridges, "Duke Pays Home Taxes, Defends Wait," *Times-Picayune*, February 8, 1991, p. B1 (both sources are continued on page 110, paragraph 1).

CHAPTER 6. *White Supremacy, Hitler, and the Holocaust*

Page 111, paragraph 1. *Udell account of visit*: interview with author, July 29, 1990.

Page 111, paragraph 2. *They shot prisoners*: Maurice Bauman, personal communication, September 26, 1991.

Page 111, paragraph 3. *Udell remembered*: interview with author, July 29, 1990 (continued on page 112, paragraphs 1–2).

Page 112, paragraph 2. *Duke would insist that the Talmud*: interview with Evelyn Rich, March 18, 1985, p. 47.

Page 112, paragraph 4. *The real holocaust was Stalin's extermination*: David Duke, "Holocaust: The Real & the Unreal," *Crusader*, no. 49 [1980], p. 10.

Page 113, paragraph 2. *Mermelstein had spent time*: David Haldane, "Holocaust Survivor Meets Push with Shove—Again," *Los Angeles Times*, November 8, 1988, p. 1, pt. 2.

Page 113, paragraph 3. *Mermelstein sued for libel*: Jason Berry, "David Duke's Role Model?" *Gambit*, September 3, 1991, p. 15.

Page 113, paragraph 4. *Duke insisted that she meet Carto*: Evelyn Rich, personal communication, September 26, 1991.

Page 114, paragraphs 1–5. *Metzger began to grow irritated*: personal communication, February 7, 1990; Evelyn Rich, personal communication, September 26, 1991.

Page 114, paragraph 6. *Duke discussed the Holocaust*: interview with Evelyn Rich, March 18, 1985. It was in this interview that Duke laid out his deepest beliefs in National Socialism.

Page 114, paragraph 7. *"You might say"*: interview with Evelyn Rich, March 18, 1985, p. 27.

Page 114, paragraph 8. *"The same reason"*: interview with Evelyn Rich, March 18, 1985, p. 33. *Duke added*: interview with Evelyn Rich, February 17, 1986 (part of interview with Joe Fields), p. 8.

Page 115, paragraph 1. *"You can't . . . was clear"*: interview with Evelyn Rich, March 18, 1985, p. 26. *"All of the . . . so Jews wouldn't die"*: ibid., p. 27. *"The so-called . . . die yourself"*: ibid., p. 30. *"Doctored photographs and everything"*: ibid., p. 31.

Page 115, paragraph 2. *"The fact . . . take place"*: interview with Evelyn Rich, March 18, 1985, p. 31. *"Did you . . . Boy! Boy!"*: ibid., p. 32.

Page 115, paragraph 3. *"He's an expert . . . funny little guy"*: interview with Evelyn Rich, March 18, 1985, p. 33. *"He goes . . . just bullshit"*: ibid., pp. 33–34.

Page 115, paragraph 4. *"He went . . . about it"*: interview with Evelyn Rich, March 18, 1985, pp. 34–35 (continued on page 116, paragraph 1).

Page 116, paragraph 2. *"You know . . . gone under"*: interview with Evelyn Rich, March 18, 1985, pp. 35–36.

Page 116, paragraph 3. *"That's why . . . into it"*: interview with Evelyn Rich, March 18, 1985, p. 28. *"I don't . . . world's flat"*: ibid., p. 29.

Page 116, paragraph 5. *"In the last . . . forget it"*: interview with Evelyn Rich, March 18, 1985, p. 38.

Page 116, paragraph 6. *"When the government's . . . country economically"*: interview with Evelyn Rich, March 18, 1985, p. 39.

Page 117, paragraph 1. *Quotations*: interview with Evelyn Rich, March 18, 1985, pp. 39, 47 ("He's been . . . really well").

Page 117, paragraph 2. *"In the media . . . not Jews"*: interview with Evelyn Rich, March 18, 1985, p. 43.

Page 117, paragraph 3. *"I want a . . . and girls"*: interview with Evelyn Rich, March 18, 1985, p. 47.

Page 117, paragraph 4. *"I believe in . . . wouldn't take"*: interview with Evelyn Rich, March 18, 1985, p. 41.

Page 117, paragraph 5. *"But as far . . . ever had"*: interview with Evelyn Rich, March 18, 1985, p. 41.

Page 118, paragraphs 2–3. *Hitler was his idol*: Gwen Udell, interview with author, July 29, 1990.

Page 118, paragraph 4. *Duke was fuming*: Gwen Udell, interview with author, November 5, 1989.

Page 118, paragraphs 5–6. *James Hintze had asked why*: Fred Hawley, "That Was Then, This Is Now," *Forum* (Shreveport weekly newspaper), March 1989, p. 5 (continued on page 119, paragraph 1).

Page 119, paragraphs 2–11. *Dearing describes conversation*: Reinhard Dearing, personal communication, September 20, 1991.

Page 119, paragraph 12. *Udell account of wedding*: interview with author, July 29, 1990.

Page 120, paragraph 1. *Duke railed*: Gwen Udell, interview with author, July 29, 1990.

Page 120, paragraph 2. *Hitler birthday parties*: Gwen Udell, interview with author, July 29, 1990. Charles Safford, Duke's stockbroker in the mid-1980s, corroborated her account in an interview with the author, July 25, 1990. *Duke denied they had occurred*: interview with author, August 16, 1990.

Page 120, paragraph 3. *Duke divorce*: Fifteenth Judicial Circuit of Florida, Palm Beach County, January 31, 1984, Case No. 7026.

Page 120, paragraph 4. *Ralph Forbes quotation*: personal communication, September 24, 1991.

Page 121, paragraphs 2–4. *Udell describes her relationship with Duke*: interviews with author, November 5, 1989, December 10, 1989, July 29, 1990.

Page 122, paragraph 1. *National Socialists view the world*: Lance Hill, *The Influence of National Socialist Political Theory in the Contemporary Political Thought of David Duke* (New Orleans: Louisiana Coalition Against Racism and Nazism, 1990), p. 5.

Page 122, paragraph 2. *Duke told Abby Kaplan*: November 29, 1989, interview published in media resource packet prepared by Louisiana Coalition Against Racism and Nazism, New Orleans, 1990.

Page 122, paragraph 3. *Wrote Hill*: Lance Hill, "Nazi Race Doctrine," in *The Emergence of David Duke and the Politics of Race*, ed. Douglas Rose (Chapel Hill: University of North Carolina Press, 1992), pp. 100–02.

Page 122, paragraph 5. *Duke told the anti-Semitic: Instauration*, February 1989, p. 36 (continued on page 123, paragraph 1).

Page 123, paragraph 2. *Duke was restating*: Hill, *The Influence*, p. 9.

Page 123, paragraph 3. *Duke had a ready answer*: Abby Kaplan, interview with David Duke, November 29, 1989. *Duke cited FBI statistics*: Kaplan, interview with David Duke, November 29, 1989; interview with Burwell Ware, March 15, 1984, p. 14.

Page 123, paragraph 4. *These beliefs explain Duke's contention*: David Duke, "Why I Oppose Race-Mixing," *NAAWP News*, no. 42 [1986], p. 10. *He has generally said*: Abby Kaplan, interview with David Duke, November 29, 1989; appearance on "Crossfire," CNN, Atlanta, February 20, 1989; "Issues and Answers," *NAAWP News*, no. 31 [1984], p. 3.

Page 123, paragraph 5. *Government loan program*: "Issues and Answers," *NAAWP News*, no. 31 [1984], p. 3. An excellent analysis of Duke's goal of creating a master race can be found in: Quin Hillyer, "'A Biology of Intelligence': David Duke's Genetic Dreams," *Gambit*, June 19, 1990, pp. 15–16.

Page 124, paragraph 1. *Duke quotation*: Duke, interview with Abby Kaplan, November 29, 1989.

Page 124, paragraph 2. *Hitler had articulated*: Adolf Hitler, *Mein Kampf*, trans. Ralph Manheim (Boston: Houghton Mifflin, 1971), pp. 403–04.

Page 124, paragraph 3. *Low-interest loans*: Duke, interview with Abby Kaplan, November 29, 1989. *Duke favored voluntary sterilization*: interview with Evelyn Rich, March 18, 1985, p. 15 (continued on page 124, paragraph 4).

Page 124, paragraph 5. *Duke praised William Shockley*: "One Imperturbable Donor: A Modern Day Galileo," *NAAWP News*, no. 20 [1982], p. 9 (continued on page 125, paragraph 1). Duke reprinted this piece in subsequent issues.

Page 125, paragraph 1. *Duke mourned Shockley's death*: "William B. Shockley, Among the Great Men of Our Time, Is Dead," *NAAWP News*, no. 57 [1990], p. 7.

Page 125, paragraph 2. *Duke also lionized Robert K. Graham*: "A Simple Beautiful Idea," *NAAWP News*, no. 20 [1982], p. 10. *George Will blasted*: "A Simple Beautiful Idea," p. 10.

Page 125, paragraph 3. *Duke looked to genetics*: interview with Evelyn Rich, March 18, 1985, p. 15. *Duke told* Hustler: Bane, "David Duke: Is the White Race Doomed?," p. 36.

Page 125, paragraph 4. *Whites choose to have abortions*: interview with Evelyn Rich, March 18, 1985, p. 15.

Page 126, paragraph 2. *Duke told Rich*: interview with Evelyn Rich, March 18, 1985, p. 11.

Page 126, paragraphs 3–16. *Three-way exchange*: interview with Evelyn Rich, February 17, 1986, pp. 11–12 (continued on page 127, paragraphs 1–2).

Page 127, paragraph 5. *Williams vowed*: John Brady and Joe Earle, "Violent Protesters Disrupt Forsyth March," *Atlanta Journal-Constitution*, January 18, 1987, p. A1.

Page 127, paragraph 6. *Duke told the crowd*: "Victory in Forsyth County, *NAAWP News*, no. 43 [1987], pp. 1, 5; John Bolt, Associated Press, *Times-Union*, January 25, 1987, p. A1.

Page 128, paragraph 1. *Duke yelled*: Eduardo Paz-Martinez, "Amid Racist Cries, Georgia Marchers Return," *Boston Globe*, January 25, 1987, p. 22. *He protested that he had not violated*: Bill Montgomery, "Anti-March Protestors Fewer than Expected," *Atlanta Journal-Constitution*, January 26, 1987, p. D1.

Page 128, paragraph 3. *Lowery quotation*: Mike Christensen, "20,000 March on Forsyth County," *Atlanta Journal-Constitution*, January 25, 1987, p. A1.

Page 128, paragraph 4. *Article quoted*: "Victory in Forsyth County," *NAAWP News*, no. 43 [1987], p. 1.

Page 129, paragraph 1. *Dispute over Forsyth County money*: Richard Barrett, personal communications, May 2, 1989, August 7, 1989; Jim Harding, personal communications, August 14, 1989, August 15, 1989; Frank Shirley, personal communication, August 16, 1989; Jerry Lord, personal communication, October 28, 1991; David Duke, personal communications, August 2, 1989, August 21, 1989; Forsyth County Defense Fund (Mark Watts) to "Friend" (residents of Forsyth County and members of the NAAWP), [March 1987]; Molly Read, "Defense League Says Suit Is Unfair," *Atlanta*

Business Chronicle, April 12, 1987, p. 1; Tyler Bridges, "Group Says It Didn't Receive Cash Duke Raised on Its Behalf," *Times-Picayune*, November 11, 1991, p. A8.

Page 129, paragraph 2. *Dozens of people sent money*: personal communications with Barrett, Harding, Shirley, Lord; Read, "Defense League Says Suit Is Unfair," p. 1. *Questions about the finances*: personal communication with Barrett.

Page 129, paragraph 3. *Mark Watts*: personal communications with Barrett, Lord; Tyler Bridges, "Group Says It Didn't Receive Cash," p. A8; David Duke, personal communication, August 2, 1989 (continued on page 129, paragraphs 4–9 and page 130, paragraphs 1–4).

Page 130, paragraph 8. *It was like a reunion*: Richard Barrett, personal communication, September 23, 1991. *Duke was running*: Duke speech to supporters at Marriott Hotel, Atlanta, June 8, 1987 (continued on page 131, paragraphs 1–2), Evelyn Rich Tapes, Political Ephemera Collection, Howard-Tilton Memorial Library, Tulane University.

Page 131, paragraph 3. *Duke boldly predicted*: Royal Brightbill, "White Supremacist Candidate for President," United Press International, June 3, 1987. *The Democrats will be tweedly-dee*: Rick Badie, "David Duke Announces Presidential Bid," *Times* (Gainesville, Ga.), reprinted in *NAAWP News*, no. 46 [1987], p. 2.

Page 131, paragraph 4. *While Jackson had the rainbow coalition*: Joe Kirby, "Duke to Seek Presidency; Blasts IRS, Welfare at Rally," *Marietta Daily Journal*, reprinted in *NAAWP News*, no. 46 [1987], p. 2.

Page 131, paragraph 5. *Duke gave himself*: Paul C. Peterson, "Duke Will Run for President," *NAAWP News*, no. 46 [1987], p. 3. *Paul Kirk denounced Duke*: East Jefferson Bureau, "Duke Aims to Shake Up Demos," *Times-Picayune*, June 13, 1987, p. B5. *He showed up the next day*: Paul C. Peterson, "Duke Will Run for President," p. 3.

Page 132, paragraph 2. *Forbes had met Duke*: Ralph Forbes, personal communication, June 15, 1989. *Forbes had been a disciple*: personal communication, June 21, 1989. *Forbes sold viciously anti-Semitic books*: Hate Groups in America, pp. 91–93.

Page 132, paragraph 3. *Forbes was bothered*: personal communication, September 24, 1991.

Page 132, paragraph 4. *Forbes recalls*: personal communication, September 24, 1991.

Page 132, paragraph 5. *Forbes found another trait*: personal communication, October 24, 1991.

Page 132, paragraph 6. *To mount his campaign*: David Duke for President, campaign finance reports (Democratic party candidacy), 1987–88, Federal Election Commission, Washington, D.C. (continued on page 133, paragraph 1).

Page 133, paragraph 2. *McCoy botched the job*: Ralph Forbes, personal communication, June 15, 1989.

Page 133, paragraph 3. *Duke began demanding loudly*: Associated Press, "Kemp, Duke Clash on Racism," *Times-Picayune*, December 5, 1987.

Page 133, paragraph 4. *Duke filed a lawsuit*: Steve Cannizaro, "Duke Loses Suit to Join in Democratic Debate," *Times-Picayune*, November 3, 1987, p. A4.

Page 133, paragraph 5. *After the ruling*: Steve Cannizaro, interview with author, New Orleans, August 16, 1991 (continued on page 134, paragraph 1).

Page 134, paragraphs 2–4. *As they arrived*: Evelyn Rich, personal communication, September 24, 1991.

Page 135, paragraphs 1-4. *The NAAWP News gushed*: "David Duke Defeats Major Candidates," *NAAWP News*, no. 51 [1988], p. 1.

Page 136, paragraphs 2–4. *Background on the Populist party: Hate Groups in America*, pp. 55–57.

Page 136, paragraph 5. *Duke also gave a speech*: Van Loman, personal communications, December 6, 1990, October 1, 1991. *Many party members*: Don Wassall, personal communication, October 2, 1991. *Duke was not enthusiastic*: Van Loman, personal communication, October 1, 1991.

Page 137, paragraph 2. *Duke still could not be found*: Van Loman, personal communication, October 1, 1991; Evelyn Rich, personal communication, September 26, 1991.

Page 137, paragraph 3. *Gritz came away convinced*: personal communication, June 11, 1991.

Page 137, paragraphs 4–6. *Thirty-minute television advertisement*: transcript of tape available from the Populist party, Ford City, Pa. (continued on page 138, paragraphs 1–2).

Page 138, paragraph 3. *He spent election night*: Sarah Laramore, interview with author, New Orleans, October 4, 1990; David Duke, interview with author, Harahan, La., October 5, 1990.

CHAPTER 7. *The Representative from Metairie*

Page 139, paragraph 1. *They stood and applauded*: James O'Byrne, "Duke: Anatomy of an Upset," *Times-Picayune*, March 5, 1989, p. A1; James Gill, interview with author, New Orleans, October 2, 1991; author's visit to bar.

Page 139, paragraph 3. *He visited*: O'Byrne, "Duke: Anatomy of an Upset," p. A1. The outline of the first half of chapter 7, pp. 139–54, comes from this article.

Page 140, paragraph 2. *Donelon told Casey*: Jim Donelon, interview with author, Metairie, La., November 26, 1991.

Page 140, paragraph 3. *A few days later*: O'Byrne, "Duke: Anatomy of an Upset," p. A1; Sam Altobello, personal communication, November 27, 1991. *When Duke appeared*: Jim Donelon, interview with author, November 26, 1991.

Page 141, paragraph 2. *Billy Nungesser clapped him on the back*: O'Byrne, "Duke: Anatomy of an Upset," p. A1. *One woman confided*: O'Byrne, "Duke: Anatomy of an Upset," p. A1.

Page 141, paragraph 5. *Neil Curran remembers seeing*: interview with author, New Orleans, November 27, 1991 (continued on page 142, paragraph 1).

Page 142, paragraph 3. *Duke told Sandy Emerson*: Sandy Emerson, interview with author, Metairie, La., November 27, 1991.

Page 142, paragraphs 4–5. *Duke began the District 81 race*: Debbie Thomas, interview with author, Chalmette, La., December 10, 1992 (continued on page 143, paragraph 1).

Page 143, paragraphs 3–5. *Background on Jefferson Parish and District 81*: Lawrence Powell, "Slouching Toward Baton Rouge: The 1989 Legislative Election of David Duke," in Rose, *The Emergence of David Duke*, pp. 15–22 (quoted passage is on p. 17)(continued on page 144, paragraph 1).

Page 144, paragraph 2. *Donna Randall recalls*: interview with author, New Orleans, March 24, 1992.

Page 144, paragraphs 4–5. *Maraniss wrote*: David Maraniss, "Winning Support with a White-Power Image," *Washington Post*, February 14, 1989, p. A1 (continued on page 145, paragraph 1).

Page 145, paragraph 4. *Charles began to note*: O'Byrne, "Duke: Anatomy of an Upset," p. A1.

Page 146, paragraph 2. *Delton Charles recognized its effect*: O'Byrne, "Duke: Anatomy of an Upset," p. A1.

Page 146, paragraphs 3–8. *Sandy Emerson kept thinking*: Sandy Emerson, interview with author, November 27, 1991.

Page 146, paragraphs 9–11. *Jim Donelon ducked away*: interview with author, November 26, 1991.

Page 147, paragraphs 3–4. *Donelon figured*: interview with author, November 26, 1991.

Page 147, paragraphs 4–9. *Neil Curran recalled*: interview with author, November 27, 1991.

Page 148, paragraph 2. *Treen had managed to offend*: Jim Donelon, interview with author, November 26, 1991. *Harry Lee summed it up*: interview with author, Metairie, La., March 18, 1993; O'Byrne, "Duke: Anatomy of an Upset," p. A1.

Page 148, paragraphs 4–13. *C. B. Forgotston spied a former classmate*: interview with author, New Orleans, November 27, 1991 (continued on page 149, paragraph 1).

Page 149, paragraph 2. *Hannan felt that a Duke victory*: O'Byrne, "Duke: Anatomy of an Upset," p. A1.

Page 149, paragraphs 3-4. *Duke spooked both of them*: Roger Villere, interview with author, Metairie, La., May 17, 1989; Bobby Savoie, interview with author, New Orleans, May 18, 1989 (continued on page 150, paragraph 1).

Page 150, paragraph 3. *Neil Curran beseeched him*: interview with author, November 27, 1991. *John Treen says*: interview with author, Metairie, La., November 27, 1991.

Page 150, paragraph 4. *Levy announced he was coming to New Orleans*: Robert Rhoden and Barri Marsh, "Jewish Group Vows to Disrupt Duke," *Times-Picayune*, January 26, 1989, p. B1.

Page 151, paragraph 1. *The incendiary statement*: Rhoden and Marsh, "Jewish Group Vows to Disrupt Duke," p. B1.

Page 151, paragraph 3. *Television was especially important*: For a good analysis of how Duke manipulated television coverage, see Gary Esolen, "More than a Pretty

Face: David Duke's Use of Television as a Political Tool," in Rose, *The Emergence of David Duke*, pp. 136–55.

Page 151, paragraph 5. *Reagan cut a radio ad*: "An Important Message from Saturday's Election from Ronald Reagan," undated statement signed by Reagan and "Paid for by the John Treen Campaign Committee"; Rebecca Theim and Kim Chatelain, "Bush, Reagan Endorse Treen in Race," *Times-Picayune*, February 16, 1989, p. A1 (continued on page 152, paragraphs 1–3).

Page 152, paragraph 3. *Beck said*: personal communication, December 6, 1991. *Duke quotation*: Theim and Chatelain, "Bush, Reagan Endorse Treen in Race," p. A1.

Page 152, paragraph 4. *"The Unmasking of David Duke"*: pamphlets published in Metairie, La., by the John Treen Campaign Committee, February 1989.

Page 152, paragraphs 5-6. *Curran was excited*: interview with author, November 27, 1991. *Duke supporters warned voters*: John Treen, interview with author, November 27, 1991 (continued on page 153, paragraph 1).

Page 153, paragraph 1. *When Duke announced*: Duke to "Dear Friend" (*NAAWP News* subscribers), letter accompanying *NAAWP News* no. 54 [1988].

Page 153, paragraph 2. *Subsisting on three or four hours*: Debbie Thomas, interview with author, December 10, 1992; Donna Randall, interview with author, November 27, 1992.

Page 153, paragraph 4. *Howie Farrell took him outside*: Donna Randall, interview with author, November 27, 1992. *Duke thought he had won*: O'Byrne, "Duke: Anatomy of an Upset," p. A1.

Page 153, paragraph 6. *Duke ran down the courthouse hallway*: Donna Randall, interview with author, November 27, 1992.

Page 154, paragraphs 1–2. *Duke announced the outcome*: O'Byrne, "Duke: Anatomy of an Upset," p. A1.

Page 154, paragraph 3. *Populist party leaders pressured him*: Van Loman, personal communication, October 1, 1991.

Page 154, paragraph 4. *The crowd stood up*: Jim McPherson, interview with author, New Orleans, January 12, 1993.

Page 155, paragraphs 1–5. *Beth Rickey's account of Populist party convention*: Beth Rickey, "The Nazi and the Republicans: An Insider View of the Response of the Louisiana Republican Party to David Duke," in Rose, *The Emergence of David Duke*, p. 63; some of the material comes from an earlier draft.

Page 155, paragraph 6. *Duke still viewed*: transcript of speech.

Page 156, paragraphs 1–2. *Account of press conference*: Associated Press, "Duke's Chicago Speech Sparks Shoving Match," *Times-Picayune*, March 5, 1989, p. A3; Art Jones, personal communication, June 19, 1989 (quotation of "You creep!").

Page 156, paragraph 3. *Duke told his colleagues*: Jack Wardlaw, "Photograph with Nazi Is a Smear, Duke Says," *Times-Picayune*, March 7, 1989, p. B10.

Page 157, paragraph 1. *When Duke at one rally*: author's notes from Duke speech, April 7, 1989.

Page 157, paragraphs 3–5. *His staff made him watch*: Debbie Thomas, interview with author, December 10, 1992.

Page 157, paragraph 6. *Duke introduced nine bills*: Zack Nauth, "Lawmakers: Duke Flunked Freshman Term," *Times-Picayune*, July 16, 1989, p. B1 (continued on page 158, paragraphs 1–4).

Page 158, paragraphs 5–6. *Anne Levy saw him*: Anne Levy, personal communication, February 3, 1993 (continued on page 159, paragraphs 1–3); Steven Watsky, "Duke in Confrontation with Holocaust Survivor," United Press International, June 6, 1989.

Page 159, paragraphs 3–6. *Rickey held a press conference*: Rickey, "The Nazi and the Republicans," pp. 66–71; interview with author, New Orleans, June 1, 1989; some of the material comes from an earlier draft.

Page 159, paragraph 7. *Duke said that he had*: Tyler Bridges, "Neo-Nazi Books Sold at Duke's Office," *Times-Picayune*, June 8, 1989, p. B4 (continued on page 160, paragraph 1).

Page 160, paragraph 2. *Dastugue quotation*: interview with author, New Orleans, August 4, 1989. *Rickey said later*: Rickey, "The Nazi and the Republicans," p. 79; some of the material comes from an earlier draft.

Page 160, paragraph 3. *Rickey cried*: interview with author, New Orleans, December 9, 1991.

Page 160, paragraph 4. *She could not accept*: Rickey, "The Nazi and the Republicans," pp. 60–61; some of the material comes from an earlier draft.

Page 160, paragraph 5. *Atwater denounced him*: Frances Frank Marcus, "Winner in Louisiana Vote Takes on G.O.P. Chairman," *New York Times*, February 20, 1989, p. A8. *This conservative majority*: Thomas Edsall with Mary D. Edsall, *Chain Reaction: The Impact of Race, Rights, and Taxes on American Politics* (New York: W. W. Norton, 1991), pp. 74–79 (continued on page 161, paragraphs 1–2).

Page 161, paragraph 3. *The Republicans pieced together their conservative majority*: Edsall with Edsall, *Chain Reaction*, pp. 140–53.

Page 161, paragraphs 4–5. *The government was aggressively pursuing programs*: Edsall with Edsall, "Race," *Atlantic Monthly*, May 1991, pp. 69–70.

Page 162, paragraph 1. *Whites in one 1980 poll*: Edsall with Edsall, *Chain Reaction*, p. 153.

Page 162, paragraph 2. *Willie Horton*: Edsall with Edsall, *Chain Reaction*, p. 224.

Page 162, paragraph 3. *Bruneau helped Duke*: Cohler, "Duke's Smooth Entry into Mainstream Politics," p. 10. Republican state legislators confirmed this in interviews with the author. *Caucus newsletter*: Spring 1989. *Duke speech in Plaquemine, La.*: author's notes, May 9, 1990.

Page 162, paragraph 4. *Nungesser denounced Duke*: interview with author, New Orleans, June 1, 1989.

Page 163, paragraph 1. *Rickey quotations*: interview with author, June 1, 1989.

Page 163, paragraphs 2–3. *Nungesser said*: Rickey, "The Nazi and the Republicans," p. 68; some of the material comes from an earlier draft.

Page 163, paragraphs 4-8. *Duke had asked*: personal communication, June 1, 1989. *Treen told Duke*: Rickey, "The Nazi and the Republicans," pp. 69–71 (continued on page 164, paragraphs 1–2); some of the material comes from an earlier draft.

Page 164, paragraph 3. *She sought out Lance Hill*: interview with author, New Orleans, June 10, 1991.

Page 164, paragraph 4. *Rickey's account of outing with Duke and his daughters*: interview with author, June 10, 1991.

Page 164, paragraphs 5–6. *Duke lost his advantage*: Rickey, "The Nazi and the Republicans," p. 73 (continued on page 165, paragraphs 1–8).

Page 165, paragraph 9. *Quotation*: Rickey, "The Nazi and the Republicans," earlier draft, pp. 24–25.

Page 165, paragraph 10. *Quotations*: Rickey, "The Nazi and the Republicans," p. 74.

Page 165, paragraph 11. *Quotation*: Rickey, "The Nazi and the Republicans," p. 74. *"This is too bizarre"*: Beth Rickey, interview with author, June 10, 1991.

Page 166, paragraphs 1-2. *Account of censure attempt*: Beth Rickey, "The Nazi and the Republicans," pp. 74–79; Tyler Bridges, "State GOP Panel Votes Against David Duke," *Times-Picayune*, September 24, 1989, p. B1.

Page 166, paragraphs 4–5. *Quotations*: Rickey, "The Nazi and the Republicans," p. 79.

CHAPTER 8. *The Senate Campaign*

Page 167, paragraph 1. *Account of press conference*: author's notes.

Page 168, paragraphs 1–2. *Donaldson aggressively challenged*: Duke appearance on "Prime Time Live!," ABC, New York, November 2, 1989.

Page 168, paragraph 2. *Workers in the capitol mailroom*: June Peay, personal communication, November 21, 1989.

Page 168, paragraph 3. *Duke blamed his reddish complexion*: Joe Beaugez, personal communication, December 11, 1991. *Mart advised him*: personal communications, November 14, 1989, November 27, 1989.

Page 168, paragraph 4. *When he attended a fashion benefit*: Chris Bynum, *Times-Picayune* fashion editor, interview with author, New Orleans, February 12, 1990 (continued on page 169, paragraph 1).

Page 169, paragraphs 3–4. *Account of IOP fundraiser*: Lucy King, IOP secretary, interview with author, New Orleans, December 5, 1989; C. B. Forgotston, IOP board member, interview with author, New Orleans, November 16, 1989.

Page 169, paragraph 5. *Dutch Morial and Duke*: Jacque Morial, son of Dutch Morial, interview with author, New Orleans, January 6, 1993; Ed Renwick, Morial pollster, interview with author, New Orleans, January 6, 1993.

Page 170, paragraph 3. *Johnston was a segregationist*: Tyler Bridges, "Johnston's Segregation Stance in '60s Downplayed by Aides," *Times-Picayune*, September 19, 1990, p. A1.

Page 170, paragraphs 4–5. *Johnston background*: interview with author, Denham

Springs, La., April 12, 1990; Rick Raber, "Johnston Quietly Gains Clout to Get La. 'More Than Its Share,'" *Times-Picayune*, September 2, 1990, p. A1.

Page 170, paragraph 6. *Geoff Garin discovered*: personal communication, January 11, 1993 (continued on page 171, paragraphs 1–2).

Page 171, paragraph 4. *Republican caucuses*: Tyler Bridges, "Bagert Wins State GOP Caucuses," *Times-Picayune*, December 10, 1989, p. B1.

Page 171, paragraph 5. *Republican party convention*: Tyler Bridges, "GOP Chooses Bagert to Run for U.S. Senate," *Times-Picayune*, January 14, 1990, p. A1.

Page 171, paragraph 6. *Duke predicted*: interview with author, New Orleans, March 10, 1990.

Page 171, paragraph 7. *Bagert background*: interview with author, New Orleans, September 2, 1990; Jack Wardlaw, "Ben Bagert Hopes to Convince Voters He's Just an Average Joe," *Times-Picayune*, August 19, 1990, p. A1 (continued on page 172, paragraphs 1–2).

Page 172, paragraphs 3–4. *As Jim Oakes sized up the race*: interview with author, Baton Rouge, January 5, 1993.

Page 172, paragraph 5. *Account of focus group*: Jim Oakes, interview with author, January 5, 1993; Geoff Garin, personal communication, January 11, 1993 (continued on page 173, paragraphs 1–4).

Page 173, paragraph 5. *Head-to-head poll*: Bill McMahon, "Johnston Could Top GOP Trio to Keep Seat, Poll Says," *Morning Advocate*, January 9, 1990, p. 6A; Bill McMahon, "Johnston Would Defeat Duke, Poll Says," *Morning Advocate*, January 9, 1990, p. 6A.

Page 173, paragraph 6. *They decided to follow*: Jim Oakes, interview with author, Baton Rouge, January 5, 1993; Bob Mann, interview with author, Baton Rouge, January 5, 1993; Hal Kilshaw, interview with author, Baton Rouge, January 5, 1993; Geoff Garin, personal communication, January 11, 1993.

Page 173, paragraph 7. *Howie Farrell*: City of New Orleans Department of Police investigatory report, September 21, 1972; City of New Orleans Civil Service Commission, Howell F. Farrell v. Department of Police, no. 645, September 6, 1974.

Page 174, paragraph 1. Billy Hankins, Duke campaign aide, interview with author, Baton Rouge, January 9, 1993; Donna Randall, interview with author, November 27, 1992. *Farrell became known*: Billy Hankins, interview with author, January 9, 1993; Donna Randall, interview with author, November 27, 1992.

Page 174, paragraph 2. *Kenny Knight*: City of New Orleans Civil Service Commission, *Kenneth Knight v. Department of Police*, no. 671, April 1, 1974.

Page 174, paragraph 3. *Babs Wilson*: Babs Wilson, "Dispel King's 'Media Mythology,'" letter to editor, *Morning Advocate*, October 26, 1989, p. B8; Billy Hankins, interview with author, January 9, 1993; "The Klan's New Look," mailing of Knights of the Ku Klux Klan [1982]. *David Touchstone*: personal communication, March 16, 1993.

Page 174, paragraphs 4–5. *Jim McPherson*: interview with author, New Orleans, January 12, 1993 (continued on page 175, paragraph 1).

Page 175, paragraph 2. *Billy Hankins*: interview with author, January 9, 1993.

Page 175, paragraph 3. *Marc Ellis*: interview with author, New Orleans, May 7, 1993.

Page 175, paragraph 4. *Don Black*: Billy Hankins, interview with author, January 9, 1993. *Bernie Davids*: Robyn Beaugez, interview with author, Harahan, La., October 5, 1990; Bernie Davids, interview with author, October 6, 1990; Irwin Suall, Fact-Finding Director, Anti-Defamation League, personal communication, July 22, 1990. *James K. Warner: Hate Groups in America*, pp. 168–70; James K. Warner, interview with Evelyn Rich, October 10, 1987, pp. 1–2; Tyler Bridges. "Duke's Klan Officer Is GOP Delegate," *Times-Picayune*, January 10, 1990, p. B1.

Page 176, paragraph 2. *Account of Monroe rally*: Billy Hankins, interview with author, January 9, 1993; Lori Lane Jefferson, "Duke Draws 750 to Monroe Rally," *Monroe News Star*, January 21, 1990, p. A1.

Page 176, paragraph 3. *Account of Bossier City rally*: Thomas Cochran, personal communication, January 10, 1993; Andy Salvail, "Over 1,000 Duke Supporters Pack Bossier City Rally," *Shreveport Journal*, February 3, 1990, p. A3.

Page 177, paragraphs 2–3. *Duke quotations*: May 9, 1990, speech, Plaquemine, La., author's notes.

Page 177, paragraph 4. *The Edsalls wrote*: Edsall with Edsall, "Race," p. 56.

Page 177, paragraph 6. *One 1990 poll showed*: Louisiana Senate Race Survey, Survey Research Center, University of New Orleans (Susan Howell, director), September 1990.

Page 178, paragraph 5. *Comparison of views*: Duke statements were made during his interviews with Evelyn Rich, March 18, 1985, and March 20, 1985.

Page 179, paragraph 2. *Hundley said*: David Maraniss, "Campaigning in Code: Ex-Klansman Duke Tones Down Race-Based Rhetoric in Senate Bid," *Washington Post*, July 1, 1990, p. A1. *One man snarled*: Adam Nossiter, interview with author, New Orleans, June 7, 1993.

Page 179, paragraph 4. *Account of fund-raising*: Billy Hankins, interview with author, January 9, 1993.

Page 180, paragraph 1. *Duke would raise*: Duke campaign finance reports, Louisiana Campaign Finance office, Baton Rouge, La.

Page 180, paragraphs 2–4. *Duke explained why to Billy Hankins*: interview with author, January 9, 1993.

Page 180, paragraph 4. *Jim McPherson grew alarmed*: interview with author, January 12, 1993 (continued on page 181, paragraphs 1–2).

Page 181, paragraphs 3–5. *Hankins said to him*: interview with author, January 9, 1993.

Page 181, paragraph 6. *Picard said*: interview with author, Baton Rouge, April 30, 1990.

Page 181, paragraph 7. *Sam Theriot*: interview with author, Baton Rouge, May 8, 1990.

Page 182, paragraph 1. *Bob Mann was told*: interview with author, January 5, 1993.

Page 182, paragraph 7. *Account of racial flareup in legislature*: Tyler Bridges, "Duke's Affirmative Action Bill Passes," *Times-Picayune*, May 30, 1990, p. B6; Tyler Bridges, "House OK for Duke's Bill Called Lottery Vote Revenge," *Times-Picayune*, May 31, 1990, p. B5 (quotations of Duke and Jones); Tyler Bridges, "Growing Racial Tension in House Blamed on Duke," *Times-Picayune*, June 1, 1990, p. A1; Jack Wardlaw, "Duke-Mania Fans a Rift Between State Legislators," *Times-Picayune*, June 3, 1990, p. B11.

Page 182, paragraph 8. *Its biggest racial dispute*: Tyler Bridges, "Growing Racial Tension," p. A1 (quotation of Accardo).

Page 183, paragraph 1. *Racial dispute*: Bridges, "Growing Racial Tension," p. A1 (quotation of Accardo). Wardlaw, "Duke-Mania Fans a Rift," p. B11 (quotation of Wardlaw).

Page 183, paragraphs 4–5. *Rusty Cantelli*: interview with author, Metairie, La., January 7, 1993 (continued on page 184, paragraphs 1–4). *Quotation of Roach*: Bridges, "Growing Racial Tension," p. A1

Page 184, paragraph 5. *Duke looked like*: Tyler Bridges, "30-Minute Ad Starts Duke TV Campaign," *Times-Picayune*, July 13, 1990, p. B4.

Page 184, paragraphs 6–10. *Duke laid out his views*: "David Duke on the Real Issues," transcript of advertisement (continued on page 185, paragraphs 1–9).

Page 185, paragraph 10. *Billy Nungesser said*: interview with author, New Orleans, January 15, 1993.

Page 185, paragraph 11. *South Central Bell*: Tyler Bridges, "Phone Company Pulls Plug on Duke Numbers," *Times-Picayune*, August 23, 1990, p. B5.

Page 185, paragraph 12. *Duke was crushed*: Billy Hankins, interview with author, January 9, 1993 (continued on page 186, paragraph 1).

Page 186, paragraph 2. *Another poll was released*: Capitol news bureau, "Johnston Favored, Poll Says," *Morning Advocate*, August 9, 1990, p. B1. *It was becoming clear*: Jim Oakes, interview with author, January 5, 1993; Bob Mann, interview with author, January 5, 1993; Hal Kilshaw, interview with author, January 5, 1993.

Page 186, paragraph 4. *Victory Tour rallies*: Tyler Bridges, "Johnston Emphasizing Unity as Statewide Campaign Begins," *Times-Picayune*, August 21, 1990, p. B1.

Page 187, paragraph 1. *Not mentioning Duke*: Tyler Bridges, "Johnston Starts Campaign with No-Duke Theme," *Times-Picayune*, August 27, 1990, p. B1.

Page 187, paragraph 2. *Bennett Johnston, Jr.*: personal communication, January 27, 1993.

Page 187, paragraph 3. *Johnston thundered*: tape recording of speech, Farmerville, La., September 5, 1990, in Special Collections, Louisiana and Lower Mississippi Valley Collection, J. Bennett Johnston Campaign Tapes, Louisiana State University, Baton Rouge.

Page 187, paragraph 5. *Johnston's Klan footage ad*: Tyler Bridges, "Duke Hits Johnston for Klan Ad on TV," *Times-Picayune*, September 22, 1990, p. B1. *Bob Mann thought*: interview with author, January 5, 1993.

Page 187, paragraph 6. *Garin poll*: personal communication, January 11, 1993.

Page 188, paragraphs 1–5. *As Lance Hill watched*: interview with author, New Orleans, January 11, 1993 (continued on page 189, paragraphs 1–5, and page 190, paragraphs 1–3).

Page 190, paragraph 4. *As Bennett Johnston midway*: interview with author, Baton Rouge, May 29, 1990.

Page 190, paragraph 5. *Bagert called Duke*: Tyler Bridges, "La. GOP Hears Bagert Blast Opponent Duke," *Times-Picayune*, March 11, 1990, p. B1.

Page 191, paragraph 1. *He had detested Duke*: Ben Bagert, interview with author, March 13, 1990.

Page 191, paragraph 2. *Bagert knocked Duke off balance*: Duke-Bagert debate, WWL-Radio, New Orleans, August 16, 1990, author's notes.

Page 191, paragraphs 3-6. *Duke called out*: author's notes. *Bagert ambushed him*: Duke-Bagert appearance before Republicans, Democrats & Others organization, New Orleans, September 4, 1990, author's notes.

Page 191, paragraph 7. *Patterson and Myers*: Tyler Bridges, "Bagert's Election Advisers Walk Out," *Times-Picayune*, September 14, 1990, p. A1.

Page 192, paragraph 1. *Bagert was finished*: Tyler Bridges, "Bagert Quits to Keep Duke Out of Runoff, Johnston a Virtual Shoo-in in Primary, Analysts Say," *Times-Picayune*, October 5, 1990, p. A1.

Page 192, paragraph 2. *A poll a week earlier*: Alan Sayre, "Poll Shows Johnston with Majority," Associated Press, October 3, 1990. *Johnston was traveling*: Bob Mann, interview with author, January 5, 1993.

Page 192, paragraph 3. *Duke was at a TV station*: Billy Hankins, interview with author, January 9, 1993.

Page 192, paragraph 4. *During the flight*: Bob Mann, interview with author, January 5, 1993.

Page 193, paragraph 2. *Johnston smiled thinly*: Jim Oakes, interview with author, January 5, 1993.

Page 193, paragraph 3. *Analysis of vote*: Richard Baudouin, "The Bennett Factor," *Louisiana Political Review*, November 1990, p. 16; Garin-Hart Strategic Research, "How 'It Can't Happen Here' Almost Happened in Louisiana: A Study of the David Duke Phenomenon in the 1990 Senate Race," Center for National Policy, Washington, D.C., March 1991; Douglas Rose, department of political science, Tulane University, personal communication, October 10, 1990 (racial breakdown of the vote).

Page 193, paragraphs 5–6. *Duke election night party*: author's notes.

Page 193, paragraph 7. *Louisiana Coalition*: Lance Hill, interview with author, January 11, 1993.

CHAPTER 9. *The Race from Hell*

Page 194, paragraphs 2–3. *Roemer was unconcerned*: interview with author, Baton Rouge, March 9, 1993.

Page 195, paragraph 2. *Roemer had won*: John McQuaid, "Stranger: Roemer Toils for Recognition," *Times-Picayune*, July 14, 1987, p. A1.

Page 195, paragraph 3. *Roemer exhorted*: Iris Kelso, "A Quotable One," *Times-Picayune*, April 26, 1987, p. B3.

Page 195, paragraph 5. *Roemer had won*: John McQuaid, "Roemer Was Raised on Public Service," *Times-Picayune*, September 24, 1987, p. A1.

Page 195, paragraph 6. *Roemer headed off*: McQuaid, "Roemer Was Raised on Public Service," p. A1; for more background on Roemer, also see Rick Raber, "Blazing Buddy Roemer," *Dixie* (*Times-Picayune* Sunday magazine), April 20, 1986, p. 7.

Page 196, paragraph 2. *Tip O'Neill quotation*: Michael M. Lewis, "Nice Guys: St. Buddy: Louisiana Gov. Buddy Roemer," *New Republic*, March 20, 1989, p. 16.

Page 196, paragraph 3. *He blamed that tradition*: Richard E. Meyer, "The Rake, the Racist, and the New-Age Reformer," *Los Angeles Times Magazine*, October 13, 1991, pp. 21–22; Steve Cochran, personal communication, June 17, 1991. *Quotation of Roemer*: Kelso, "A Quotable One," p. B3.

Page 196, paragraph 5. *It was a crushing blow*: Meyer, "The Rake, the Racist, and the New-Age Reformer," p. 22.

Page 197, paragraph 1. *Quotation*: Meyer, "The Rake, the Racist and the New-Age Reformer," p. 22.

Page 197, paragraph 2. *He brought books*: Tyler Bridges, "Roemer: Gaffes Make Enemies, Mystify Allies," *Times-Picayune*, July 3, 1991, p. A1. *Raymond Strother marveled*: personal communication, April 14, 1993.

Page 197, paragraph 3. *Roemer went into a shell*: Meyer, "The Rake, the Racist, and the New-Age Reformer," p. 22 (quotation); P. J. Mills, interview with author, Baton Rouge, February 28, 1993 (quotation); Billy Rimes, interview with author, Baton Rouge, February 28, 1993 (quotation).

Page 197, paragraph 4. *Walker organized*: Meyer, "The Rake, the Racist, and the New-Age Reformer," p. 23 (quotation); Steve Cochran, interview with author, Metairie, La., March 20, 1990; P. J. Mills, interview with author, February 28, 1993; Peter Nicholas, "Is Roemer Growing Soft or Simply Growing Up?" *Times-Picayune*, December 9, 1990, p. A1.

Page 197, paragraph 5. *Roemer didn't give up*: Meyer, "The Rake, the Racist, and the New-Age Reformer," p. 23 ("Honor," read the sign); P. J. Mills, interview with author, February 28, 1993.

Page 197, paragraph 7. *Roemer apologized*: Meyer, "The Rake, the Racist, and the New-Age Reformer," p. 23 (quotation); Iris Kelso, "The Roemer Stance: Goodbye Negative, Hello Positive," *Times-Picayune*, April 19, 1990, p. B15; Jack Wardlaw, "Roemer Makes Plea for Unity," *Times-Picayune*, April 17, 1990, p. A1.

Page 198, paragraph 1. *Roemer speech*: Meyer, "The Rake, the Racist, and the New-Age Reformer," p. 23; Wardlaw, "Roemer Makes Plea for Unity," p. A1.

Page 198, paragraph 2. *Roemer and his advisers thought*: Buddy Roemer, interview with author, March 9, 1993; Billy Rimes, interview with author, February 28, 1993; P. J. Mills, interview with author, February 28, 1993.

Page 199, paragraph 1. *Edwards quotations*: Errol Laborde, "The Return of the 'New Edwin Edwards,'" *New Orleans Magazine*, May 1991, p. 42.

Page 199, paragraph 4. *Edwards dismissed the complaints*: Iris Kelso, "'Outrageous' Edwards Plans to Remain in Public Eye," *Times-Picayune*, March 9, 1980, sec. 1, p. 1 ("It was illegal"; "I think people"); Donna St. George, "A Last Hurrah," *Philadelphia Inquirer*, June 1, 1991, p. 1C ("No, it wasn't").

Page 200, paragraph 1. *Trip to France*: Roy Blount, Jr., "What Does Edwin Edwards Do When He's $4 Million in Debt? Take 617 of His Closest Friends to Paris," *People*, February 13, 1984, p. 69. *"In bed with a"*: St. George, "A Last Hurrah," p. 1C. *"So slow it takes him"*: Meyer, "The Rake, the Racist, and the New-Age Reformer," p. 21.

Page 200, paragraph 3. *Edwards trial*: Bridget O'Brian and Mark Schleifstein, "Casino Debts $2 Million, Court Told," *Times-Picayune*, November 8, 1985, p. A1; Mark Schleifstein and Bridget O'Brian, "Exec: Edwards Won at Casino," *Times-Picayune*, November 27, 1985, p. A1; Mark Schleifstein and Bridget O'Brian, "Edwards Grilled on Gambling," *Times-Picayune*, December 3, 1985, p. A1; Mark Schleifstein and Bridget O'Brian, "Edwards Case Ends in Mistrial," *Times-Picayune*, December 18, 1985, p. A1.

Page 200, paragraph 5. *He would run again*: interview with author, March 9, 1993.

Page 201, paragraphs 3–5. *Edwards declared his candidacy*: Jack Wardlaw, "Edwards Promises to Be a New Man," *Times-Picayune*, February 9, 1991, p. A1.

Page 201, paragraph 5. *He joked that he and Duke were similar*: Billy Hankins, interview with author, January 9, 1993. *Edwards joked to a crowd*: Edwards fund raiser, New Orleans, author's notes, August 2, 1991.

Page 201, paragraph 6. *Jim McPherson told him*: interview with author, New Orleans, March 4, 1993.

Page 202, paragraph 1. *Duke had been impressed*: Duke's informal campaign announcement, January 16, 1991, tape recording; Duke's formal campaign announcement, March 13, 1991, tape recording; interview with author, March 27, 1991.

Page 202, paragraphs 4–5. *Buddy Roemer was preoccupied*: interview with author, March 9, 1993.

Page 203, paragraph 2. *Quotation*: Buddy Roemer, interview with author, March 9, 1993.

Page 203, paragraph 3. *Dinner at governor's mansion*: Buddy Roemer, interview with author, March 9, 1993; P. J. Mills, interview with author, February 28, 1993; Billy Rimes, interview with author, February 28, 1993.

Page 203, paragraph 4. *He wanted to run for president*: interview with author, March 9, 1993.

Page 203, paragraph 5. *Nungesser thought Roemer was too liberal*: Billy Nungesser, personal communication, May 14, 1991. *Roemer shouted*: Buddy Roemer, interview with author, March 9, 1993; P. J. Mills, interview with author, February 28, 1993; Billy Rimes, interview with author, February 28, 1993 (quotation).

Page 204, paragraph 4. *These developments thrilled David Duke*: personal communication, May 3, 1991.

Page 204, paragraph 6. *Account of convention*: Tyler Bridges. "Holloway GOP Pick for La. Governor," *Times-Picayune*, June 16, 1991, p. A1; author's notes of convention.

Page 205, paragraph 2. *Unnerved Neil Curran*: interview with author, November 27, 1991. *Some friends he called*: Al Donovan, interview with author, Metairie, La., February 28, 1993; Bob d'Hemecourt, interview with author, New Orleans, March 2, 1993.

Page 206, paragraph 2. *Lawmakers called him a liar*: Peter Nicholas and Ed Anderson, "Lawmakers Livid over Roemer's Change of Heart," *Times-Picayune*, August 4, 1991, p. A1.

Page 206, paragraph 3. *The House adopted*: Peter Nicholas, "Duke Bills Gain Some Acceptance," *Times-Picayune*, July 15, 1991, p. B1.

Page 206, paragraph 5. *Roemer announcement*: Tyler Bridges, "Roemer Enters Race, Says Dark Days Are Over," *Times-Picayune*, August 28, 1991, p. B1 (continued on page 207, paragraph 1).

Page 207, paragraph 4. *Duke at Free Speech Alley*: author's notes, tape recording of speech.

Page 208, paragraph 1. *Shannah Smith quotation*: David Maraniss, "Duke and the 'Hidden Vote,'" *Washington Post*, September 15, 1991, p. A1 ("Amen, I'm tired"); other quotations: author's notes.

Page 208, paragraph 2. *The students chanted*: author's notes, tape recording of speech.

Page 208, paragraph 3. *Hankins said*: interview with author, Baton Rouge, September 11, 1991.

Page 208, paragraph 4. *Duke ad*: Tyler Bridges, "30-Minute Duke Ad Expands Platform," *Times-Picayune*, September 19, 1991, p. B4 (advertisement transcript p. 2).

Page 209, paragraph 1. *Duke portrayed himself*: Advertisement transcript p. 16.

Page 209, paragraph 2. *He admitted this several days later*: David Duke, interview with author, Metairie, La., September 25, 1991.

Page 209, paragraphs 3–6. *Caroline Roemer*: personal communication, March 17, 1993 (continued on page 210, paragraphs 1–7).

Page 210, paragraph 8. *Raymond Strother had been warning him*: personal communication, April 14, 1993.

Page 211, paragraphs 2–19. *Account of focus group*: Raymond Strother, personal communication, April 14, 1993; Steve Lombardo, personal communication, April 30, 1993; Sam Dawson, personal communication, March 7, 1993.

Page 212, paragraphs 1–8. *Ads*: Raymond, Strother, personal communication, April 14, 1993 (continued on page 213, paragraphs 1–4).

Page 213, paragraph 5. *His aides chafed*: Raymond Strother, personal communication, April 14, 1993; Sam Dawson, personal communication, March 7, 1993; P. J. Mills, interview with author, February 28, 1993; Billy Rimes, interview with author, February 28, 1993. *Roemer didn't feel comfortable*: interview with author, March 9, 1993.

Page 213, paragraphs 6–7. *When Roemer was growing up*: interview with author, March 9, 1993.

Page 214, paragraphs 1–10. *Account of Jack Kent ads*: Deno Seder, interview with author, New Orleans, April 7, 1993.

Page 214, paragraphs 10–11. *Kent sent an emissary*: P. J. Mills, interview with author, February 28, 1993. Mills agreed with Roemer's opposition to the deal.

Page 215, paragraph 2. *Sam Dawson got hold*: personal communication, March 7, 1993.

Page 215, paragraph 3. *Duke was rising*: tracking poll courtesy of Buddy Roemer and Fred Steeper. *Duke's campaign staffers*: Jim McPherson, interview with author, March 4, 1993; David Touchstone, personal communication, March 16, 1993.

Page 215, paragraph 4. *Gill wrote shortly before the primary*: James Gill, "Keeping the Unthinkable in Mind," *Times-Picayune*, October 11, 1991, p. B7.

Page 215, paragraph 5. *Roemer quotation*: Jack Wardlaw, "Final Two? Voters to Trim Field," *Times-Picayune*, October 19, 1991, p. A1. *Edwards spent the day*: Al Donovan, interview with author, February 28, 1993. *Duke told a cheering throng*: author's notes (continued on page 216, paragraph 1).

Page 216, paragraph 4. *Analysis of voter returns*: Bill Walsh, "Blacks, Republicans Eluded Gov. Roemer," *Times-Picayune*, October 20, 1991, p. A1. *Caroline Roemer walked into*: personal communication, March 17, 1993 (continued on page 216, paragraphs 5–7).

Page 217, paragraph 1. *Marie Serrat said*: quotation in a graphic, *Times-Picayune*, October 24, 1991, p. A1.

Page 217, paragraph 2. *Registrars of voters throughout Louisiana reported*: Tyler Bridges and Christy Harrison, "Crowds Swarm Voter Registry Offices: It's Duke: For or Against," *Times-Picayune*, October 22, 1991, p. A1. *People began queuing up*: Steve Culpepper and Curt Eysink, "Runoff Sparks Run on Registrar," *Morning Advocate*, October 23, 1991, p. 1A; James Hodge, "Thousands Rush to Claim Right to Vote," *Times-Picayune*, October 23, 1991, p. A1. *Altobello quotation*: personal communication, November 27, 1991.

Page 217, paragraph 3. *James Heckathorn quotation*: Hodge, "Thousands Rush to Claim Right to Vote," p. A1.

Page 217, paragraph 4. *In Baton Rouge*: Culpepper and Eysink, "Runoff Sparks Run on Registrar," p. 1A.

Page 218, paragraph 1. *Heggin had last tried to register*: Associated Press, "87-Year-Old Man Registers to Vote for First Time," October 25, 1991.

Page 218, paragraph 2. *Fowler said*: Mary Foster, "Louisiana Voters," Associated Press, October 22, 1991. *68,335 Louisianians*: Associated Press, "Campaign Notes," November 1, 1991. *The large numbers of blacks*: Jim McPherson, interview with author, March 4, 1993; David Touchstone, personal communication, March 16, 1993.

Page 218, paragraph 3. *Duke press conference*: Jack Wardlaw, "Scramble for Roemer Voters Starts," *Times-Picayune*, October 21, 1991, p. A1; author's notes.

Page 218, paragraph 4. *Edwards felt confident*: Al Donovan, interview with author, February 28, 1993; Bob d'Hemecourt, interview with author, March 2, 1993.

Page 219, paragraph 1. *Edwards quotation*: Guy Coates, "An Uneasy Coalition for Edwards," Associated Press, October 31, 1991.

Page 219, paragraph 2. *Raymond Strother by chance*: Raymond Strother, personal communication, April 14, 1993; Billy Broadhurst, interview with author, New Orleans, March 6, 1993.

Page 219, paragraph 3. *David Treen*: interview with author, New Orleans, March 8, 1993.

Page 219, paragraph 4. *Treen statement*: Christopher Cooper, Peter Nicholas, and Ed Anderson, "Down on Duke, Treen Supports Edwards," *Times-Picayune*, October 30, 1991, p. A1; transcript of statement (continued on page 220, paragraph 1).

Page 220, paragraph 2. *Mills admonished him*: P. J. Mills, interview with author, February 28, 1993. *Roemer told reporters*: Ed Anderson and Jack Wardlaw, "Roemer: I'll Vote for Edwards, Urges Former Backers Not to Sit Out Election," *Times-Picayune*, November 1, 1991, p. A1.

Page 220, paragraph 4. *Pres Kabacoff*: interview with author, New Orleans, March 7, 1993.

Page 220, paragraph 5. *David Dixon*: interview with author, New Orleans, March 10, 1993 (continued on p. 221, paragraphs 1–2).

Page 221, paragraph 3. *Jim Bob Moffett said*: Charley Blaine, "Duke Victory Would Cost La., Execs Say," *Times-Picayune*, October 26, 1991, p. A1. *Tourist leaders chimed in*: Bruce Eggler and Christopher Cooper, "Tourism Leaders: Duke Will Be Costly," *Times-Picayune*, November 2, 1991, p. A1.

Page 221, paragraph 4. *Thinking of editors*: author attended October 21, 1991, meeting but played no role in deciding editorial coverage for the runoff.

Page 221, paragraph 5. *Editorial*: "It's Time to Think Straight," *Times-Picayune*, October 20, 1991, p. B10 (continued on page 222, paragraph 1).

Page 222, paragraph 2. *Five-part series*: "Choice of Our Lives," *Times-Picayune*, October 27–31, 1991. *Duke broadcast a television commercial*: Howard Kurtz, "New Orleans Paper Plays Central Role in Contest," *Washington Post*, November 16, 1991, p. A12.

Page 222, paragraph 4. *Men fell over themselves*: Jim McPherson, interview with author, March 4, 1993; Keith Woods, "Missing the Point about Duke," *Times-Picayune*, October 28, 1991, p. B5.

Page 222, paragraph 5. *A parade of Roemer supporters*: David Touchstone, personal communication, March 16, 1993. *Reported C. B. Forgotston*: interview with author, New Orleans, October 31, 1991.

Page 222, paragraph 6. *Born-again Christian*: author's notes of Duke campaign appearances on October 18, 1991, and October 20, 1991; Mark Schleifstein and Tyler Bridges, "Duke's Christian Fervor Contrasts with Past Views, Religion Grows into a Key Issue," *Times-Picayune*, November 1, 1991, p. A1.

Page 223, paragraph 1. *Duke Quotation*: Schleifstein and Bridges, "Duke's Christian Fervor Contrasts with Past Views," p. A1.

Page 223, paragraph 2. *Lance Hill thought*: interview with author, March 9, 1993.

Page 223, paragraph 3. *Mason-Dixon poll*: Christopher Cooper, Peter Nicholas, and Ed Anderson, "Edwards Pulls Ahead in Poll," *Times-Picayune*, October 30, 1991, p. A1; poll.

Page 223, paragraph 4. *AARP appearance*: Ed Anderson, "Retirees Back Duke at Forum," *Times-Picayune*, October 31, 1991, p. A1; Guy Coates, "AARP Members Cheer Duke, Shout Down Edwards," Associated Press, October 30, 1991.

Page 224, paragraphs 1–5. *Quotations*: Coates, "AARP Members Cheer Duke, Shout Down Edwards."

Page 224, paragraph 6. *Exulted Jim McPherson*: interview with author, March 4, 1993.

Page 224, paragraph 7. *Edwards was rattled*: Al Donovan, interview with author, Metairie, La., March 21, 1993.

Page 224, paragraph 8. *Duke was nervous*: Jim McPherson, interview with author, March 4, 1993. *Quotations*: Tyler Bridges, "Duke and Edwards Spar on Familiar Issues," *Times-Picayune*, November 3, 1991, p. A1.

Page 224, paragraph 9. *Account of first debate*: Bridges, "Duke and Edwards Spar on Familiar Issues," p. A1; Guy Coates, "Duke Wants Louisiana to Fight Federal Government," Associated Press, November 3, 1991.

Page 225, paragraph 1. *Duke quotation*: Coates, "Duke Wants Louisiana to Fight Federal Government."

Page 225, paragraph 2. *Hirsch said*: Tyler Bridges, "The Rush Is on for Roemer Supporters," *Times-Picayune*, November 4, 1991, p. A1. *Duke and his aides celebrated*: Jim McPherson, interview with author, March 4, 1993; David Touchstone, personal communication, March 16, 1993.

Page 225, paragraph 3. *Account of debate preparation*: Edwin Edwards, interview with author, March 9, 1993; Billy Broadhurst, interview with author, March 6, 1993.

Page 226, paragraph 1. *Quotation*: Edwin Edwards, interview with author, March 9, 1993.

Page 226, paragraphs 2–10. *Account of Duke before the debate*: Jim McPherson, interview with author, March 4, 1993.

Page 226, paragraph 10. *The four journalists*: Jeff Duhe, interview with author, New Orleans, May 30, 1993.

Page 227, paragraph 2. *Account of debate*: Ed Anderson, "Duke, Edwards Let Sparks Fly in TV Debate," *Times-Picayune*, November 7, 1991, p. A1; Carl Redman, "Debate Heats Up," *Morning Advocate*, November 7, 1991, p. 1A; quotations on debate transcript pp. 1–11.

Page 227, paragraphs 3–5. Quotations come from the debate transcript, p. 11.

Page 227, paragraphs 6–7. *Norman Robinson*: interview with author, New Orleans, April 1, 1993 (continued on page 228, paragraphs 1–2); transcript and videotape of debate.

Page 228, paragraphs 2–9. Quotations from debate transcript, pp. 12–13.

Page 229, paragraph 3. *David Touchstone exulted*: personal communication, March 16, 1993. *Henry Dillon III cheered*: interview with author, Baton Rouge, March 9, 1993.

Page 229, paragraph 4. *Edwards's closing statement*: debate transcript, pp. 19–20.

Page 230, paragraph 5. *Donald Spector*: personal communication, March 27, 1993.

Page 230, paragraph 6. *Steven Ross*: Donald Spector, personal communication, March 27, 1993.

Page 231, paragraph 1. *Actors' contributions*: state campaign finance reports, Louisiana Campaign Finance Office, Baton Rouge.

Page 231, paragraph 2. *When Edwards visited New York*: Donald Spector, personal communication, March 27, 1993 (quoted). *Eating lunch*: Bob d'Hemecourt, interview with author, March 2, 1993 (quoted).

Page 231, paragraph 6. *State Democratic party ads*: Deno Seder, interview with author, April 7, 1993; videotapes of ads.

Page 232, paragraph 2. *Raymond Strother said*: Paul West, "Louisiana Airwaves Clogged with Anti-Duke Ad Blitz," *Baltimore Sun*, November 14, 1991, p. 1.

Page 232, paragraph 3. *Timothy Russert was determined*: Colette Rhoney, "Meet the Press" producer, personal communication, May 2, 1993.

Page 232, paragraphs 4–7. *The show*: Tyler Bridges, "Pat Answers Falter in Debate," *Times-Picayune*, November 11, 1991, p. A1; transcript of show. *Hilton quotation*: "Employers Speak Their Minds: Letters from the Boss Implore Workers to Stop Duke," *Times-Picayune*, November 14, 1991, p. A17.

Page 232, paragraphs 5–7. *Quotations*: transcript of show, p. 10.

Page 232, paragraph 8. *McPherson said*: interview with author, March 4, 1993.

Page 233, paragraphs 2–3. *Russert followed up*: transcript of show, p. 10.

Page 233, paragraph 4. *A playful Edwards*: interview with author, March 9, 1993.

Page 233, paragraphs 5–6. *Duke said to Edwards*: Edwin Edwards, interview with author, March 9, 1993.

Page 233, paragraph 6. *"Heavens to Betsy"*: Bridges, "Pat Answers Falter," p. A1.

Page 233, paragraph 7. *Bob Hawks*: Staff and wire reports. "Aide Criticizes Duke Over Religion, Quits," *Times-Picayune*, November 12, 1991, p. A1; Tyler Bridges and Michael Perlstein, "Ex-Aide Saw Little Faith," *Times-Picayune*, November 13, 1991, p. A1; Mark Schleifstein and Sheila Grissett, "Religious Leaders Doubt Duke's Christianity," *Times-Picayune*, November 13, 1991, p. A1.

Page 233, paragraph 9. *He said it had happened*: interview with author, New Orleans, November 10, 1991.

Page 234, paragraph 1. *Neil Curran quotation*: Associated Press, "Duke Attracts Crowds as New Allegations about Money, Religion Surface," November 11, 1991.

Page 234, paragraph 2. *Ros Davidson*: Tyler Bridges, "New Reports of Racism Dog Duke," *Times-Picayune*, November 13, 1991, p. A1.

Page 234, paragraph 3. *Duke shouted*: Sam Attlesey and Todd J. Gilman, "Louisiana Foes Blitz Voters, Edwards, Duke Stir Up Emotions," *Dallas Morning News*, November 14, 1991, p. 13A (Duke quotation). *Edwards at a New Orleans rally*: Lisa Frazier and Christopher Cooper, "Duke, Edwards Attend Rallies as Campaigns Draw to a Close," *Times-Picayune*, November 15, 1991, p. A12 (Edwards quotation).

Page 234, paragraph 4. *A woman told*: Todd J. Gilman and Sam Attlesey, "Duke-Edwards Spar Until End, Louisianans to Decide Acrimonious Race Today," *Dallas Morning News*, November 16, 1991, p. 1A. *Duke predicted victory*: author's notes.

Page 234, paragraph 5. *Henry Dillon III*: interview with author, March 9, 1993 (continued on page 235, paragraphs 1–2).

Page 235, paragraph 3. *Jay Jackson quotation*: Mary T. Schmich, "Duke Trounced at Louisiana Polls, Edwards Wins 61% of Vote in Record Turnout," *Chicago Tribune*, November 17, 1991, p. 1.

Page 235, paragraphs 4–5. *Dillon was at the headquarters*: interview with author, March 9, 1993.

Page 235, paragraph 6. *David Touchstone saw*: personal communication, March 16, 1993.

Page 236, paragraph 1. *A dozen Duke supporters*: Kevin Bell and Chris Adams, "Time for Peace, Duke Foes Say," *Times-Picayune*, November 17, 1991, p. A6.

Page 236, paragraph 2. *Bob d'Hemecourt shook Edwards's hand*: Bob d'Hemecourt, interview with author, March 2, 1993.

Page 236, paragraph 3. *A brass band materialized*: Carl Cannon, "Duke Concedes as Edwards Elected Governor of Louisiana," Knight-Ridder newspapers, November 17, 1991.

Page 236, paragraph 6. *Exit polls showed*: Bill Walsh, "Anti-Duke Voters Help Edwards Win," *Times-Picayune*, November 17, 1991, p. A1.

Page 237, paragraph 2. *Edwards told a cheering throng*: transcript of speech (the transcript was published by Associated Press on November 16, 1991).

Page 237, paragraph 3. *Duke Quotation*: Peter Applebome, "Fearing Duke, Voters in Louisiana Hand Democrat Fourth Term," *New York Times*, November 18, 1991, p. A1. *Brief interview*: author's notes.

CHAPTER 10. *The Presidency or Bust*

Page 238, paragraph 1. *He said on CNN*: transcript of show.

Page 238, paragraph 2. *Duke told reporters*: Tyler Bridges, "Duke: A Shot at the Presidency May Be Next," *Times-Picayune*, November 19, 1991, p. A1.

Page 238, paragraph 3. *Presidential announcement*: All major newspapers covered the event; transcript of speech. *One woman screamed*: Thomas B. Edsall, "Duke Announces Bid for the Presidency," *Washington Post*, December 5, 1991, p. A1.

Page 239, paragraph 1. *A sign that read*: Robin Toner, "Duke Takes His Anger into 1992 Race," *New York Times*, December 5, 1991, p. B18.

Page 239, paragraphs 2–3. *Quotations*: Toner, "Duke Takes His Anger into 1992 Race," p. B18.

Page 239, paragraph 4. *"We must go"*: Toner, "Duke Takes His Anger into 1992 Race," p. B18. *"From a 'New'"*: Federal News Service transcript, p. 3–1.

Page 239, paragraph 5. *Edsall wrote*: Thomas B. Edsall, "Duke Latest to Capitalize on George Wallace's Political Legacy," *Washington Post*, December 6, 1991, p. A4 (continued on page 240, paragraph 1).

Page 240, paragraph 3. *Duke had supported*: interview with author, New Orleans, September 10, 1991.

Page 241, paragraph 6. *Duke thought*: Jim McPherson, interview with author, New Orleans, May 10, 1993.

Page 242, paragraph 3. *Phillips wrote*: Kevin Phillips, *Boiling Point: Democrats, Republicans, and the Decline of Middle-Class Prosperity* (New York: Random House, 1993), p. 236.

Page 242, paragraph 6. *Moynihan quotation*: Paul Taylor, "Carrots and Sticks of Welfare Reform," *Washington Post*, February 4, 1992.

Page 243, paragraph 1. *The impact of this rule*: Peter Brown, "Buchanan, Duke Face Built-In Disadvantages," *Washington Times*, November 30, 1991, p. A4.

Page 243, paragraphs 4–5. *Buchanan column*: Patrick Buchanan, Tribune Media Services, "David Duke's Challenge—to the Right Wing," October 22, 1991 (continued on page 244, paragraphs 1–3).

Page 244, paragraph 4. *Greg Mueller said*: personal communication, May 17, 1993.

Page 244, paragraph 5. *Buchanan and Duke on issue after issue*: Sandy Grady, "Pat, Dukester Saying Same Thing Two Ways," *Philadelphia Daily News*, December 10, 1991, p. 7; Clarence Page, "And Now, the Pat and David Show," *Chicago Tribune*, December 11, 1991, p. 27; Tyler Bridges, "Buchanan Sounds Like Clone of Duke," *Times-Picayune*, March 6, 1992, p. A1.

Page 244, paragraph 6. *Quotation*: Buchanan for President campaign brochure, Kenner, La., p. 4.

Page 245, paragraph 1. *"I think God"*: Grady, "Pat, Dukester Saying Same Thing Two Ways," p. 7. *"Does this First World"*: Bridges, "Buchanan Sounds Like Clone of Duke," p. A1.

Page 245, paragraph 2. *Quotation*: Grady, "Pat, Dukester Saying Same Thing Two Ways," p. 7.

Page 245, paragraph 4. *Lacy quotation*: Tyler Bridges, "Analysts: Buchanan's Gain Comes at Duke's Expense," *Times-Picayune*, February 20, 1992, p. A14.

Page 245, paragraph 5. *Duke quotations*: Associated Press, "Ex-Klansman, Legislator Sees Bush as Vulnerable," February 19, 1992.

Page 246, paragraph 1. *Marc Ellis scheduled*: interview with author, May 7, 1993. *Jewel Tardiff quotation*: interview with author, New Orleans, May 11, 1993.

Page 246, paragraph 2. *President Bush's advisers*: Charles Black, personal communication, May 19, 1993; Mary Matalin, personal communication, June 4, 1993. *Marlin Fitzwater and B. J. Cooper quotations*: Thomas B. Edsall, "Duke Announces Bid for the Presidency," *Washington Post*, December 5, 1991, p. A1.

Page 247, paragraph 1. *John Powell quotation*: personal communication, March 10, 1992.

Page 247, paragraph 2. *Duke quotation*: David Maraniss, "Demanding 'Respect' from GOP, Duke Warns of 3rd-Party Run," *Washington Post*, January 10, 1992, p. A4.

Page 247, paragraph 3. *The Republican party had laid a trap*: Charles Black, personal communication, May 19, 1993; Mary Matalin, personal communication, June 4, 1993; Warren Tompkins, personal communication, June 8, 1993.

Page 248, paragraph 2. *He visited Dallas and Houston*: author covered Duke in Texas. *Mark McKinnon quotation*: personal communication, February 26, 1992.

Page 248, paragraph 3. *Knight quotation*: Peter Applebome, "David Duke Battling in Dark As Spotlight Trails Buchanan," *New York Times*, March 6, 1992, p. A1.

Page 248, paragraph 4. *Earl Black quotation*: Tyler Bridges, "Bush, Clinton Roll to Victory in S. Carolina," *Times-Picayune*, March 8, 1992, p. A1.

Page 248, paragraph 5. *Final rally*: Tyler Bridges, "Duke's Swift Ascent Matched by Fast Fall," *Times-Picayune*, March 11, 1992, p. A1; author's notes at two rallies.

Page 249, paragraph 2. *DiFalco quotation*: personal communication, March 11, 1992.

Page 249, paragraph 3. *Buchanan said*: Bridges, "Duke's Swift Ascent Matched by Fast Fall," p. A1.

Page 249, paragraph 4. *Duke said*: Bruce Alpert, "Duke Calls It Quits on Campaign Trail," *Times-Picayune*, April 23, 1992, p. A1.

Page 250, paragraph 1. *Holly Sarre quotation*: personal communication, November 12, 1992.

Page 250, paragraph 2. *Van Loman quotation*: personal communication, November 11, 1992. *Duke tried his hand*: Tyler Bridges, "Duke Sells Wares to Slim Audiences," *Times-Picayune*, November 15, 1992, p. A1.

Page 250, paragraph 3. *Duke wrote his followers*: Tyler Bridges, "Duke Pleads for Money from Followers," *Times-Picayune*, August 14, 1992, p. A1.

Page 251, paragraph 1. *Katie Nachod said*: Bridges, "Duke Sells Wares to Slim Audiences," p. A1.

Page 251, paragraph 3. *Robert Namer said*: J. E. Bourgoyne, comp., "David Duke Fine-Tunes Act for Radio Show, Ex-Politician Snags Spot on WASO," *Times-Picayune*, April 13, 1993, p. A9.

Page 251, paragraph 5. *He told listeners*: Duke on WASO radio, New Orleans, May 3, 1993.

Page 252, paragraph 1. *He told friends*: Jim McPherson, interview with author, May 10, 1993; Jewel Tardiff, interview with author, May 11, 1993.

INDEX